George, being George

GEORGE,
BEING GEORGE

RANDOM HOUSE

NEW YORK

GEORGE, BEING GEORGE

—

George Plimpton's Life as Told,
Admired, Deplored, and Envied by
200 Friends, Relatives, Lovers,
Acquaintances, Rivals–
and a Few Unappreciative
Observers

EDITED BY

NELSON W. ALDRICH, JR.

For Dee and Arabella with love

Published in the United States by Random House,
an imprint of The Random House Publishing Group,
a division of Random House, Inc., New York.

RANDOM HOUSE and colophon are registered
trademarks of Random House, Inc.

LIBRARY OF CONGRESS CATALOGING-IN-PUBLICATION DATA

George, being George : George Plimpton's life as told,
admired, deplored, and envied by 200 friends, relatives, lovers,
acquaintances, rivals—and a few unappreciative observers /
edited by Nelson W. Aldrich, Jr.
p. cm.
ISBN 978-1-4000-6398-7
1. Plimpton, George.   2. Authors, American—
20th century—Biography.   3. Editors—United States—
Biography.   4. Journalists—United States—Biography.
I. Aldrich, Nelson W.
PS3566.L5Z68 2008
818'.54—dc22   2007046215

Printed in the United States of America
on acid-free paper

www.atrandom.com

2 4 6 8 9 7 5 3

Title-page photograph by Otto van Noppen

Book design by Barbara M. Bachman

Photos on pages 184, 237, 274, and 292 copyright © Jill Krementz

CONTENTS

—

GEORGE,
BEING GEORGE

PROLOGUE:
A PLAUSIBLE METAPHOR

—

BUDDY BURNISKE I don't know whether most people have a yearning for ecstatic experience, but George certainly did, and it was no secret. You saw it most sensationally in his love of fireworks. He really did live a life punctuated by fireworks, his fireworks, which produced ecstatic oohs and aahs but then instead of burning out would somehow generate the energy for another explosion. Ecstasy after ecstasy. But again, there was nothing secretive about this great appetite of his. He wanted to share it with as many of his friends as possible. I remember watching him in the Hamptons at a Fourth of July picnic. That's when George seemed to me most at peace—he was just, "Look at this, golly, this is marvelous!"

PIEDY LUMET Long ago, when George was in his mid-twenties and in Madrid hunting for Hemingway to do an interview for *The Paris Review,* he and I went out one evening and happened upon a square where four little ancient medieval streets came together. There were homemade fireworks going off, and big pieces of the shell would drop down in flames from above. I found it quite terrifying, these strange flaming particles with a lot of weight to them, falling onto the crowd, but George was transfixed with joy. I remember his face, his mouth wide open in a smile of pure delight.

FELIX GRUCCI, JR. Our family came to know George when he used to drive out to the Hamptons during the summers in the early 1960s and stopped off at my dad's fireworks factory in Bell-

Fortieth Anniversary celebration for *The Paris Review,*
East Hampton, 1993. *Photograph © Sara Barrett.*

port. He struck up a conversation with my father and began a relationship. Eventually it grew to the point where George—this
was when he lived in Wainscott—would have us to his Bastille Day
party, and we brought a fireworks show, a little one, just a tiny
backyard fireworks show. George was supposed to take care of the
details of getting the permit. That never happened, but since it was
little pops here and there, it never bothered anybody. But over the
years it became a mammoth fireworks show in the potato fields
behind his house. So much so that the municipality said to George,
"You can't do this anymore." And George said, "Well, why not?
We've been doing it now for many years." And they got into a little bit of fisticuffs because the woman at the municipality said, "If
you do this, we're going to arrest you, we're going to arrest the
Gruccis, we're going to stop your party, and there's going to be

lights flashing and everything else." So we get there, we're setting up, and the next thing you know, as the party is unfolding, wailing fire trucks and police guards come, they hose everything down, all the fireworks, so that you can't fire them. No one got arrested, but it was the end of the fireworks behind George's house.

WILLIAM STYRON   It was just a moment which was so perfectly George. He was doing the Bicentennial of the City of New York. There was a huge parade from the Battery up to Washington Square, a monster parade. And George asked Rose and me to sit with him in a horse-drawn carriage with a sign, a very big sign on the side, saying, "Fireworks Commissioner City of New York." I just recall the absolute delight that he took—the three of us, as a matter of fact, but especially George—in bowing to the crowd, passing people who were saying, "Jesus, I don't believe it, a fireworks commissioner!" I remember that as an example of George's joy in being George.

SARAH DUDLEY PLIMPTON   George loved parades. He grew up on Fifth Avenue and could see the St. Patrick's Day parade from his apartment. This was close enough to his birthday, he told me once, so that he thought for a while that the parade was for him. I thought of this many years later when George had to go to MacArthur Airport to do a fireworks show, and asked me to come along. The limo arrived to pick us up with, for some reason, a motorcycle escort. Here we are screaming down Second Avenue with sirens and lights, and into the Midtown Tunnel. George was so pleased with himself. He winked at me and said, "Stick with me, kiddo!"

RICHARD PRICE   The thing that I liked about George was that he was this combination of Long Island lockjaw and "Why can't I do that?" We were put on this earth to go on safari, and fly on a trapeze, and put on football helmets, and be commissioner of fireworks. I have a hard time having fun, period, and he was the paragon of fun.

REMAR SUTTON   The first time I met George was back in—oh God, in '71. I knew of him, of course, but we also had a good mutual friend, Bill Curry, the great football player he wrote *One More July* with. I invited George to fly down to Florida to have some fun. I've always liked to do things for fun, and our county, Brevard County, where the Kennedy Space Center is, was in a lot of trouble—the space program was winding down, the place was going to pot, so I decided we had to bring some good publicity to the county. So with George and the Gruccis we set off the biggest firework ever, one ton. This was the famous Fat Man [actually George's second of that name; his first, on Long Island, had been a dud, "the world's lowest firework," according to the Guinness record book; the original, of course, exploded over Nagasaki]. We were going to hide it in the middle of the Indian River. We took the mortar out to a small sandbar, buried it, and on the appointed day we took all the press out there, along with Fat Man. It was supposed to be shot off in about ten to fifteen minutes, when all of a sudden, by mistake, one of the Gruccis accidentally hit the delay starter and he yelled, "My God, it's going to go!" There were about fourteen of us who had to fit in one boat, which got stuck in the sand for too, too long. But then we gunned it and away we went. As we're tearing away, the Fat Man explodes and sends a shock wave that cracked the foundations of two houses and broke ten thousand dollars' worth of windows and set off every alarm within twenty miles. By the time we came to shore, the police were there to arrest George and me. George leaned over to me and said one word: "Marvelous."

KURT ANDERSEN My family called me "Explodo." I was mostly into big explosions, and that's what George planned for a *Lampoon* festivity in 1976. We made the largest explosive fireworks ever [Fat Man III]—over Boston, anyway. It was a folly, as much of the *Lampoon* is a folly, in the best sense. George's interest in pursuing beautiful, purposeless ventures of various kinds was what I admired most about him.

ROSE STYRON The first thing I remember of George's love of fireworks was when he brought a display to John Marquand's place on Martha's Vineyard. He carried the fireworks in his bag across three borders, illegally—by plane, train, and ferry. When he got to

Martha's Vineyard, we went out to Marquand's beach. It was the day before the Fourth of July, and we set it up on the beach, and it all went off and was tremendous fun. George was breathing a sigh of relief that nobody had arrested him. And all of a sudden, all these Army planes flew over. It was the same year they had the movie *The Russians Are Coming*, and somebody had alerted Otis Air Force Base that they'd seen fires, rockets, bombs, explosions of all sorts—but not fireworks. And they sent the whole Air Force over to see what was happening. And George thought, "Oh, my God," and packed everything up and fled the island, leaving John Marquand to face the music with the cops.

FREDDY ESPY PLIMPTON One year, George decided to do a Bastille Day fireworks because Ted Kennedy was coming to stay. We were renting on Gardiners Bay at that time, and George wanted to do a party for Ted, a dinner and fireworks. Well, the long and short of it is that the cops and fire department came, of course, and, after noting that Ted Kennedy was there, they arrested George, who

Fat Man III, Indian River, Florida. *Photograph © Bill Kilborn (1977).*

hadn't, of course, got a permit. It wasn't a major show, but it was major enough that neighbors saw it and complained. There was a lot of talk that they hated Kennedy out there. Perhaps Chappaquiddick was still on people's minds. Anyway, George got dragged off in handcuffs and slammed into the back of a police car. We were flabbergasted. We were saying things like "You can't do that! You can't—that's George Plimpton!" The cops were really mean. Teddy got him out, because, needless to say, he had a lawyer with him. When Ted's lawyer brought George back, he was very pale and very much in shock. He said, "I don't understand, I don't understand why they had to do that. If they do that to me, imagine what they do to poor people." He was going to make sure to get a permit from then on. Soon afterward, though, he turned it into a lighthearted story.

PATRICIA STORACE His attachment to fireworks—I mean, I can understand that; I love them, too. But look at how extraordinary they are, and how ephemeral. They're beautiful, beautiful, but sometimes you can think there's nothing sadder than fireworks. They're beautiful feats, but there is no more mortal art.

I.

GEORGE'S STORIED BACKGROUND

—

George talked about his family background end-lessly. The whole family, his mother especially, had an extraordinary knowledge of the glories of their past generations. As his wife, I heard all the stories many times. One story George loved was "Pull up your bowels, sir!" which is what General Adelbert Ames, "the Boy General," used to say when reviewing the men of the 20th Maine, maybe at Gettysburg when they drove back Pickett's Charge. It was George's way of saying, "Get a grip!"

—*SARAH DUDLEY PLIMPTON*

ANCESTORS

SARAH GAY PLIMPTON Our mother may have looked down on Daddy a bit. It wasn't his fault, of course, but Daddy wasn't an Ames.

TIMOTHY DICKINSON It is something to be an Ames in New England. The Ameses have been around, making themselves felt, for a substantial time in that part of the world. But the fact that the two prominent Ames families in George's family tree were called the "Maine Ameses," for their non-Boston origins, and the "shovel Ameses," for the homely origins of their wealth . . . well, that tells you something about their position in the New England hierarchy. It's not like being a Winthrop, a Cabot, a Forbes, a Lowell, a Saltonstall, or a Lawrence—to be one of the families whom one is never surprised, no matter how questionable their manners, to see in the Somerset Club. I guess George embraced that New England identity, with the Ameses carrying the Plimptons—socially, so to speak. But it was, as I say, not that *final* New England eminence, which features no more than a dozen families.

PHOEBE LEGERE I don't know how George and I got into a discussion about genealogy—at Elaine's!—but we were talking about how both of our mothers are in the Mayflower Society. At Society meetings, you know, they read off the names of the *Mayflower* passengers, and when the name of your ancestor comes up, you stand. So I asked George, "From whom are you descended?" He said, "I don't know, but my mother stands up five or six times." I just loved that.

OAKES PLIMPTON   Adelbert Ames, our great-grandfather, was
the hero in our family tree. He was the youngest general in the
Civil War, a Medal of Honor winner, and the officer who trained
and commanded the 20th Maine at Gettysburg, in fact throughout
the war. Afterwards, under Reconstruction, in the South, he became governor, then senator, then governor again of Mississippi.
He married Blanche Butler during this time, a daughter of another famous general, Benjamin Butler, who was a Radical Republican congressman from Lowell, Massachusetts. Adelbert and
Blanche Ames had a daughter—also named Blanche—and she
married a shovel Ames, Oakes Ames. Grandfather was a serious
Harvard professor of botany who was the son and nephew of
Oliver and Oakes Ames of the Crédit Mobilier scandal. Grandma
and Grandpa Ames lived in Boston and in North Easton, Massachusetts, where they built this big stone house on the shovel Ames
family estate, near the factory. They had four children, one of
them our mother, Pauline, who married our father, Francis T. P.
Plimpton, and they had four children: George, "T.P.," me, and
Sarah, in that order.

JOAN AMES   I never knew our great-grandmother Blanche Butler, Adelbert's wife, but she must have been a remarkable woman.
She and Adelbert wrote hundreds of wonderful letters to each
other. Before their wedding, she warned him, "I have not the least
intention of making that promise," meaning the vow of obedi-
ence. In another letter to Adelbert, who's in Mississippi now, she
recounts her adventure of going swimming "boy fashion" with
her sister Kate one night at the Butler summer place on Cape Ann.
It's beautifully written, seductive really, and Adelbert writes back
that he took a night swim in the Gulf of Mexico a few weeks later,
so as to share in her experience.

OAKES PLIMPTON   Adelbert Ames came from Rockland, Maine,
from a family that wasn't so fancy as the shovel Ameses or so rich
as the Butlers. As a great champion of black civil rights in the
South he failed, for sure, but only when the establishment Republicans up in Washington, many of them hot abolitionists before the

Top: Benjamin F. Butler.

Above: Adelbert Ames.

Bottom: Blanche Butler Ames.
All courtesy of the National Archives.

war, deserted the cause in the 1870s. That's when the North began turning against Radical Republicans like Adelbert and Butler, picking up the South's curse word for them, "carpetbaggers." You can find the same sneer, directed at Adelbert, in Kennedy's *Profiles in Courage,* published in the late 1950s. In the South, Adelbert was so hated that Jesse James and his gang of bank robbers, all ex-Confederates, rode all the way up to Northfield, Minnesota, where they heard he was visiting, in hopes of killing him. They didn't get him, of course. He lived to be ninety-seven—the oldest surviving Union officer—and George actually met him. He was only six, but he always liked to say, "I've looked into the eyes of the man who repulsed Pickett's Charge at Gettysburg."

SARAH DUDLEY PLIMPTON   George told me they'd met in the garden. George was terrified of him, he was so very old and so severe. His great-grandfather leaned over and picked up a stick and fiercely snapped it in two and said, "Life ends like that, boy."

WILLIAM BECKER   I remember one time in the early 1960s when George and I visited his grandmother Blanche in North Easton. She was an extraordinary woman. According to George, she became incensed at JFK's characterization of her father, General Ames, as a carpetbagger and wrote letter after letter to the president, demanding that he rectify the calumny in subsequent editions. Finally she asked George to intercede with Kennedy, who he knew, of course. As George told the story, JFK approached him at a White House party begging him to persuade his grandmother to stop writing these scolding letters. George said he told the president that it might be easier to remove the slander. JFK said he would but in fact did not. Whereupon, at age eighty or so, Blanche Ames commenced writing a massive biography of her father. I have it, and it's quite good.

OAKES PLIMPTON   Grandmother Ames was a lot of fun and figured out all these projects. She thought of this whole idea of a composting toilet and actually got patents for it. She prospected for oil on the Butler ranch in New Mexico; the company was called the Praying Mantis because that's what the oil rigs reminded her of. Unfortunately, they never struck oil. She was a suffragist and was also one of the people who started the Birth Control League in the 1930s; I think she even invented a contraceptive device. When some people began talking about eugenics, she quit. She was also an artist. She painted these incredible, lovely paintings of her husband's orchid collection; and she did landscapes and portraits. One drawing that this curator woman found was of a woman on the cross. Her feminism was one of those generational things. My mother was not a feminist.

JOAN AMES   Some part of George's income (and mine, for that matter) surely came from trust funds established by our great-great-grandfather Butler. Some came from the shovel Ameses, too, but Butler made lots of money as a lawyer after the Civil War. He was a social and political upstart in Massachusetts—most definitely not a Brahmin—and his wealth didn't stop him from winning the governorship of Massachusetts on the slogan "A friend of the working man." Which I believe he was: As governor, he appointed the first Irishman and the first African American to judgeships. There is a strong streak of unconventionality in the Butler line of our family.

ROWAN GAITHER   Butler is most famous, I suppose, for that infamous order which he promulgated as military governor of New Orleans. George kept a framed copy of it on his kitchen wall. It said that any woman who disrespected a Union soldier would be assumed to be a lady of the evening and treated as such. George also loved the story that Butler had been asked by Lincoln to be his vice president and that Butler had said, "I will agree to do so only if you promise to die." So the job went to someone else.

OAKES PLIMPTON   George didn't talk as much about the Plimptons. By an amazing coincidence, they came from a village in Walpole, just a few miles from the Ameses in North Easton. But our Plimpton grandfather, George Arthur Plimpton, decided he could do better in New York City. And he did, which is how come our father came to be born there—his mother died giving birth to him—and eventually settled there with Mother. Grandfather Plimpton was president of Ginn and Company, the textbook publishers, and a trustee of everything from the New York Philharmonic to Barnard and Exeter and Amherst. Amherst and Exeter, in fact, were sort of Plimpton family schools. Smith, too: Mother went there, and so did Sarah. Our grandfather and father and uncle [Calvin Plimpton, Francis's much younger half-brother, a doctor and college president] and my brother T.P. went to both of them. I went to Amherst, but Milton before that. George went to Exeter but then to Harvard. Daddy went to Harvard, too, to the law school. So did I, actually. Anyway, our father wasn't as "family proud" as our mother was, but Grandfather Plimpton was a good man. He collected stuff, old books and portraits of great writers, and cigar store Indians, and he gave Exeter some playing fields and Barnard a dormitory and God knows what else to other institutions.

SARAH GAY PLIMPTON Mother kept scrapbooks of all our doings, everything that got into print, from school yearbooks to the newspapers. Actually, I started it. When I was young and worshipful, I started a scrapbook with George's writings and achievements in it, but then Mother took it over. Naturally, George's scrapbooks grew hugely fatter than ours. I think the scrapbooks were an extension of her family pride. She also wrote books about, or compiled speeches and articles by, Benjamin Butler, her father-in-law, and our father. George wrote introductions for all of them, of course. And she wasn't shy about getting friends and strangers to buy them. George was like her in promoting *The Paris Review.*

OTHER GIVENS IN FAMILIES LIKE HIS

OAKES PLIMPTON George always used to say that there were two halves to the Plimpton family in our generation, the lower half and the upper half. George and our brother T.P. were "Irish twins," less than a year apart, and they're five and six years older than me. That's quite a gap. Sarah is almost four years younger than me, but we sort of formed a pair. George was born in 1927, a jazz baby, in

New York; I was born in 1933, a Depression baby, in Washington, D.C., where my father had gone to work for the Reconstruction Finance Corporation. Before Washington, they'd been living in France, where he worked for some law firm, so George and T.P. grew up speaking French. From Washington they went back to New York, where Daddy joined the firm that eventually became Debevoise Plimpton.

Francis T. P. Plimpton and Pauline Ames Plimpton.
From the collection of George Plimpton.

MEREDITH BROWN By middle-class standards, Francis and Pauline Plimpton were very well-off indeed. A profile in *The New Yorker* about George's father, when Kennedy appointed him deputy ambassador to the UN, totted up the various clubs he belonged to and concluded that most people in the United States didn't make as much money as the combined annual dues that Francis was paying for his club memberships. Francis was not a

Sam Walton rich person, but his running rate had to be pretty substantial, just to keep him in clubs and clothes and travel, his children educated, his houses kept up. On the other hand, lawyers in his day didn't make anywhere near as much money as they do today. Bear in mind, also, that Whitney Debevoise, *the* founding partner of Debevoise Plimpton, was getting twice what Francis was getting, I'm told. In the Plimpton household, my guess is that it was mostly her money.

SUSAN MORGAN I remember going to little musicales at George's mother's, and the maid would serve these dusty Pepperidge Farm Goldfish that they poured back into the bag. Six months later, you could swear it was the same Goldfish.

SARAH GAY PLIMPTON We spent our childhood at 1165 Fifth Avenue, a duplex apartment. The bedrooms were on the second floor, and mine looked out over St. Bernard's School, where my brothers all went, and over to the East River and the Triborough Bridge. From a side window, I could see the Central Park reservoir. On the first floor there was a library, a living room, a dining room, and a kitchen. Lots of windows, lots of light everywhere. Mother had a series of devoted Irish maids, including the one who took care of her for her last few months. We always had Sunday lunch after church, St. John's Episcopal Church in Cold Spring Harbor on Long Island in the summer, the Presbyterian (the Brick) Church on Park Avenue in the winter. I'm not so sure they were believers. Daddy thought it was a good thing to do. There was always the social aspect to it.

OAKES PLIMPTON In the summers, we lived out in Long Island, in a place called West Hills, near Cold Spring Harbor, which is not far from where Walt Whitman was born. At that time it was country, there was no one around at all. It was a shingle house with a peaked roof and a lot of windows. Our parents entertained there a lot. George came by his social appetites honestly—our parents were very social people—but I guess he outdid them and then some. Duke Sedgwick, Edie's father, was one of the people who used to come all the time. And when my father became deputy ambassador to the United Nations in 1961, all of a sudden there were all these parties out there entertaining the second tier of United Nations groups. He had everybody playing tennis, going swimming, but also Ping-Pong and touch football. One famous time, some ambassador from Africa got a football in his face, and nobody would own up as to who threw it. Next door there was a high hill, all natural, the highest hill in Long Island. Our neighbors could see Connecticut. We could see the Great South Bay twenty miles away. During the war, we used to bicycle to the Beach Club in Cold Spring Harbor, which was six miles away, all downhill.

JOAN AMES   My parents [Amyas and Evelyn Ames, Pauline's brother and sister-in-law] lived in the same small tribal community as the Plimptons. I remember this little telephone table in my parents' bedroom that held the *Social Register;* it was the only phone book we ever used. It was a time when you grew up in a circle of people who were very similar to you, a tribe of WASPs who were lawyers and bankers and brokers and architects. In the summer—in the winter, too, some of them—they all rode in the club car together to and from the city. Wherever you lived, up and down the north shore of Long Island, there were all these people you just *knew* or were related to. We often had Sunday dinner at the Plimptons' place in West Hills. For me it was heavenly, because they had their own tennis court and swimming pool and a beautiful meadow that swept down from the house. Oakes and George would just be killing each other on the tennis court, along with my brothers, Oakes and Ned, or other visitors and friends. Sarah, George's sister, was the youngest in the family, and she was always very sweet to me. After tennis, we'd go up the long path to the house and have roast beef and Yorkshire pudding and all the fixings, with a maid and a cook in the kitchen. And my uncle Francis would pontificate. I can remember my parents sometimes rolling their eyes about lawyers: Lawyers were just definitely a lower breed.

SARAH GAY PLIMPTON   During spring vacations, we loved visiting our Ames grandparents at Ormond Beach, in Florida, which had a wonderful natural world, and at North Easton, which was also a wonderful nature preserve: a thousand acres of ponds, grass-lands, and forests, which were full of interesting birds and animals and fish. Ormond Beach was the family compound where our grandmother Ames and her sisters had houses. It was on the inland waterway of the Halifax River, near Daytona Beach. Everyone fished there, especially George, who became something of a young naturalist at that point. There was a wooden trestle bridge from Or-mond to Ormond Beach, and George told stories about going out there and fishing with all these black people who were also fishing off the bridge and also telling stories. He was introduced to bird-watching, too, by our cousin Jack Stevens, whose favorite swear word was "Oh, fish hawks!" When Stevens pointed out an osprey to him, a kind of fish hawk, George became so entranced by the big bird, with its slightly naughty association, that he determined to become a bird-watcher. He was never as fanatic as Oakes and I, but he was a good one; we used to give each other bird presents at Christmas. George started out as a naturalist, though, and one sum-mer when he was fourteen he went out to California to collect an-imals for the Cleveland Museum of Natural History. He had these skins and skulls and so forth in the West Hills house, in a glass case.

GENE SCOTT One of the nice things about having a good up-bringing is having enough resources to have tennis lessons. By the time you're sixteen, seventeen years old, if you're playing against someone who didn't have lessons, you're going to beat them, no matter how gifted your opponent is. And it stays with you, too; you're not going to lose it. George was competitive; he had some grit. And he was cagey. Many people have no idea that some points are worth more than others. They may be very smart off the tennis court, but they are boobs on the court. George wasn't one of them.

ELISSA SCHAPPELL George was such a competitor, but also a gentleman. In tennis he took his game up just a notch higher than the person he was playing with. He wouldn't cream you in tennis; he'd just play slightly better than you. He always won, but he would never humiliate you, because he had this sense that that's not what one does.

Advantage, George.
From the collection of George Plimpton.

MARY LEE SETTLE His manners were almost southern. In Paris one time, we went somewhere in this tiny Citroën. George was driving along when a car cut in front of him, and he cried, "*Espèce de con!*" and then turned to me, and said, "Oh, I'm very sorry. I shouldn't speak that way in front of you."

FREDDY ESPY PLIMPTON I was always amazed at his lack of vanity. Part of it was that WASP background, but George carried it to extremes. One did nothing ostentatiously, so it was very, very hard to get George to buy a car that actually worked, or a new jacket, or to replace his torn and stained pants. It was even very hard to get George to look in a mirror when he was getting dressed. To him, it was vanity to have to watch himself put on a necktie or shave, so he was sort of hmm, hmm-hmm-hmm—looking around, looking away.

P. J. O'ROURKE Ideologically, George was of a piece with a certain segment of his class—a patrician liberal, a kind long gone. He wasn't terribly political, but he believed that people needed help and that the government should provide it when they needed it. I believed that people should be left alone; and that was the core of our argument. He would say, "Well, you just can't leave people alone, they need help." And I would say, "George, when we set about to help them, it's almost always disastrous." But George's was a munificent and beneficent and decent kind of liberalism. Part of that was the age difference between us. He had at least some sort of childish memory of the Depression. He had an adult memory of the war. He of course had a more mature memory of the civil rights struggle, which I have a child's or adolescent's

George in the Sierra Nevada.
From the collection of George Plimpton.

memory of. And then my leftist passions, when I had them, all had to do with the Vietnam War, with always the subtext of saving one's own butt.

SARAH DUDLEY PLIMPTON   He would have hated my saying this, but George had a deep sense of noblesse oblige. It knew no bounds. He loved swooping down and rescuing people. His compassion and loyalty were almost pathological, which got him in a lot of hot water from time to time.

WANDA URBANSKA   He had, so to speak, trace assumptions of the old ruling class. I came to work at the *Review* just when President Carter botched his Iran hostage rescue attempt. We were in the *Review* office, below the apartment, and George came down in his pajamas, I think, or maybe his boxers (it was often one or the other), and he was just in a rage. He said that he had fired off a telegram, or maybe he had called the White House, and he quoted himself as saying, "What on earth are you boys doing down there?"

NORMAN MAILER   He had a gift of a sort I never had: He never felt unimportant in the scheme of things. That was something to get worked up about. You know, where does this guy get that absolutely extraordinary, unique sense of cool? That's why blacks loved him.

BASIC EXPECTATIONS

JAMES GOODALE   George's father's primary motivating desire in life, I would say, was to be respected by the then governing class of his country, and he was. For lawyers in that class, what Francis did was an extraordinary achievement. Debevoise Plimpton isn't just any old firm; it is still consistently thought to be the top ten, top seven, firm in New York. In fact, it was recently voted the number one firm in the United States by *American Lawyer*. He wanted to be respected for the quality of the firm's product. It was as important to Francis to have something perfectly performed as it was to make a lot of money, and the high standards he had with respect to drafting and writing carried Debevoise for twenty or thirty years. That sort of perfection is no longer relevant in this age, but in his age it was, to a great degree, what made Debevoise a giant. I also think that he wanted to be respected for having a firm that had a sense of public purpose. Personally, too, he wanted to be respected for the fact that he did things other than draft documents, such as lead the march against the Vietnam War on behalf of the city bar association and being deputy ambassador to the UN.

SARAH DUDLEY PLIMPTON George told me that his father's favorite lecture at family dinners was the beauty of the mortgage indenture: "Accuracy is everything! One comma in the wrong place could cost millions!"

MEREDITH BROWN Debevoise Plimpton was a "white shoe" firm, which I think referred to the people who wore white buckskin shoes in the summer, which meant that they probably weren't scuffing their shoes too much in the dirt. But even when I joined, in 1966, I would say that Debevoise Plimpton was moving towards being a much more diverse place. One of our main partners was Jewish, which was a big deal in those days. It used to be that there were firms that were almost entirely Jewish and almost entirely not Jewish. Debevoise was a little ahead of the curve, similarly with women and African American partners. Only a few firms were more diverse. I don't think Francis was a snob in that sense at all.

SARAH GAY PLIMPTON Father cared about where someone went to college. That was more important for him than who the person actually was. If you went to Harvard, Amherst, Yale, you were obviously good. If you went to some college he didn't know about, it was already a strike against you. I think, later in life, he loosened up; but I remember bringing home a boyfriend who had gone to Union College, and this just wasn't possible. Part of it was snobbery—Union wasn't the "right" sort of college—but for him I think the college you went to was an index of how smart you were or how hard you were prepared to work, especially the latter.

MEREDITH BROWN   As a distinguished graduate of Amherst, Francis was a longtime trustee of that institution—as indeed he was of Exeter, the Philharmonic, the Metropolitan Museum, though these I think he sort of inherited from his father. At Debevoise Plimpton, there was the story about when Francis was head of the search committee at Amherst, looking for a new president. He looked and looked and looked and after an exhaustive search came up with a recommendation that his brother Calvin be the president.

OSBORN ELLIOTT   Francis and I were at a Harvard Board of Overseers meeting that advised the president on suitable recipients of honorary degrees. When Robert Lowell's name was put forward, Francis pulled a sheet of paper out of his briefcase and, with a great flourish, read a few lines from the famous poem—I forget the title—that Lowell set in Nantucket. "Those lines were cribbed from Thoreau," said Francis, very severely. "We can't give a degree to a plagiarist." When it was explained to the distinguished lawyer that Lowell was deliberately reflecting Thoreau's work, I remember Francis seeming more offended, perhaps, than embarrassed.

OAKES PLIMPTON   My father had a prejudice against stockbrokers and other people who just made money. I think the real question was whether someone had a true profession, whether they'd acquired a whole bunch of learning. He was a Puritan in that respect. For example, he belonged to an awful lot of clubs, but he looked down upon the Piping Rock Club to a degree, because it was filled with these stockbrokers and people who displayed their riches. He felt that they didn't deserve the money they got, and he made it obvious. He preferred the Beach Club in Cold Spring Harbor, which had clay courts, not grass, and you couldn't eat lunch there; no drinks, either. The beach was of rock, so you had to swim from the docks, essentially, and the clubhouse was nothing special.

TONI GOODALE   Pauline had a gang of women, about eight of them, and they ruled New York. They knew they did and they liked it, and they were very intimidating. When Jim went to De-bevoise Plimpton from *The New York Times,* I was told that I had to join the Cosmopolitan Club; they shepherded me in there, then watched me while I went through the tea ritual. There was no questioning it. I would never say, "Well, gee, that's not really where I want to spend my time."

SARAH DUDLEY PLIMPTON I liked his mother. My first real en-counter with her was the summer before George and I got mar-ried. I was living in a tiny penthouse on Sixty-ninth Street, and one hot August afternoon she invited herself to tea. She wore a linen dress with stockings and heels, and her hair had a fresh blue rinse. I, on the other hand, was sweaty and dirty from digging in my tiny garden. She was very direct: "Sarah, I just want to know one thing—what are your intentions with my son?" Most people would have been appalled by her bluntness, but I found it refresh-ing and blurted out something like "Well, Mrs. Plimpton, I am

George with his mother, Pauline. *From the collection of George Plimpton.*

deeply in love with your son and I want to marry him." From that moment we got along wonderfully. I remember she used to exhort me, "Sarah, take control of that household!"

JEANNE MCCULLOCH   The *Paris Review* staff had this running joke about his mother, who used to come by all the time, and we always called her "George in pearls." She was this vision of a Plimpton at the prow of a ship that would sail forward with the pearls first, going, "Ge-orge!"—"Yes, Mutha!" and they would go

George, "T.P.," and Pauline with Oakes and Sarah Gay at Borderlands, the estate of Oakes and Blanche Ames. *Courtesy of Sarah Gay Plimpton.*

off to lunch together. I always got the sense that he was never going to come into himself fully until she died. She hung around for way too long.

RUTH TALBOT PLIMPTON   The truth is that Pauline adored George far and away above her other children, so much so it was almost shameful, criminal.

REMAR SUTTON   George loved to tell the story about how his mother once saved his life. It was the time he and Freddy went rafting with Bobby Kennedy on the Colorado River, and he fell overboard. The water was rough and running fast, and George seemed to be making no headway swimming toward shore. In fact he went under—twice, as he told it—but then, as he was going under for the third time, he had this vision of his mother collecting his things after his death, poking around the apartment, and finding a few reels of a movie called *The Nun's Delight* that he'd stashed away in a wooden box. Instantly he found the strength to struggle to the surface and swim to shore.

OAKES PLIMPTON   Our parents were both very puritanical and believed in hard work. My report cards from Buckley are full of parental jottings saying, "He has to work harder." I think George received some of the same advice. They didn't believe in coddling kids at all. We were spanked with hairbrushes and belts and things, by either my father or my mother, depending on who was around and how serious it was. Of course, being belted by your father was more unfortunate. They definitely believed in corporal punishment, no doubt about that. My mother was the type who did not accept apologies. If I broke a lamp or something and said, "I'm sorry"—well, that just wasn't going to work. One weird thing: My parents believed in not getting clothed all the time, so we actually saw our parents naked, which is sort of different from the way I brought up my kid. There was some sort of doctrine that they'd read that it was important for kids to see grown-ups without their clothes on.

SARAH DUDLEY PLIMPTON   If you read some of his classmates' notes in Francis's yearbooks from Amherst and Exeter, people thought of Francis almost as a minister, incredibly pious and scholarly. He was chained to his sense of obligation, so naturally he thought George was having way too much fun—not making the academic grade. On the other hand, Francis's letters to George when he was working his way up the ranks in the Army were full of pride, and by the time George was in his thirties, writing well-received books, hobnobbing with the Kennedys—the people, after all, who appointed Francis deputy ambassador to the UN—they were actually very proud of each other. Yet I don't think George ever accepted that—that his father could actually be proud of him.

SARAH GAY PLIMPTON Everyone in the family had to live up to Father's standards of performance. Achieving them wasn't complicated; he thought: "If you work hard enough, you should do very well." That's the sort of person he was. All his children came up short at one point or another, and his solution was always "Work hard." It's a very simplistic way of looking at things. George, Oakes, T.P., I—we all bore the brunt of it when we were growing up. Sarah [Sarah Dudley Plimpton] thinks George was a textbook case of attention deficit disorder. T.P. had a lot of difficulties. We all did. I think it skewed how we approached things, too. We were supposed to grow up to be like him: overachieving WASPs who fit into New York Society; and none of us did—rebelliously or not—except George, in his odd way. Odd, I mean, in the view of New York Society.

GEORGE BECOMES GEORGE

PETER MATTHIESSEN George never ventured very far from his family background. Any child in the household of Pauline and Francis T. P. Plimpton had excellent manners or else. He never used four-letter words and was generally circumspect in his language. Even when drunk, he very seldom turned himself loose entirely, and his dress was faithful to his upbringing. One had to admire his unflinching loyalty to the shirt and tie, V-necked sweaters, sports jacket, gray flannels, and fedora. He kept a tight rein on himself and minded his mother. I remember the time in the late fifties when George and I were both involved with beautiful, very smart, funny young women. George was absolutely nuts about his girl, but at a certain point, he let it end or let her end it for him. I remember he blurted out, "Well, y'see, old fella, she wasn't quite . . . *socially acceptable!*" I was aghast. I said, "This is ridiculous!" and George said, "I know." He was truly miserable.

JOAN AMES   You might not have seen him for years, but George's family feeling was strong and warm. All of his cousins would call him periodically, even though we weren't *au courant* with him in any way. He would treat me like a long-lost sister. He'd be there for me on the other end of the phone—he'd call me "love" and my heart would melt, that's all I could say. You know, he was this older cousin, he was famous, he was busy, but he had all the time in the world for me.

SARAH GAY PLIMPTON   How did George cope with parents like ours? Well, he tried really hard to live up to their standards; and maybe he got credit for trying. We all did. But maybe George was more sensitive to their intellectual challenges, to being reprimanded, to being called to account, than the rest of us were. I know that except for games he hated contention and criticism, not only to protect himself, but all of us. Of course I was much younger than he was, but by the time I came along, whenever he was at home, I saw how extraordinarily good he was at deflecting even the possibility of confrontations. He did it with stories, with self-deprecating humor, with a gentle sense of absurdity, with unfailing good humor. He coped with our parents by entertaining them. He made them happy. This required tremendous emotional self-control, especially in someone as young as George must have been when he began. It also required a great gift from somewhere. The rest of us didn't get it.

CHARLES MICHENER   George was someone who figured out early on that it was easier to get through life with a persona. He *became* George Plimpton.

JAMES GOODALE   In the St. Bernard's alumni bulletin, there are some great stories about George. One that struck my fancy was about George as the pitcher on the St. Bernard's baseball team. Apparently, he read books on how to pitch, or perhaps studied

George as Prospero, St. Bernard's School, 1939.
Courtesy of St. Bernard's School Archives.

other pitchers very carefully, and one day came to school with a pitch that no one else at St. Bernard's could throw: an underhand fastball. Now, what sort of kid thinks of throwing a fastball underhand, other than a person who is conscious of his own persona? So, as a young fellow who is developing a particular persona, and if you've got a gift for telling stories in a charming way, a gift of great charm, charisma even, why wouldn't you work on that, too, especially as it might be an effective way of keeping your parents off your back? He could really charm his way out of, and into, almost anything. He probably figured that out as a little kid, and he got away with things, even with someone as tough as Pauline. He discovered a way to make room for happiness, his own and others'.

FREDDY ESPY PLIMPTON   George never tried to change anybody to make himself comfortable, not for a minute. He worked
his own way through to a point of comfort, and if he could do
something to make others comfortable, which he almost always
could, he did that, too.

JEANNE MCCULLOCH   He must have spent so much time trying
to keep his parents at a bearable distance, by keeping things light,
by keeping them amused; he had no choice but to keep doing it all
his life. But, God forbid, don't go to the deeper emotions.

NANCY STODDART   Was it Mailer? I don't know, but *somebody*
called him a smokeless Vesuvius—anger, but no sign of it. But because George was so genial and charming, he could pretty much
make things purr along in a manner that pleased him. There
wasn't much reason for anger. Anger was for when someone
nipped the edge of a boundary of his, and then he let you know.
He was like a well-trained animal. Well-trained animals will behave perfectly well until you violate a boundary. He was a strong
person in that way. Otherwise, being so genial and charming, if he
didn't have that boundary thing, he would have been awful.

BLAIR FULLER   I used to think of George as a psychological
tragedy. The unfailing courtesy, generosity, curiosity, the insistent
self-deprecation. Yes, of course, that was the secret of his charm, as
a storyteller and as a social creature, but how much self-deprecation
can an ego take before it becomes self-mutilation?

HIS ACCENT

MICHAEL FRITH   I remember a number of years ago *New York*
magazine ran one of those "Best of New York" articles, and for
"Best Accent" they chose George's. There was a little footnote
saying, "By the way, where did he get that thing?" But of course,
if you'd met George's father, you'd know exactly where he got
that thing. If anything, it was even more patrician than George's.

ANTONIO WEISS   You would never understand his accent until you spoke with his mother. Whatever you thought of his accent, it was a very watered-down version of hers.

SUSAN MORGAN   He was the only person I know who could say Gore Vidal's first name as though it had four syllables in it, the pitch rising and falling—"I think we should talk to Go-ah-r-ahh." You should see the TV show he did, on the making of *Rio Lobo*, the one where he's playing a cowboy: He's trying to say his one line in a cowboy accent, and it's hilarious. He can't do it. He couldn't *not* speak in that accent.

HUGH HEFNER   When we were planning a *Playboy* twenty-fifth anniversary TV special for ABC, I wanted George to read a voice-over. ABC didn't want him. I insisted, and they used him. I liked the fact that George had a kind of Kennedyesque, eastern voice, and I thought it was right for an overview, not only of the history of *Playboy,* but the history of pop culture and politics of the past twenty-five years. He was the perfect choice, and as a result he was offered a whole lot of work, voice-overs and commercials.

JAMES ZUG   He told me that at Cambridge [University] he'd read for a production of *As You Like It* and was rejected because they thought his accent was so bad, he must have grown up in Brooklyn.

CALVIN TRILLIN   I had this strong feeling that it wasn't an affectation. It was an accent that might exist elsewhere; you just hadn't met any other people who spoke that way, and you probably hadn't met them because you really weren't *haute* enough to be allowed into their presence. They surely existed somewhere, but only God knows where. It was exciting, the idea that he was a representative of a people who would one day come here to be with us.

HARRY MATHEWS   He never talked any other way to anyone. George was candor itself. Anybody who was with him for more than one minute knew that he wasn't trying to act superior, that that was just the way he was. He was a model example of the fact that being very open about who you are is the best way to inspire people's trust.

BRUCE JAY FRIEDMAN   When I closed my eyes and listened to him, it was like listening to Katharine Hepburn. I never heard anything quite like it. I thought if you woke him in the middle of the night, he'd say, "You talkin' to me?" He'd sound like De Niro.

DAVID MICHAELIS   All I remember of George's own description of his accent was "eastern seaboard cosmopolitan." Something like that. I thought that it must have come from St. Bernard's and that it was very much a part of his self-created persona, but something that he was entirely comfortable with. At the same time, there was this whole sense of, as Don Hall said, "You can't have a voice like George's and be taken seriously." Was he entirely comfortable with that, with George Plimpton being a kind of joke? It's hard to imagine, but perhaps this was the plan, or a happily unintended consequence of the plan. I don't know: I just always understood the accent to be part of himself.

II.

SIGHTINGS OF GEORGE
AT SCHOOL: 1934–1952

—

We do not mind the winter wind
Or weep o'er summer's bier,
Nor care a jot if cold or hot,
So long as football's here;
And fat and thin can all join in,
The sport is all the same;
There's health and fun for every one
Who plays the good old game. . . .

There's naught to choose
'Twixt win and lose—
The game's the game for all.

—ST. BERNARD'S FOOTBALL SONG

ST. BERNARD'S

BUZZ MERRITT St. Bernard's School at that time was one of the three best private boys' schools in New York City. It's on East Ninety-eighth Street, right next to where the Plimptons lived. The faculty was almost entirely British. When George and I started, there was only one American, and he was the athletic director. The fellow who headed the school—Mr. Jenkins, by name John Card Jenkins—had come over as a young teacher from Britain with a partner named Tabor after World War I and started this school, really as a moneymaking venture. Mr. Jenkins was very attractive, as were his number two and number three, and they were constantly asked out to dinner parties by kids' parents. Their marketing was very low-key. There were two other good schools at the time: Buckley and Allen-Stevenson; but they were not British, and St. Bernard's had a cachet all to itself, which we're quite proud of.

PETER MATTHIESSEN One good thing due to the presence of British teachers was that we learned how to parse a sentence. We were given sentences of increasing complexity, and we were able to assign the grammatical function to every word, which was invaluable for a career in writing. To my amazement, ages later, I found that many of my college students had never learned this, and they were incapable of saying what part of speech "however" is.

BUZZ MERRITT We had our own little caps, along with the traditional uniforms of gray flannels and white shirts, and in the summer, gray flannel shorts. We always had to have our caps on when we came to school or there were serious consequences. The academics were very rigorous, and we were generally quite terrified of our teachers. There was one little fellow, a Mr. Edwards, an English teacher, a very high-blood-pressure type, who would stand us up and kick us in the butt whenever we did bad things. In Latin, we were lined up against the wall every morning to recite our vocabulary—five or six new words, every day. Those who missed went to the end of the line. At the end of the line, we got either a whack with the ruler or we had chalk thrown at us, etc., etc. It was the British "public school" attitude, where there was a lot of discipline and a good deal of fear. George and I had a teacher who actually kept a shillelagh prominently propped against his desk. He never used it, but the threat was always there. In hindsight, we received a great education, particularly for memory.

BILLY GRAHAM We had a lot of interesting people in our class— or, at least, the children of interesting people. Punch Sulzberger was one of them, who later became the publisher of *The New York Times*. Who else? Charlie Morgan, whose grandfather was J. P. Morgan. I remember a teacher once said to him, because Charlie was rather slow, "Charlie, the Morgan family is like a baby carriage rolling down a hill." Charlie just smiled. I think we kept up with each other more than most elementary school classmates do, but I'd guess that the longest-running friendship was between George and Peter Matthiessen. They were both literary, and of course Peter gave George the editorship of *The Paris Review*, which was as close to a "real" job as he ever had.

BUZZ MERRITT George was extremely good at baseball. He was a pitcher, a little wild, but very good. I think he won every game he pitched in the two years we were on the so-called first team. I was his catcher. When I would go out to the mound to steady him down, George reacted well. He got better. We were also great fans, and we got into collecting autographs any way we could. We would go downtown to all the hotels where the visiting teams were staying and try to get their autographs in the lobby in the morning. Usually we'd be thrown out by the floorwalkers and try to sneak back in. We knew every single doorway, the garbage entrances, the service entrances, of all the hotels. We were rabid collectors.

George pitching for St. Bernard's.
Courtesy of St. Bernard's School Archives.

NELSON ALDRICH George told me a story once about going out for a weekend in the country with Punch Sulzberger. They were driven, of course, by a uniformed chauffeur in a limousine, but about midway in the journey, they got a flat in the right rear tire. What followed was not the worst of George's lifetime of mortifications, but he vividly recalled his squirming embarrassment in the backseat as the chauffeur got out of the car and set about changing the tire. He remembered how the tails of the man's black uniform jacket flapped crazily in the wind of the passing traffic and how the sweat stood out on his face as he worked the jack up and down, up and down, while the rear of the car, with the little boys safe in their soft gray seats, went up, up, up.

BUZZ MERRITT   In those days, our class enemies, so to speak, were the Irish, known as "Micks"—a terrible scourge. On weekends, they would come out to Central Park where we were playing and challenge us to football games. They always insisted, "You kick off first, and we'll receive." Of course, if you went with that, as we did the first time, you kicked the ball, and it ended up miles away in what is now Spanish Harlem. The blacks were way up in the north of the city, so it was the Micks who taunted us. Our caps were what did it. One day, I remember this particular group came up to steal a baseball bat or something, and a tough-looking big Irish kid, with six or seven others, confronted us. We were all trembling, wondering what to do, and suddenly Toby Wherry cracked and surged forward—he was a big kid, but always very retiring—and started quoting *Macbeth,* I think it was: "Out, damned spot!" This Irish kid just melted. They all ran away.

PETER MATTHIESSEN   George was a good student. I had evidence at one time: a report card from the school, and it showed that one of us had 95 or 96 in Latin, and that wasn't unusual. When he applied himself, George was very bright and got good marks.

BUZZ MERRITT   We had a couple of cutups, including George. I remember one time some scatological stuff had been written in the toilet, and Mr. Jenkins announced that there'd be no more of *that.* He was going to inspect it. One day, Plimpton and another fellow got the idea of putting soccer shoes on the top of the door, and leaving the door a bit ajar, and balancing a full cup of water on it, too. We were all happily doing our homework one evening when suddenly Mr. Jenkins came into the room and then walked purposely into the locker room. The next thing we heard was a great clattering, and out came Mr. Jenkins, soaked with water. Terrifying event. George was quite instrumental in that. By and

large, though, he was in the mainstream. I mention this prank because of course he diverged considerably from the mainstream
later on.

PETER MATTHIESSEN George cut the same figure from start to
finish. In photographs, right to the end, he mostly had that inquis-
itive, pointy-nosed, mischievous look that I seem to recall from
when we were little boys.

BUZZ MERRITT A great event at St. Bernard's was the annual
Christmas Shakespeare play at the Heckscher Theatre, which used
to be on 104th Street. The play was chosen in the spring, and we
had to learn our lines during summer vacation. Our mothers will
never forget. We were given progressively bigger parts as the years
went on. George was a good actor and always had very significant
parts. My senior year we did *The Tempest,* and he was Prospero. I
was Caliban. That was a very, very good show. Of course, it was
absolutely terrifying, but you realized that everyone who had gone
before you had done it, so you could, too.

TOBY WHERRY, JR. St. Bernard's is where that famous story
comes from, which I've heard over and over again, about George
being discovered as a writer by my father. George had written a
short story; I think it had something to do with the chauffeurs'
race, the annual Field Day footrace for the chauffeurs that many St.
Bernard's families employed in those days. He'd gotten a C on it,
I believe, and my father ripped it from his hands. I'm not sure if he
read it then and there, or they read it out loud, or whatever, but he
angrily crossed off the C and wrote an A, and said something like
"You're a real writer."

PETER MATTHIESSEN Our paths split in the fourth or fifth grade,
and years would pass before George and I saw much of each other
again. However, we must have stayed loosely in touch because
when I was in Paris in the early 1950s, and the time came to find
someone to edit the as-yet-unnamed *Paris Review,* I knew where
to find him.

EXETER

BUZZ MERRITT I went to Exeter because George and so many St. Bernard's boys were going. I guess George started it because of his father's and grandfather's connection. His father was president of the board of trustees, as his grandfather had been before him. The "Plimpton playing fields" tell the rest of the story. We were pretty young. I had just turned thirteen.

TIM SELDES Exeter and Andover were brother and sister schools. We always thought that Andover was where the rich boys went and Exeter was more democratic, but I would imagine that the average income of parents of Exonians was fairly high.

BUZZ MERRITT The first big thing, which occurred when we were freshmen, was when George became interested in taxidermy. That summer, he had gone on a trip with the Cleveland Museum to California, where they were collecting rodents, which they skinned and stuffed. When they got back to New York, there were a lot of extra skins, so George said he'd take them, and he brought them back to his room at Exeter. He had them scattered all over the place and was practicing taxidermy on them from a book. I remember a whole lot of rodents with cotton sticking out of their mouths. We had maids in those days who came in and made our beds and cleaned our rooms, and one of them opened the door to George's room and screamed and ran down to the dorm master, who went to investigate and encountered all of George's rodents with cotton sticking out of their mouths. George thought that was a lovely prank, even though he hadn't really intended it.

> *Dear Mother,*
>   *Sorry not to have written for such a long time, but I thought I would summarize all the things that have happened in just one letter.*
>   *I joined up with the Exonian today, to my great surprise, with [Warren] Leslie. My first job as a heeler was to pick a penny off the floor.*

A few days ago, the Blue team (which I am on) played Emerson. We beat them 19–0. . . .

I have not yet found a birthday present for Sarah. I went shopping the other day but Exeter is not New York.

I hope you will come up soon.

My first job for the Exonian is to write a, quote—n'everything—unquote. This is an article in the Exonian which is filled up with curious happenings in and about the school.

I think the first quote—n'everything—unquote, I shall write is as follows: Two enthusiastic juniors, Buzz and myself, were seen kicking field goals (sometimes) under the light of the moon.

My radiator had quite a few visitors last night. It seems as if the radiator is not turned off the whole way it begins to knock all the other radiators to bits. So a few masters broke in at four o'clock a.m. and turned it off.

My subjects have been going along fairly well except for Algebra. I am a little careless, but I am sure that I will improve.

Boys almost fall over at the sight of my rattlesnake. I am so glad I brought it up.

If my squirrel skin is ready, that is with no flesh on it, please send it up. (In laundry bag.)

Grandma called while I was seeing a football game and I could not see her. She left me a basket of apples. Do thank her for me. . . .

[no date]

FARWELL SMITH I first met George at Exeter in 1941. He had come with a crowd of St. Bernard's and Buckley kids, who were pretty fast for my Chicago speed. George wasn't one of the fast, though. Maybe I'm hard on New Yorkers, but at the age of thirteen and fourteen they were kind of clubby and looked down a little bit on the outlanders who came from other parts of the country, particularly the Midwest and the West. But George was less snooty. He was also a wonder to behold because he was very tall at a fairly young age. One of my first vivid memories of him was of him at six feet three playing the maid in a play at Exeter. He was very noticeable, and he was funny. He had a way of tripping across the stage, and although it was a small part, it was a very memorable one. He got write-ups on it because his whole manner of doing it was enhanced by his gangly size. He was sort of like a shaven Abe Lincoln.

GORE VIDAL We sat next to each other at chapel. I remember he was a rather uncouth-looking boy and always sort of on the outside of things. Of course, he had the cachet of the Plimpton playing fields, which had been given by his family to the school, where games were played and where, you can count on it, I never set foot in four years.

TIM SELDES Most of us were ordinary boys, and George was extraordinary. He saw things in his own wonderfully imaginative, idiosyncratic way. And especially compared to the rest of us insecure ragged little muffins, George always seemed to be sophisticated. He and Gore Vidal seemed to be the two who knew the great world in a way that none of us did at all and could barely aspire to.

BUZZ MERRITT I was athletic, and George was athletic, so it was easier for us. None of us were any good at football, though. We played club football, and with a great friend of ours, Ted Lamont, we all finally ended up in the Exeter band, where I played the cymbals, and George beat the bass drum, and Ted Lamont carried the bass drum.

TIM SELDES George and I were the two pitchers, and even at this late date I cannot help but say that I was the number one pitcher. George used to envy my accuracy because I could also throw the ball quite fast. George had this absolutely gigantic curveball. This great angular figure would be almost parallel to the ground and this great arm would uncoil and this enormous curve would come. And on the prep team, the freshman team, we were the two pitchers. I think we were the only freshman team in Exeter's history that ever placed higher than fourth. We finished first. It was a triumph that George and I were largely responsible for and inordinately proud of.

BUZZ MERRITT Of course, the war was very much in our minds. I remember on Sunday, December 7, George and I were over in the gym playing pickup basketball, and we ended up walking back to our dormitory, and everybody was yelling, "They bombed Pearl Harbor, they bombed Pearl Harbor!" We all gathered in our social center, the Butt Room, where you smoked downstairs. I remember everybody just being in stitches about the Japanese navy. What are these people doing when they had absolutely no navy? It showed a real gap in our knowledge of the Japanese. The Germans were supposed to be on their way to bomb New York. We couldn't figure out how they could get their planes there. That was all in the flash of the moment, but then things simmered down. School went on, except that we were obviously engaged in the day-to-day progress of the war.

TIM SELDES Exeter was an academic pressure plate. The first thing that comes to mind about that tension is that they marked us on an A, B, C, D scale, except they would go below that. You could get an E, or in a worst-case scenario you could get an E-Q, which meant not only that you were irredeemably stupid, but also that you didn't even care. I doubt that George had very good grades, except in English. In English, he was remarkable even then.

BUZZ MERRITT Exeter had a famous phrase—"There are no rules at Exeter until you break one." And George pushed the edge of that envelope, considerably. He was getting into a little trouble here and a little trouble there. Just generally raising hell on the edge of dorm discipline—fooling around in the halls when he was supposed to be studying and that sort of thing. But George was always a bit of a rebel. He liked to trick authority figures, you know. People who got away with things like that had a certain cachet. As at all schools, there was a faculty versus students rivalry. George played to that, but I think some of it was, frankly, that his mind was not set up for strict schedules. It was his innocent vagueness. In fact, I think his nickname at school was "Vague," "Vague George."

SARAH GAY PLIMPTON He didn't do very well at Exeter, and he talked about the letters Daddy sent him. "Work hard. Do this, do that"—one of them with a fifteen- or twenty-point program to follow, everything specified from the type of paper he should use

January 1, 1944

Resolutions

1. To work hard at any task which is given to me, not trying to fool others, or, more important, myself.

2. To write a letter to Daddy every evening, to tell him what I have done during the day.

3. To keep a diary - faithfully - so that I may have a chance to look back over the days and reprimand myself on tasks done poorly and congratulate myself on a task done well.

4. To rise early, to be on time, to go to bed early.

5. To never waste time - to keep an appointment book.

6. To answer letters immediately.

7. To appreciate the judgment of those older and experienced.

8. To follow the above faithfully, knowing that I can fail no longer, that I stand before an abyss, but realizing at the same time, that through faith and work, there must lie ahead happiness, and above all, satisfaction in a success.

Supplementary Resolutions

1. I will drive my work - and not let it drive me.

2. I will be completely and absolutely honest in my work and to my teachers and to myself.

3. I will work first.

4. I will not postpone - I will do it now.

5. I will not read the newspaper more than 15 minutes a day.

6. I will take nothing into study hall except my work.

7. I will not read any trash of any sort.

8. When I am studying I will concentrate, concentrate, concentrate.

9. I will not day dream.

10. I will answer letters promptly.

11. In class I will pay attention every second, so that I won't miss anything.

12. When I write anything, I will read it over carefully (just as though someone else had written it) and catch the mistakes myself before handing it in.

13. I will learn to say NO - to others, and to myself.

14. I will remember that nothing counts except results.

15. I will not sponge - I will stand on my own feet.

16. I will not make excuses.

17. I will not be easy going - I will push myself.

18. When I have finished reading a chapter, I will read it through again, marking the things to remember.

19. I will not be discouraged by my mistakes and failures; I will learn from them, and determine never to let them happen again.

20. I will watch my health, and try to make myself strong.

21. I will be neat about my appearance - hair cut short, hair combed and brushed, face and hands clean, clothes clean and not mussed or torn, clean shirt, clean under-wear, shoes shined.

22. I will eat plenty of sensible food - milk especially, and lots of variety.

23. I will be interested in my work, and try to understand the why of things.

24. If there is something I don't understand, I won't let it alone until I do understand it.

25. I will stand up straight, and walk as if I were carrying a pail of water on my head.

26. I will change the pattern!

Any of the following will be regarded as justifying immediate withdrawal

1. Any unprepared recitation - the teacher is to be the judge.

2. Any paper handed in late.

3. Any failure in any marks.

4. Any failure to write us every day - a letter must be post marked by the post office each day.

Francis Plimpton to George: resolutions for success at Exeter.

From the collection of George Plimpton.

to rules on how to concentrate. Toward the end when George was on probation, Daddy demanded that George write him a short letter—all on the same blue stationery! every day!—accounting for his time. And George would sit down to try and do all this, and of course he couldn't.

> *Dear Daddy,*
>
> *Passed a very lazy Sunday. Heard a very poor preacher at the Phillips Church. His sermon pointed straight at me though, but that doesn't surprise me anymore.*
>
> *Wrote my Exonian story in no time flat, cleaned up the room so it looks unbelievable.*
>
> *Saw the Dean tonight. He says he['s] glad to have me back, and thinks I can do it. I know I will satisfy him.*
>
> *Followed schedule perfectly.* [January 9, 1944]

> *Dear George,*
>
> *The two blue envelopes I found on my desk downtown this morning were a welcome sight. I'm glad that things have started out all right—now let's have them go right along the same way.*
>
> *Suggestion no. 1 is that you send letters up here to the apartment, for Mummie is just as interested in them as I am. Suggestion no. 2 is that you write them in ink. A letter in pencil inevitably looks sloppy and blurred, no matter how carefully you write it.*
>
> *I'm glad that the dean thinks that you can pull through. So do I, if you pull. That is something you must do yourself—it's up to you and no one else.*
>
> *We never did finish talking out whether or not you should resign from the Exonian, but I think it's all right for you to keep on if you'll do your work on it efficiently and promptly, and not waste time fiddling around. Indeed, you must train yourself to be efficient about time—I don't like the sound of a very lazy Sunday; it's all right if the laziness means no sports, for that's OK until your ear mends, but let's have no lazy minds ever!*
>
> *I'm delighted to hear that the room is cleaned up—now let's see you keep it that way. I know that I find it ever so much easier to work and think and live if things are neat around me. If they're*

neat I know that I'm their master, but if they're a mess I'm never sure who really is in charge here, to quote Mr. Darrow's cartoon.

Affectionately, Daddy
[January 11, 1944]

Dear Daddy,
    I have been a little slow on starting off my everlasting stream of epistles but I thought I'd wait until I got back all those tests that I was studying violently that weekend. So from now on, your letters come in daily.
    Believe it or not I knew my Greek well enough to get an 80 on the test, an eighty. Mr. Phillips is shocked, and so am I. That gives me a C in Greek. Got a C– in the English theme, but [the English teacher] *is going to give me an incomplete because I missed two very important tests.*
    I got a C– in the second History test, which will give me a D in that course. And finally a D in the French test, which will give me the same mark. Mr. [Bull] *Clark is pleased, but won't take me off any of my restrictions. I guess he wants better, and I'll be fighting to give it to him. . . .* [February 9, 1944]

Dear Mummy,
    . . . I suppose I might start off with the bad news to make you feel happy. Apparently the crime of staying out after eight is a great deal more serious than I had ever dreamed of, and especially with regard to me. The faculty put me on disciplinary probation:—now all the loopholes are closed, and I must be very careful. So much for the bad news. I feel most wretched about the whole thing, for it was so completely needless. I apologize—that is my first apology.
    I have never worked so hard in my life as I have this last week. Three nights out of four I have stayed up almost the complete night. I fell asleep at my desk at 3:00 o'clock this morning, and was found there by Mr. Clark, who remarked somewhat stoically that I looked like a ghost. . . . I should get a C in French, perhaps a C in history, and if [I] *get a 100 on a Greek test, which I am setting as my*

mark, I will get a B in Greek. English is my worst, somewhat of a
shock when [I] realize I am the class poet. My chances are rather
dim for passing this marking period.

Baseball is in full swing now, and I think I'm doing very well.
I have not been doing a great deal of pitching, but I think Mr.
Clark is pleased. I missed [getting on] the squash team by a hair.
I'm playing in the Lockett Cup tournament, and may get my letter
if I win. . . . [February 11, 1944]

BUZZ MERRITT The key figure in George's career at Exeter was
Bull Clark, who coached football, hockey, and baseball. He taught
math, and he was not very good at it, but he was a very good
coach. He saw George's potential in baseball early on. He wanted
George to go out for the team in his second or third year, but
George didn't like the idea of all the practice and the running
around the track and so on, so he opted for tennis instead. Tennis
at Exeter was the big catchall for the people who couldn't or
wouldn't do anything athletic. You could go to the court and bat
a ball around and tell stories. From there, you'd either go back to
the Butt Room or just screw around. George did that once or
twice, and Bull Clark heard about it and took it badly. He was already unhappy that George wouldn't go out for baseball. I must
say that Bull Clark, who was a great friend of mine, was very hard
to get along with. Most people didn't like him. He was a blue-
collar guy from Amesbury, Massachusetts, an old mill town. He
had cauliflower ears. He had been a very big athlete himself, on
scholarship at Dartmouth. He was a really gung ho coach who
couldn't understand why some people might not want to be on
the varsity. He wanted to win.

FARWELL SMITH He was kicked out in the spring of 1944,
somewhat prior to graduation. George never could sit still, and, as
I remember, he wanted very much to go to some lecture or drama
meeting or something like that, but he was on probation already
and he got caught. Exeter had no tolerance for anything like that.
The motto then was either sink or swim. Of the class that I went
into, about a third of it never graduated. George was deeply upset

Bill "Bull" Clark, Exeter housemaster, teacher, and coach.
Courtesy of Phillips Exeter Academy.

when his father called and dressed him down. I think he was hoping he'd get some sympathy.

BUZZ MERRITT   As luck would have it, in his last year George had found himself in Bull Clark's dormitory, one of the most prestigious. It had circular stairwells between both floors, and therein lay George's undoing. Someone had given George a Revolutionary musket, and one night, after lights out, they were having a battle in the ground-floor hall. When George heard the noise, he grabbed the gun and ran down the stairwell, and as he did he heard someone coming up and thought it was a student. So he came down the spiral pointing the gun and yelling, "Bang bang! You're dead." It was Bull Clark coming up to see what the excitement was about. According to George, Clark yelped in fright when he said "Bang bang!"—a very unmanly reaction. He said that Clark knew that George knew that Clark had yelped. As who wouldn't—the man was probably scared out of his wits, all keyed up. Well, the end of that story is that a faculty committee voted on the matter (the principal was a marvelous man named Lewis Perry who left discipline to the faculty) and asked George to leave right away, not many weeks before graduation. And even though Clark "prosecuted" George before the committee, the rumor is that he recommended that George not be thrown out.

TIM SELDES   It was horrible to be thrown out of Exeter. It is probably best that if it had to happen to someone, it happen to George, because he could handle it. The rest of us would have been just horrified at the idea of going back home and saying we flunked out—especially as wartime came, because if you did get kicked out, you pretty much went straight into the ranks.

GORE VIDAL   We were all surprised when he was expelled. The Plimpton playing fields, we thought, carried more weight. The last time I saw George, we talked about his expulsion. (Actually, he always talked about it.) One day he wasn't there anymore. I only noticed because I knew what seat in chapel he was in.

SARAH DUDLEY PLIMPTON   After George died, I found the correspondence with his father and his report cards. I guess that the real reason was that he was failing. He'd been a naughty boy, certainly, and he had tweaked the lapels of some very self-important people, but the bottom line was he was failing. The Bull Clark thing was the last straw. So it was just a way of the school making a point, setting him up as an example. Not that he saw it that way. For him it was a hugely significant event in his life. He told me his father didn't speak to him for a year after his expulsion, which devastated him. I think it was at the heart of much of what he did in his career. I think it was a prime motivator—"I'll show the world—I'll prove to the world that I can succeed and that they were wrong. I *am* good."

OAKES PLIMPTON   It happened right before he was going to graduate, in April or something. So he had to spend the months of April, May, and June with our Ames grandmother in Ormond Beach at Sea Breeze High School, and that's where he graduated. Then he went to Harvard. Of course, it was a little easier to get into Harvard in those days than it is now.

HARVARD I

FARWELL SMITH   None of us did very much work the first year at Harvard. Nobody would have thought of working on Saturday or Sunday, except right before exams. We arrived in the fall of '44 and would be going off to war in the spring. There was a feeling of maybe we'll be dead in six months. You didn't dwell on it, but there was a certain sense that we weren't going to complete Harvard anyway. We had friends from Exeter who were immediately used for cannon fodder in the Battle of the Bulge and got killed. So there was a very pervasive feeling to not take it all very seriously. There was a mix of people. There were some who were working very hard to stay at Harvard, some of whom had come back from the war and perhaps been wounded there. Then there were a lot of people working very hard to *not* stay at Harvard. There was a lot of drinking. Maybe part of our friendship was that we were all in the same pickle, we were all kind of waiting.

> *Dear Daddy,*
>   *As I think I told you over the telephone, I was initiated into Pi Eta. Perhaps I have made a mistake, but there was something about the pleasure of being asked to join a club, that I just couldn't seem to think properly. But the boys there are a wonderful bunch, as far as I can make out from my two visits to the club. . . .*
>   *PS: I've been asked to join the Phoenix SK Club, Daddy—I'll follow your advice this time. If you disapprove, let me know quickly, because I have a good mind to join. . . .* [Fall 1944]

MICHAEL THOMAS   George was mad for clubs. I think it was sheer gregariousness with a bit of Tom Sawyer thrown in. But

don't forget, once upon a time a man was measured by the number of clubs that were in his obituary in *The New York Times*. You
also tended to join clubs that your father was a member of. Certainly Francis T. P. Plimpton was a member of the Century for
about a hundred and thirty-two years. Uncle Cal, I'm sure, was a
member of the Century. There are things you do that run in families. Of course, George's father didn't go to Harvard. Still, I imagine there were multitudes of Ameses in the Porcellian Club, so
why he joined the Pi Eta (a jock club, I'm told), and the *infra dig*
Phoenix, I can't imagine, unless it was something to do with
wartime—the Porcellian not taking any new members for the du-
ration, some such thing.

BRONSON CHANLER   The Porcellian Club is the oldest club in
continuous existence in the United States, founded in 1791. It is a
purely social club, nothing like Skull and Bones and that kind of
club, which have to do with virtue of some sort, or accomplishment. It's based entirely on friendship and sociability, and George
became a devoted member after the war. The Latin motto of the
club is *Dum vivimus, vivamus,* or "While we live, let us live."

WALTER SOHIER   To join the PC he had to renounce the Phoenix, which put him under a little bit of a cloud. I think joining
the PC was indicative of the importance he attached to his social
position and acceptability at the highest level. He saw an opportunity there and he took it, and I wouldn't argue with him about
that.

JAMES RIGHTER   It's true that there's a sort of club hierarchy at
Harvard, with the PC being the most prestigious. But what
George is supposed to have done—joining the Pi Eta and the
Phoenix SK and then, after the war, the Porcellian—was nothing
shameful. I'm not sure the PC was taking freshman members in
1944; sophomore year was the rule. And he didn't have to snub the
two other clubs when he did join the PC. Neither of them was a
"final club"; in fact, my father joined the Phoenix SK and then the
Porcellian, with no sorry consequences at all.

Dear Daddy,

I had a good smashing talk with Gordon and we pulled all the stops out. I would look for the best in the future. I have pledged myself to finishing this term up with a bang—in character, honesty, financial problems, and study.

I'm afraid I've fallen into Goethe's pit for a time, in this question of honesty. That is to be no more.

I'm going to do my best with finance and my checkbook. The statements have come in, and I shall look them over and let you know how in Hell I ever came to rock bottom.

I've fallen into that rut of self-complacence and no sense of responsibility. I've pulled out once—I'll do it again.

I've sent the Lampoon *down and hope you will enjoy it. The next issue looks better by far, but the one here is a start, and I hope carries great significance. . . .* [May 4, 1945]

FARWELL SMITH   I'll never forget going out into the suburbs of Boston toward the end of freshman year and swinging birches. It's kind of a Robert Frost thing. You climb a young birch and get up quite high off the ground, maybe about twenty feet, until it bends over slowly, slowly, till your feet finally touch the ground. It's the damnedest thing, especially the sight of George, this long, hanging object, finally touching the ground. It's just one of these visions I have of George—the whole grace of doing it, but also the hilarity. We were rolling on the ground. It was a beautiful spring day, the wildflowers, the grasses were up, the birches were just beginning to turn, to leaf out. It was a wonderful time of life, the spring before we all went into the Army or the Merchant Marine or whatever. There was a gaiety to it, and George fit into it perfectly.

ARMY

Dear Mummy and Daddy,

Well, I'm safely situated in the Army now, and I must say it isn't half as bad as I expected it would be. After the softness and late hours at Harvard, it is hard at first to find yourself in a chow line at

5:30 in the morning, and it is hard to work at physical jobs all day, but the life is beginning to become second nature to me and thus, very enjoyable indeed.

My comrades in arms are pretty nice fellows. They're a little slow and a little uncouth, but they're good men and we all get along wonderfully. One of the funniest people I've ever met is a huge Negro who sleeps in the same barracks and convulses the rest of us thoroughly. He calls me Long John! My other names are "Slim," "Stretch" and "Harvard." No one has called me George yet. The sergeants call me Plimpton and very loudly, and ten minutes later I find myself in a warehouse.

I found the German pin in the warehouse yesterday, and am sending it along as my first trophy of war. . . . [no date]

TED LAMONT   It was late in the fall of '45. George was in the Army, and I was still a midshipman in the Navy. We were both in uniform, attending a holiday dance in New York. George was at Camp Kilmer in New Jersey, where his regiment was temporarily stationed before going overseas, indeed the following morning. The dance was at the Plaza Hotel, and everybody was dancing and the wine was flowing. It was getting pretty late, and you know George, let's face it, had had a fair amount to drink and wasn't alert in watching the time. We said, "George, you've really got to get back to Camp Kilmer because your regiment is leaving to go overseas in the morning." Phil Potter [another St. Bernard's boy] and I took him outside the Plaza, and the only way to get to Camp Kilmer we could figure out was to get a taxi. It was snowing. And it was the middle of the night. Taxis were extremely hard to come by. Lo and behold, a taxi drove up and we jumped in and the driver said, "Sure, I'll take you to Camp Kilmer"—I think the fact that we were in uniform helped. So we drove along; and at length we realized that the taxi driver was dressed in a tuxedo and that he had a lovely girl sitting beside him in a white evening dress. And we said, "What's the story here?" He said, "Well, my girlfriend and I were at a party uptown earlier, and I wanted to take her home, so we jumped into a cab; but the cab-driver said he was off duty and he was going to the taxi garage. We stayed in the cab all the way to the taxi garage, and when the cabdriver left we borrowed the cab so I could take my girl home, which was the only gentlemanly thing to do." Off we drove, into the night. We always remembered crossing the George Washington Bridge—the strange look the guy who collected the fare gave us as he looked at the incongruous crew of people assembled in this cab. The snow was coming down onto the highways of New Jersey, and finally the cab ran out of gas, but we were close enough—maybe ten miles or so—from Camp Kilmer. George found another cab, just his luck, and we hitchhiked back to New York. A couple of days later, when I was back at the naval base, there was a little article in *The New York Times*—cab stolen, garage police investigating.

ANDREW LEGGATT He was fond of declaring that he had arrived in Europe two weeks after the cessation of hostilities, and then the story went that he was put to work clearing mines; but then they had the better idea of making the German and Italian prisoners clear them. So he transferred to tanks, I think. I believe that's what happened. And after his tank duty he had the stupefying good luck, even for George, to be assigned to teach social graces and military techniques to his fellow soldiers at a *caserna* on the Lido, if you can believe it, in Venice.

> *Dear Sarah,*
>
> *I haven't had much chance to go birding and I'm pretty sure the Army would frown on such practices and I'm not sure one's officers would feel very happy about the whole thing if a G.I. began raving about having seen a White-Throated Sparrow. Everybody's a little too keyed up around here for that sort of thing.*
>
> *I have had, though, trouble with two species of birds, the barn swallow and a screech owl. I used to hold my public speaking classes out underneath a huge maple tree just outside the walls of the Caserna. It was a terrible place to hold a class. Italian curiosity is enormous and I usually found that I had more Italians listening than soldiers. There was a pair of goats that was tethered right behind my class and they were prone to making noises at the drop of a hat. A flock of geese held forth in the class area, and the Lido airport was to the rear and on the main channel to the front*

of my class. It was pretty hard to concentrate. But the worst trouble of all came from the barn swallows. You've seen them; they love to skim along the ground, twisting and dodging in search of insects. In Italy, they are the bravest birds you ever saw. They actually would dodge in and out among the students at incredible speeds and many a time they'd grab an insect two or three inches off your nose. What with the geese, the goats, and a herd of cows that I forgot to mention, that class was almost a joke. . . .
[Venice, July 4, 1946]

BERNARD CONNERS I served with George on the Lido. His relationship with his parents was a little unusual, I thought. It was this huggy-kissy stuff and, you know, this guy is nineteen. "Dear Mummy and Daddy"? This is not wartime, but close to war, right after the war. I never understood them. They were very endearing letters to a mother and father, but I can't help but think that the troops would not have liked it if they read these letters. They were written like they were coming from a fourteen-year-old kid who had just gone away to school. But that's not a very nice thing to say. He loved his mother and father so much, and he had such respect; it all came out in the letters of his that I read.

> *Dear George,*
>   *The Lido Training Center sounds like West Point itself! But don't, in the flush of discovering the great merits of discipline and neatness and obedience, forget that they are somewhat minor virtues. Virtues, yes, and important ones, but not nearly as important as character and awareness of the dignity of man and intellectual curiosity and independence of mind and judgment—the very things that* do, *and I hope always will—distinguish Americans from Nazis and Fascists and Communists. They are the things that count more than inculcating discipline, important as discipline is. Much love from us all—*
>
>   *Affectionately, Daddy*

BERNARD CONNERS We were young male animals. We had all of the drives, but we were in leadership roles on the Lido, with a vis-

George with fellow officers, the Lido, Venice, 1946.
From the collection of Bernard F. Conners.

ibility that I think mandated that we act like total gentlemen at all times. But I remember these two women we met during the summer of '46 or whenever it was, and they were deliriously handsome, these two girls. George and I fell in love with them, but they were from very nice families in Italy, and they always had some kind of a chaperone, an aunt or someone, disappointingly. But we spent a great deal of time on the beach with them. We always conducted ourselves with great propriety, but there were moments when we were boys. One night, I came home, and it was very dark in my quarters. I began groping around for my bed, and my hand landed on a leg. It was not George's leg. Somewhere he had found this woman and had brought her home and put her in my bunk as a joke on me. I don't know what her profession was, but she was a very elderly woman for me at the time.

HARVARD II

FARWELL SMITH We happened to come back to Harvard at ex-actly the same time, the fall of '47, and we roomed together in Eliot House. We were in the class of '48 but graduated in 1950. We had another roommate, Josiah, called Mickey, Child, a Bostonian with a very cultivated accent. I think he went to St. Paul's School. George was the same old George. None of us had been through anything close to combat or seen a bullet or heard a big noise. What happened is we matured two years, which was probably a positive thing. I'd say that we were not running around getting drunk all the time or going to parties as much. We took our homework a bit more seriously, and we were a bit more cultivated. We drank sherry instead of gin, I suppose. We might have had music in our room. But life had not radically changed.

BLAIR FULLER Eliot House had a somewhat posh reputation. There was a rather snobbish professor named John Finley who was the housemaster, and he liked to tell you about the glamour of the boys in his house.

CLEM DESPARD My last year, John Finley called me into his study and said, "I wonder if you wouldn't mind relinquishing your apartment to a very unusual group of three who want to come into the house. They need a ground-floor apartment." I didn't ask him why. It turned out that one was Stephen Joyce, grandson of James, and the others were Paul Matisse, grandson of Henri, and Prince Sadruddin Aga Khan, as Finley put it, "the grandson of God." Finley said he thought it was the perfect union of arts and money. So I had to move up to a fourth-floor room, having been in a first-floor apartment. Sadri Khan couldn't quite make it to move his trunks down to the basement storage area, so I was asked by his mother's lovely assistant to do it for him. Sadri had been spending the summer in Ireland working at his brother's horse farm to get a recommendation to allow him back into college, be-cause he failed everything in his second year. He got all A's in his first year and all F's in his second year. The dean said that if he got a good recommendation from some employer, he would consider allowing him back in.

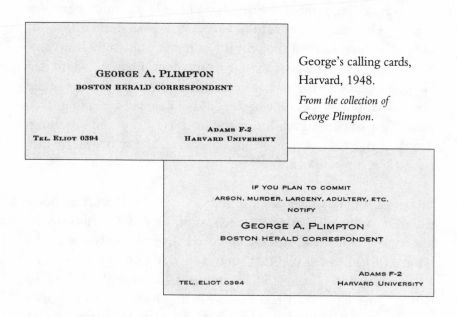

George's calling cards, Harvard, 1948.

From the collection of George Plimpton.

WILLIAM BECKER   In those days—it's all changed now and, I think, very much for the worse—the houses all had an individual character. Eliot House, while John Finley was its master, was the literary house and also, to some degree, the social house. George was the ideal Eliot House resident, because he was socially prominent on the one hand and had all the serious literary inclinations on the other. He was bright, and charming, and he played squash and tennis. In those days, the literary faculty at Harvard was mind-boggling: F. O. Matthiessen, I. A. Richards, Douglas Bush, Harry Levin, Theodore Spencer, and Archibald MacLeish, whose famously selective creative writing course George took. Most of those people were connected with Eliot House. Oh, and Jackson Bate, the great eighteenth-century scholar—we mustn't forget Jack Bate. He lived in the house. It was a heady place, Eliot House, in those days.

BLAIR FULLER   I thought of George as someone witty and interesting. I was of a more serious mind than George seemed to be.

He was actually a very serious fellow, a stringer for the *Boston Herald,* I believe, and extremely well read, and so on. But my ambition was to be printed in the *Harvard Advocate,* and here was George, clowning around at the *Harvard Lampoon* stunts and looking giddy in costume. I thought it was rather undignified and embarrassing. It surprised me that he would do it. I have to admit that George seemed to me not quite bright in those days. George did not talk about books. He never said, "I've been reading Turgenev," or something. A lot of the people I knew did say things like that. But George was bright, of course, and whatever he did, he made it his kind of thing.

CHRIS CERF The *Lampoon* inspired George. The Common Book is a great example. That's a *Lampoon* tradition, and *The Paris Review* just took it over lock, stock, and barrel. Everybody wrote in the book. If I had to tell you that so-and-so was going to drop off an ad this afternoon, it would be in the Common Book, but so would some silly idea I had for something I wanted to write, or something clever and nasty that I wanted to say about somebody. There were lots of running jokes, often about Elmer Green. Elmer was the *Lampoon* janitor. He was an incredible ham. He appeared in just about every issue of the magazine, and they always photographed him—often in costume—for every *Lampoon* parody. He was remarkably good-natured about having to clean up the mess the students would leave for him after their weekly dinners (someone would invariably write "I KWIT. ELMER" in the Common Book on such occasions). Some of the "Poonies" would torment him in other ways, too—I remember John Berendt rolling logs down the metal staircase to the basement apartment where Elmer lived in semisqualor year after year. But Elmer never complained.

FARWELL SMITH To get on the masthead at the *Lampoon* you had to pull some sort of prank, so I entered the Boston Marathon about four hundred yards from the finish line. I looked like a runner. I had a sign on my rear that said, "Property of the *Harvard Lampoon,*" but it looked to everybody like I was in the race, actually behind the number three guy. The crowd was screaming, "You can catch him, kid!" I started to catch up to him, and this guy who

With Farwell Smith outside the *Lampoon* building,
costumed for a prank. *Courtesy of Farwell Smith.*

had just run twenty-six miles looked around, saw me, and he put
on a burst of speed that could have killed him. The crowd was
screaming. So I started catching up again. When I got to the finish line, the guy, with every ounce that he hadn't wasted putting
on that last burst of speed, took a swing at me. The cops didn't
know what to do. They could see the sign on my rear. I never felt
more out of place in my life. They finally just threw me out; I
didn't get into any particular trouble. Postscript: Very close to the
end of George's life, my daughter went to see him perform in
Seattle. George starts out—I have a recording of this—telling how
he once ran in the Boston Marathon, my story. Laura went up to
him afterwards and said, "You just stole my father's life!" And
George said, "It's just too good a story. I couldn't turn it down."

He wasn't embarrassed at all. I don't care at all, either. I thought it was very humorous. I was a little surprised that he had to go outside of his life for an amusing story; God knows he had plenty of his own.

CLEM DESPARD   George, the editor at the time, would preside over dinners at the *Lampoon*. Every Thursday, you'd pay two bucks, and you'd have a dinner at the *Lampoon*. Sadri Khan was the secretary, and he had to arrange the dinner, and the only place he knew where to get the food was from some fancy place in Cambridge. All you had was a tiny little breast of chicken and a hard roll. That was the whole thing. I came up with a game called Kick the Khan, which he didn't like much. Then, when he served that dinner, I said, "Let's all have a vote of thanks to Sadri for this marvelous dinner by getting up and throwing our hard rolls at him," which we all did. Sadri was a little pretentious, but he had a good sense of humor. He'd wear a snap-brim hat and these big-lapel suits, and he would drive into Boston for arrangements made by Ilio Bosco for teenage girls to entertain him. Bosco was touted as the chairman of the Damon Runyon Cancer Fund; but he also supplied the *Lampoon* with "sporting films," porno films, which were quite yellow and dusty and not so good. He would always show up at the *Lampoon* with his violin case with these sporting films in it, and he would set them up. Plimpton arranged that, and Sadri carried it on the next year when he became secretary.

BLAIR FULLER   You'd never have taken George for a jock at Harvard. He never went out for any varsity team, not even tennis or squash, which he was very good at (as I learned to my chagrin early on) and which he played every chance he got before he died. You wouldn't have taken him for much of a student, either. He was in [Archibald] MacLeish's creative writing class—as was I; as Doc Humes was, and as was the first *Paris Review* poetry editor, Donald Hall—and this carried tremendous cachet in literary circles, at Harvard and beyond. I think he was also on the *Advocate,* the "serious" literary magazine, as well as the *Lampoon*. But he didn't seem very literary, either, any more than he was a jock. I think he was much too busy with the *Lampoon,* with his club life and social life, to get all caught up in anything that demanded a lot of arduous concentration—which, of course, serious writing and serious athletics do. He was having too much fun.

TEDDY VAN ZUYLEN What did we do at the Porcellian? Well, the drink was copious; the food was better than in the houses; and you could study there. But mostly you went there to be with your club-mates. There's a peculiar sort of social distance that's observed in clubs like the Porcellian, in most men's clubs, I think. It's somewhere between intimacy and acquaintanceship but far from both. There's actually a word for it, clubbability, that goes back to the eighteenth-century coffeehouses. George was bred to be clubbable. I don't see George talking about problems he had with his wife or his girlfriend or anything else. It was not the correct thing to do. You don't talk about money in clubs. You don't talk about women. That's your problem. There's no way one would have brought it up: "Oh, by the way, do you ever sort of comfort your girlfriend when she's feeling down?" I can't imagine even thinking of saying that to him. He would have said, "What? I don't know what you're talking about. She never has bad moments." That was off bounds with him, completely off bounds. I think that he was brought up that way, and it stuck with him, in his clubs and out in the world.

NANCY TUCKERMAN The coming-out party circuit was pretty elaborate. There was a stag line, and the men there would go and cut in on people. George liked to hang out in the stag line, talking to friends and not getting into the dancing part, because you might get stuck with a girl and then never be able to get away. The ones that were the most attractive and appealing, like George, would spend a lot of time in the stag line until they saw some really glamorous woman, like Jackie [Bouvier then; Kennedy and Onassis, to be], and they'd go up to dance with them.

BEE DABNEY I was seventeen. I think it was 1949, and I was invited to a party in Long Island by Lucy Aldrich, and it was a beautiful party. I was very excited because it was the first time I'd ever been to a party in Long Island. That was just before I came out. I took the train down from Boston with a friend of George's named James Walker. Jackie was there, and Alexander Aldrich—it was very exciting. At the piano was George. I was immediately attracted to him—this romantic figure playing the piano with his long wrists and fingers. He was singing a song, something like "Her hands wandered over me like huge busy whiskbrooms. Now, what's got into me since I got into you," or something like that. It was terribly amusing, and soon people began to gather around the piano, and George began to look up at me, and I really don't remember too much more about this party, excepting that I really thought he was extraordinary. It stuck in my mind all the way back to Boston on the train, and I started to draw little sketches by memory of who I'd met there. To my great excitement, soon after this, George called me up in Dover, and he began to take me out. He was at Harvard, and I was about to graduate from Beaver Country Day School and then go to the Museum School of Fine Arts. That's when I met him, and we saw a lot of each other. He would come out to Dover in his gray Pontiac convertible car. Mother thought he was wonderful. Everyone always thought he was wonderful because he was enchanting. Every time he spoke, something extraordinary would come out of his mouth. He had a way and a style about him that was just glorious.

BLAIR FULLER I don't know how long I'd been at Harvard when I first met Bee Dabney, but there was a football game, and George was going to have a party after the game, and I was asked to go to it, and into the room—fairly crowded—came this charming little person. She looked about fourteen, fifteen at best. She had on saddle shoes and bobby socks and a pleated gray flannel skirt, and she had a little suitcase in her hand that had stickers on it, and the stickers said "Colgate" and "Yale." This was my introduction to Bee Dabney. From the first, I thought, "Oh, George! This person is too young."

BEE DABNEY One of the most entertaining moments that I had with George was on one of our first dates. He always had a sense of adventure about him, and he said, "I want to take you to North

Bee Dabney.
Photograph by Otto van Noppen.

Easton, where my grandmother has a house." This was in the cold of the winter. So we drove to North Easton, and the house—an enormous stone house—was totally locked. I don't know if he had a key or how we got in, but everything was covered in white sheets. We crept around and went into this extraordinary room where there was a balcony that went all the way around the room, a library on the second floor. It was all open. There were these extraordinary books about nature, birds, flowers. I think his grandfather was a botanist. This was an extraordinary collection, so we spent hours looking at these things. Then George said, "Now we're going to go ice fishing!" So we put on what we could find in the closet, and we tramped out to this frozen lake and went ice fishing for pickerel, or would it be perch? Some such fish. It was very exciting, and he seemed to know exactly what to do. It was freezing out there, so when we got back into the house, George said, "We have to get under the covers, and I'll cook you up something warm." He was fantastic at cooking spaghetti or rice. Those were his favorite things to cook. I think we had spaghetti in this case, but nothing much on it. We got warmed up, we got *very* warmed up. After that, as we progressed with seeing each other, there were declarations of how much we cared for each other. That was my first big outing with him, and it was an adventure in every way.

BLAIR FULLER   One of the complications of going to college after having been in the service during the war was sex. Girls were available everywhere I went in the Navy, but there were things about being in college which seemed to make you juvenile again: debutante dances out in Manchester-by-the-Sea or someplace where every girl was a virgin, or behaved like one. I didn't feel like courting those girls, attractive though they were. I kind of stopped. One girl and I became friends, but when you courted somebody, they expected you to marry them. I didn't want to be married. George certainly didn't want to get married. On the other hand, he wanted Bee Dabney, who, if not a virgin—well, I don't know anything about that. He may have felt some of the same confusion that I did, but I don't know. I did find Bee alluring, but she was always taken, so to speak. We were friends. Later, when Bee was involved with Michael Canfield, a cousin of mine, he went to Boston, and he saw, not just Bee, he saw the mother. Her mother said to Michael, looking at Bee crossing the lawn, "Delightful little strumpet, isn't she?"

BEE DABNEY   We went to lots of *Lampoon* parties, and that was always very exciting for me because I could meet other artists. Fred Gwynne, the actor, was a great friend. We were involved with pranks a great deal and mischief. John Updike was there, and Michael Arlen, and Mickey Child. I liked that group. Those were my favorites. The people in the Porcellian Club were great fun also. I liked them very much. So we saw a great deal of each other, this group. I saw George constantly. Everyone else I knew dropped and paled by the wayside. We went to functions on the weekend a lot: football games, and baseball games in the spring; gatherings of the brothers.

CLEM DESPARD   George didn't always have Bee to himself. Sadri Khan and he were always competing for Bee, but Sadri had the better car, a Daimler convertible. That went on for some time, especially after George graduated and went to Cambridge University.

> *Dear Mother and Daddy,*
>
> *I have been talking to many people here at college about the advisability of going abroad next year to college. In particular, I've been trying to find out whether Oxford or Cambridge would be best suited for my needs. The evidence seems pretty conclusive that Cambridge would be far better. There are fewer Americans; the facilities for English study seem better.*
>
> *I've talked to Archibald MacLeish about it. He far prefers Cambridge, thinks it would be an enriching experience. He is trying to find out what college would be best and under what tutor I should study. However, I won't be seeing him for two weeks, so in the meantime, I'm going to write letters to Jesus and Trinity Colleges, Cambridge, and since Oxford is easier to enter, Merton and New Colleges there, in case of difficulty with Cambridge.*
>
> *I've also applied for two scholarships to Cambridge, the Lionel de Jersey and the Fisk, and one for study in France. Though I applied on the recommendation of Mr. Finley and Dean Bender, I'm not relying at all on the possibility of being chosen.*
>
> *The Colleges are hard to enter and it will need your help, Dad. I will send you carbon copies of the letters I write and receive from England to keep you posted on my progress.*
>
> *May I again say that I am more particularly interested in Cambridge at the moment, and the epistolary offensive should be directed towards that University.*
>
> *Squash season is over. With the Championship of the Ivy League at stake, we lost at Yale last weekend. I played no. 5 and lost after a two hour five set match which I came within a whisker of winning.*
>
> *Everything else continues to go well. They're selling violets in the subway stations now, so spring must be just around the corner.*

I plan to join you [in Florida]; *my Havana plans are nebulous since I'm way behind work on my novel, and might spend the vacation at Ormond working on it. Will need money for trip to Fla., regardless. . . .* [spring 1950]

BEE DABNEY When George said he was going to King's College, Cambridge, he asked me if I would wait for him, which I thought was terribly romantic. He wrote me a great deal from Cambridge that [school] year [1950–1951], and I wrote him; but in the meantime I had become great friends with Sadri Khan. He knew George, so this caused a big friction in my life, because I'd found these two people who were fantastic, really unusual, so I was very absorbed with both. Then, Sadri invited me to travel in Europe with him and his mother and father for the summer. I thought this

Portrait by Bee Dabney.
Courtesy of Bee Dabney Adams.

was an extraordinarily exciting invitation. I had always wanted to go to Europe. It was one of my dreams, and I also wanted to see George, who said he would be spending the summer in Paris between terms.

WILLIAM BECKER George told me this wonderful story about his graduation at Harvard. It seems that for his last term, he had to satisfy a science requirement, so he took a gut course in geography and dutifully read all of the texts, but he never went to class. He took the final examination and thought he did quite well. But the professor flunked him. George went in to see him, and the professor looked across the desk at him and said, "Mr. Plimpton, do you realize this is the first time I've ever set eyes on you? If you think for one minute that I'm going to pass a man in my course who has never set foot in my classroom, you've got another think coming!" George flunked. That caused all kinds of problems because it meant he couldn't graduate. He didn't have the credits he needed for graduation. So he went back to summer school in the summer of '50 and was ignominiously handed his degree in September. I've always loved that story, and George took great pleasure in telling it.

FARWELL SMITH One weekend we went down to Narragansett Bay in Rhode Island; somebody had a house there, and maybe a dozen of us went down and had a picnic on the beach. It was one of those beautiful spring days. We put our baskets down, and George and I went walking; he was looking at birds. Everybody else had scattered, too, and when we came back to the picnic site, there were two kids, maybe about ten years old, stealing our stuff. You could see them as we came around a corner; they were rifling through our stuff and taking things. George and I came roaring at them, and one kid went one way and George followed him, and the other kid went the other way and I followed him, and we caught them both. I remember being outraged that somebody would do anything like that and cuffing this little kid. I came back dragging him screaming by the hair. I don't know what I was going to do with him—give him to the cops or something like that—but I was really treating him roughly. And George came back from the other direction, hand in hand with the little kid, who kept calling him Georgie. George's way of dealing with it was to persuade him that he'd been bad and to not do it again. It was one of the most touching, true parts of George, and it made me feel like a terrible bully.

KING'S COLLEGE

WILLIAM BECKER   I went to see George in Cambridge at least once, maybe twice. He was in King's College. I was at Oxford on a Rhodes, but I'd never seen Cambridge, so I went over and he showed me around King's Chapel, which was one of the most breathtaking buildings I've ever been in. Oxford, which is a rather dirty, somewhat industrial town, is not a thing of great beauty; but Cambridge, with the Cam flowing through it and all these trees, was a thing of unbelievable beauty. I was rather jealous.

ANDREW LEGGATT   He was twenty-three when he arrived at Cambridge. We first met when we were both freshmen at King's. We lived in the Garden Hostel, which held, I think, fifty-two of us, in single rooms—each room probably had a shower and a place to boil a kettle. It opened in the year in which we went up. So we were two of fifty-two first occupants. We both had rooms in this hostel for a year, and of course we had to get to know each other pretty damned well because by the end of it we decided in the following year we would apply to share rooms when we moved into college.

MILTON DEVANE   King's College Hostel, as I recollect, was of rather ordinary architecture, three stories high. The architect didn't know how to signal that the building had come to the top when it did. So he put granite balls on the top of it, and since the chapel was well known to have been done in the perpendicular style, the undergraduates promptly named the new hostel as being in the "testicular style." George told me that they put the heating in the floor, which was a new venture, because most of the places didn't have heating at all. George showed me with great delight on one occasion a communication from the bursar saying, "Gentlemen will please be careful, as they step out of bed in the morning, to test the temperature of the floor before putting full weight down."

ANDREW LEGGATT We had a rather tiresome housekeeper during our first year. She'd been chatting to George for a long time in his room one day when he had been recovering from flu. After a while, in order to get rid of her, George said, "I must ask you to leave now, Mrs. Denton. My favorite radio program is just coming on." As she paused expectantly in the doorway, George switched on the radio and the sprightly announcer said, "Come now, children, clap your hands!"

> *Dear Mother and Daddy,*
> *   . . . There is no mountain climbing here, East Anglia being notoriously flat, but there is a wonderful sport called roof-climbing. Roof-climbing is not to be confused with wall-climbing which every undergraduate is forced to do to get back into his college if he is out after midnight. Roof-climbing requires cat-like nerves coupled with extraordinary bravado—both acquired, I'm told, from a bottle of Gilbey's gin. The favorite target for roof-climbers is the King's College chapel and the height of success to put some article on one of the four spires of the tower 160 feet in the air. Articles discovered in the light of dawn (all climbing is done at night) have included umbrellas, a "Save Ethiopia" banner, glass tumblers, and a Union Jack. The college has to pay a steeple jack 20 pounds sterling to get the articles down, and of late an expert with a shotgun has been shooting them off. He demurred, however, when faced with the Union Jack. . . . [October 27, 1950]*

ANDREW LEGGATT The only sense in which we would have been in class together is attending the same lectures. I don't recall if we did, mainly because George didn't go to many. I don't remember him ever going to a lecture, but it would be an exaggeration to say that he never did. One can only say he would have been extremely selective. He never worked as studiously as some. He would sit at the table thinking, and writing when the inspiration occurred to him, and he read a good deal, of course. But I don't have a memory of him studying very intently.

———

BEE DABNEY   I saw George in Paris that summer of 1951 [after George's first year at King's]. My mother and I took the boat from Canada, and we landed in Le Havre, and Sadri came and met me, much to the discouragement of George, who was in Paris on vacation. George knew Sadri and liked him, too. Mother and I stayed in this hotel together, the Bristol, and there seemed to be lots of people from Boston around. I think people knew about these two men in my life, and there came this discussion of "What in the world is she going to do?" This was really a dilemma for me. George and I had a wonderful, happy reunion. But I kept on with my trip, and said good-bye to Mother, and went off to Switzerland with Sadri and Princess Andrée, his mother. We met his father in some extraordinary hotel on Lake Geneva, and then we all seemed to be following each other around by car on this tour all over Switzerland and ended up in the South of France at Sadri's mother's house, where I spent the summer. I was already struggling to stay forever in France and threatening my parents that I would never come home, but that didn't work. Then I realized that the Atelier des Beaux-Arts would be the place for me to transfer to, to get to Paris, where I really wanted to be, because George was there. Sadri introduced me to his cousin, who was absolutely lovely, and she connected me to the right person at the Atelier to whom to send my portfolio.

PIEDY LUMET   I think George just loved Bee. She always moved on—George, too, though I imagine with Bee in possession of more of his heart than he possessed of hers. He was always so devoted to her. She loved him, too, but I couldn't make out where Bee stood most of the time. It was too confusing. But she was adorable and engaging—everybody loved her. She had a smile that went right around the corner—a little bit off center, very beguiling.

BEE DABNEY   I came back to Boston at the end of the summer of 1951, and I told my great friend Jeanne Hannan, who was studying at the Museum School with me, that our dream of going to

Europe would come true for sure because we had this name, Sadri's cousin. So we put together our portfolios and sent them to Europe. Our families, meanwhile, said, "No way are we going to send you to Paris." My father was adamant: "Bee, you're going to go back to Boston. You're going to get a job. You're going to do what everybody else does. You don't need to be traveling around in Europe." Well, when the Atelier des Beaux-Arts sent the acceptance, all in French, this document on parchment with this embossed ribbon with a gold stamp on it saying, "Mademoi-selle Beatrice Dabney has been accepted," all in French, "to this Atelier des Beaux-Arts," etc., and Jeanne got one, too, I showed mine to my father and he almost died of excitement. He went around to all of his cocktail parties and said, "Look! My daughter has been accepted to the Beaux-Arts in Paris!" And this ribbon flowed out of this document, and everyone was agog, and so off we went. That was how I got back to Paris in the summer of 1952.

ANDREW LEGGATT During his two years at Cambridge, George read English and derived great encouragement from Dadie Ry-lands, the great Shakespearean scholar. Dadie supervised me one-to-one for my first year at Cambridge, because I had thought to read law for all three years that I was up, but they wouldn't allow that thinking. They required that you read something else for first year, so that at least I would have an element of humanity in my education. Supervision by Dadie was the greatest teaching experi-ence that I have ever had. I used to leave his rooms on occasion lit-erally leaping in the air because of the physical uplift of the experience.

> Dear Mother and Daddy . . .
>   I completed a short story the other day and read it aloud to Mr. Rylands during a supervision. He was very excited about it and suggested sending it off to a magazine called the Cornhill, a quar-terly with an ancestory (sp.) of three centuries. . . . [no date]

MILTON DEVANE George and I were drinking other people's sherry all over the college. We decided in the spring that we had to do something to pay back all of our debts, and George came up with the idea that we would introduce the English to the American martini. We did it in his quarters at King's College. There wasn't much ice in England in those days. We left it that I would take care of the liquor and George would take care of the ice. George's search for ice was much more adventurous than mine for liquor because all I had to do was go down and buy the stuff. George found the ice in the fish store, because that was the only place where you could get a block of it. We stuck it in the bathtub and proceeded to lose about half of it as we tried to get the smell out. We finally did. Gin in England in those days was a lesser proof than it was in the United States, only eighty proof, I think, so George decided that the true introduction of the martini should be at full strength. We mixed the things and stuck them in the icebox and only served them after they came out. The damn things were lethal! After we said good night to our supervisor, Dadie, who had stopped by for a drink, we closed the door and then opened it up five minutes later to let somebody in. Our supervisor of studies lay there, passed out, in the rain. That's the way we introduced the martini.

Dear Mother and Daddy,

. . . I'm spending the first part of Easter Vacation with the Dowager Lady St. Just who was one of the people Mr. Lamont gave me an introduction to. She ought to feed me up a bit. Don't for heaven's sake send over any gin. That addition of the gin to the list was not supposed to be taken seriously at all. I was trying to be funny. I shall not again. . . . [no date]

Dear Mother and Daddy,

. . . Somewhat to my surprise I've been elected to a Cambridge club known as the Pitt, a sort of large scale Porcellian filled with (as Andrew puts it) "decaying horse-men." Andrew thinks I was elected because of my plum-colored waistcoat (called in some circles "Old Wine") and that seems to me as good a reason as any. . . . [October 27, 1951]

ANDREW LEGGATT Morgan [E. M. Forster] had rooms in Cambridge when we were up; we used to see him there, of course, and talk with him when we were undergraduates. And that's how George had the connection to do that first *Paris Review* interview. It was typical of George's luck, wasn't it, that he should have known personally such a great literary figure from the past who would be prepared to give him the kind of interview that would subsequently become a classic.

PETER STANFORD George had this worshipful attitude toward Forster, which I didn't share at all. Forster was well known for despising Americans for their warlike ways and their perpetuating another empire to replace the British Empire, which he hated. He lived just one floor above me, and he never spoke to me, even to say hello.

GEORGE PLIMPTON, UNPUBLISHED INTERVIEW WITH FRAN KIERNAN Bowden Broadwater called me one day and said he'd been browsing around in the Strand bookstore and he bought a book and he opened it up and out fluttered a postcard that had some writing on it. He read the postcard, and it said, "Dear Lou, No, I do not wish to have dinner with your friend Plimpton tonight." And it was signed "Morgan." And of course, that's E. M. Forster. It had the King's College crest on it. Bowden said, "George, this thing fluttered out and there's your name and there's Morgan Forster. Can you remember about this?" And I said, "Bowden, I certainly do. It was when I'd just arrived at Cambridge." I was at King's College there, which is a very snooty college. Most of the Etonians go there, and when I went there they didn't talk to me. I was just shunned. For about two weeks, no one would talk to me, not even the guy who was sitting next to me in Hall. At any rate, I had a friend there called Lou Connick, who was an American, and E. M. Forster had asked him to have dinner with him. So he thought that he could bring me along. There were no phones in the college. Everything was passed around in these sorts of notes. And Lou had gotten one and slipped it into a book. Of course, then I became a great friend of E. M. Forster's, but not at that time, and I did not go to that dinner. Lou prob-

E. M. Forster in his Cambridge rooms.
Photograph by Edward Leigh, Cambridge, held at King's College Archive Centre, Cambridge.

ably sold all of his books, and it ended up here in the Strand. I've always
thought I should write an explanation—otherwise scholars will think I
was sort of a pariah.

ANDREW LEGGATT During our second year in college, we lived
five floors up at the top of a winding stone staircase. It was mighty
cold in winter, and I vividly remember how George's day used to
begin crouched over the gas fire, wearing nothing but his khaki
underpants, relics of his military experience. He would then toast
a slice of bread on a toasting fork and proceed to prepare himself
for the day. You have to remember that when I say we roomed together, we had one bedroom with two beds in it and one living
room. And a place where you could boil a kettle. So we lived in
pretty close quarters in that cold ambience which is Cambridge in
the winter. He was particularly tidy. That's right. And he was
slower to recover from the night before, I always used to think. It
took him some time to warm up. Some of us spring to instant ac-

tion, don't we, and others only do it slowly, and George was a supreme example of the slow beginner to the day.

> *Dear Mother and Daddy,*
> *. . . The books also arrived after being held up by a Customs Official under the impression I was running a book shop. Your choice was excellent. I was particularly impressed by the Maxwell Perkins letters. A really engrossing fine Yankee character shines through them. I have almost definitely decided (not because of the Perkins letters mind you) to go into publishing when I return to the U.S. whether or not my writing pans through. . . .* [no date]

ANDREW LEGGATT On weekends George would go up to London and stay at the Cavendish Hotel, which in those days was still presided over by Rosa Lewis, the Duchess of Duke Street, as she was known, famous if not infamous for her hospitality as well as for her cooking. Most of his accounts of his visits began with the words "The door opened and there stood this wonderful girl." After one of these expeditions, when he had a stick on account of a skiing accident, there were dog-bite marks on the handle. According to George, the dog had been occupying itself with the stick while he enjoyed the ministrations of its mistress.

> *Dear Mother and Daddy,*
> *. . . Last Sunday I had a very pleasant day in London with the Cowles'. We had lunch at Claridge's and then were shown through the Holbein exhibition in the Royal Academy by Oscar Kokoschka, the famous German painter who has done a portrait of the Cowles which raised quite a controversy in Minneapolis circles. His interpretations of the Holbeins we looked at were interesting if rather over-arty and abstract. Mr Cowles was bewildered at times, I thought. At one point he interrupted the verbiage to ask, "Well now, let's see, Oscar. Just whom is number one in this painting business?" Kokoschka's artistic sense was obviously shaken by this question but after considerable hedging suggested Titian as his choice for "number one." "Ah," said Mr Cowles. "Well now, if Titian is Number*

One, who then might we call Number Two." "Tintoretto," barked
Kokoschka curtly, quite angry now. Fortunately, Mr Cowles didn't
continue the progression. He said: "Well now, if Titian is 'Number
One' and Tintoretto is 'Number Two' I guess we can consider the
rest of 'em sort of supernumeraries." . . . [no date]

Dear Mother and Daddy,
    . . . I put on grandfather's white tie and tails last weekend and
went to a dance at the Savoy where I sat opposite Princess Elizabeth. I, unfortunately, did not make the most of the occasion.
    My one conversation with her occurred in the reception line prior
to the dinner when I bowed (rather stiffly in grandfather's white tie
and tails) and said "How do you do, Ma'am?" She smiled at me but
had nothing to say as to the state of her health. She, however,
looked pretty, and very healthy.
    Halfway through dinner I leaned across the table and lit her cig-
arette for her with a French match that sputtered badly and gave off
that obnoxious odor peculiar to French matches. She again smiled at
me. I had nothing to say.
    By about midnight I had steeled myself to asking her to dance. I
was just rising out of my chair to go around the table to ask her when
the orchestra gave vent with a Mexican Hat dance—certainly not
the sort of music suited to the occasion of one G. Plimpton dancing
with the future queen of the British Empire. I sank back into my
chair.
    There then followed a cabaret during which I composed a very
amusing hypothetical conversation which presumably would take
place between the Princess and myself on the dance floor following
the end of the cabaret.
    When the cabaret ended, I rose and went around the table. The
Princess rose. I bowed (stiffly) and the Princess smiled at me and
swept out of the ballroom, home to Buckingham Palace.
    The orchestra was playing a slow and very danceable tango. . . .
[no date]

PETER STANFORD   Lou Connick, an Iwo Jima veteran, and
George decided to hold a "going down party"—going down from

university, that is—in my rooms, because they were going to be torn down to make way for some other facility there. The idea was that they could smash it up. They went out and bought a lot of dead chickens and dead rabbits, which they put in glass aquarium bowls. So I had these dead animals hanging out of these bowls. That was the beginning. Then they gave out little hammers so the guests could hammer all of the plaster in the rooms—this mock medieval room with a big fireplace and so forth. This was in June, during the summer vacation, and I can remember George coming in with Jacqueline Bouvier, suited up with her sister—quite a different lady than the great woman we knew as President Kennedy's wife. She spoke in a rather shrill voice, smoked a cigarette, and sat on the piano. I was terrified that she would put out the cigarette on the piano! That was another George party; George was always the animator of these things.

SARAH DUDLEY PLIMPTON   George told me that before he left Cambridge he had to sit for a three-hour final exam on one topic. The question was: "Who was Charles James Fox?" George drew a blank, so he began to improvise: "Charles James Fox was a rather mediocre second baseman for the Cincinnati Reds . . ." and spent the next three hours describing his career.

ANDREW LEGGATT   As soon as we came down from Cambridge I got married, and George gave a speech at our wedding. He was, of course, an incomparable speaker, and the speech was an inevitable success. Nothing untoward occurred. But I did remember with apprehension a wedding in which he was an usher and the seat of his pants split as he was unrolling the red carpet down the aisle. George asserted that thereafter he had to walk upright down the aisle, clutching his trousers to his backside and kicking the carpet before him. I was, of course, never quite sure to what extent situations like that were embellished in the telling.

PETER MATTHIESSEN   With the future *Paris Review* still germinating in Paris, and still unnamed, it occurred to me that George

Plimpton, my old buddy, might be good for the job of editor. He was in England, winding down his last year at Cambridge without knowing what he wanted to do next. This would be midspring 1952. The first issue was still months away. I took a chance and rang him up. I wanted him to come and take over as editor: I doubt if anything less would have attracted him. I didn't want the job, and I didn't think my colleagues in the venture, Doc Humes and Billy du Bois, were, for very different reasons, up to it. Did George imagine being a magazine editor? I doubt it. But he was an extremely curious and energetic guy, and he thought it was a great excuse to come to Paris—why not?

> *Dear Mother and Daddy,*
> *   . . . I shall be leaving here next week after degree day and prob-ably go straight to Paris. In the interests of the magazine, I should have left as soon as term ended but after so many years of fruitless at-tempts to march in a Commencement I'm not going to pass this one by. I have to wear "black boots, a black suit, black stockings, a square in a good state of repair" and a piece of rabbit fur about my neck.*
>
> *   I didn't do particularly well in my exams—an honours degree third class which could sound impressive but isn't. I thought the exams hard and was pulled down by an essay paper which got out of hand, as essays written to a time limit will, and a difficult three hours of French translation.*
>
> *   I went down to Oxford after the exam to stay with Don Hall, a friend of mine from Harvard and the Newdigate Poetry Prize-winner (see last week's* Time*). He's given me his prize-winning poem for the* Paris Magazine *and has collected a startlingly good portfolio of Oxford verse and prose, mostly verse, which should be successful. . . .* [June 12, 1952]

III.

CREATION MYTHS OF
THE PARIS REVIEW: 1952–1955

—

I am struck by how it must have been when they started the *Review,* how unencumbered and free and bold they were. It was a work of love among friends. They were publishing each other at first, as well as their heroes. Even as the years have gone by, you never lost the sense that George was doing it out of love. He took some glamour from it, but he gave it glamour. That was all because it was a work of love. It's not something you do because it's a good career move.

—PHILIP GOUREVITCH

THE FOUNDERS CONVERGE

RUSS HEMENWAY We were all in the right place, at the right time: postwar Paris. We felt just as important as Scott Fitzgerald and Hemingway and all the expatriates did after World War One. Some people were very productive, some people were not; some people were relatively rich—they had the GI Bill, plus a little money from home, maybe more than a little—some were flat-out poor. Myself, I could do things. I could access Paris. If I wanted to go to the theater, I could go to the theater, whereas many people would sit around and say, "Gee, I wish I could eat out at a restaurant instead of eating over this Bunsen burner," you know? But we all felt like family. There was some division; the Montparnasse crowd was a little different from the Saint-Germain-des-Prés crowd, and there were some people who actually lived on the Right Bank—we couldn't understand them at all. They actually *lived* over there.

WILLIAM BECKER We were living like kings. In Paris, on the black market in the mid-1950s, you could exchange a dollar for six hundred francs. My hotel room cost three hundred francs. For a hundred and eighty francs, you could get a steak *pommes frites,* with a bottle of Beaujolais. Paris was filled with GIs who were living on their seventy-five dollars a month GI Bill money. I had GI Bill money, plus my Rhodes stipend, which was converted into dollars. So I would go cash my Rhodes money into American dollar traveler's checks and head off to the Left Bank. But it was astonishing how well you could live in Paris even on seventy-five dollars a month.

PETER MATTHIESSEN I went to Paris after I graduated from Yale in the class of 1950. I was an English major, and by senior year, my favorite professor was a brilliant guy named Norman Holmes Pearson. He and I were members of something called the Jacobean Club, as was a man named James Jesus Angleton, who was already an important CIA officer. Pearson recruited a lot of people for the CIA, including me. My main reason for signing on was that I could insist on being sent to Paris when I graduated. I'd met Patsy Southgate there in the junior year abroad program, from '48 to '49, so Paris was very romantic for us; and by 1950 I was beginning to publish short stories, and I wanted to write my first novel. So here was the CIA, as it turned out, offering to send me to Paris for its own reasons. I should mention, back then, that the CIA was brand new, and they were not yet into political assassinations or the other ugly stuff that came later. I had no politics. I was a Yaley greenhorn as far as politics went. This was 1950. The cold war had hardly started, but Paris was a hot spot of anti-Americanism, which Communists were happy to exploit to benefit the Soviet Union. So there was the appeal to my patriotism, to work for my

Max Steele, Peter Matthiessen, and Richard Wright, Paris.
Photograph by Otto van Noppen.

Harold L. (Doc) Humes.
Photograph © the Estate of Harold Louis Humes

country against the Communist menace. Mainly, I was interested in being a writer.

RUSS HEMENWAY When I first saw Harold (Doc) Humes, he had just arrived in Paris, in 1949. I was doing my graduate work there, but doing the required café sitting as well, and there was this guy walking down the boulevard Saint-Germain in this incredible outfit. It was summertime, so it was hot—Paris gets hot—and he had on this black wool suit, a homburg hat, a white shirt, and a black tie, and he carried a cane with a silver handle. Everyone was saying, "Who's *that* guy?" We had no idea, but he was obviously crazy. It was hot as hell out, and he had this beatific smile on his face. This darling, cute face; he looked like a little boy in a grown-up suit. It turned out that he was a remittance man—he got money from his father. It's the only money he ever had. He didn't like to talk about it. His father was a Puritan: nice, very nice; loved Doc and dearly wished for him to go straight; get a job and have a conventional life.

He wanted Doc to take care of his own children, when they came, whereas he and his wife had to take care of them.

DOC HUMES TO GAY TALESE, 1963 *I went to Paris because Paris is where you go when you want to think. I wanted to hide out and think, and maybe learn. Paris is the University of the West, and anybody who doesn't understand that doesn't need to go. I went to Paris because I was ignorant; I went as a matriculator, not a pilgrim.*

DAVID AMRAM Doc sometimes wouldn't say anything, he would be really quiet, and then in the middle of a conversation he would come blasting out with this torrent of argument. It wasn't that he particularly cared about what he was arguing about, I thought it was just his way of keeping himself in shape. He would go into some crazy monologue or start screaming about something that I think made him feel good so he could go home and write about something else. It would relax him. Doc had his own language, combining hip talk with some expressions of his own. He would start speaking about something that had happened two months ago or would continue a conversation from three weeks ago. A lot of people were confused by him.

JOHN TRAIN I arrived in Paris a year before George in the early summer of 1951 to get a doctorate at the Sorbonne after getting an MA at Harvard. I settled at a splendid place on the avenue Franco-Russe that belonged to an English writer. It was a studio transformed into a library, with two floors and a minstrel's gallery.

WILLIAM STYRON After my first novel was published, *Lie Down in Darkness,* in 1951, I received a prize called the Prix de Rome, which entitled me to spend a year at the American Academy in Rome. This seemed like a fine thing for me to do since I had de-livered myself of a novel and was footloose and fancy-free. *Lie Down in Darkness* was a modest bestseller, so I had made a bit of money, enough for a bachelor. So I headed, as one did at the age of twenty-six, for Europe. I first went to England, and then to Denmark of all places, and figured this was a good way to get to Rome. It was a long journey but a pleasant one, and in the spring of '52 I ended up in Paris for eight months, I found a little room in a small hotel called Liberia. I wrote *The Long March* there. I think it was Blair Fuller, whom I had met in New York, who told me to look up a good friend of his, Peter Matthiessen. So in the course of events, not long after I arrived in Paris, I met Peter. But first I met Doc Humes, who heard that I was in Paris, sought me out in my hotel on the Right Bank, before the Liberia, and said, "You can't live on the Right Bank. You've got to live on the Left Bank." So he got me situated in the Liberia. And about this time I met Peter.

PETER MATTHIESSEN   Bill Styron showed up on the dingy fourth-floor landing of our apartment at 14, rue Perceval, with no French and a thick Tidewater accent and a scrawled note of introduction from our friend John Marquand, Jr. Patsy and I gave him a drink and then took him to Ti-Jo's (Petit Joseph), a little Breton café that served big, fresh, delicious Belon and Marenne *huîtres* (a French word derived, or so I informed Bill, from the sound made when one's first oyster is spat across the room: hweet-tre!). We were also sloshing up a good deal of rough *vin de table,* and at a certain point, overcome by dire homesickness, he fell face forward into his platter and lay lachrymose amongst the oysters, uttering the immortal Styronian words: "Ah ain' got no mo ree-sistunce to change than a *snow*-flake; ah'm goin' home to the James Rivuh and grow *pee*-nuts." But by this time, we were already fond of this well-read, humorous, and very intelligent man: We became fast friends on that first evening and from that time on.

RUSS HEMENWAY   The first time I actually spoke to Doc—well before Peter or George arrived—I asked him, "What are you doing in Paris?"—the obvious question. He said, "I'm an art dealer. I'm over here buying paintings." In fact, he didn't have any money to buy paintings. But then he met Sinbad Vail, Peggy Guggenheim's son, and suddenly he was a publisher. Sinbad had a little magazine called *Points.* Everybody knew *Points,* everybody talked about it, it was the beginning of the "little magazine" period, and he was by himself, with his own dough, publishing this little mag. It wasn't a lot, but it was a little magazine, and Doc thought Paris needed another little magazine. That was the beginning of *The Paris News Post*.

IMMY HUMES My father told me he had been thinking about starting a magazine for years—that the idea had sort of been germinating—he credits it to a conversation with Jimmy Baldwin, a conversation that happened sometime in '48 or '49, before he hooked up with Matthiessen. Doc *loved* James Baldwin, absolutely idolized James Baldwin, and he says they talked about making a magazine—how great it would be if there were an outlet and a safe space for writers by writers. Doc always talked about *The Paris Review* as an antianxiety measure. In other words, it was going to be this protected space, and it was going to be criticism free; there would be no academic jargon, just fiction, and this was going to be a measure against this "age of anxiety," a phrase he got from Randall Jarrell, I think.

JOHN TRAIN By the time George came to town, I had abandoned my studies at the Sorbonne and had already discussed starting a magazine with Rosamond and Georges Bernier. I had a distinct entrepreneurial bent, even then; indeed, I started a car credit company for GIs in Europe. But I liked magazine work, having done it at Groton and at the *Lampoon*. So I had discussions with the Berniers about starting a *New Yorker* sort of magazine: a commercial publication, not a "little magazine." Little magazines, by their very nature, cannot make money. They discover authors. Very few people want to read undiscovered authors. They want to read reliably good authors they've already read. Anyway, we made some progress on that project, but then the gang appeared— George, Peter Matthiessen, and Doc Humes, who had been running *The Paris News Post*—and we sort of coalesced.

PETER MATTHIESSEN Tom Guinzburg, my roommate at Yale in senior year, had been managing editor of the *Yale Daily News* and was going around with Bill Buckley's sister, whom he planned to meet in Paris; that's how he got mixed up with the new magazine. Tom's editorial input was always welcome, and in addition, he knew a good deal about publishing since his father was head of the

Viking Press, as he would be himself. Terry Southern was another member of our group and later became a great friend of George's. In those days, he smoked so much hash that he passed for a junkie, and his spoken word was suspenseful, to say the least. "Yeah, man, uhhhhh . . ." then three minutes might pass before he resumed, picking up the thread where he'd left off. He had to *lean;* that was my phrase, he had to *lean* for three minutes.

MARY LEE SETTLE   Max Steele was another *Paris Review* writer in the earliest days, a funny person, a big-eared southerner who wrote for the *Review* in the early days. He was very funny, actually, but also odd. Max got his little touch of fame too soon, to tell you the truth. It's a bad thing that happens to some people. Another early figure was Alfred Chester. He had had some kind of fever that he'd caught when he was growing up, and all his hair fell out. He had a red wig, which he used to put on like a beret. Never gave a damn if it was straight or anything. God, when I think of Alfred, I can see him with squinty eyes and that wig he wore all the time. Later, I gather, he gave up on the wig, but it was very much a part of life for him when he was in Paris. He went to Tangiers, and then things got from bad to worse.

BEE DABNEY   Let's see. Pati Hill was one of the people around the *Review* very early on. She was beautiful, absolutely beautiful, and wrote beautifully. She was once a model. I think she wrote quite a few stories for the *Review.* Eugene Walter was another. He was called "Tum-te-tum." I used to walk in the Luxembourg Gardens with him, and we would have picnics. He was always inventive about something to do, and he had the most wonderful imagination, an artful way of whipping up parties and gatherings together. He was full of whimsy. Brilliant. Fascinating, I thought. Very original. Sally Higginson arrived. She was from Boston, and she started out on the Left Bank. I think she stayed in the same hotel that Eugene Walter was in, across the street practically from the *Review.* Soon after her arrival, she moved out of that hotel and into rather sumptuous quarters at the Hôtel Vendôme, and she was wonderful because she gave parties. We'd all dress up in costumes and had champagne, and it was terrific fun and luxurious for all of

Party at the Hôtel Vendôme, Paris, 1953. From left: Eddie Morgan,
John Train, three persons unknown, Bee, George, and Eugene Walter.
Photograph by Otto van Noppen.

us. She had red hair. She was comfy looking and had a comfy way
of speaking.

PETER MATTHIESSEN Patsy and I had a poker game at the apartment one evening a week with Terry Southern and others. One
night, Terry brought a young black writer named Jimmy Baldwin,
whom we didn't know. During supper, there was quite a lot of
talk about how certain jobs in the art world, ballet, and the theater were now almost entirely the province of gays. We were all
drinking and excitable—Jimmy, too—and suddenly, deep into the
evening, he announced that he was gay and furthermore very offended, although the talk had not been homophobic in the least. I
was very annoyed, but being the host, I felt I had to respond, and
I said, "Look, I'm sorry, but we don't know you and you came on
like you were straight: Why didn't you speak up earlier instead of
waiting all this time, then acting offended?" Not long after that,

his first book, which was *Go Tell It on the Mountain,* was published in the U.S. He was too broke to go home, so we all chipped in and got him a ticket and sent him off. When he came back, he went out of his way to avoid those who had helped him out, perhaps because he thought we thought he owed everybody money. We didn't. Jimmy's first novel was very good, and he was a fine polemic writer, and in later years, he came to Bill Styron's defense in the uproar among black writers over *Confessions of Nat Turner,* but I'm afraid I never quite trusted him. This may have been partly because I was friends with Richard Wright, who was also in Paris at that time, knew Baldwin, and admired his talent but found him ambiguous, too.

RUSS HEMENWAY Matthiessen's the only guy I know who was there in Paris for "you know who." But it was not an opprobrious thing. Those of us who had been in World War Two realized that we had no intelligence service at all, just the OSS. So we were delighted with this thing they called the Central Intelligence Agency, which was going to be the central gathering place of intelligence. We could now make judgments based on something other than talking to the British ambassador. So Peter was never derided for this. Also, you've got to remember that from 1949 to 1952, we were living in high anxiety. The Korean War was a major threat, and we were losing. As for the Russians, every night we thought, "Well, they will come off the steppes and march into Western Europe, and there's absolutely nothing there to stop them." Meanwhile, back home, the Republicans had taken over the Senate, and Joseph McCarthy was to be chairman of the subcommittee on investigations, and he decided that he had to have a hundred accountants, fifty lawyers, this whole expanded staff, and he came in with a budget of four or five times what the committee budget normally had been. There was one vote against it. One vote against it! Bill Fulbright.

DOC HUMES TO GAY TALESE, 1963 *Exile is like unrequited love. Ours was a sick nation in those terrible days. I left my native land because I couldn't stand watching the rape of justice and murder of decency. I left America because the alternative to leaving was suicide or madness.*

PETER MATTHIESSEN Sometime in the winter of 1951–1952, in the cafés, I ran into Harold L. Humes, Jr., who was running a magazine called *The Paris News Post*—a restaurant and theater guide, like the old *Cue* magazine. He wanted me to get fiction for it, which I would not have done except that I needed more cover for my nefarious activities, the worst of which was the unpleasant task of checking on certain Americans in Paris to see what they were up to. My cover, officially, was my first novel, but my contact man (who met me in the Jeu de Paume, of all places) had said, "Anything else you can do while you're here?" I could now say, "Well, yes, I'm an editor on a magazine."

RUSS HEMENWAY Anybody Doc chose to get to know, he got to know. For instance, besides the Matthiessens, he got to know Ambrose Chambers. I think Chambers was the number two man in the Marshall Plan or something, but he was also working for the Agency. He and Doc became very close friends. *The Underground City*, Doc's first novel, owes something to those conversations.

IMMY HUMES Matthiessen and George tell the same story: that *The Paris News Post* was a "*Cue*-like magazine"—or sometimes a "fourth-rate *New Yorker*." So it was quite a shock for me to see *The Paris News Post* when I was researching my documentary on Doc. It wasn't terrible, it really wasn't; but over the years their story became ossified.

PETER MATTHIESSEN I discovered Terry Southern in the pages of Doc's *Paris News Post;* it was a very good story called "The Sun and the Still-born Stars," and I thought it was too good for Doc's magazine. I also realized that *The Paris News Post* was a flimsy vehicle. Doc's staff was ready to mutiny. All three of the guys Doc had working there were furious with him. I too wanted to kill him half the time, although I remained very fond of him. But I saw that his magazine was going absolutely nowhere, so I said, "Doc, I'm not interested in doing this. If we're going to publish fiction, let's publish a real magazine." He agreed, almost overnight, and *The Paris News Post* came to an end. So we had this idea, and I worked with Doc for a month or so, and I realized, and Patsy realized, that it wasn't going to work. Doc was too erratic to manage it, and too opinionated. He liked to hold forth; his whole life was about holding forth.

A COVER STORY

PETER MATTHIESSEN   My call to George in Cambridge had been a stab in the dark. If that call hadn't worked, the *Review* might have died on the vine. But the call did work; as soon as George came over to Paris and signed on, he began collecting poems from Donald Hall for the first issue, and we all began talking about funding. We got a hundred bucks from Ellen Berry, who was Philip Berry's widow. She was in Paris at the time, seeing a friend of my folks and of George's folks.

JOHN TRAIN   George, when he finally arrived in Paris, in '52, I believe, lived down the street. The concierges all knew each other, of course, and knew everything happening on the block; that was the Napoleonic function of concierges, to keep control over the population. One day, my concierge told me, "If your friend wants to get his mail, he should give something to his concierge." It seems that his concierge was withholding it pending a *douceur*. George started tipping her, and all was well. But then he moved on, as George seemed always to do.

> *Dear Mother and Daddy,*
>   *. . . I've decided to stay over here in Paris and run this magazine. I think I'd be a fool not to. Here's the quick background: It's to be called* The Paris Review *and is one of the literary quarterly genre; 3,000–5,000 copies are to be printed and distributed in England, the U.S., and France. We are to be printed by La Table Ronde, one of the best publishing houses in France and with a famous quarterly printed bi-monthly of the same name. La Table Ronde is interested in publishing us in that their name (the review and the house) is introduced into American literary circles. We in turn (far more advantageous to us really) through them have*

knowledge of the particulars of magazine publishing born of seventy years of successful enterprise in this field. This should put us immediately out of the realm of the fly-by-night literary magazines that blossom and die with mushroom rapidity here in Paris.

The editors are John Train, president of the Lampoon *after me; Peter Matthiessen, winner of the Atlantic First last year; Harold Humes, William Pène du Bois, a successful book illustrator (his famous bears appeared in* Life *two years ago; his latest work is Peggy Ashcroft's* The Young Visitors*); William Styron, the Prix de Rome Literature Prize winner for his novel* Lie Down in Darkness. . . . *[no date]*

RUSS HEMENWAY   The rumor around the cafés was that they had no money and no sign of any coming in. Then they began to talk about this figure named George Plimpton. Plimpton was going to come over from Cambridge, and he had tons of money. He was really well connected; he knew everybody. He knew Sadruddin Khan. The money was going to pour in, and they were going to have this big publication. He was supposed to have all this money, "the Plimp," but it turned out he didn't. Still, he faced up to the problem of budget better than the others did. At that point, I was leaving Paris. I was involved with the Adlai Stevenson campaign. Doc began to drift away from the *Review* to do other things and soon left for the States.

DOC HUMES TO GAY TALESE, 1963   I really didn't like [George] at first, mistaking the apparent snobbishness and studied front for gratuitous thoughtlessness rather than recognizing the necessary camouflage of an almost tenderly vulnerable man. I know a lot about [him] now that I didn't when I first met him [in Paris eleven years earlier], and he is a complex, lonely, rather brave human being.

ROBERT SILVERS   George refused to be perturbed by money matters. There was a day when a letter arrived, saying, "I write on behalf of the Banque de Paris. We have need of your help because we have been asked by *Horizon* magazine to make a payment to Mr. Eugene Walter for an article he wrote in that journal; but, by mistake, we have sent him five hundred dollars too much, so we seek your help in recovering the five hundred dollars that was sent in error." George then wrote: "In reply to your letter, I've been asking myself just who you are referring to. In the café the other day, I saw on the street one of the denizens of the *quartier* who I recognized as Eugene Womble. I greeted him, as I always do, '*Ça gaz*, Womble?' Womble did seem distinctly more prosperous than usual; so while I can't be absolutely sure, I think he may be your man." The bank wrote him back saying something like "*Merci pour un bon moment dans notre journée.*"

PETER MATTHIESSEN For many years I have stated flatly that the chronic rumors that *The Paris Review* was founded or influenced by the CIA are simply untrue. Though I still believe that, it now appears that some of our start-up funding may have come from an acquaintance of George's and mine, Julius Fleischmann, a rich, cultured Chicagoan living in Paris who, many years later, around 1966, turned out to have been associated with a CIA-sponsored outfit called Congress for Cultural Freedom. His foundation served the CIA as a conduit of funds that Congress deployed to sponsor conferences and publications like *Encounter*, to oppose Communist influence among European intellectuals. Julius—"Junkie"—was one of several friends of our parents who donated money to help print and publish the first issue of the *Review*. George and I had no idea of his connection to the CIA—not then, certainly—and by the time we learned of it we'd forgotten about his donation. Now, of course, I've seen the letter George wrote his parents about our fund-raising efforts, and, difficult though it is to believe that an utterly unknown apolitical magazine of laughable potential circulation was a likely recruit for ideological warfare, the name "Fleischmann" in that letter muddies the picture a bit. What muddies it even more, though, is that the Fleischmann George refers to—Raoul, the publisher of *The New Yorker*, who was Junkie's cousin, I believe—was a man who as far as I know had no connection with either the Congress or *The Paris Review*. Perhaps George confused his Fleischmanns; perhaps we both did. Or perhaps, as I think, the CIA is not in this picture at all beyond having casually approved my use of the *Review* to strengthen my cover. Meanwhile, around this time, I was becoming disillusioned with the CIA. Anticommunism was breeding witch hunts in the States; [Roy] Cohn and [David] Schine were snuffling through our embassies in Europe, and Paris itself was seething with international and ideological conflicts—all of which was politicizing me leftward, as happened to many Americans living in Paris in those days. By the winter of 1953 I was ready to quit, and did. And I have to say that among the many adventures in my life, my paltry experience as a spy in Paris is the only one I remember with distaste and regret.

ALISON HUMES My father believed there were secret, vital, terrible things that "they" had given him to understand about the world. But "they" were Doc's only way of making sense of what was happening to *him*. He couldn't face the idea that he was just crazy, so instead he reasoned that he must have been really on to something and had become a guinea pig for the government from the time he was in high school. That was his cover story, you see: "They," the evil forces of the CIA, they wanted to take someone intellectually gifted and turn him into a pawn to be manipulated.

PETER MATTHIESSEN In the mid-1960s, with the Congress for Cultural Freedom being exposed everywhere as a CIA front, I decided that George deserved to know the truth of the *Review*'s origins. I assured him that I'd kept my two Paris activities strictly separate and that the *Review* had never been contaminated by the CIA. Even so, he was shocked and very angry, understandably so. Who, after all, wants to hear that the "love of his life," as he himself would call it, had been conceived as a cover for another man's secret activities? I had wanted to tell Doc, too, but had put it off because, as George and I agreed, he might not be able to handle it. He had become so paranoid and dangerous by this time that Anna Lou, who was with him in London, was finally obliged to take the children and flee back to the United States. Not long after that, in 1967, I think, when I tracked him down there with the idea of bringing him home, he was in desperate condition and I was at a loss as to how I might pierce the murk. But my instinct was that hearing the truth about a trusted friend's CIA connection might retrieve his fantasy-CIA from the lenticular clouds that followed him everywhere and make it as real as this flesh-and-blood old pal walking by his side on the concrete sidewalk. Ill-advisedly or not, that's what I did. We had an amiable dinner, after which I gave him the other bed in my hotel room, where he also enjoyed a long-overdue bath.

ALISON HUMES   I know from seeing some of Doc's old papers that he felt betrayed when Peter told him that he'd been working for the CIA. But Peter's revelations certainly didn't *cause* Doc to go crazy, as Peter sometimes feels accused of doing; Doc was already quite mad. The news just fed into his paranoia. In a way, Doc may not have felt betrayed so much as confirmed. His response may have been closer to "Yeah, of course, I always suspected that" than confusion or anger. But Peter's story must have been a pretty heavy thing to drop on all the other guys at the *Review*.

IMMY HUMES   Researching the film I made on my father, I found a letter from Doc to George in March of the year when Matthiessen had come to London and told Doc that he, Matthiessen, had been in the CIA when *The Paris Review* was founded and *The Paris News Post* abandoned. The letter from Doc was extraordinarily lucid for somebody who had literally lost his mind and was listening to implanted broadcasts from his furniture. He says he's going to resign from *The Paris Review* unless Peter goes public with his story—he's to be congratulated on coming out on all this, but he needs to write it in public in *The Saturday Evening Post* or, God help us, in *The Paris Review*. Peter never did. George's response to that letter was the most extraordinarily sweet letter to Doc saying, I absolutely refuse your resignation, you can't possibly resign; come back to New York and you can stay with me in my apartment for as long as you want. Then he sort of puts little asterisks and said, Well, okay, let's say one year. What a good attitude he had! Just refusing to draw invidious distinctions between people or throw people away; that extraordinarily smart way of being warm.

DAVID AMRAM George was very good with Doc. If George wasn't sure what Doc was saying, he would cock his head, like he was listening to some music. I think when Doc would get on one of his particular crazed rants, George seemed able to turn on a different receptor, and instead of listening to what Doc was saying, he would just listen to the sounds as they were bellowed.

PETER MATTHIESSEN In her film documentary on Doc, his daughter Immy leaves the impression that my London confession in the late sixties, fourteen years after the event, was somehow related to Doc's longtime CIA paranoia and helped send her dad around the bend. As a narrative device, this distortion of Doc's chronology is useful, but sadly (for me, at least) it ignores the fact that Doc's paranoia had been well established for many years before my revelation. George compounds the damage by yelping on-camera that Doc had been "outraged" by my news. That was not my experience, either: It was George who'd been "outraged." Doc was not upset by my perfidy, if that's what he thought of it. That the CIA had in some ghostly sense been present at the creation of the *Review* must have seemed to him perfectly natural, given his sense of his centrality in the way the world worked. Eventually, somewhat recovered, Doc returned to the U.S., where our long telephone discussions and occasional visits over the years remained friendly, although mostly limited to Doc's oratory, which was still bizarre but never "outraged."

GEORGE ON BOTH BANKS

CHARLES MICHENER George once said to me, "You know, the great thing about Paris in the fifties was you could go anywhere; you could get into any level of society you wanted; so long as you had a black tie and evening clothes, you could go anywhere." He loved that.

Dear Mother and Daddy,

My window looks out on a bleak host of smoking chimneys. I'm on the fifth floor, a very small room, but warm and with a little pot-bellied stove. Still, Paris is cold and today I [am wearing] *my hideous Army underwear. I spend most of my day at the office on the rue Garancière, reading proofs, meeting artists, writers, and other editors, and arguing, of course; arguments seem to be the basis on which these magazines start. Don't worry, Mother. I'm not going to seed here. This whole project, at least from here, is too enthralling to consider going to seed.* . . . [no date]

MARY LEE SETTLE George lived two lives. He lived a Right Bank life, as you know, and he lived a Left Bank life, and one day I got pretty bloody fed up with this, let me tell you. I said, "George, I'm a nice girl from America. I went to Sweet Briar, for God's sake. I want you to come get me in a taxi, and I want you to take me to the Ritz for a drink, and then to dinner. I'm sick of this slumming life." He said, "I didn't know you wanted to do anything like that. Of course!" So when the time came for me to sally forth from my Left Bank hotel in the one black dress I had left from a Right Bank life, there was George with the oldest taxi in Paris. He had found a suit, I swear to you, that he had worn at Exeter. We got into the taxi, a little embarrassed with each other, like we didn't know each other very well. We started out, amid the derisive jeers of the whole clientele of the Café le Tournon [the *Review* hangout on the rue de Tournon, around the corner from their tiny office on the rue Garancière], who watched. We got to the Ritz and we sat down. I had just published *O Beulah Land*. As soon as we sat down, a waiter came over and said, "Miss Settle, will you and Mr. Plimpton join Mr. So-and-so of the Viking Press?" From that time on, we were drinking carafes, though we had to listen to this old fool. That was our evening on the Right Bank. It was very funny, and for George very lucky, because George didn't have as much money as people thought he had.

PETER MATTHIESSEN In that summer of '52, the hard drinkers besides Patsy and me were Styron, sometimes George and Tom

Guinzburg, and Cass Canfield, Jr., a friend of ours from New York (also the son of a well-known publisher of Harper & Row). We'd cross over to the Right Bank to the bar of the Hôtel Crillon, which made excellent dry martinis; then in the evening we might repair to Montparnasse and Le Chaplain.

DAVID AMRAM I was playing in a jazz band at the time, and one evening we were invited to a party at this huge château. We began playing, and there were all of these society people, and they expected us to play dance music. Instead, we began to play our great Thelonious Monk, Dizzy Gillespie, Charlie Parker music, and our own free-improvised music, and managed to clear out the entire garden. I was so upset that I went behind a hedge to calm myself down by taking a little smoke—when suddenly from behind, I saw George Plimpton peeking through the hedge, taking in the whole scene. I said, "George, what are you doing here?" "I'm a guest," he said, "but I'm doing a little reportage."

PATI HILL George sometimes said things that sounded simple enough but followed you around afterward. One that comes to mind now was about Sadri Khan and it was the result of a slight altercation. George had asked me for the second or third time to some event with Sadri, and I had refused, saying I thought it would be just boring, and George said—sharply—that he would imagine it would be rather hard to be bored by an evening with somebody who was in line to be the absolute leader of millions of Muslims, and from my point of view, that was puzzling. However, George did manage to make me see that he didn't live in the same world I did. And maybe not in the world most writers live in. I mean that whereas in general writers are trying to keep the door shut so we can get on with counting our bedbugs or whatever we hold dear at the moment, George saw everything out there as one huge old swimming hole to plunge seriously into and come up with a fish in his mouth.

RICHARD SEAVER *The Paris Review* wasn't the only English-language literary magazine founded in Paris in 1952. Alex Trocchi, Austryn Wainhouse, Patrick Bowles, Christopher Logue, and myself—a Scot of Italian origin, an Englishman, a South African, and two Americans—started a magazine called *Merlin*. *Merlin*'s raison d'être was to discover new writers, to publish serious fiction and poetry and critical essays—on French existentialism, for example, and on Samuel Beckett, both of these the first in English. Thereafter we published a lot of Beckett. I said to Alex Trocchi, "You know, if we go down in history as the organ of propaganda of Samuel Beckett, that ain't so bad."

JEANNETTE SEAVER   The *Merlin*ites thought that the Harvard boys, with their good looks and their money, were playboys, really—*pas du tout sérieux*. And they weren't—that was a fact. They were having fun pulling their beautiful bodies around Paris. George looked the same as he always would—tall, dashing, handsome. He walked about like someone who was born feeling good with himself, with money and aristocracy, whereas our group were like lepers. They were good-looking, yes, but not at all the same thing. Pennies mattered; with George they never mattered. Doors opened from the day he was born, which does make you look different and move about differently. The head of *Merlin* was also a very tall, handsome, brilliant Scot named Alex Trocchi. He was not a good man at all, a junkie, but he was irresistibly intelligent and charming, and we were all under his spell at one point or another. And so was George. When Alex showed up in New York in the late 1950s, George was extremely generous to him. Housed him, gave him money. Then, when Alex fled to Canada, he put on two or three of George's suits, went to Canada, and from there back to London. I'm not clear whether George gave the suits to him or if he stole them. I wouldn't be surprised if he stole them, because that's what he did.

WILLIAM STYRON   We were a world apart from the *Merlin* people. They were in the avant-garde and we were not. I certainly respected the avant-garde, but I felt there was also a place for some conventional stuff, like the stuff *The Paris Review* would publish.

RICHARD SEAVER   We had a deal with Maurice Girodias, publisher of the Olympia Press. We brought him Beckett's *Watt,* and of course he also published Nabokov's *Lolita*. Mostly, though, he published porn. Some of us wrote for him, Trocchi more than the others. George also wrote a dirty book—I can't remember the name—but it was not published. It was terrible. I read it. George had too much Harvard in him. Girodias wanted down and dirty: "It's page five already, let's get on with it." But George was doing elaborate plots and romantic things and just couldn't do it. Christopher Logue was doing a dirty book at the same time as George,

The Café le Tournon crowd. Front row, left to right: Vilma Howard, Jane Lougee, Muffy Wainhouse, Jean Garrigue. Second row: Christopher Logue, Richard Seaver, Evan Connell, Niccolò Tucci, unknown, Peter Huyn, Alfred Chester, Austryn Wainhouse. Last row: Eugene Walter, George, Michel van der Plats, unknown, James Broughton, William Gardner Smith, Harold Witt. *Photograph by Otto van Noppen.*

and he had a nervous breakdown, it was so hard for him. He and George were sort of the two cats who couldn't do it—their minds were not there, they just couldn't steel themselves for that kind of book on command. You know, to have a wide-ranging sex life and to write about it—there's a difference.

BEE DABNEY He was always struggling with his stories. I would go to his flat and cook rice because he lived on rice, along with all the cats he'd collected. Wherever he was living, he had to have a cat. I remember one time he read to me a story he was struggling with, and it was so pornographic and so shocking to me, I said, "George, you simply can't!" I don't know why I became so prissy about it, but it upset me so much that I burst into tears, persuading him to please, please not write that story. His other stories were really much more elegant and stylish, and I didn't want him to be known for that story.

RICHARD SEAVER I found *The Paris Review,* when it appeared in the fall of 1952, to be a real competitor to *Merlin*. "First of all," I said, "the magazine looks better than *Merlin*." And Alex Trocchi said, "Yeah, but look at the inside. Don't be worried, these people are not serious. They won't be on the Left Bank very long, and when they leave Paris after their stint here, their magazine will not exist. And we will. We'll still be here." And, of course, we had nine issues and George had two hundred and thirty or whatever it was.

A LOVE STORY

BEE DABNEY After the first trip with Sadri and his parents I went back to Boston, only to return, of course, with my beribboned admission to the Atelier the next fall. I stayed in Paris for two years. That's when I again saw a lot of George. We were either at Café de Flore or the Deux Magots, with hundreds of writers and artists, people like Orson Welles and Truman Capote. But we scattered ourselves *all over* Paris. We were one minute dressed up as best we could be on the Right Bank at some very pompous French thing, struggling with our French; or going off to an outing in this little tiny house in the country. It was wildly exciting. He lived on the Left Bank in a series of freezing cold little apartments, and I lived on the Right Bank, with a very serious French family. I was constantly getting on this bus to the Left Bank to see George and creeping home at the wee hours, because whenever I saw George, there was no bedtime, ever. My French family could hear the bathtub running in the wee hours, because I was so frozen cold that I wanted to take hot baths, and they kept reprimanding me.

PATI HILL Bee was marvelous looking. She looked like a little animal. If you had a squirrel or a marmot or something for your own, you might want it to look like Bee Dabney. She was very seductive in the way of giving smiles and admiration all around, but not making you feel as if you had to deserve it. She wasn't a close friend of mine. I just admired her and felt like explaining to her how to make pound cake or something. How to do some very simple magic trick, as if she didn't already know all she needed.

TEDDY VAN ZUYLEN Flirting was part of Bee's charm. I think that she was obviously, seriously interested in George, but he never showed anything of that kind. He did not wear his heart on his sleeve as some people do and caress the lady, call her "darling," say, "Ah, you look so lovely." She was so cute, so feminine, and so charming that it was a mystery to me to see how indifferent he seemed. I'm sure that part of his New England lineage would never allow him to show any affection in public to the woman he happened to be with. He was perfectly polite to her. He never treated her badly. But you never would have known they were together, if you didn't already know it.

BEE DABNEY I left the serious French family I was staying with when I first arrived in Paris and found a flat on the Left Bank, right next to this wonderful, imaginative nightclub on the rue du Bac. When I would go to George's for dinner, he would always concoct this rice dish. So I said, "George, why don't you come over and have dinner in my little apartment here." I did *not* know how to cook particularly well, but I got my dinner together: a piece of meat, and some salad, and some cheese and bread, and a perfectly delicious bottle of Rothschild wine that I had been given by this relative of the Rothschilds, a most interesting man named Karl Hans Strauss. Fascinating man. He had sent a whole case of this wine, which I used to give to that family I was living with, and they were mortified, because by then I think they thought their table wine that we'd been drinking was not up to snuff or something. Here I was, taking hot baths and presenting them with a bottle of Rothschild wine. I didn't realize—well, anyway, I think that's why I moved out and into my little flat. So, George was having difficulties carving the meat, and it was just adorable. The table I set up with the candle, and everything was so romantic, except for this terrible piece of meat that kept flying around. George asked me what it was, and I told him. Of course, George made a huge story out of it and said I'd served him cat lung with a bottle of Rothschild wine. That was the end of my dinner parties.

CHRISTOPHER LOGUE   I was looking at a photograph of Bee Dabney yesterday. She had this beautiful oval face with her hair that came down like that, also oval. She knew very well what she

George with Baron Teddy van Zuylen.
From the collection of George Plimpton.

was doing with George. But I don't think she was really very keen. It was very difficult to tell with Bee how interested she was in men. She was kind of distant—at least, I thought so. George was dotty about her; at the same time, he was always pretending to be somewhere else, free all the time, you see. He *didn't* want to be emotionally committed, and he *did* want to be emotionally committed. Very common. He was elusive, George was.

BEE DABNEY I got a little fussed over George's attentions to others. I was quite jealous of Zadie Parkinson. I thought she was very good-looking, and George seemed to like her, and that irritated me. At the same time, Jimmy Goldsmith was paying a lot of attention to me, so I suppose I was being just as irritating to George. I don't know what came over me, to find Jimmy so interesting. He could be so charming, and yet he was a gambler, an incredible gambler, which was a total bore. He was also terribly jealous of George. Still, no matter what, George and I were with each other throughout all this time in Paris. We would go to our little bistros, whatever they were called, where they would be willing sometimes to take the paper tabletop that we had been painting or drawing or writing on and frame it, and give us a free meal. We were always inventing children's stories together. He would tell the story, and I would illustrate it right then and there. We were also always making wedding plans. Who are our ushers going to be, and who are our bridesmaids going to be? We were always making these lists and dreaming away of wedding plans.

ROBERT SILVERS George and Bee would travel together, sometimes to George's family's villa on Lake Como. In fact, we would all go down there Teddy Van Zuylen, John Marquand, and several others. George's sister, Sarah, would join us, and then George's father and mother.

BEE DABNEY All the time, of course, the greatest thing in George's life was, really, *The Paris Review.* I felt it, what with all of these late nights all the time, it was always *Paris Review, Paris Review.* The focus was *The Paris Review,* really. I knew this. We used to joke about it. As time went on, I realized that I was getting unable to stay up that late, because I'm an early person. When your time clocks are different from someone, it isn't as easy. So I began to realize that those late nights were extraordinary, and I couldn't keep up with that.

THE FIRST ISSUE

GEORGE PLIMPTON DIARY   Elected editor, chairman, president, what-have-you to magazine. Position of no authority except position of whip, hardly one which I can do well. Decisions I don't mind. That's what I wanted. If Humes, Matthiessen, and du Bois had agreed to that we'd have no trouble on the magazine, though perhaps hurt feelings. . . . A composite accumulation of agreements through vote in a magazine results in its death. . . . Therefore there must be an absolute boss if one agrees that the magazine is more important than feelings. Example is argument about cover. I know The Paris Review is a sensible and safe title. It may not sell a million copies but it's safe. It has snob appeal. Paris—God what that connotes

"They were the most glamorous quartet you could imagine." George, Bee Dabney (obscuring Dune Plunkett), Sadruddin Khan, and Princess Andrée (Sadri's mother). *Photograph by Germaine Traverso, from the collection of George Plimpton.*

everywhere, and its life and its literatures, and its eccentrics. But not quite enough for them. Merde, Phusct, Venture, MS, Manuscript, Counterpoint, Baccarat, *all these evocative names which symbolize countless magazines with similar names which have failed in one respect for that very reason*—zero, Blast, Transition *(although that a fine one),* Wake, *etc. I said I'd never read a literary magazine of any sort with a one name supposedly striking title which hadn't folded within a year or so.* "Time, Life, Fortune?" *asked du Bois. Well, he may be right but we shall see. The title can certainly ruin it. We're all thinking about it. I hope if there's a better one and a safer one than* The Paris Review *I can open my mind to it.*

PETER MATTHIESSEN In my wonderful flat on 14, rue Perceval, we tried to thrash out the name of the magazine-to-be—"we" being George, Humes, Styron, du Bois, perhaps Train, and me. This was also, I think, the first meeting in which we agreed on our editorial philosophy and content, which excluded literary criticism in favor of fiction and poetry—or agreed, anyway, to the point where we could start to put it together.

JOHN TRAIN A magazine seemed to all of us like a good thing to do; that was a given. Not so given was exactly what sort of magazine it would be. Matthiessen favored a magazine to be called *Baccarat*—hyperliterary. I claim to have come up with the name *The Paris Review* and lobbied for that because it seemed very logical.

IMMY HUMES There was a skirmish over the title; they were all kids, and they were all fighting over who would get the credits for *The Paris Review* right from the start.

PETER MATTHIESSEN I was very proud of the magazine and was petty enough to bristle occasionally when, over a period of many years and almost to the end, George permitted people to describe him in interviews and elsewhere as "the founder and editor of *The Paris Review.*" This was technically untrue. The magazine was under way when George was invited to Paris, but that founding was nebulous and mostly talk: The real founding did not take place until after George and Billy du Bois had joined us. Patsy Southgate made many contributions, including a fine translation for the first issue, and Styron, Guinzburg, and Train were also important participants and contributors in that spring and summer of 1952.

> GEORGE PLIMPTON, DIARY *Meeting of editorial board here in the afternoon. Went much better. Humes a bit difficult but argument always led to an understanding far deeper than a snap agreed judgment would have given us. Title agreed upon:* The Paris Review. *Closing date agreed upon. 15 July. Issues per year decided. Six. Cover agreed upon. Humes broke one glass.*

PETER MATTHIESSEN At another meeting at 14, rue Perceval, we were talking about what we wanted to do with the contents of the magazine. Because I was a short-story writer, my whole thing was to push new, young talented fiction writers. And I had this idea about interviewing established writers, and I didn't realize how successful that would be, but it did seem to work. I wanted Irwin Shaw, who was living in Paris then, but George had two well-connected literary friends, Francis Haskell and P. N. Furbank, friends of E. M. Forster at Cambridge, and they did an interview with Forster. That was the first interview, for issue number one, very impressive indeed.

PATI HILL I believe George didn't actually do the Forster interview, but he could have. He was very good at getting people to talk about themselves. Writers like to talk about themselves anyway, but I think George was really interested in what they had to say, even in the boring bits. He stayed optimistic that something interesting was bound to turn up and, sooner or later, it usually did.

> *Dear Mother and Daddy,*
> *. . . What we are doing that's new is presenting a literary quarterly in which the emphasis is more on fiction than on criticism, the bane of present quarterlies. Also we are brightening up the issue with art work. An "Art Portfolio" by a young American artist in Paris is to appear in each issue. The first is by Tom Keogh who has an excellent reputation both here and in America. Appearing with*

it in the first issue are: the Newdigate prize poem from Oxford by
Donald Hall, an essay on the technique of the novel in dialogue
form by EM Forster, some unpublished poems by the Chilean poet,
Pablo Neruda, four short stories, and a section of a novel to be pub-
lished next year by Simon & Schuster. . . . [no date]

WILLIAM STYRON Peter asked me to write an introduction to
the first issue, setting a general tone, which was that this was going
to be a literary magazine rather than a magazine of heavy-duty literary theorizing like *The Hudson Review.* It wasn't going to be political, either, like the *Partisan Review.* We just wanted to make this
a creative magazine. Matthiessen and I worked that out—George,
too, I think.

RICHARD SEAVER Trocchi used to try and get George more interested in the political concerns of Europe and our country, but
George could not get existentially involved in that. He was a terribly positive person, even if postwar Paris wasn't. Cohn and Schine
were traveling through Paris in those days—Roy Cohn and David
Schine. They were visiting consulates throughout Europe, sent by
Senator McCarthy to see if any Communists might be lurking in
our embassies and so forth. They were creating a climate of unrest
and fear wherever they went. But George was sort of above all that.

GEORGE PLIMPTON, DIARY Bill Styron's preface arrived today
from the American Academy in Rome. It is short, to the point. Peter
thinks it suffers from overwriting. That is Bill's style, Jamesian, in
which occasionally the structure is so ornate that one is kept in sus-
pense until the finish—like German which must await the qualify-
ing verb at the end of the sentence. But regardless, Bill's preface is
what sets the issue up. It is now all in.

JOHN TRAIN Tom Guinzburg, who was businesslike, was supposed to be the first managing editor, but then he became para-
lyzed with love for Francine du Plessix, now Gray, and was unable
to proceed. He was lifted gently from behind the desk. I knew
about magazines already from having run the *Lampoon* and indeed
the *Grotonian,* so I was promoted from nonfiction editor. My ten-

ure was not uncontroversial. An early story by Terry Southern had a traffic cop addressing a doctor, whose car he'd stopped. The doctor began to protest, so the cop says to the doctor, "Okay, Doc, don't get your shit hot." I pointed out that this would create trouble in Boston, where the post office was exceedingly prudish, so after heated debate we compromised on: "Don't get your crap hot." The same story stirred another question: One fellow hits another, who falls to the ground, knocked out. In the tale, his feet and legs are "vibrating," which I thought highly improbable. George and I went on my standard stroll down the Seine and then up to the Pantheon and down to the Jardin des Plantes—a zoo as well as a botanical garden—and we happened to be discussing this exact issue of the vibrating legs when we passed by the vulture cage. To my amazement, there was a vulture lying on his back in the cage, clearly dying, and his feet were indeed vibrating. George looked at me significantly, and I nodded in submission. The other vultures were staring at him with proprietary interest, waiting for him to stop kicking, undoubtedly before gobbling him up. We went around to the little cabin where the keeper was, and I said, "One of your vultures is dying." He replied dismissively, "That's the other service. You have to wait until two o'clock." Having no intention of doing so, we resumed our walk. I assume nothing good befell that poor bird.

PATI HILL   I would never probably have had anything to do with *The Paris Review* if it hadn't been for George. I had a picture in my mind of a lot of men who were mainly sitting around in front of the Café le Tournon, all very macho. That was the big word at the time, said without irony. Peter Matthiessen was supposed to be very macho, but he was also great-looking in his lanky way and funny enough so you could forgive him for always being off down the world's canyons in a canoe. John Train was just a mystery. He was so young he seemed more a captive of his three-piece suit than he probably did once he got the upper hand of it. I liked George immediately. He was incredibly stylish—like a praying mantis. It was his mantis movement, breaking sort of wildly and elegantly in the middle, that you noticed. That and his bunged-up hat that he wore as if it were a kind of subtitle:

The Intrepid News Reporter, brim pushed back—oh gosh, how could I have forgotten that appointment—brim pulled down over his ears.

IMMY HUMES Doc went back to the States before the first issue was printed and shipped, so he never knew that the editors decided to remove his name from the masthead. I can imagine that the rest of the guys were furious with him because he didn't do enough work and didn't pony up the five hundred bucks that they did, even though he ponied up the original magazine. I don't know what other real grievances there were. But they couldn't deal with it. Doc was probably always mentally ill, and always manic-depressive, and always a talker like you've never seen, and they didn't know what to make of him. George was better able to deal with that. He was less competitive. Or he was just better natured.

JOHN TRAIN My supreme moment as managing editor was when George had to return to the States to seek funds, leaving me to get out the first issue and ship some of it to the States. I negotiated a deal with U.S. Lines, swapping passage on a ship, the *United States,* for a free ad—standard stuff in the magazine business. Then I had to get the magazine boxed for shipment. The agency asked whether it should be in one big carton or in smaller ones. I said I had no idea, and I asked them for the ins and outs of the matter. They said the smaller ones were easier to transport, but one big one would be reusable, being heavy and substantial. I said, "Let's do it with one big one." Alas, I had not calculated how heavy that would be. As a consequence, several thousand copies of *The Paris Review* were plopped down by crane onto the New York docks in an immense, immovable carton. The dockworkers refused to touch it, so we had to assemble a kind of ant army of volunteers to break up the crate on the dock and carry the copies into a warehouse. That was when Doc Humes turned up. He got hold of a rubber stamp and stamped them all "Harold Humes, New York Representative." He was miffed that his role consulting on the inception of the magazine, even though he didn't appear in the office, had not been acknowledged on the masthead.

First issue of *The Paris Review.*
Courtesy of the Morgan Library & Museum, New York.

GORE VIDAL I read the first issue of *The Paris Review;* somebody —not George—gave me a copy and asked me what I thought of it. I said, and perhaps I was unfair, that it looked like a number of well-to-do boys who'd got together because they'd all heard about the 1920s in Paris. So now in the 1950s, they were going to be

Hemingway and Fitzgerald and all the others. They were so self-conscious. And much impressed by what they were doing. But it doesn't happen like that. You don't make a great magazine from the top down.

WILLA KIM On my way back to New York, I stopped in Paris at a dinner that Tom Keogh and Theodora Roosevelt Keogh gave. It

At La Table Ronde: from top, Peter Matthiessen, Colette Duhamel, George, Louisa Noble, Billy Pène du Bois.

Photograph © *Estate Brassaï–RMN; Réunion des Musées Nationaux/Art Resource, N.Y.*

was a Thanksgiving dinner—Thanksgiving 1952—and I met Billy Pène du Bois. He said there was going to be a party, and it was the inauguration party for the first issue of *The Paris Review.* Shortly after the party, I was catching a plane, and Hal Prince was on the train with me to get to the airport. He said, "Something awful happened to me. I was invited to a party by George Plimpton, and then he called up and canceled my invitation, so I didn't get to go." I guess George had invited too many people. Of all people to cancel on! I knew Hal because he was the stage manager on *Wonderful Town.* Everyone else was at the party: Styron, George, Peter Matthiessen, Tom Guinzburg, John Train. Billy designed the magazine. He always said that all the editors had been dithering about it forever, until he finally lost patience and took all the material, did the layout, and had it printed and gave it to them, and they were astonished that they had a magazine out.

RUSS HEMENWAY   Billy Pène du Bois is the reason there is something called *The Paris Review,* I'm convinced. Because even though the first issue didn't have much content, it looked great, and it looked great because Billy Pène du Bois worked over the stone with the printer for days. I remember it was coming down to a deadline, and he made it look beautiful. This was no amateur. He spoke French, and he had six or eight children's books in circulation and was one of the great illustrators. He had great style. *The Paris Review* looked great. That's what everyone talked about.

TWO RESCUERS; HUNTING FOR HEMINGWAY

Dear George . . .
   The latest issue of the Review turned up a day or two ago. I have only had a chance to glance at it, finding the first piece not to my liking, by reason of a certain exhibitionist quality of substandard taste. I recognize an incorrigible tendency in the young toward épater la bourgeoisie, *but I must say that I think it is a tendency, which, if it affords any gratification to anyone, affords it only to the author. . . . Affectionately, Daddy* [December 17, 1953]

Dear Mother and Daddy,

Here is another Paris Review, *the fifth. I'm not sure as usual that you're not going to be shocked by most of the content. It is hard to say why such stories are being written or why editors find them the best being done—best, that is, in terms of literary quality. William Styron in his interview discusses the matter at some length. He has an answer to give; no solution though, and that probably is as it should be. The contents, you'll be glad to hear, are hardly reflections of my own character, which remains merry enough and full of hope and enthusiasm. You'll have to wait for* The Rabbit's Umbrella* *for proof, which in its way may make you laugh twice, or even three times, and I doubt will be considered the product of a tormented mind. . . .* [March 20, 1954]

Dear Mother and Daddy,

I am still not quite sure of my plans for the future. I quite realize I must come back and fairly quickly. I must admit that I don't like to live in Paris in tiny breathless hotels. I can never tire of working on this magazine, though. Unlike the others I have a sense of mission about it. There is no-one else here now. If I left without getting a good replacement the whole business would collapse like a house of cards. I owe that neither to myself nor to those like yourself, grandma, and others who have helped; nor to the subscribers, or authors who so believe in this enterprise.

We have been in serious financial difficulty for the past two months. It is mostly the fault of the New York people who have been, for one reason or another, unable to catch hold and do the things that must be done. Their office is running at a loss, which is incredible, considering they have no expenses to speak of other than distributing [a product] *which is supplied them by us. There is nothing I can do about it by letter, though I've tried. I must return to do it myself, probably at the close of the summer. In the meantime I must find a replacement—someone like John Cowles for example, or Blair Fuller, responsible people who would have not too hard a job to do now that the operation here has finally been pretty well streamlined. Perhaps then the magazine can run without my hav-*

---

* George's first book, for children, whose main character is said to be much like his mother.

ing to spend so much time on it; but I hope you'll understand that I
must work very hard to set it right. Of course, this might go on in-
definitely, but I promise you I don't intend to let it. Some recent
events suggest that the magazine may be put on a firm financial
footing, and that of course must be the basis for any permanence I
feel we must have before I throw over the traces. . . . [no date]

JOHN TRAIN Obviously, there was always a problem about money.
George had a very valuable conception approaching the *Paris
Herald,* as it was then called—it's now the *International Herald
Tribune*—about scrapping the stock page, which was only one page
in those days, and replacing it with a literary page, which we
would design and edit for a huge amount of money. As you might
imagine, this idea met with very little favor at the *Paris Herald.*
More fruitful were the hawkers we employed to peddle the magazine in the streets. In French, such people are called *camelots.* Our
best *camelot* was named Abrami. He was a poet, and he would walk
in front of the Deux Magots and the Flore handing out to the
drinkers on the sidewalk copies open to some interesting illustration, preferably off-color; then he'd come back, retrieve them, or
collect payment, if possible. He was particularly effective. You had
to catch up with him at frequent intervals, because if he collected
too much money from the customers, you risked having him go
into hiding and on to a spending spree. So you had to keep up
with him. It was like emptying a cormorant every few fish. Of
course, we are talking about units of a few dozen from time to
time, not hundreds of thousands. Unfortunately, Abrami became
enamored of a girl student, and by way of attracting her attention,
he shaved his hair, like van Gogh cutting off his ear, which gave
him a particularly hideous appearance and reduced his capabilities
as a *camelot.* We also sold the magazine in kiosks and bookstores
and daily came up against the Hachette Company, which fancied
it had a monopoly on that activity. We had these big sit-downs, à
la Mafia, in which they said we had to get out of the hawking
business, and we said, No, it was a free country, and so on.

RUSS HEMENWAY I wrote a piece for their fifth issue, an interesting piece on the *livres d'or* of Paris. These were guest books

kept by the better Parisian restaurants. In those days, at some point in the course of your meal, the maître d' would come over and say, "Would you sign the gold book?" If you're Charlie Chaplin, you might make a little illustration; or if you're Prévert, you might write a little poem; or if you're Matisse, Chagall, or Picasso, you might draw something. They were a treasure trove, as you can imagine. I did a piece for the *Review* on these. I went around with Billy and we took photographs that we thought would appeal to a general audience. We had a page of clowns: Grok, Chaplin, and Tati, for instance, on one page. It was a nice little piece. And the head of the Paris bureau of *Life* magazine called me up and said they'd like to do a piece on this subject as well—they wanted to know, did I have a lot of pictures? George was thrilled, because the *Review* would be mentioned in *Life* magazine; I was very pleased to be in *Life* magazine, too. My deal with George assumed that I owned the photographs and was therefore entitled to a share of *Life*'s fee. So we sold them to *Life* for—I've forgotten what it was now, but it was something substantial for those days, two hundred and fifty dollars or something like that. The check came to the *Review*—at which point, George decided that there had been expenses involved in doing all this and kept the money. They invented the word *parsimony* for George.

JOHN TRAIN   Literary magazines are like churches and political parties and opera houses. You can count on donors. If you have a church, you would never expect to make enough money in the plate to pay for the whole thing. You expect a devoted donor to come along and endow it. The same is true of a political party. Some fat cat appears and gives you millions of dollars. The same is true of an opera house, in response to what's called a "named gift opportunity," some huge sum that pays for a new *La Bohème*. With a literary magazine, if you play your cards carefully, you can sometimes find someone to come along and back it—for a time. George was the ringmaster of these good folk and extremely effective.

> *Dear Mother and Daddy . . .*
> *A splendid Managing Editor has turned up—one Bob Silvers—*
> *a discharge from the Army, a good business man, perfectly willing to*

sacrifice a couple of years running the Review—*in fact it's his dream in life. It's a stroke of great luck for us. He's intelligent, very interested, and is that new infusion of blood so necessary to combat apathy, laziness, and downright disinterest that seems to have struck everybody in the concern save your indefatigable son. So after spending a short time as his tutor, overseeing him bring out an issue or two I ought to be able to come home. I will be coming towards the end of October,* [but] *will have to make one more trip back to Paris. Then my full-time activity with the* Review *should be over. It is beginning to look as though it would be possible for me to leave the enterprise without its tumbling flat to the ground.* . . . [October 6, 1954]

ROBERT SILVERS I was in the Army, at SHAPE headquarters, just outside Paris, working in the library. One of the nice things about the headquarters was that you had every Wednesday afternoon off. You got on the bus and before long you were at the Arc de Triomphe. I had some friends in New York, Cecil Hemley and Arthur Cohen, whom I'd known at the University of Chicago, and they had a publishing venture called Noonday Press. When I saw them before I went abroad, they said, "Why don't you represent us in Paris, and see if you can find some French books for us?," and on Wednesday afternoons I would visit French publishers. This was in 1954, the last year that I was in the Army. *The Paris Review* had been started the year before, and I'd been reading it in the barracks; and one afternoon I went around to the rue Garancière where La Table Ronde, a small publishing house, had allotted *The Paris Review* a very small office. I walked in the door and there was George. I said, "I'm with Noonday Press and I'm looking for books." We talked about some of the writers in the *Review*, Terry Southern and others, who might be of interest for Noonday, and I'd found a French writer who interested him. I had the impression of someone who was immensely alert, yet relaxed at the same time. Then at the end of the day, George said, "I'm going around to a friend's. Why don't you come with me?," which seemed wonderfully welcoming and generous. So we walked over to the Île Saint-Louis to see Pati Hill, a young woman who had been a fashion model and was now publishing fiction in *The Paris Review*. She had a charming flat overlooking the Seine with white walls and mustard velvet couches. There were various people about drinking tall glasses of wine, among them John Train, at that time the managing editor of the *Review*. I knew something about him because he had an essay in the first issue. In a certain way, it set the tone of the *Review*, because he pointedly seemed to avoid such matters as the bitter controversy between Sartre and Camus that was dividing Paris intellectuals at the time. The *Review*, so the essay implied, was going to concentrate on the best young fiction writers and poets that the editors could find, and that would be that.

BEE DABNEY   Bob Silvers was there with us. We were all just amazed at his history. I think he graduated from college when he was in his teens or something extraordinary. I always thought that he never flaunted his brilliance. He was cozy and fun, and to this day, I think he's one of the most attractive, bright people I ever met. Pati Hill was there; she was absolutely beautiful and wrote beautifully, although I can't remember exactly what she wrote. I think she wrote quite a few stories for *The Paris Review*. Francine du Plessix was there, and she was rather brilliant and very beautiful also. I feel like we all sort of belonged in a little family together.

ROBERT SILVERS   At Pati Hill's party, I told John Train I was getting out of the Army soon and thought I would stay in Paris and go to the Sorbonne on the GI Bill, which paid more than enough to live in Paris at the time. When we met a little later at his flat at 2 bis, avenue Franco-Russe, John said, "Why don't we start a publishing house together?" We might begin, he said, with a book of letters and writings by James Joyce's brother Stanislaus in Trieste, with whom he'd been in touch. Then he said, "By the way, at the same time, you could have my job as managing editor at *The Paris Review*. I have the work of getting the paper out pretty well organized, so there's not a lot to do, but you'll have to keep an eye on things. I've talked to George about this." I saw George later at the Café le Tournon and he said he was glad I was joining the paper, and we went to the office around the corner and there I saw a wire basket that said, "Managing Editor." Across the basket were two strings, and there was a sign on the strings saying, "Don't Put Anything in This Basket." George said, "Well, you see, there's the basket of the managing editor, but it has these strings on it." He rather ceremoniously took off the strings. Then we rummaged around and found a number of things in drawers, which we put in the basket—bills from the printer, a note on bookshops where we might sell the *Review,* a list of people we might approach to get more advertising, and so on. So we put the things in this basket, and, thanks to John Train, I became managing editor.

DEWITT SAGE   George relished telling the story of his quest for a Hemingway interview for the magazine. He said it began in the spring of '53 when a bunch of reprobate Harvard Porcellian types, as he described them, were in town for the wedding of Joan Dil-

George and Hemingway at a *tienta* outside Madrid, 1954.
Photograph by Mary Lumet.

lon, whose father was U.S. ambassador to France, to Jimmy Moseley. The enormous reception took place at the embassy, just off the
Place de la Concorde, I think. George said they were behaving
"terribly"; people were drunk, throwing tables out of windows;
there couldn't have been more ghastly behavior. Douglas Dillon
had more or less hidden away from the whole thing. Meanwhile,
George, with a bottle of Dillon's finest Bordeaux, goes in through
the front door of the Ritz, not far from the party. He's walking
down a long corridor to the bar at the rear of the hotel, which is
now called the Hemingway Bar but then, I believe, the Little Bar.
He looked up, he said, and he saw this apparition. "For the first
and almost the last time in my life," he said, "I saw someone actually reading *The Paris Review.* It was the first issue. And then I saw
that the apparition in front of me, with the gray beard and the unmistakable profile, was none other than Ernest Hemingway. I became immediately sober."

JULES FEIFFER It's interesting how George deified Hemingway:
On a personal level, you'd think that George's world and his persona were much closer to F. Scott Fitzgerald.

> *Dear Mother and Daddy . . .*
>
> *I came down* [to Madrid] *ostensibly to interview Ernest Hem-
> ingway. He is not well, sadly, and I'm not sure he feels up to an in-
> terview. I've had lunch and drinks with him, and yesterday with
> his helpful advice I was able to stay in a bullring on a bull breeding
> farm outside of Madrid and successfully pass with the cape a fight-
> ing calf the size of a small spaniel. Bullfighting, I'm sure you'll be
> glad to hear, is not a profession for me. At one point during my fight
> my right foot got under the cow's hoof and the cow stood on it for an
> appreciably long time while she looked for me with her horns. I have
> a profound admiration for the professionals fighting here in the
> Playa de Toros every afternoon. . . .* [spring 1954]

PIEDY LUMET I saw him in Madrid in '54, maybe. Peter [Gimbel,
her husband at the time] and I were there because we were going
to see the bullfights in San Isidro, you know, that bullfighting thing
in Madrid in May—like Pamplona, but much more sedate. George

was looking for Hemingway, and because Peter's father had been friends with Hemingway, we went each day to the bullfights with him. When George heard that, he sort of hung around. And he did find Hemingway, obviously. We used to go in the morning to the Palace Hotel opposite the Ritz in Madrid, and Hemingway would be there, this mountain of pink pajamas in the bed—it was very dramatic to me, who was just this person from the Connecticut suburbs—and Hotchner would bring a huge pitcher of martinis— ice all melting by the time he got to the room, and the bullfighter Ordóñez came in with Ava Gardner. They'd never met, she and Hemingway, and they just reclined together on the bed and talked. She hopped onto his bed; he beneath the covers and she beside him on top of them—murmuring, laughing. The language! So obscene! They had a fine time. George must have come with us, and then we all went for a big lunch after the three martinis in Hemingway's bed. Then, on to the bulls.

> *Dear Mother and Daddy . . .*
>
> *I had a very splendid time down there* [in Madrid]. *I didn't get much of the interview done, simply because Hemingway doesn't much like to talk about writing and I didn't press him, not* [want-ing] *to talk about writing when there's a man around who'd rather tell you about elephants and the shooting thereof, big game fishing, and who has much to say about the Mau Mau and the hyena. Spain is a country I loved, and of course I had the best guide in the world to show it to me. Not that he did, but I saw him enough to feel I understood one large facet of it. . . .* [no date]

A. E. HOTCHNER One of the first times I met George was when he came to Madrid to talk to Hemingway about maybe doing an interview. He did the interview later, then sent it to Ernest, and Ernest really rewrote a lot of it in order to conform to whatever Ernest thought he should be saying. So that was the beginning of the time George came to Hemingway. I don't think he really was around Ernest all that much.

ROBERT SILVERS George described to me being down in Pamplona with Sadri Khan, the youngest son of Aga Khan, who had been at Harvard with him, and there, sometime after the running of the bulls, George put it to Sadri that *The Paris Review* needed a publisher, and Sadri said he would do it, which meant that he was going to pay the bills. It was a marvelous moment a few weeks later when Sadri arrived at the offices of *The Paris Review,* a very well-dressed, smiling, very diplomatic, very courtly young man. We took him in to meet Colette Duhamel, the publisher of Éditions de la Table Ronde, who was immensely happy to meet him for many reasons, one being that the heavy debts of *The Paris Review,* for which she as *gérante* was ultimately responsible, now seemed very likely to be paid. I don't know just what arrangement George worked out with Sadri after he left for New York, but from then on we had money in the bank to pay the bills.

Sadri's decision to back us was a crucial point in the life of *The Paris Review,* and this was all George's doing. I remember Colette saying to Sadri, *"Est-ce que vous êtes à Paris maintenant?"* He said, *"Mais oui, en principe,"* and I saw an immediate relief in her eyes. Here we had found for a publisher the son of one of the richest men in the world; indeed, Sadri was a candidate at that time to be his successor. But these crises continued all George's life. He would find a new publisher, a record producer or an heiress, and he'd tell you, "I've just found So-and-So and he's going to take it." But then their businesses didn't go on as they wanted or they grew bored, and they would quit. George never seemed disheartened. I'd see him again and he'd say, "Well, I found another one!"

LEAVING FOR NEW YORK

JOHN TRAIN I left Paris when I got mobilized and had to go back to the States. After a while I got out, but because I had started this company in Paris, I went back and forth often. In fact, I was pretty responsible for the office that the *Review* occupied after the one on the rue Garancière. It was on the rue Vernet, parallel to the Champs-Élysées where our credit company was. The man who owned the building was a part of the enterprise and found the room for them. Oddly enough, I also found an office for the *Review* in New York, on First Avenue near where I was then living.

It was fifty bucks a month, not a bad price. That was in 1955 when George had moved back to New York himself, leaving Bob Silvers managing things at the Paris office.

ROBERT SILVERS The second night I was at the *Review,* George and I went over to the printer, a dark, oily shed of a place, smelling of very cheap wine which the pressmen drank rather steadily. We had on the press a long story by, of all people, Pati Hill. The pressmen spoke not a word of English, by the way, so the words *no one,* for example, looked like *noone.* Proofreading these long galleys, full of these errors, George would cry, "Golly, another one!" and the typesetter would say, *"Quel ennui, votre journal."* Not the most congenial atmosphere, and later, when the issue was printed, we were horrified how many "noones" we had missed. About this time, too, I was introduced to the Common Book. It was a legacy of George's *Lampoon* days. It was a big, ledgerlike volume where we would enter messages, jokes, or anything that occurred to us. George spent quite a lot of time writing in it, but its big champion was John Train. I remember reading a letter that Train had posted

The Two Rescuers, Robert Silvers and Sadruddin Khan, and George.
From the collection of The Paris Review.

in the book, from the manager of the American Library in Paris, a small library on the Right Bank that had some of the latest English novels and biographies. The letter said, "Dear Mr. Train, I'm writing you because Miss Jane Wilson [not her real name] has given your name as her reference, and she has not returned five books to the American Library. We ask that you contact Miss Wilson and have her return these long-overdue books as soon as possible." Beside this was pasted Train's reply, saying, "Dear Mr. ____, I'm sorry to be writing you in my own hand, but the machine on which I am used to compose these letters was last seen in the hands of Miss Jane Wilson. Yours faithfully, John P. C. Train."

PATI HILL   George wasn't overbearing as an editor and he didn't seem all that persistent, but he usually got what he wanted. Once he came to see me at my tiny apartment on the Île Saint-Louis to try to scratch up a piece for the *Review*. He had already published excerpts from both my books and I didn't have anything left over to give him. George said, "Well, you can just sit down and write about anything at all." I said, "I don't have anything at all to write *about*," and he said, "You like cats, write about cats," and I said all right. But George said, "I can see you're not going to do it so I'm going to sit here until you've written about the cats." And he did. He sat there until I wrote it and it wasn't that bad because he hit on the right subject for me. He didn't try to order things to his wishes. He never tried to get people to write *his* ideas for him. I think he valued surprises.

> *Dear Mother and Daddy . . .*
> *I've written Cabell Greet that I'm definitely coming back next fall and will take up the post at Barnard College teaching* [creative writing]. *At least until midyear (January 15th). I'm not satisfied at all in my mind that I'll want to continue teaching—in fact I quite definitely don't want to—but at least it will give me a chance to inspect the field. The classes are on Tuesday and Thursday—another half-day for conferences—and that should certainly give me enough time to continue my own work both for the* Review *and my writing. Much more time really than I've had here. I'll be leaving*

the magazine in good hands, at least so it would appear at the mo-ment. It is still a mill-stone to the extent I must always be prepared to save it if a real need should arise, but it is worth it whatever the circumstances. I cannot let something die I've worked three years to start. It is not a play-toy for an interim period in my career. . . .
[spring 1955]

IV.

MOUNTING CELEBRITY:
1955–1963

—

George knew so many more people than I did; he was having so much more fun in New York than I was having. I felt that whatever enjoyment I was having, I had earned; and there is nothing that excites envy like the feeling that you received no more than you earned, while there was George, who had received so much more than he had earned. . . .

—*NORMAN MAILER*

SOCIALITE

HARRY MATHEWS George had a funny reputation in Society. He was from a distinguished family on both sides, but he was too glitzy for those people, even before he became a celebrity. He was still a prankster, as he had been at St. Bernard's and Exeter. Rules, traditions, conventions were excellent things in his view, but never to be taken too seriously. Others might never know what they could get away with, but he did, and he did get away with it. He may have felt that the strictures of Society—what was left of it— were *pour encourager les autres,* not him. But I doubt it. He didn't have that sort of arrogance. Still, Society sensed something mischievous and anarchic about him and vaguely disapproved.

PIEDY LUMET One time, he came to a birthday party in East Hampton that I gave for Sidney [Lumet], and it was all Sidney's friends, most of them Jewish, except for the waiters. Everybody made toasts, and George said, "I look around this room and there's Gene Saks, and Saul Steinberg, and Peter Stone, and I see that I'm in a minority. I'm not really used to that, and I don't really like it. So could all those people who are not Jewish please wave to me?" So the waiters all waved, and I waved, and Keren Saks, who is half Jewish, gave a half wave, and George said, "Thank you." It was terribly funny, because they were all friends of his.

Dear Dave,

I believe Marion Capron has called you on this sad matter— not teaching next year. I was prepared to come back to it, but at the last minute Sports Illustrated *offered me another job to do—a profile on Jock Whitney. I'm not sure that in accepting the offer I*

*haven't committed a blunder of sorts. I certainly don't want the rep-
utation of being a writer whose only topic is the sporting life of the
extremely rich. But I've done it.*

*And in doing so recall almost nightly Prof. Greet's description of
free-lance writers finishing out their days at the bar of the Century;
pathetic, frayed, tremble-handed drunks, all of them regretting the
day they decided to undertake an article on Jay Gould's court-tennis
prowess.*

*I hope that if you sense one day that I am about to join their
ranks you will take me back where I probably belong. . . .* [Janu-
ary 26, 1957]

GAY TALESE There are places in New York that define your social position, none better than the Racquet Club. People that belong to the Racquet Club, they might also belong to Sure Fire
Bowling Lanes and they might also be out with the fishermen in
Staten Island, you know, but their defining place was the Racquet
Club, George's Racquet Club. He could be at ringside in Sunny-
side, Queens, watching José Torres beat up some Puerto Rican,
and he could have his arm around Torres and have dinner with
him in some little place in Brooklyn. But there was still a time
when George was going to be at the Racquet Club. But I never,
never saw him insult anyone. I never saw him mean-spirited. He
wasn't snooty, he wasn't arrogant, he wasn't full of himself—well,
he was full of himself, but in a nice way. It isn't often that you get
from that privileged background a man who would be almost always acceptable and approachable.

ROBERT PARKS There's a very interesting letter of Donald Hall's
in the *Paris Review* archive at the Morgan Library. It's from the late
fifties, I think, in which Hall says, "Dear George, I picked up
Vogue and there you are. I look at something literary and there you
are with Ginsberg and Corso and others. I really don't know who
you are." It really gets at something that people have noted about
him and have been perplexed about.

ANN WINCHESTER At one point, he was listed, in *Esquire* I think,
as one of the most attractive men in America. He was stunned and

a bit embarrassed. He just didn't quite understand it. I don't think he had any sense of his own attractiveness, so he didn't know how to deal with this concept of himself as a male sex symbol. Eventually he decided that it was terribly funny. He always thought about following his dreams, but he really didn't think about how he appeared.

GEOFFREY GATES I thought George was broad-gauged but also subtle and elegant in his pursuit of women. When I was taking out Candy Bergen . . . no, I was feeding her, I wasn't taking her out, by which I mean only that whatever my intentions or desires were, I ended up paying for dinners. Anyway, there were a couple of other men in her life at that time, one of whom was George; none of us knew about this. George certainly had an active eye. There were all these little cuties, pretty girls from the lit world, and a few of the Muffies and Alisons from old WASP Society with a capital S, and the odd Café Society woman, like Nan Kempner; but George never showed any of that kind of focused, aggressive, or predictable behavior. He was always laid-back, cool, very charming, with great manners, and of course he was a good-looking guy. In the early days, you didn't know who he was with. He never stood with his arm around a woman or some gauche thing like that. You never knew who was his date that night, or if he even had one—unless Bee was there, and even then you couldn't be sure.

BEE DABNEY George and I came back on the plane together to the United States. That was in 1955. I think it might have been the spring. Then George and I continued to see each other. He'd take the train to Route 128, near Dover, with his books and his work, and he'd spend weekends with me and my mother. Once we went to Bermuda together. At the same time, I was thinking that I needed to get away from Dover immediately and go to New York, because that's where all my friends were then. All the people in Paris were coming back. I had started drawing people's children around Boston, and I found that I could get good likenesses, and I continued that when I went to New York. That was 1956. I lived in a perfectly wonderful apartment that I rented from a friend on Eighty-first Street. I continued to do portraits of my friends and people's ponies and horses and dogs and children. I had a show at the Westbury Gallery, and from then on, I always painted seriously: murals, commissions of any kind. In that way, I made enough money to stay in New York.

PIEDY LUMET I think that when Bee came home, she was just broiling with suitors. She was so particularly charming. And so was George. That's not a good couple, when they're both the star. Somebody has to defer. Still, I know that a good deal of George's life was spent daydreaming, a lot of it about Bee. I don't know in what sense he thought they would be a couple. It may have been over before they came home from Paris, where I think she took up with Sadri and probably others. I remember asking him when he was back in New York, "Do you ever see her and talk to her?" "Oh," he said, very emphatic, "oh, I talk to her, I talk to her often." More than that was the fact that the connection existed and was important to him. I think she was annealed onto his life. There was almost a severity, an edge to his voice, when he said, "I talk to her often."

JOHN HEMINWAY The last time I saw George, in the late 1990s, I was about to get married. I called him up and said that I'd love him to meet Kathryn, my fiancée. He'd met a number of my girl-friends along the way and always had lovely things to say about them. We went to Elaine's, of course. He sat down and he wanted to find out about Kathryn's background. And the question of her mother came up and she said, "Well, she's divorced from my father, but she's living with somebody called Dougie Burden." And he went, "Oh, my God." You could see a story coming in behind his eyes. And it went like this: Years before, he was in love with this woman called Bee Dabney. He just adored Bee Dabney. They had an engagement party, and everybody came, including Dougie Burden, who George said was the handsomest man in New York (I heard him say this several times about several different people, so take it with a grain of salt). Dougie had never met Bee. George watched out of the corner of his eye as she and Dougie introduced themselves, got into a conversation, and talked and talked all night long; and that was the last time George saw Bee Dabney. To me that was quintessential George—he took such pleasure in telling a story about what great sadness he'd had.

DOUGLAS BURDEN Well, it happened when George invited me to his engagement party to Bee Dabney. It was a lovely party, on Fifth Avenue with a lovely view out the windows, I think it was his parents' apartment. It was a crowd of people that I knew very well, though I had never seen Bee Dabney before. I knew that George had taken Bee away from Sadruddin Aga Khan—and vice versa—and that she was really a dazzler. At any rate, I ended up sitting down next to her on this couch in the middle of the party. We got talking and had a better and better time, roaring with laughter. And then, sort of instantly, we became terribly attracted to each other. I guess you'd call it falling in love instantly. She was looking at me and laughing and giggling—we both were. And I think I said to her, "You wanna split?" And she burst out laughing and got up off the couch and we ran for the elevator. Of all the horrible things to do on earth, that was it. We were together for five years. I never asked her to marry me for some reason, maybe because of how it started. I felt terrible about it. Peggy Bancroft hired Bee to come and do a mural on the wall of their apartment, going up these beautiful round stairs from the main entrance. The picture she painted was of me on a white horse, with a great javelin, and I had speared George and he was lying on the ground in his armor; you could see his face, and you could see my face, and so you knew who the figures were. And Bee was in the picture, too, all dressed up as a little goddess, and she was smiling. Everyone who came to the many, many parties that Peggy gave instantly recognized what had happened. The picture was the topper—that really did it. At some point I called George and apologized profusely for the terrible rudeness and the horrible thing I'd done, and amazingly enough, he was very, very nice about it. I was just stunned at how kind and nice he was. I never heard about what happened afterwards. I think some of George's friends never forgave me, like Peter Matthiessen. I think they were always angry at me and still are to this day. It's a terrible story about a shameful deed.

BEE DABNEY There was too much competition for George's time. Harold Vanderbilt entered George's life and whisked him off to Palm Beach and heaven knows where else. George would go because he had a commission to do this story on Harold Vanderbilt and the America's Cup races, and bridge, and that occupied George's time, very much so. I began to realize that I didn't want to get married anyway. The domestic life of having babies—I wasn't really ready for that, because I was getting so many commissions, and I didn't want to settle down into a domestic situation. I didn't feel that George was going to be the domestic person, and my time clock was so different from his. I was an early-bird riser, and George didn't want to go to bed too early. Nighttime was when George's morning blossomed, almost. I didn't think that would be helpful. We always remained very close friends for the rest of our days. I got married first in 1965 to an Italian artist/photographer named Gianni Penati, who entered my life with a camera because he was doing a story on me for *Vogue,* during which time he had to retake all the pictures because *Vogue* wasn't satisfied, so he came back a second time, and by then he was taking me to museums and telling me about his paintings, etc., and we became great friends. By then I was thirty-three, and I felt this was a very fascinating man, and George was very occupied with his world. Although we were great friends and had affections, I decided that was that.

KATE ROOSEVELT WHITNEY I got to know George because he was my school classmate Sarah Plimpton's older brother. I was a freshman entering Barnard College in New York City in 1954. A few friends and I had launched a literary magazine in high school, so, naturally, I registered for the freshman creative writing course to be taught by George Plimpton. I believe it was George's first foray into a college classroom as "the professor." About fifteen female students were seated, awaiting our twenty-seven-year-old teacher, who loped into the room slightly bent over the stack of ten or so books he was carrying in his arms. From the pages of each book were sticking a forest of paper markers. The students were intrigued and curious about his eager yet hesitant and vulnerable manner. At the end of class, besides the assigned reading, he asked each of us to start a journal (just start writing!), which he would review with us individually on a regular basis. When my turn came two weeks later, George wanted my advice, as a friend— what should he do about the very personal messages some students were writing to him in their journals? If I offered advice I don't now remember, but George did not teach beyond the first semester. Maybe George the perennial student of life, having tried on the academic mantle, was ready to move on.

KATHY AINSWORTH I met George within three days of arriving in New York for the first time, in the summer of 1958 or 1959. I was sitting in El Morocco with Dick Sabat, who was a lover of my mother's, and George just walked across the room from where he was sitting and introduced himself. We were very young. I was eighteen, and he was twenty-five [actually, thirty-one or thirty-two]. He told me later that I looked like a little girl dressed up in my mother's clothes, and he had to find out who this little girl was, sitting in El Morocco with Dick Sabat, who was *the* man about town at the time. In those early years that I was in New York—modeling with Eileen Ford and becoming well known, I suppose, the girl of the year—he was the first man I made love with. He didn't look the part of a lover at all, he was like this big, lanky cowboy, like Gary Cooper: tall, lanky, hair flopping in his face, really thin, whip-thin. He didn't speak with a drawl, but he sort of walked with a drawl. I'd had some heavy petting, as they said in those days, in the back of a car or something like that, but I'd never had an adult gentleman with beautiful manners, lots of fun, a wonderful dancer, who took me everywhere. He was my first sort of knight errant. He introduced me to everything. He told me what to read. Whether it was culinary, literary, or in bed, he taught me everything. I expected there to be another George in my life, but there never was. There was either passion and no manners, or there were lots of manners and no passion, or they didn't read, or I don't know. He was a whole man.

MARION CAPRON I was introduced to George in 1955 or 1956 by a professor at Barnard when George was teaching there. I did not have a class with him, but I was taking a course with the professor, who was a mutual friend. We met, and George started going on about *The Paris Review*. Very soon he said, "Would you like to come aboard?" I was on scholarship at Barnard, and I was already working at the public relations office there, and I liked working a whole lot better than I liked studying, so that's what I did. I dropped out in my fourth year and went to work at *The Paris Review*, first at the office on Columbus Circle, then at the one on First Avenue. I also lived in these offices. Of course, when he got his apartment at 541 East Seventy-second Street, I stayed there quite a lot. It beat the hell out of my cot at the office. George would be seeing other girls, but I didn't care. I wanted him to be with me; I had a terrific crush on him; but, no, I didn't care. It was just a separate thing. Also I began to see other people. He didn't mind; in fact, he rather liked it, especially when I saw rich or famous people. Once I accused him of wanting a triangle setup. I was kind of appalled. When I stopped adoring George, it was because of that. To me, it meant that he wasn't sure enough of himself, whether he liked me, if he had to have it reinforced by the fact that other richer, more famous men liked me. That made it okay for him to like me. That meant that his judgment was okay.

MAGGIE PALEY   I was having an affair with a man named Bill Cole. He was a publicist at Knopf. One morning I was at Bill's, and he said, "By the way, George Plimpton is coming over, and we're doing an interview with P. G. Wodehouse," who was a friend of Bill's. I said, "Who's George Plimpton?" This was 1963. I had never heard of him. I don't remember how Bill described him exactly, except that he said, "He's a neuter, and I know that because he's with a different woman every night. He couldn't be screwing them all." George came over, and here was this handsome, long-necked man, and we sat around in the kitchen for a while and talked and laughed. He was about thirty-five. He was really beautiful. Beautiful skin. They went off to see P. G. Wodehouse, then Bill called me and told me that George had said, "Who was that enchanting girl?" George began inviting Bill to parties, asking him to bring me. Bill and I were not in love. It was just a wonderful, companionable relationship. Then, I think what happened was that I got a strange card, a black-and-white photo-graph of people who looked like nomads in the desert, and it was signed, "George." I couldn't figure out what this was. It turned out it was George in *Lawrence of Arabia*. He was sending out a pic-ture of himself in the film as his Christmas card. He phoned me up and asked me for a date. Because Bill had told me that George was a neuter, when he made a pass at me, I thought, "I'm going to save this man. [laughs] Oh, boy! This neuter likes *me*." I think he took me on our first date to Le Club. Le Club was one of the first dis-cos in New York. It was run by a man named Olivier Coquelin, and it was a chic place for young people to go and dance, although I don't remember dancing with George, but I started having an af-fair with him which went on for a while. Do you remember the big piece about the *Paris Review* crowd that Gay Talese wrote? It was called "Looking for Hemingway," it was in *Esquire* in 1963, and it sort of stamped George as a national celebrity. He described a party at which George was the host, but he left to go out with Mrs. Kennedy. I was George's date when he came back from Mrs. Kennedy. So it was clear to me, fairly early on, that I was not the only woman in George's life. I thought he was a wonderful lover. Of course, I was very young. I've heard that some girls thought that George was awkward as a lover, but I don't remember that at all. I remember him being enthusiastic, and I really enjoyed him. I *remember* sex with him. There have been a lot of men in my life, and many of them were forgettable [laughs]. But not George.

FRANCINE DU PLESSIX GRAY   At this time in my life, I seemed to have a particular taste for *Paris Review* boys: first Tom Guinz-burg, then Blair Fuller, then, a year later, George. I was going to Barnard, and George invited me to one of those big cocktail par-ties that his parents used to give for the young people at their apartment on Ninety-eighth Street, where George was still living after coming back from Paris. So it must have been 1956 or 1957. Of course, in that milieu, we used to drive everywhere, and George picked me up in his little convertible at my parents' house on East Seventy-eighth Street. I have no memory of where we went, but he drove me home and gave me a good-bye kiss, and it was the most asexual kind of butterfly kiss I've ever had from a

Times Square. From left, Robert Silvers, Didi Ladd, Luisa Gilardenghi, George.
From the collection of George Plimpton.

man. And it had nothing to do at all with the way a homosexual kisses you on the mouth, either, which is a totally different thing. It was like alighting on your lips for a second. And I thought to myself, "This man will never commit himself to a woman."

MARION CAPRON   George was a strange mixture. Part of him sneered at Society, and part of him was in absolute awe of it. Part of him thought his father was the best model, and another part idolized Harold Vanderbilt, who was busily doing things like getting monkey glands to improve his potency. That was his rage, and George would go to Palm Beach to visit Vanderbilt and listen to this stuff seriously. And then he would come back, having been bored to tears, and would say so but still be enormously pleased that he was included. I disapproved, because I was this earnest, deadpan pain in the ass. Part of it was probably envy. But Norman Mailer once said that I had a built-in shit detector, and I knew I had better instincts about people, certainly, than George did. I think the secret was, George was genuinely fascinated by anything for a while. He could talk to almost anybody. He had that gift. But he was also in awe of money and high social status. At one point, he went to one of these Vanderbilt things or something else, and I said, "George, you're rather like a used toothbrush. You just park it anywhere." And he reached across the table—we were at some bar—and slapped me. He was probably drinking; it was the only time he ever did that. I guess it was the nastiest thing I could have said, but I thought somehow he should be earnestly editing books, writing, working harder, applying himself, whatever that meant. Meanwhile, what was I doing? Unloading *Paris Reviews* from the dock into a Mercedes. That was my high moral vantage point. . . .

LITERARY ENTREPRENEUR

TOM GUINZBURG When I went back to New York in 1953, I got some help from family lawyers, and we went through the whole business of setting up a little company for the *Review*, and working out the distribution, and dealing with the postman—all the stuff that occupied us for the next year or two and which was critical to our success. The resonance was already there—*Time* and *Newsweek* had reviewed us enthusiastically, and people were talking about the magazine. We had an office at Two Columbus Circle, used mostly for storage, mail, and so forth, except I think Marion Capron actually lived there, and then we got another office, or she did, or John Train did, on First Avenue. But Peter [Matthiessen] became much less involved with the magazine very quickly. He was pursuing his own writing and environmental concerns, tracking the bad guys in the world. He was also out in the country, living in Sagaponack, almost from the time he came back from Paris. Humes and Train were in town and still concerned about the magazine even as they, too, got caught up in other things. So it was still George who carried the major weight of the thing.

MARION CAPRON The Columbus Circle office was an incredibly filthy place, through which flashed the neon Chevrolet sign. My pittance of a salary was paid personally by George, and when I complained of being cold in the night, on my cot, his mother trotted down and brought me a blanket. To get to that cot, I had to climb eight flights of office-type stairs—very long stairs—because no one was allowed to use the elevator at night. We hauled *Paris Reviews* up these eight flights. I went down to the docks to get them in the company car, George's 250 Mercedes, which he was very proud of. It was a subdued gray, with red trim, so that was a perk for me. We were distributed then by Eastern News. I remember the guy's name, even: Drucker. George was mighty intimidated by Drucker, who was a burly, quasi-waterfront guy, but Drucker and I got on just fine. At any rate, I went down, and Drucker would help load up the car with boxes and boxes of issues. Lillian von Nickern helped, too. Nicky was the secretary, and the glue, I may say, of the *Review* at that time. She kept all the records, and without her it really would not have functioned. She and I, we had fun. A nifty lady.

LILLIAN VON NICKERN My first introduction to George must have been at the Columbus Circle office; he didn't strike me like a bolt of lightning. George would call me up: "So-and-so needs his money! We printed his work! We promised him!" I would say, "We can't pay him. I mean, it's nice to promise him, but I don't have the money to do it. He's on the list." And they were. I did not pay in installments—that's just not the right way to do it—but many a payment had to be delayed because we just did not have the funds. And because *The Paris Review* was *The Paris Review*, to be in it was such a wonderful thing for so many of the young writers that they didn't really object to a late payment. The agents, of course, were different. They made me "business manager," which sounds so good. It was bookkeeping work, detail work that nobody likes doing. I didn't mind doing it, I found it interesting, but most everyone else associated with the *Review* was certainly not interested in subscriptions and ad payments and writer payments and paying the printer and all the rest of it. For that, there was nobody else but me.

MARION CAPRON I had no title in the beginning. I read manuscripts and sent them back mostly, or sent them out to Rose Styron, who was reading at that time. George read many, too. Don Hall read the poetry. I was an associate editor later on, at the same

time that Jean Stein was made associate editor—me on the strength
of the Dorothy Parker interview, and Jean on the strength of her
money and the Faulkner interview. I remember one priceless
scene involving *both* those great interviews, the Hemingway and
the Faulkner. Faulkner was notoriously shy of interviewers. Nevertheless, there he was one night in Jean Stein's apartment on Sutton Place, ostensibly to be interviewed by her. George and I were
there, George to lend a little moral support or seriousness or lightheartedness or *something* to the proceedings. But for some reason,
maybe just a prop for our mission, we had brought the Hemingway interview to work on. It was not a very large apartment, and
the living room had a black rug with rosebuds on it, like the car-
peting in a hotel corridor. I remember that rug vividly because
George and I were on it most of the time, cutting and pasting our
interview (late, of course) to send back to Cuba for the approval
of the great Papa. Meanwhile, I gathered that Faulkner wanted
to go back to his hotel; why, I couldn't imagine. Jean was amply
endowed, and braless, and kept soothing him with drinks, bend-
ing over him with these giant . . . It reminded me of the Walter
Matthau movie with the lady who threatens to open her dress and
he says, "Oh, please don't let them out! Please!" The novelist,
however, appeared to be mesmerized by Jean's cleavage, and
there's no question but that he succumbed to her allure at some
point. But that night, I thought he might be frightened of her or
maybe put off by the work on his chief rival's interview going on
around his feet, or maybe he just didn't want to be interviewed
himself. He wasn't under much pressure, though. The talk was
pretty informal, chatty. Eventually we left, and sometime later I
took the Hemingway interview down to Cuba, for the great man's
approval.

ROWAN GAITHER George told me he was down in Havana just
after the Cuban revolution, when Hemingway was still there. Kenneth Tynan was there, too. They were all out at lunch, drinking
heavily, probably, and a revolutionary appeared and said, "You're
Hemingway. We're about to execute a prisoner. We would like to
invite you to the firing squad to watch this execution." As George
tells the story, Tynan, being an opponent of capital punishment,

declared that he was going to go to the execution and throw himself in front of the firing squad. Hemingway was just drunk. George said he was going to go along. They all set off. And along the way, it suddenly occurred to them that at the end of the execution, somebody was actually going to die. And it all got a lot less interesting. Then they began to think of some way to get out of it. According to George, it took them a surprisingly long time to realize what actually goes into an execution.

DONALD HALL There was irritation among the founders with the way George was running the *Review*, the way we would miss issues. I remember taking one poem, which we held on to for two years. But in the meantime, the poet sent me six revisions of it. I kept sending them to Paris marked "This is the new revision—substitute." When it came out, it was the original version. The poet was furious. Naturally. So it wasn't going well, and there was sentiment, not overwhelming definite sentiment, to end the *Review*. But then I was suddenly overcome with my early enthusiasm for the magazine, and I made an impassioned speech for it to continue. And George felt that saved the day. Whenever we saw each other, he would bring it up.

MARION CAPRON I think I know why George stuck with the *Review*, but I'm not sure he knew. George was clueless about his own character. True, he was complicated. It was hard for him to know himself, I'm sure. He didn't know what he wanted, and certainly in that period, he had no idea what he wanted to do or what he wanted to be. He was writing in those days, but not as Norman Mailer did or as Peter Matthiessen did. He knew what he didn't want. He didn't want nine to five. He didn't want a regular life, but he needed a calling card; he needed a peg to hang himself on. That's what *The Paris Review* was. It served as something he could say he did. The fact that he only spent an hour a week on it didn't matter. There it was, in print.

PETER MATTHIESSEN After I came back to the States in '53, I never lost the thread of *The Paris Review*; I stayed in touch. I think

The Paris Review in New York, 1965. From left, bottom row: Dorothy Fielding, Freddy Espy, Maggie Paley; second row: Susan Fielding (with horn), George, Tom Guinzburg, Sally Belfrage; third row: John Filler, an unknown person; fourth row: Billy Pène du Bois, Victoria Arends, Neil Wolf, Penelope Lee, Donald Hall, Frank Simon. *Photograph © Richard Marshall.*

George still thought of me as an editor, and I did work on certain stories. But I'd read somewhere that the natural life span of a little magazine was about eight years, so sometime in the late fifties or early sixties, I suggested to George that it was time to fold our tent. He had been saying, "Nobody works on this thing except for me, and I never would have gotten into this if it weren't for you." I said, "If you really feel that way—that you're doing all the work and nobody's helping you—then shut it down. It has had a very noble career already, it's made its mark, we've published some very good stuff. I don't see why we're agonizing over it. It's lived longer than most little magazines anyway." This shot down his little argument. He needed the magazine. *The Paris Review* was the armature for everything he did.

GEORGE PLIMPTON, UNPUBLISHED 1979 INTERVIEW WITH DAVID MICHAELIS *We had one big fight over* The Paris Review, *here in New York in about 1960. Peter and Tom wanted to close it down. We had too much to drink one night during a meeting, and tempers began to flare. I kept trying to get people to stay on and work harder. I kept trying to hold them together, and I think they finally were impatient. So they said, "Look, we don't want to work anymore, so let's close the thing down." And then I had to make a big choice in my own mind—do I want to go along on this alone and bring in other people? And of course that's what happened.*

PETER MATTHIESSEN, UNPUBLISHED 1979 INTERVIEW WITH DAVID MICHAELIS *I was amazed how concerned everyone still was about the magazine. But I don't think* [the meeting] *is really important, to tell you the truth. It didn't change anything; it wasn't any watershed. Of course, at that time, you know, nobody but George really was still with the magazine.*

GEORGE PLIMPTON, UNPUBLISHED 1979 INTERVIEW WITH DAVID MICHAELIS *I would feel like a limb was gone if* The Paris Review *stopped—like a crutch had fallen out from underneath me. And I think that's one of the reasons I've never stopped it. I mean, there are choices you have to make, and it's odd that of all choices I've made in my life, the most sensible one would probably have been to drop* The Paris Review *so I could put all that energy into something else. But I've never been able to do it.*

MARION CAPRON We had meetings, often at restaurants. There were no great policy decisions made at these meetings. I was so terribly self-conscious in those days that I couldn't remember for the life of me why they were held at all. The main thing I remember was when Sadri, our publisher, came to visit the Second Avenue office (and my pad by that time). I remember he walked into our bathroom, which had a tiny, tenement-sized bathtub, and he said, "Oh, that's just like the one I had as a child, but mine was in gold." I said, "Sadri, I'm five feet eight, and it doesn't do." The strange thing is I *don't* remember anything about our relations with the Paris office. This is strange because it could be argued that they

were doing most of the work over there—putting the issues together, layout, cover, illustrations, the art portfolio, the ads, the
printing and shipping. All we were doing was selecting the short
stories and interviews—and paying the bills; and Nicky was doing
that.

———

JOAN DE MOUCHY I met George in Paris April 1953, a month
or so before my unfortunate marriage to Jimmy Moseley. A year
and a bit later I would be divorced and back home, which was the
embassy, with an infant daughter and not much of a clue as to
what I wanted to do. A few months later, Peter Duchin, a childhood friend, turned up in Paris with Bob Silvers, and during dinner Bob asked if I would like to come work at *The Paris Review.* I
said, "Sure, why not?" The office was at 16, rue Vernet, just off the
Champs-Élysées. There were some odd characters in that office.
One of them was a man named Art French, who did the long
march with Mao and was married to a colored woman with whom
he had two mulatto children. I remember when Art decided that
his children didn't have souls until they were seven years old and
that he could bump them off if he wanted to. I spent hours with
Eddie Morgan, Sam Farrell, a wonderful Irish fellow, and several
other colleagues persuading Art French that he could not bump
off his children and that they did have souls even though they were
not yet seven years old.

TEDDY VAN ZUYLEN Silvers and Duchin lived on a barge that
was tied up somewhere near the Place de l'Alma, if I remember
correctly. It was probably the most uncomfortable setup you've
ever seen in your life. I don't know how people could live there—
even one person was difficult, but two seemed absolutely miserable. Peter didn't have any money; he had an allowance, which he
squandered on women, probably, taking them to nice hotels: I
don't know if he had very much money left over to go to restaurants. In any case, my apartment in Paris became kind of a refec-
tory. When people were hungry, they would come to my place
and have dinner. By 1954–55, George, of course, was back in
New York, but when he was in Paris, he'd come to dinner as well.

We had a very good chef, so it was kind of nice. I thought, "What the hell? I have to give them back something. We're part of a gang here. Everybody contributes what they have." Bob didn't have any money, either, but don't forget, this was very much a bohemian era of our lives, and we didn't care in those days how we lived. We had been to boarding schools, then college dorms, so we were used to living uncomfortably. The charm was that there were other barges very close by, so there was a communal barge life, in a way. In those days we were looking desperately to be as unidentifiable, in a social sense, as possible. So living on a barge was great.

JOAN DE MOUCHY   We were also always in need of new mailing lists, to encourage people to subscribe. I remember having drinks with Art Buchwald in the bar across from the *Herald Tribune* and talking with him about the *Review.* He suddenly said, "You want a mailing list? Hold on." He walked across the street and came back with a large pile of the brown paper strips that went around the newspapers for mailing to their subscribers and just handed them to me. Such things happened in those days.

NELSON ALDRICH   I came to Paris in the fall of 1957, right out of college, to go to Sciences Po [Institut des Sciences Politiques]— a foolhardy thing to do for someone who knew very little French. However, relief appeared that Thanksgiving when Joan Moseley, as she then was, invited me to dinner at her apartment. A few other Americans were there, among them Bob Silvers, who allowed as how he was soon going back to the States to work for *Harper's* and needed someone to take his place on the *Review.* I don't think he'd finished his sentence before I raised my hand, and to my great delight he took me on, at least provisionally. I actually had some experience editing a literary magazine, a mildly incendiary thing called *i.e., the Cambridge Review,* which I'd helped put out at Harvard. I also got the best possible tutorial in magazine publishing from Bob, who, as Joan used to say, had the patience of Job when it came to explaining anything, and not just the niceties of keeping the Dutch printer happy. He did keep postponing his return to the States, though. At that point he'd been in Paris, happy, extremely well connected, for seven years. One more, he told me, and he might have stayed forever. In any event, one day not long before he left, I got a welcome-aboard letter from George, whom I'd never met, written almost entirely in Porcellian Club jargon. This was odd, since, if he knew I was a member, he should also have known that I was so ghostly a presence in those precincts that I couldn't be counted on to understand what he was saying. Nevertheless, I was overjoyed—as much as anything to have an excuse to stay in Paris for a few more years.

JOAN DE MOUCHY My most vivid memory of Nellie Aldrich's term at the *Review* was the day that Allen Ginsberg and Gregory Corso appeared at rue Vernet and proceeded to bugger on the office floor in an attempt to get me to leave. I was alone working late when they showed up, obviously quite drugged. They chorused together, saying, "Oh, we want Ezra Pound's text." I said, "We don't have Ezra Pound's text." "Oh, we know you have Ezra Pound's text." "We don't have Ezra Pound's text." This went on for a while. Then they looked at each other and said, "Let's do it." So, with lots of lurching, gurgling, and mumbling, they undid their trousers and proceeded to get on with it on the office floor. I remember that just before they had gotten totally into it, Nellie called up to check in. I could not describe my predicament but said, "Will you please come over to the office and tell them that we don't have Ezra Pound's text?" Nellie gasped, "Oh, my God, I have a black tie on! That won't help at all!" Ultimately, I passed the telephone to Corso, who Nelson knew from Harvard, God knows how, and he told them, "We don't have Ezra Pound's text," very firmly. But they were still so drugged and cross with me that they kept on buggering. I decided not to move, because I knew that if I left, they'd rip the whole office apart, and I was going to have to clean it up. So I just sat at my desk licking stamps for future mailing-drive envelopes and pretended to ignore them.

NELSON ALDRICH As it turned out, I stayed at the *Review* for only a year and then went on to a better-paid job at the Congress for Cultural Freedom, which by 1959 was already a well-known CIA front, but no less admired for that. Two things I recall of my tenure at the *Review:* my shame at not getting out more than two issues a year and my gratitude to George for being so forgiving.

JOAN DE MOUCHY   George would show up about once a year. His first prerequisite was to organize a party at my apartment, to which he would invite every writer, artist, plus down-at-the-heels bums and anybody else he had come across in the last year. The guests came in droves, looking forward to free drinks and food. They were a motley crew to look upon but were representing talent of all sorts beneath their various guises. Nonie Phipps, who was living with me at the time, announced yearly that she wasn't going to stay when we had these parties, because revolting people kept going down the hall and throwing up in her bathroom. First of all, it seemed as if the people George invited hadn't eaten since 1902; and as for the booze, their only idea was to get totally loaded as quickly as possible. Riffraff aside, one found Bill Burroughs, Jimmy and Gloria Jones, Maurice Girodias, Irwin Shaw, and everybody you could possibly think of in Paris in those days that had anything to do with writing or art. Sadri Khan, then our publisher and a good and understanding friend, was extremely kind and would regularly extricate me when things got fraught, leaving George to cope. One year all the paintings in the entry hall were stolen. Lady Granard owned my building and was the twin of Nonie's great-aunt Gladys Phipps. Thanks to this Phipps link, the lawsuit that they were about to embark on was canceled.

————

MAGGIE PALEY   By the time I came on George's scene in the early sixties, there was no longer any official *Paris Review* office in New York, just George's apartment on the third floor of 541. (I think Bob Silvers was still living in the one-bedroom on the first floor that later became the *Review* office.) George's place had a thin little kitchen and a thin little guest room where Terry Southern would crash, plus his own bedroom and an office where he would write and make phone calls. It was the huge living room that everyone remembered who saw the place; it had maybe six windows overlooking the river. I used to think that George spent an awful lot of time watching the boats go by, but then I thought,

"Who wouldn't?" I remember a couple of Bernard Buffet paintings on the wall, souvenirs of Paris, but dating by the minute. There were also some odd chairs and drab sofas where he and I would sometimes work on interviews he'd done for the *Review.* This was after I'd made the transition from girlfriend to assistant editor.

LILLIAN VON NICKERN As business manager, I went into the office at 541 occasionally, but most of the work that I did for them, from the 1960s on, was at my apartment in Woodside, Queens. The address was on the front of the magazine, so for years people sent unsolicited manuscripts to my home (a few came in person, unannounced). I had married by then and had a young baby. Even-

1965 *Paris Review* Revel at the Village Gate.
From left: Andrei Voznesensky, Allen Ginsberg, George.
Photograph © Henry Grossman.

tually, I had three children in the house. And at one point five dogs. My husband and I owned two Baskin-Robbins [ice-cream stores], so I was doing that, too. Manuscript work was done out of George's apartment. George always was the final say on everything that went into the *Review*. Whoever was in charge of the office over there in France would decide on certain things, and they would be sent here, and George—well, it was a back-and-forth thing.

MAGGIE PALEY George was always coming up with ideas of how to make money for the *Review*. "Enterprise in the service of art," he called it. The Revels were one idea he had. The first one was in 1965 at the Village Gate. It was a "hot ticket," the first fund-raiser I knew of in New York that mixed the Society world, the entertainment world, the literary world, and people who couldn't afford to pay—artists and various other bohemian types. I don't know if we made any money, but it was a great success.

LILLIAN VON NICKERN The Revels were a lot of fun—one at the Village Gate, then another on Welfare Island, then another at the South Street Seaport—and they brought a certain amount of attention, which was very good for raising big donations. In that respect they worked out, but as for the Revels themselves, we were fortunate if we broke even.

MAXINE GROFFSKY My involvement in *The Paris Review* began in 1962 when I announced to George that I was running off to Paris with Harry Mathews. George said, "Oh, wonderful! Do you want to do *The Paris Review*?" I told him that I didn't know if I was going to stay there, since I had only known Harry for two weeks. Bennett Cerf had given me a leave of absence, saying I could come back whenever I wanted to. So I suggested a friend from Random House: "Larry Bensky's going to Europe. Ask him." When Larry started as Paris editor, I helped him. We first worked out of a dingy space at 16, rue Vernet, off the Champs-Élysées. In 1964, thanks to Colette Duhamel, the *Review* moved to a wonderful courtyard office on the rue de Tournon, down the block from the Luxembourg Gardens and Café le Tournon, where everyone hung out in the founding days. So we had come home in a sense. By 1966, Larry wasn't really around much anymore. He wasn't very happy at the *Review,* or didn't seem to be, and I was doing all the work. So then I told George that I wanted the job, and he gave it to me.

HARRY MATHEWS   It was fine, Maxine working for George, because they never had anything to do with one another. George had the final say on everything that went into the *Review,* but then Maxine took extraordinary initiatives on her own and confronted George with them. For instance, in one issue, I wrote a poem that incorporated lines from all the poems in that issue. I told her about this. I don't think George ever noticed, but one reader did notice, and wrote to the magazine. Her boldest initiative was—I had written *The Sinking of the Odradek Stadium,* which was just unsellable, and Maxine, out of the goodness of her heart, published it in four issues of *The Paris Review.* I don't think that George minded at all her putting in the first installment, but I don't think he realized there were going to be three more installments. In George's memoir of those years, which he published several years ago in *The Paris Review* itself, the question around the New York office was "Is that shit still going down?"

MAXINE GROFFSKY   When friends in Paris asked, "What's *The Paris Review?*" I jokingly answered, "*C'est moi.*" I put out issues thirty-six to fifty-six, and I was proud of the fact that I was the first editor who actually produced four issues in one year. For each issue, George sent me the interview, which was often delayed, and short stories. Tom Clark, the poetry editor, sent me his selections. I commissioned the art—the covers, the portfolio of drawings or photographs—and put in my fiction choices. So when George received the printed issue, it was sometimes a big surprise. Not sometimes, all the time.

TOM CLARK   I became poetry editor in the fall of 1963, on Don Hall's recommendation. One snag was that my predecessor, X. J. Kennedy, had accepted about six issues' worth of poems in the final months of his editorship—against the calamities to come, I later surmised. I immediately wrote George to point out that unless that

The Paris Review in Paris: Maxine Groffsky.
© *Harold Chapman / The Image Works.*

whole backlog could be summarily dumped, he'd have no need for a new poetry editor for at least another year or two, in which case, why did he need me? George, characteristically, said, "Fine, go ahead and dump it all." So I wrote to all those professor-poets, and out went their poems. It was a horrible thing to do, of course, and I'm surprised that only two or three of them complained, to the effect that their hoped-for promotions hinged on their being published in *The Paris Review,* etc. Of course I felt bad about that, but probably not bad enough, and I was sure George didn't care at all.

RON PADGETT Tom Clark was in some ways a surprising pick for Don Hall to make, since Don had coedited, only a few years before, a somewhat conservative anthology, *New Poets of England and*

America. Whatever the reason, Don was able to like a poet like Tom Clark, and Tom published Frank O'Hara—posthumously, of course—and Kenneth Koch, Kenward Elmslie, Joe Brainard, Ted Berrigan, Aram Saroyan, John Ashbery, himself, and me. And let's see, who else? Tom loved Jimmy Schuyler's work. Oh, also poets such as Philip Whalen, Gary Snyder, Michael McClure, and Allen Ginsberg. Tom did the *Paris Review* interview with Allen and published a really wonderful poem of Allen's to go with it. I can't recall if he published Olson, Charles Olson; he might've. But that was generally Tom's aesthetic at that time.

ARAM SAROYAN   George coordinated the NEA's annual, *The American Literary Anthology,* of the "best" poems and stories and essays that had appeared that year in literary magazines. There was a small cash award of five hundred dollars to each author and two hundred fifty dollars to the little magazine that printed the piece. Three writers in each category selected the work, and my poem "lighght," from the *Chicago Review,* was chosen by Robert Duncan, one of the great American poets, if you don't mind my saying so. Well, a Republican congressman from Iowa, William Scherle, brought the poem up on the floor of Congress, and they started gutting the NEA budget because you don't give seven hundred fifty dollars for a single misspelled word. Henceforth they would use the word "lighght" whenever they wanted to cut the NEA budget; it was like a fiscal laser surgery tool. Then in the eighties when Reagan brought the poem up, George called me in Bolinas. And when I wrote a piece about it for *Mother Jones,* he did an intro for it, which was very kind of him. The piece was called "The Most Expensive Word in History," by which I meant the millions denied the NEA, not the seven hundred fifty dollars. George was very open-minded and generous. The poem was fine by him. Only a few years before he died, he told me he'd gone to Iowa to campaign against Congressman Scherle when he was up for reelection. What a guy, I thought.

> *Dear Maxine,*
>   *The new issue has arrived, a handsome and interesting cover and it is a surprise and pleasure to find so many ads.*

We are upset here on a number of counts. Why wasn't the masthead changed as per a number of requests? There is going to be something of a stew here because of it. I am speaking specifically of letters written by Dan Lloyd, Molly and myself, all of which stated that Dan Lloyd, Laurie Sobel, Michael Newman and Molly McKaughan were to be added to the masthead in designated slots. You can imagine the disappointment at working very hard for the magazine, with recognition promised which for unaccountable reasons was not granted. Very awkward.

I find the fiction contents mediocre this time. I am literally ashamed to read the Phillip Lopate junk—badly written, and lacking in any value at all as far as I can see. The Jong, the Roche and the Perec at least have the quality of experimentation and a command of the medium. Cohen bores me, but once again a gift is evident . . . though I'm blessed if I can see why we must promote it as much as we do. This is the fifth time he has graced our pages— which may put him at the top of the list for frequency of publication. He's simply not that good. But it's the Lopate that disturbs me. I have written so many times that as the Editor I must see what goes into the magazine under the category "fiction." Why do you deny me this? I've always stated that if you in Paris find a piece of material selected here second rate or questionable, it would be very much my principle to remove it. Apparently I cannot express to you the horror of opening up the magazine and finding a piece in it so thoroughly embarrassing.

I have not had a chance to look at the poetry yet but the names seem appallingly familiar. I wrote a long tough letter to Tom Clark the other day in which, among other things, I pointed out that in the compilation of the index the poet who has published more work in The Paris Review *than any other is indeed Clark himself. I urged him to cast his net in different waters, and his reply suggested that he had done so, but it's certainly not evident in the present issue. . . .*

I do apologize for what may seem somewhat snippy remarks about #56. But I cannot bear the procedures that somehow get the issue spoiled by the mawkish, amateurish nonsense [by] this cat Lopate's. I presume he is of the same school as that friend of Kenneth Koch's, Mitchell Sisskind, whose work we apparently published because it is so marvelously bad. I reread Sisskind just to see if

he and Lopate might not be the same person and discovered that Siss-
kind is considerably better. Really, we must never do anything like
that again. It won't be the guilder-dollar crisis that drives us under
but selections made by some other authority than their integral ex-
cellence.

Incidentally, we have been having discussions here about the
considerable strain put on the magazine by the dollar crisis and I'll
try to get a memorandum to you about this as soon as possible. En-
closed is the quarterly check—and I hope things aren't so bad there
that it will disappear in an evening of café hopping. . . . [August 14, 1973]

MAXINE GROFFSKY Why did the *Review* move back to New York? For several reasons. Although I loved living in France and working with George on the magazine, by fall 1973 I acknowledged that my job in Paris was not a career and that it was time for me to do something else. And at the very same time, George was having his own doubts about the future of the magazine. Since we owed a lot of money to our Dutch printer and it had become cheaper to print in the States, we both knew it made sense to close up shop in Europe. George was even considering closing up shop altogether or getting someone else to take over. I told him, "George, you're the magazine, and if you don't do it, it's another magazine." He decided to find a way to pay our debts and bring the *Review* to New York. So I started packing up the office and in the middle realized I wanted to go home, and left almost as precipitously as I had originally gone to Paris. The *Review's* trunks were shipped in mid-January and I followed by plane two weeks later. George gave me a great welcome-home party, and since I had to get my new life in order, I had little to do with the magazine afterwards—except, of course, for going to those fabulous parties at George's.

———

BLAIR FULLER Looking back on it, I feel that the *Review* actually reached a turning point long before it was moved to New York. It was when George decided to have a contest. He talked Sadri Khan into putting up a thousand dollars in the name of his father—so it was called the Aga Khan Prize for Fiction. It seemed just laughable, but it turned out that George had done a very, very intelligent thing. Till then, the magazine had published mostly unknown writers of the sort that would remain mostly unknown. Now, with this contest, all that would change. He had gotten three excellent people as judges of the contest—Saul Bellow, Hiram Haydn, and Brendan Gill of *The New Yorker.* He also wrote a letter, which I never saw, to all the agents and so forth, announcing the contest and the "big name" judges. Then, sometime in the middle of the winter, we got a letter from George saying, "Well, we have winners of the contest and the judges have chosen all the wrong people." I'm not kidding. That's just what he said. "They made all the wrong choices." One story was by a very good short-story writer named Gina Berriault; another was by a guy who taught poetry at San Francisco State named John Langdon, and as far as I know, it's the only short story he ever wrote. The third one was by a black writer whose name I've forgotten, but I thought that story was interesting, too. So what was George complaining about? Well, it turns out that while those guys got the prizes, George saw the real gold in at least four other writers who had submitted stuff that hadn't won anything. There was a wonderful story by Richard Yates called "A Wrestler with Sharks." Jack Kerouac had sent a chapter of *On the Road,* really the most lively, attractive chapter in that whole book. Evan S. Connell had submitted a part of *Mrs. Bridge,* and Nadine Gordimer, future Nobel Prize winner, had a story. We did publish the winners, of course, but George had every reason to be proudest of publishing the losers. He was a damn good editor, you know; he'd spotted those people.

WRITER

RAY CAVE Most of sport is what the people competing are going through, what they're thinking, what they're doing, and nobody approached George's ability to write about that inside of the game. It takes a George to ask the question "What's it feel like, if you're the quarterback, when you put your hands up under that guy's ass? How'd you do that?" People find that sort of question irresistible. You'd spend an hour telling him how you did it, right?

PAT RYAN I followed Ray as George's editor at *Sports Illustrated* in the seventies. With his distinctive voice, it's really ludicrous to say you edited George. You'd agree on a story and cheat on his deadline so it got delivered on time, but after that you didn't mess with his distinctive voice. You might ask a question, and he'd immediately rewrite the sentence or paragraph. He loved clarity. What I did mainly was protect George and his copy from legions of less talented and envious staff. They had no conception how hard he labored at his writing. (How could they? It looked effortless.) And because they didn't know him, they slammed him as a dilettante. That was the knock.

MAGGIE PALEY I think George earned his first serious income as a writer from *Sports Illustrated*. I don't know how this happened, whether he approached them with a proposal or what, but I am sure he was thrilled to get an assignment. There was a lot of financial anxiety when I was with him in the early sixties. He didn't share it with me, of course, and maybe anxiety is too strong a word. I suspect he had a small income, and Sadri was still publisher of the *Review*, so George wasn't carrying the whole of that obligation. On the other hand, New York was a lot more expensive than Paris, and what with his club dues, and his nightclubbing, and his rent at 541, George's lifestyle wasn't getting any cheaper. So there was a good deal of scrambling for money in those years. Scrambling was part of his nature, of course, and writing was the thing he most loved to do in the world, but still, he was happy about the money that would be coming in from *Sports Illustrated*.

BLAIR FULLER To someone of George's class, wealth came in many forms. The first thing he thought to do for *Sports Illustrated* was a piece about Harold Vanderbilt, the great prewar defender of the America's Cup and the inventor of contract bridge. Well, it happened that Nina [Fuller's first wife] and I went to Florida one winter when George was down there interviewing Vanderbilt in his mansion in Palm Beach. I called George and he invited us to come to lunch. We arrived and went over to a tennis court within a courtyard where Vanderbilt was playing with a pro. The pro, of course, was hitting the ball right to where the old man could hit it back, while his wife was on the sidelines, crying, "Good shot, Harold!" The most striking thing to me was that "Harold" was wearing makeup. Maybe it was sunscreen of some sort, but it looked like makeup that an actor would be wearing, foundation sort of stuff. It all seemed a little cockeyed. We had a perfectly pleasant lunch, but then, that evening, we went to this party where the Duke and Duchess of Windsor turned up, surrounded by toadies. George was quite at home there, in his element, really. He seemed to have struck up a good relationship with the duchess; in fact, I had a conversation with her myself during which she actually made a good impression on me. She was straightforward, apparently intelligent, and curious, while my impression of the duke was appalling. He looked like a sad little boy feeling deprived. He couldn't take his eyes off the duchess wherever she was in the room, as though he was always looking for her affirmation. I talked with him, too. I was standing next to him and he asked me, "Where are you staying?" I said, "Well, my wife and I have just been in Miami. We came up here for the day." He said, "Miami?" I said, unbelievable, that someone known to have been a Nazi sympathizer would say such a thing only ten years after the war. But, you know, in the end George got something out of this besides a four-part laudatory piece on Harold Vanderbilt. Shortly after that part, Mrs. Vanderbilt, apparently in her cups, complained to George that she had read the stories in the *Review* and she was disgusted that everybody was so bizarre, so poor, so wretched, so crazy, that she would put up a prize for the best story about nice, normal people. George was really in some anguish about this. He said, "Golly, we would really like to have that prize money, but I don't think we can give it out for the kind of story she has in mind." I said, "No, we really can't." And I had the idea—well, at least I believe it was my idea—to say to him, "I wonder if she could be persuaded to make it a humor prize." And she was persuaded.

RAY CAVE   Nobody else in sports journalism, only André Laguerre of *Sports Illustrated,* would have listened to a proposal from an amateur, even a passionate amateur like George, to do a story about another amateur like Harold Vanderbilt. All the other guys, though brilliant writers, were pros. George was an amateur pro, the best. André Laguerre was the best, too, the best magazine editor I've ever known. He was a writers' editor; and *Sports Illustrated* was known in the Time-Life Building as by far the best written of their magazines. Laguerre was *Time*'s London bureau chief when Luce asked him to come back to New York to run a sports magazine. People thought this was a bit bizarre, because Laguerre was a man of some eminence. He had been de Gaulle's press aide. I asked Laguerre once why he came back to take charge of a bungling sports magazine, and he said, "It all happens in sports. Sports, competition, is more important to our lives than some damn U.S. Senate committee hearing or the prime minister of England saying X and then two months later Y. It matters a great deal." That's why he was willing to undertake it. Now, the key to this—and Plimpton benefited from it—is that Laguerre's definition of sport far transcended anything that you and I could imagine. It encompassed any activity that engaged us in a competitive sense. The corollary was that there was no writer in the world that he didn't feel free to approach: Steinbeck, Dos Passos, Doctorow, O'Hara, Fowles. You'd ask them if there was anything they'd like to write for us, and they'd say, "Of course we have something we'd like to do." That's the proof that Laguerre was right.

ROBERT SILVERS He didn't want to be an outside observer; he didn't want to be a reporter, although he could write superb pieces for magazines if he wanted. His idea was to go into the secret world of the professional; the reporter would stop at the locker room door, then go to his perch in the press section, while George would be in the locker room putting on his uniform and going out with the players. Completely different. On the other hand, he did an enormous amount of research for each piece, on each sport. He tried to pick up everything he could.

Dear Mr. Commissioner [Pete Rozelle]—

I have sent you under separate cover a copy of Out of My League, *an account of an afternoon I spent in the Yankee Stadium pitching to some of the best players in the business. The book grew out of a series of articles I was commissioned to do for* Sports Illustrated, *a series describing what happens to the average week-end athlete competing at the highest possible level of athletic prowess. In this capacity, during the past two years, I've suffered not only at the hands of the baseball players, but in the ring against Archie Moore, on the golf course against [Sam] Snead, on the tennis courts against Pancho Gonzalez, and in a number of other contests, all of which, I need hardly say, have been equivalently unequal. I have experienced, however, what everyone imagines himself doing from time to time—getting out there and trying it—and I have put it down in words as truthfully and seriously as I can.*

It is my hope, of course, to do something for Sports Illustrated *(and a second book) on professional football, and it's to this end that I'm taking the liberty of writing you. . . .*

But anything I do with the League, before tackling the owners and coaches, must start with your permission. I hope that can be forthcoming. The point is, I think, that I'm doing this series not as a stunt, but as a serious inspection of a world of great athletes, which, while carefully observed by reporters, is rarely described by participants—and hardly ever by a representative of those myriads of onlookers, devoted to the game, who often imagine what it would be to train with a team and try it for an afternoon. . . . [July 29, 1961]

CHARLES MICHENER In Francis Plimpton's generation, journalists were from a rougher background. They tended not to be Ivy League, white-shoe boys, which George was certainly the epitome of. When I came into that world, I was at Yale and people would say, "Why do you want to be a journalist? It's sleazy. That isn't for people like you." But then came the New Journalism, so-called—Tom Wolfe, Gay Talese, George. They all developed a personal style, a persona, that covered everything from the clothes they wore (Wolfe's and Talese's eight-piece suits, George's schoolboy Brooks Brothers) to their quirks of punctuation and syntax. George became the most unlikely sort, the Brahmin as amateur journalist, the man who loves his subjects, who wouldn't be caught dead rummaging around in someone's dirty laundry. Indeed, he was sometimes criticized for dodging the dark side of things.

ROY BLOUNT George was always more literary than we were, but without writing literarily. André loved that. Back then they liked quirky things. Frank Deford wrote a great story about a traveling whale—a man who carried a whale around the country, a dead whale, to show people. George fit right in.

PAT RYAN George never did his expense accounts. At *SI,* if you go back into the Time Inc. records, it will look like George had a lot of stories fail, more than you would think; but that was because he'd go to Manila or someplace, and he never drew any money in advance, and he wouldn't save any receipts. So he was out all this money. You'd call the *Paris Review* office and you'd say, "I need these expense accounts so that he can get some money." It was hopeless. So I finally thought to give him kill fees for various imaginary articles that we turned down, supposedly. The kill fees were meant to cover what I thought was probably his expenses.

TIM SELDES I think the first time I became aware of this partici-patory journalism that George had in mind was when he told me, "I'm going to do some rounds with Archie Moore and write about it." He was the middleweight or heavyweight champion at the time. We all said, "You've got to be joking," but not at all. We all showed up at Stillman's Gym, and Archie was very nice and sort of bomped him around, and that was the beginning of George's amateur-among-the-pros thing. I wasn't his agent at the time; he called me as his friend to come and carry him away if necessary.

BLAIR FULLER Archie Moore was at the absolute peak of his ca-reer, the light heavyweight champion of the world after many a year in the boondocks. He had just won a terrific bout up in Montreal, defending his title against a French-Canadian fighter named Yvon Durelle—by a knockout, I think, in the eleventh round. So people began to collect at Stillman's Gym. George had asked some, and Archie some, Miles Davis, for one, who was dressed in a camel's-hair coat. George had asked me to be in his corner with George Brown, a gym owner who taught boxing, a good guy. Hemingway had put George in touch with him. Eventually Archie comes into the gym, just beaming. We go back to the dressing room, a plastic cubicle with a bench over here and a bench over there. Archie is in his fight clothes; he just takes off some sweats, and there he is. He starts taping his own hands; he didn't need anyone to do it for him. George did. George Brown is taping his hands, and Archie says, "Kid, I just wanna tell you something. Just go out there and do the best you can. I'm gonna make you look good." Well, that was a relief. But then, having relaxed us a bit, Archie thought he'd better tighten the anxiety a bit and began telling stories to his entourage. "Say, what happened to that last guy I knocked out? Is he still blind?" That kind of stuff, and horrific anecdotes came one after another. George, meanwhile, looked kind of zoned out. But then Archie, having taped his hands, got up and came over to the wall that George and I were sitting against and socked that wall with such force that the medicine cabinet jumped its moorings and flew all the way across the room. Finally we go out to the ring. There is a clock—three-minute rounds. There is a ref, but I've forgotten his name. People were in both corners with their buckets and sponges and stuff. And the bell rings. And George simply goes out there, no little dance you see boxers doing at the outset of a fight, he just goes forward toward Archie Moore, sticking his left hand out. Trying, in fact, to box. For quite a while in that first round, Archie clowned. He wasn't really trying to make George look good, but he was trying to make him look like an amateur, when he wasn't even that. Archie, on the other hand, was a great professional. When George tried to hit him with a left jab, Archie would just knock it away. And then he would just kind of tap George, showing that he could do it, you know. It seemed to me a very, very long round, and toward the end of it Archie's clowning really wasn't so funny now, because George kept coming at him. I mean, George didn't enter into the spirit of the joke, shall we say. He simply went on doing what he could, which was to keep moving forward. The second round was more of the same, with George moving forward, still forward. But then—I couldn't see what happened—but then suddenly the champion of the world slipped onto one knee. In other words, he's down. That's terrible, of course, and George stood there looking surprised. So up gets Archie with a smile and breaks George's nose. Blood is streaming out of his nose, but George does not stop. On he went doing this forward shuffle. Archie did not go any farther, thank heaven, because he could have put George away. He didn't, and then the bell rang. George Brown uses the styptic pencil on George's nose, and out George goes again for the third round. It's the same thing as before. But then I see something moving in my peripheral vision: George Brown is advancing the clock. Maybe he thought Archie was getting bored and might do something drastic, just to get out of there. I don't know, but I believe I was the only person in the place to notice what he did. I never said anything to George. But Brown was advancing the clock. And he saw that I saw it, and he winked at me.

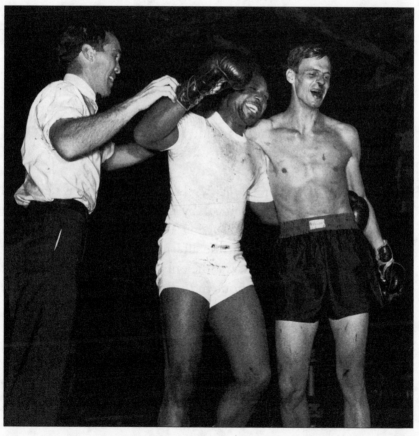

George v. Archie Moore, Stillman's Gym, 1959.
© *Herb Scharfman*/Sports Illustrated.

DAVID AMRAM When George and Archie Moore were going to fight, someone apparently told Archie that George was a champion boxer in college and was going to try to knock him out, for a book George was writing. None of this was true, of course. Archie Moore got a different look on his face and said, "That ain't gonna happen." So, the first few moments of the fight, Archie started flicking a few little left jabs. George had a good-sized nose, and splat, George's nose was bleeding almost from the beginning. Miles Davis was there, and he came up afterwards and said, "George, is that black blood, white blood, or red blood?" George turned to him and said, "That's blue blood." That was the story as George told it to me, but there are many variations of it.

MYRA GELBAND It was *Out of My League,* with that terrific blurb from Hemingway—George as the explorer of the dark side of Walter Mitty—which launched him as a *literary* sportswriter. But he didn't really make his mark until the early sixties, with *Paper Lion.*

MARION CAPRON That was a title I gave him, by the way: *Out of My League.* He never liked it. It was brilliant on my part.

ROBERT SILVERS For *Out of My League,* the idea was that we'd prepare for this pitching ordeal by standing on either side of Seventy-second Street and throwing a baseball to each other. I'd leave the office at *Harper's* in the afternoon and we would throw these balls across the street. It was the only way to do it. You couldn't do it on the sidewalk without hitting pedestrians, but *across* the street was all right, as it dead-ended right there at 541 East Seventy-second Street, overlooking the East River.

I shared the flat there with George for over a year. The night I arrived from Paris after seven years abroad I went to 541 East Seventy-second Street from the airport and George said, "Where are you going to stay?" I said I was about to phone some hotels. "No," said George, "you can stay here." He had the kind of instinctive generosity you never forget.

A. E. HOTCHNER About that great blurb Hemingway gave him for *Out of My League*, I was with Hemingway when he wrote it. It was toward the end of his life when he was at St. Mary's Hospital, attached to the Mayo Clinic. George had sent him galleys of his book. So Ernest says, "You know, George sent me a galley of his book and I read it and he'd like me to send a comment, but I'm having a lot of trouble being able to get things on paper." And so while I was there for two days, he fretted about it a couple of times, and I said, "Well, why don't you just do a couple of sentences, whatever you think," and I sort of urged him to give

George pitching to the All-Star lineup, Yankee Stadium, 1959.

© *The Estate of Garry Winogrand, courtesy Fraenkel Gallery, San Francisco.*

George a quote. It was a very good quote, but it was difficult for him.

DONALD HALL One year after *Out of My League* came out, several writers were invited to try out for the Pittsburgh Pirates, and I was one of them. I was a terrible athlete, and I knew it. I weighed two hundred and fifty pounds. Anyway, the night before I suited up for the first time, to meet the players, I called George in New York and I said that I was nervous. George talked to me very soberly and very practically; he advised me to get to know a particular player, make him into a friend. Then he said, "Above all, Donald, don't be sullen." I said, "George, do I sound sullen?" He said, "Donald, you sound as though you are walking into the valley of the shadow of death." And of course, I ripped it off. I printed that whole dialogue. It was the beginning of my essay.

JAMES SYMINGTON You knew that George boxed Archie Moore, I'm sure, but did you know that George drove a sulky for the Travis Stakes at Saratoga? Well, he did. A sulky is perfect for George. You sit stiffly erect and the horses go pitter-patter-pat down the track, gliding along in a wonderful way, and George actually came in first. So I had the pleasure of awarding my old St. Bernard's classmate this enormous silver cup. It must have been the first time in his career as an amateur among professionals that he actually won something.

STARLING LAWRENCE Sportswriters are a pretty earnest bunch of folks. By and large, they take the home run and the no-hitter very seriously. Then there's George, who has a wonderful way of mocking himself and everything else. I don't know another sportswriter who was coming from quite the same place or had the same touch.

JONATHAN DEE By the late 1970s *SI* had changed a great deal; as the years went on it became harder and harder for George to sell them his sort of article ideas, with the huge exception of "Sidd Finch."

HOST

GEOFFREY GATES I was just back in New York from the Marine Corps in the late 1950s, really ready to go. My mother had thrown me out of her house, because my first night out on the town, I had behaved badly and slept on the doorstep of the little brownstone where we lived. I moved in with a friend of mine, and he knew George, and he knew a little bit about *The Paris Review.* He said, "What we've got here are a lot of young editors and writers, and a lot of girls, and all the liquor you could drink." I said, "I'm very interested," and that evening, we went up to the apartment at 541, small as it was then. This was what I'd been waiting for since college: this waft of conversation, liquor, perfume, smoke, and the exact noise level I've always liked. Then there was this great tall guy who, when we were introduced, acted as if I was the greatest thing that ever happened to him. For five seconds, I was in heaven. We did the "Do you know?" a little bit and then broke to the cheese platter and the bar. He told me he had these parties quite often. I wasn't shy, and I managed to get the dates of each and

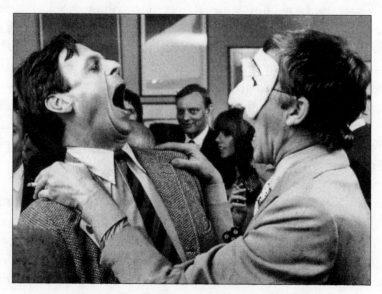

George's characteristic party greeting. The masked man is
actor Patrick O'Neal. *Photograph © Henry Grossman.*

every one in the next month or two. After that, I simply started crashing them. Despite that, and the fact that I was not quite on the intellectual level of some of the more serious lit types, we became very good friends. I made a lot of noise and laughed and had a good time.

DAVID AMRAM I came back to New York from Paris in the fall of 1955. The second week I was there, I was playing with Charles Mingus, by a miracle, and going to Manhattan School of Music in the daytime and sleeping even less than I did in Paris. I got a phone call, and I heard that unmistakable voice. I was living on the Lower East Side, where there wasn't even that much English spoken, between Avenues B and C on Eighth Street. I heard those cultured tones, and he said, "Hullo, boy! David, I see you're in the phone book. Welcome to New York! This is George Plimpton." I said, "Oh, my God, George, how are you?" He said, "I thought you were going to call me." I said, "George, I've been so swamped," and I told him all the things I'd been doing. He said, "You've got to come up and see me. We're having a little party up here." I said, "Where are you?" and he said, "My friend Norman will come and pick you up. I gave him your address in the phone book. I assume that's correct." I said, "Right, 319 East Eighth Street." He said, "Well, I imagine you don't have a bell in that neighborhood. Just come down in front of the building. He'll be there at two p.m., and he has curly brown hair. You can't miss him." So I went down, and sure enough, at about quarter to two, this guy shows up, and he had curly hair. I said, "Are you Norman?" He said, "Yes, you're David. Hop in! What's your full name, David?" I said, "I'm David Amram." He said, "I'm Norman Mailer."

NORMAN MAILER I don't know when I first met George, but my earliest memory of him may be of arm wrestling with him at a diner on Sheridan Square. And I remember he won, which irritated me. It went on for a while, but he won. Normally I didn't care whether I won one or lost one. But I didn't really like George at that point. I didn't trust him particularly. He seemed so, oh, I don't know. Much too—I have to think what the word is that I didn't quite like about him. Part of it, the lower part, was probably just a touch of envy. Here I've written a couple of novels, this and that, and here's this guy who strikes me as a bit of a skillful playboy who is putting out this magazine with a couple of other playboys. Through the years I knew him, there were so many things about him that I had to respect more than I wanted to. But these were all undercurrents. They never flared up. There was never any verbal artillery when we met. Nor did we work with foils in terms of wit. When we met, we enjoyed seeing each other, but there was a false element. He never did anything unpleasant, but there was something that I felt was just not fair. The gods had given him too much. From his side he may have thought, for all I know, "Why the hell did the gods give all that talent to that guy over there when I could have done so much more with it?" Which he could have, too, if he'd had a huge literary talent.

DONALD HALL I went to two or three parties at George's after he became the Elsa Maxwell of his time. Artie Shaw would be there, and Peter Duchin, and there was a big black guy and a little black guy. The big black guy was Archie Moore, light heavyweight champion, and the little black guy was Jimmy Baldwin. These contrasts were incredible. I was never there with Jackie. I was there when Boris, the drug dealer, came by sometimes. Boris was a guy with a Brooklyn accent, well dressed, with a little case; he would go back into the study with certain people who were there and close the door. I was there the night Brendan Gill of *The New Yorker* told Norman Mailer that he, Mailer, didn't know anything about the Irish. Mailer was terribly drunk. There were suggestions of a fistfight. One time I went to one of his parties and I passed out for the night on a spare bed that he had. When I woke up in the morning, my wallet was still there, but all the money was gone. So George loaned me twenty bucks to get to the airport. I had the ticket.

GEOFFREY GATES I was going out to these black-tie events with my friend Peggy Bancroft, who needed an escort, because her husband refused to go to them. George knew Peggy and went to her parties, so did Dougie Burden. But it was a different kind of connection. The whole point of George's parties was really George's beatitude. You walked in and he could be hosting the most solemn folks, like his parents' friends, old and gray, quietly muttering to each other, and George would act as if, "Thank God, Geoffrey's here!" Then Jim would come in, and Ed, and Sally, and it would be, "Thank God, they're here!" He made everybody mix. It was effortless. He just said, "You must meet So-and-so," then shuffled you on to So-and-so.

CHRIS CERF   George didn't categorize people. Of course, he probably noticed what categories they might fit into, but he didn't make a point of it. José Torres is a good example. He was the light heavyweight champion of the world and a real interesting guy, but I'm sure there were members of the Porcellian Club who had never met him (and probably wouldn't have wanted to). George was very comfortable with all people.

ANNE ROIPHE   In '60, '61, George was having parties just about every Friday night, and we were invited, my first husband, Jack Richardson, and I. This was before there was an Elaine's; in fact, George's apartment served at the time as an Elaine's. There were painters, most of whose names I don't remember because painters were not my thing; also they don't talk a lot. There were other writers—Styron, Mailer, Roth, Terry Southern, Doc Humes, etc.—and a few Wall Street and Society people. Were all these people brilliant? Probably not. My own feeling is that most of the time everybody was too drunk to be brilliant. What was going on was social-sexual interaction. It was interaction among intellectuals, yes, but did I ever hear a conversation that I found so absorbing that I never forgot it? I think it was more about one big bull bumping up against another big bull. A lot of joking, a lot of talk about who's the most famous person in the room. Women were not considered full participants in these parties. In fact, despite the sexual overtones, I think the most important intimacies at that time were male to male, not male to female. I'm absolutely not suggesting homosexuality. I'm suggesting something much more serious. It wasn't about sex; this was about love and hate and ambition and other things that get the fires burning, and I don't think that any woman I met there was particularly central to those matters.

RUSTY UNGER Obviously there were exceptions: Some of the women went on to become notable, but that's not why they were there in the first place; they were there because they were hot. On the other hand, these guys were the last gentlemen, most of them, George above all. It was a great thing, that gentlemanly quality. I'd come down the stairs into the crowd and George would catch sight of me and throw up his arms and call out, "Great Russ." Well, that made me feel like a million dollars.

NANCY STODDART I came to New York from Philadelphia, and I guess you could say that George launched me. In retrospect, I see that the only power I had was the way I looked. I mean, it's really sad, in a way, to be a person whose only power is in their looks, unless you find a way to turn it into something else. I was very shrewd about getting entrée. I wanted to get inside, inside all those houses and all those families. So I had a pretty wonderful time, being nobody in particular. Over the years I got myself pretty well educated, and I am pretty interesting to sit next to at a dinner party. If you give me an assignment to get something done, I am a very can-do person. But if I had devoted more energy to that back then, imagine what I'd be doing now—like, ten times more. So I think it's kind of a curse to be a hottie or to be more beautiful than is normal. I think it's good to be nice and pleasant and attractive-looking, but not more. That's what I think.

JULES FEIFFER People were just coming out of the Eisenhower years—the postwar somnolence, the consensual repression that hung around even after McCarthyite repression dissipated. It was almost as if this entire generation of well-educated young men and women had never been told they had First Amendment rights. So what parties like George's did was to allow them safely to let it all hang out, to let it all go, to be explosive. Booze was a great way to let things happen that might not ordinarily happen. You could be, or at least feel, more dangerous, more playful, than you'd ever felt in your life. But George's literary world was part of a general cultural revolt—against conformity, against sexual constraint—but which was also, in the arts, seriously ambitious. There was an excitement at the time that these writers were part of—think of Mailer's "The White Negro," Roth's *Portnoy's Complaint,* Friedman's *A Mother's Kisses,* Heller's *Catch-22.*

RON PADGETT   I remember an article in *New York* magazine about a George Plimpton party. In it was a photograph of me sitting on a couch wearing a suit and tie, holding my son, who must've been nine months or a year old. In those days, if you were a downtown New York poet, you just didn't go uptown to a party with your *baby,* and yet it was perfectly all right at George's. That was George.

IMMY HUMES   Do you remember the famous photo taken at George's with Ralph Ellison, Jonathan Miller, Ricky Leacock, Truman Capote, Willie Morris, Bill Styron, Chandler Brossard? My mother was in it, and Maggie Abbott, and some film producers, Frank and Eleanor Perry. Jack Richardson was in it, and Mario Puzo. It was quite a lineup. Well, all of these writers had signed up as members of Filmwrights Incorporated. Filmwrights Incorporated was another great Doc idea that didn't go anywhere. It was supposed to get writers involved in Hollywood, to get the best of fiction writers working on film scripts in some kind of a cooperative structure. I'm not sure exactly what the structure was, but it was like what United Artists turned into. So with his gift for publicity, Doc put together that extraordinary party at George's apartment. It was just another business thing of Doc's that fizzled out. Nonetheless, I'm told that everybody had a grand old time.

SARAH GAY PLIMPTON   George's parties were intimidating if you didn't know people or you weren't with somebody. I remember those early years in the sixties I just couldn't deal with what was going on. I didn't have a steady boyfriend, and I was always going to the parties alone. It was tough for a girl. I think it's different for a girl. I think it's hard to try and be a star in those circumstances, in those days.

JULES FEIFFER If you liked parties with political people, especially Kennedy people around 1960, you went to Jean Stein's parties. George was an old friend of Jackie's, of course, but Jackie wasn't political in my sense of the word. I don't think the two salons, Jean's and George's, were competitive; I thought they were very complementary. Jean had sit-down dinners, and in a way she had the more famous people. George had the up-and-coming generation, the people you really had a better time with. Jean's parties were fun; I loved being there. But they were fun in the way that sitting next to and talking with powerful people is fun, people after all who would be most cautious about what they had to say around perfect strangers. George's parties were fun for the opposite reason, because no one was on their best behavior.

TEDDY VAN ZUYLEN I thought George's parties were wild. He gave one for some mafioso, and one of these guys came up and said, "Hey, do I know you from somewhere?" and I said, "I don't know," terrified. And he said, "Yeah. Chicago. Aren't you Vito's son?" I said, "No." He said, "Oh, that's too bad. Hey, George, who is this character?" George said, "Well, he's from Europe, Bugsy." "Oh, you're from Europe?" "Yeah, I am. Yes, sir." "Tell me something, do you know any bankers in Europe?" I said, "I have a bank in Europe." "Oh!" he says. "What's your name?" I said, "Teddy." "Teddy? Ted. Big Ted. Now tell me, Big Ted, how would your bank like to get a couple of million dollars coming in, a couple of million smackers? You know, if I bring them over like this, just to have?" I said, "I've never known a Swiss person to refuse ten smackers, so two million must really make quite an impression." "Oh, Big Ted, you're great! You're great! I'm giving a big party in three days down in the Village. You've got to come." I arranged for the two million smackers to go to the bank; I called them up and they said, "Yes, please." Bugsy was delighted, and he said, "Big Ted, when you get Bugsy as a friend, you've really got a friend. Don't forget to come to the party. It starts at one o'clock in the morning. That way we get all the pretty dames from the shows, you see. Before that, nothing is going on anyway." I went, and his place was exactly like a speakeasy. Bugsy came up to me and said,

Cocktail party at George's apartment, 1963. George is seated at left with Maggie Abbott; behind her is Anna Lou Humes. At top, left to right: Jonathan Miller, Gore Vidal, Ricky Leacock, Robert Laskey, and Paul Heller. In background, left to right: Ralph Ellison and Peter Matthiessen. Center: William Styron (seated facing couch with back to camera), Doc Humes (behind Styron to right), Mario Puzo

(leaning against mirror), Jack Richardson (tall man, front, right foreground), Arthur Kopit (foreground, right), Frank Perry (left of Kopit), Eleanor Perry (left of Frank), Arthur Penn (obscured behind Eleanor), and Truman Capote (center, on couch).

© Cornell Capa C/Magnum Photos.

"Hey, Big Ted, are you alone?" I said, "Yeah." And he said, "Oh, don't you like women?" I said, "Sure, I like women." He said, "Pick one out. She's yours for the night." This gorgeous redhead with green eyes, the goddess of autumn, came in—and I looked, and I saw Bugsy's face get very dark, and I said, "No, no, Bugsy, that's your girl. We don't do that in Europe. We respect the other person's property. I will not do it." "Well said," says Bugsy. "She's worth two, so you take two of them. I'll choose them for you." So he brought in two girls, shoved them over to me, and said, "You take care of them. How long are you staying, Big Ted?" "Three days." "You've got them for three days!" Those were George's parties: You never knew what you were going to come across.

NORMAN MAILER Doc Humes and I got into an altercation once, at one of George's parties. This was before he decamped to London with his family. We were about ready to have a fight, and I re-

Norman Mailer, George, and Alice Roosevelt Longworth.
Photograph © Henry Grossman.

member George seizing me from behind in an iron grip that I could not get out of. He wasn't seizing me so that Humes could hit me; quite the contrary, somebody was pulling Humes away— we were being pulled apart. George had great strength in his arms; I remember that, for what it's worth. Because he was around so many people, boxers, football players, who were stronger than him, he never bothered to discuss his strength. But I remember thinking, "Goddammit, that guy is strong."

JOHN GRUEN Jane [Wilson, his wife] gave our parties. Our crowd was less intellectual than George's. We did not have the literary crowd. We had the actors and the painters and the musicians. Betty Bacall and Angela Lansbury and the young Jasper Johns, the young Rauschenberg. Andy Warhol came and brought along his super-stars; Viva came and Joe Dallessandro, who promptly took his shirt off and paraded around with Andy sitting in a corner saying, "Gee, wow." Of course Edie Sedgwick came with her hair all bleached. Later on we had Bernstein, and he would play the piano. George's parties were not any more raucous or full of drink, because we drank and smoked, too. We tried to make out: People were having little intimate talks in corners and might go home together. Always sexy, and of course, we were all gorgeous.

GAY TALESE I led my *Esquire* article on George and *The Paris Review* with the scene at one of his parties. It was a typical Plimpton evening—only made different by the fact that Jackie Kennedy walked in. But aside from that, it could have been any other of a dozen nights. Average Plimpton crowd. You saw the same people there, which was wonderful because there were a lot of them, and they were from downtown, uptown, East Side, West Side, or more faraway places at times. He had that capacity to embrace, or at least give the appearance of embracing, this eclectic gathering of strays and straights and very social people. And yet, in reality, he had a discerning eye. In that apartment, there were two or three steps where you came in, down to where the pool table is now. When Jacqueline Kennedy walked in, as the First Lady, I remember George stood on the third step; and, tall as he was, he could survey from afar, from above the head level of all the people below, clustered in, jammed into the main living room. And as he looked around this room full of all his associates and friends—Styron, Mailer, everybody—I could see the judgmental George. I could see the eyes moving, and he was thinking to himself, "Now I have my friend Jacqueline Kennedy with me here, as a guest in my house: Who am I going to take Jackie over to meet?" He had a choice of a hundred, hundred and twenty people. As he stood on that kind of stage, at the top of those steps, and with all his life— his nighttime life, his private life, his side street life, his main street life, all the people that his personality and his curiosity had drawn to him at different times—all of this spread out before him. Suddenly within a matter of seconds the appearance of the First Lady had prompted him, provoked him, demanded of him that he decide who it was that he was going to introduce to her. And I could see that the long guest list suddenly got very short. I remember one guy he wouldn't introduce Jackie to, and didn't, was Norman Mailer, who was probably the most famous writer in New York at the time. You never knew what the hell Mailer was going to do.

NORMAN MAILER I remember one evening at George's when Jackie came in. Well, in 1961 or 1962, I had written a piece about Jackie's televised broadcast from the White House, her tour of the place. I wrote about how she could have been marvelous but wasn't marvelous enough. Here was this wonderful, marvelous woman, and she hadn't been all she really should have been. It was a pretty mean piece, actually. Anyway, Jackie walked into George's party, and I remember she made a point of talking to Styron for the longest damn time. I was dying. One of the reasons I enjoy talking to you about all this is it's so nice to be eighty-two and have these sorts of meanness long out of me. But I died seeing those two together. And of course Styron enjoyed it!

GAY TALESE People seem to think that my *Esquire* article of '63 extended George's celebrity far beyond 541 East Seventy-second Street, the Racquet Club, Debevoise Plimpton, and a few apartments on the Upper West Side. George was much upset about it, not by the confirmation of his celebrity in a prestigious national magazine, but by certain characterizations of the *Paris Review* crowd as easy, pleasant, handsome, fit, and mostly WASP—in short, upper-class. George's upset took the form of an easy, pleasant, extremely long letter to me, most of it quibbling with inconsequential details of fact. Doc Humes weighed in with a letter almost as long but far more supportive, contrasting the atmosphere of Paris as it actually had been in the mid-1950s—boiling with barely suppressed political tensions and literary hatreds—with the amiable, comfortable coterie gathering around the nascent *Paris Review*. No harm came of this three-sided difference of opinion, but that was George's great gift, wasn't it, to throw sweet-smelling oils on troubled waters.

GEOFFREY GATES Not all of George's parties were at 541. Most notably, the *Paris Review* Revels—money raisers, supposedly for the *Review*—were not. At the first spring Revel for *The Paris Review* at the Village Gate, flushed with vodka, I felt that my duty was to sort of be the bouncer. Bobby Kennedy, Ethel, and their entourage were coming. That word was surely leaked by George. So around the Village Gate, there was just a ring of paparazzi, and as Bobby and his entourage came in, I was waiting, like one of those beefy security people you see in the lobby. I was waiting and eager to please. The paparazzi surged forward, and George noted this: "Geoffrey, they're coming in." He didn't say to do anything, but apparently I stretched my arms out and started going this way and that and knocked them all down. I pushed them back about ten feet into a corner. As they came in, I saw this threat to the integrity of George's guest list, and for some reason, I was inspired to play bodyguard. I didn't really give a shit about the Kennedys. I mean, I knew them, but . . . But see, the Kennedys got safely downstairs, you know, and the paparazzi were shouting.

WALTER SOHIER I was living in Washington during the 1960s, and I saw George a lot there. The Kennedys had a number of dances and parties, and George and I went to one of them, the famous time when Bobby Kennedy supposedly took Gore Vidal's finger and twisted it because Gore was putting his arm around

Jean Kennedy Smith, Jacqueline Kennedy Onassis,
and George, New York, 1971. Photograph by Jill Krementz.

Jackie or something. Everyone was very drunk. Not the president,
but the rest of us. That evening, the president took me around and
showed me the pool downstairs. I remember Lyndon Johnson fell
down when he was dancing with Jackie, and there were all kinds
of funny incidents. Going home, George and I were in a cab with
Ken Galbraith and Gore Vidal. Galbraith was upbraiding Gore,
saying, "Hey, fuckin' faggot." It was very amusing. Nothing personal intended. Very funny. It's funny about George's memory,
though, because I reminded him about that incident five years ago,
and he didn't remember it at all. Then, not long afterward, he
came and stayed with me in Washington for President Kennedy's
funeral. We went to it together.

FAYETTE HICKOX Was he a snob about anything? I think he was
a Kennedy snob. I think he really quite preened himself on knowing that family.

PIEDY LUMET Once we were going to a party in Washington at Bobby Kennedy's house and got stuck in the mud. The speedometer kept going, but we weren't going anywhere. There we were, I in my party dress and George in his black tie, trying to get this car out of a muddy ditch, with the wheels up off the ground. It was hilarious. That was the party where they pushed Arthur Schlesinger into the pool with all his clothes on, and George sang all his St. Bernard's songs: "We do not mind the winter wind so long as football's here, so dribble and kick and block the ball, the game's a good old thing!"

MARION CAPRON There's one point I want to make about George's celebrity. It has to do with his father and his supposedly repressive role in George's life. That may have been true when George was a schoolboy, but by the time I knew them it wasn't true. I knew George's father; in fact, I adored and admired him, and he thought well enough of me to offer to send me to law school. George didn't get pressure from his father; he was not a disappointment to his father. His father thought it was terrific that George was this creature that was foreign to him in a way, but his father rather admired it—probably envied it. That's my take on it. George did all the things that Francis Plimpton certainly never had the time to do, nor was allowed to do, in his rigid upbringing. He was programmed for one thing, and George was left, miraculously, unprogrammed, as were Oakes, T.P., and Sarah.

MAGGIE PALEY Once, sitting in his little office with him, I saw that he was putting in a new address under X in his address book. He said it was his first X: Malcolm X.

FREDDY ESPY PLIMPTON I didn't get involved with George until 1963, the year of Gay Talese's article on him in *Esquire* and the *New Yorker* cartoon of the patient on the operating table rearing up and saying to the surgeon in his mask, "Wait a minute! How do I know you're not George Plimpton?" It was the year, I always thought, when he became an official celebrity.

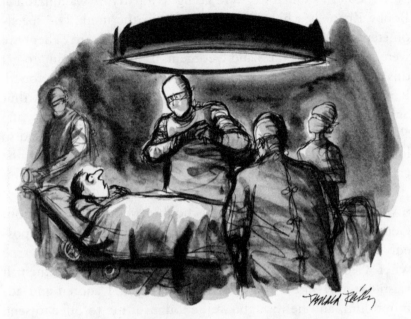

"Wait a minute! How do I know you're not George Plimpton?"

CELEBRITY ATTAINED

GERALD CLARKE   George was very annoyed by the piece Gay Talese wrote for *Esquire*. He was rather bitter about some of the things he said were inaccurate—which I thought was odd because the piece seemed delightful to me and was certainly favorable to George.

WALTER SOHIER   I remember the early sixties when I was first living at 541 East Seventy-second, just below George's place. Sometime around then, Frank Sinatra had an apartment across the way, and when I took a taxi home the driver might ask, "Is that Frank Sinatra's apartment building?" But it wasn't very long before they started asking me, "Is that George Plimpton's building?" He'd gotten into that league.

DAVID AMRAM   It was a strange sort of celebrity he had, in the context of his writing. He was always the observer with a sense of adventure that made him able to be part of any event but not the event itself. He was just like you, the reader. So for him to suddenly become any part of the story himself, as a celebrity, was so bizarre to him. It was such a surprise that he, the amateur among the pros, should become the point of it all. He used to say, "Isn't this amazing? I don't know quite how to handle it."

BOBBY ZAREM   For George it just happened. I don't think he consciously, actively sought publicity. His books and articles were unique. They always got great publicity because the story idea was great, and the publication he got his pieces in would publicize it. He would also create events that would lend themselves to great publicity, like the *Paris Review* Revels. I think he became quite conscious of his image and sometimes had to try and protect it, but his image was so close to being himself, doing just what he loved to do, he didn't have to run after publicity. It just happened.

GEOFFREY GATES   Later, you began to hear people whispering that as a celebrity he sometimes got paid to go to people's parties. Well, they got their money's worth. He entertained people. People paid him to come to events to give some sort of festivity, some sparkle. To my mind, he had a lot to sell—more than the Windsors, anyway. Then, of course, he did those commercials. I've seen a couple of them. There was a terrible one he did late in life about a pool. Some people snooted George about this, but it's not exactly some sort of disgrace. This is the twenty-first century. Image is everything.

JAMES SCOTT LINVILLE   The only time I saw George nervous was when he was about to interview Andy Warhol for the magazine. There was something in Warhol's voice, which had always been so flat, almost inhuman-seeming, but here . . . well, I thought: My God, he really wants George to *like* him. I realized he'd have had to have been hurt by the *Edie* book years before, and here he was talking to him. And George, George clearly did not like him, but he was fascinated by him. I suddenly realized these two guys had in some sense studied each other, for decades, how the other fashioned himself in the media—George of course with his effortlessness, the patrician thing, and Warhol . . . well, whatever he was. It was clear they had each paid attention to how the other had moved through some grid of public awareness.

PETER MATTHIESSEN In those years, when he was first gaining his celebrity, there was something very driven about George. He had to keep on being seen; he couldn't stop. I do not remember him being like that when he first got to Paris, because he wasn't a celebrity then. He deserved to be a celebrity if he wanted to be one; he'd earned it. He certainly put in the hours. But I think that the heart of it, if you trace it all the way, goes back to *The Paris Review.* Without it, what would his celebrity have consisted of? He was a good-looking, charming, very well-mannered son of the WASP establishment. But an awful lot of people fill that category, nothing very unique about it, so there had to be some other element that set him apart.

TIMOTHY DICKINSON George wanted always to be seen to be "George Plimpton"—the whisper that goes through a room, "There's George Plimpton"; the heads turning. George was "George Plimpton" all right, but the question was *conveying* "George Plimpton." There was necessary artifice in injecting "George Plimpton" into the national bloodstream; but this did not involve changing George. Some people, you feel, lose their inner identity precisely by it being consumed by their outer identity. George never felt consumed by his public. He was at a great distance from his public. He was not going to get worn out by his fans. His superb manners were largely a protective mechanism, preserving, in Burke's phrase, "the unbought grace of life." Yes, George had that. It showed, above all, in his ability to live off a public, but neither to despise it nor to owe it more than the basic service.

V.

GEORGE AGOG:
1963–1973

—

To me the most Georgish of expressions that you'd see on his face was when he was looking *agog*. What does that mean? Well, here's the Random House dictionary definition of it—"1. highly excited by eagerness, curiosity, anticipation. 2. In a state of eager desire; excitedly . . . Syn. awe-struck, enthralled . . . MF *en gogues; see A GOGO.*" That's George. A display of skill, an eccentric character, a great deed, a fine folly, a beautiful woman, a splendid paragraph—all left him agog, and he loved them for it.

—*FAYETTE HICKOX*

RIVER GIRL

FREDDY ESPY PLIMPTON I first met George when I was seventeen or eighteen years old. I remember sitting at a table at P. J. Clarke's, in the middle room. There was a round table reserved for VIPs. There were three of us, Bennett Cerf, the founder and publisher of Random House, his son Christopher, whom I'd known all my life, and me. It was the summer I worked at Random House for Jean Ennis, in the publicity department, doing things like babysitting Moss Hart's kids in the park while he was having lunch with Bennett. Anyway, that evening at P. J. Clarke's, I was facing away from the back room, and Bennett was on my left, facing that room, and all of a sudden he looked up and half stood, and from behind me came this tall man wearing a cape. I remember the cape very well. My mouth dropped open, because he was quite an apparition—I mean *very* dashing. Bennett introduced him all around as George Plimpton, and I remember George sort of leaned over to Bennett and conspiratorially, looking at me, said, "Aha, and what do we have here?" I had no clue who he was. I just thought this was some odd, wonderful, romantic figure.

LARRY BENSKY I think George and Freddy met at my good-bye party in the summer of 1963. She was my girlfriend at the time—or rather my soon-to-be-ex-girlfriend. I went to George's parties, but I didn't hang out with him much. I just was sort of doing my life at Random House and rising through the ranks there. And then, sometime in 1963, early in '63, I decided that I didn't want to work at Random House anymore. I wanted to live in Europe. Anyway, I think that's how Freddy and George connected, through me at my good-bye party.

ANNA LOU ALDRICH Before he married Freddy, I always thought there were two sorts of girls in George's life. It was a curious thing about him that you could never tell, at one of his own parties, who his girl was—if indeed he had one that evening. He was the host; there was no hostess, and never would be. But in the early days, the fifties and sixties, you would see him out often enough with someone who was probably his date. I thought of these women as George's "Society girls" because you knew them from the social gossip columns—Nan Kempner, Candice Bergen, Jane Fonda, Jackie, Kathy Ainsworth. Whether there was anything sexual going on there, I never knew. But with the other sort of girl—like Marion Capron, Maggie Paley, Freddy—we all knew that sex was part of it. I thought of them as the "river girls" because that's where the sex went on, presumably—at his apartment by the East River. Freddy of course eventually made the leap from river girl to wife, but how she did that was one of the great mysteries.

Freddy Espy and George.
Photograph © Henry Grossman.

FREDDY ESPY PLIMPTON   The second time I saw George was when Larry Bensky was going to Europe—eventually to manage the *Review.* I was Bensky's girlfriend at the time. There was this huge good-bye party for him; the whole publishing world was there. I was on the balcony, having had quite a few drinks, and was feeling a little maudlin, when out comes this man who looks familiar to me, this very tall, handsome man. George had called several times after that first time we'd met at P. J. Clarke's, but I didn't go out with him. I had read that Gay Talese piece in *Esquire,* in 1963. I'd fallen madly in love with him; but when I read that piece, I thought, "Oh God, here's a guy who's full of himself, and full of shit, and I really don't want much to do with him, because I can tell he's a bad one to focus on." My father knew George and really wanted me to go out with him, and I remember how stubborn I was about saying, "No, no, no. I really don't want to go out with him; he's a snob, famous, rich, you know. I don't want to go out with him, I'll have my heart broken." So anyway, there we were on this balcony. It was a little bit cold. I said some stupid thing like "I'm going to miss Bensky so much that I should jump off this ledge right now!" George said, "I know a better way down," and he took me from the party. Waiting downstairs was a car, and he asked me where I lived, and I told him, and he took me home. He got my telephone number and said, "I'll call you." Now, how many times have I heard that? But he did.

HARRY MATHEWS   It seemed evident to a lot of people why Freddy would have liked to be with George, but it wasn't very clear why George would have liked to be with Freddy. Freddy was very glamorous. I found myself looking at her legs a lot. But there were many good-looking women around. I felt that she was frail somehow and that this touched him in some way. She didn't look frail. She was dazzling. But I sensed that there might be some kind of vulnerability in her that brought out an otherwise undetected older brother in George.

CHRIS CERF   Freddy Espy was my very, very good friend. She and her three sisters lived one road away from me in Mt. Kisco. They were all attractive, Freddy by far the most so, and they were all flirts, every teenager's dream and nightmare. I had a crush on Joey as much as on Freddy, and Joey was the first girl I ever kissed. My father [Bennett Cerf] had nicknames for them. Freddy was Miss Upper Plate, Joey was Miss Lower Plate, and Mona was known as Bite. He knew them well. Whenever there was any drama in the family, and there was a lot of drama, they'd all come and talk to my parents. Freddy was delightful but there always seemed to be a streak of trouble in her life. This made her all the more lovable to me, because she seemed so vulnerable. But there was a dark side of Freddy, always.

FREDDY ESPY PLIMPTON How he found me, to invite me on our first date, I'll never know. I was working for a photographer, Jacques Simpson, as a stylist. We were shooting in a bowling alley in New Haven, doing men's pants for Sears, Roebuck catalogs. I had to pin their crotches, so the models were standing spread-eagle, with this bowling alley going straight through their legs. A phone rang in a booth in the corner. It rang and rang until finally one of the assistants picked it up and said, "Freddy, it's for you." It was George. He said, "Can you get back to Manhattan to have dinner with the president this evening? We *must* be there before the president arrives." This was at four in the afternoon. He said, "I'll make a reservation for you to fly into Newark, and then I'll send a car, and you can go home and change." This guy's got the whole evening figured out. It was just amazing. So I said bye to the bowling alley, got into the cab, flew from New Haven to Newark, was picked up by this limo and taken to my stepmother Louise's house, who had run out to get me something to wear for dinner with the president. And George and I managed to get there ahead of the president—I was a complete nervous wreck. The dinner was at Jean and Steve Smith's. It was a very small party, and the president was with his favorite friends, smoking cigarillos and being utterly charming. George seemed delighted that I was there. I was so nervous, all I could think of to do, in talking to the president, was to ask him how to do things, like "How do you remember names?" He said he asked himself, on meeting someone, who or what he or she reminded him of and later remembered their name from that. He went around the room, pointing out everybody, and said, "Okay, her name is . . . because she reminds me of blah, blah, blah." George just left me with the president and went over and talked to the other people. After dinner we went down to Raffles, and the president was very happy because he had eluded the Secret Service. Now it was just about escaping, going to a fun place. George and I got up and danced. The president just watched because his back was not in good shape that night. I really can't remember how it all ended, but I do remember getting into a cab with him and going around the block and up Madison Avenue and back to Fifth Avenue, dropping the president off at Fifth, at the back entrance. It was early October, I remember, because the president died a month later.

MAGGIE PALEY Freddy came on the scene gradually, as I remember it. There were always a lot of beautiful women at these parties, and which one would stay was always just a matter of who would outlast the others. I saw these other women. I didn't know who they were, but I imagine a lot of them would have been happy to stay. I of course assumed that George had invited me to stay. But when Freddy came on the scene, things changed. She dawned slowly. He and I were still having an affair, and he was still seeing other women. I remember one afternoon, I was there in the apartment, and we were in the middle of something. Freddy came in and knocked on the door, and then just walked in. I guess she wasn't being paid enough attention. Anyway, she stomped out and George went running after her. I thought, "That's the kind of thing that I would never be able to do," but Freddy did it, and it worked. He moved her in next door.

FREDDY ESPY PLIMPTON One of our best, weirdest memories of that time before we were married was being robbed. We were constantly robbed by this guy who would come in from downstairs, then open the bedroom door—which was the whole upstairs living room area—he would open the bedroom door in the early morning, always, around four. If you were awake—George and I were usually dead drunk asleep, but sometimes we would have just gotten home—in would come Mr. Peterson, as we called him. The first time Mr. Peterson arrived, he stole a Universal Genève watch with all kinds of diamonds on it that George's family had given me as a gift. I put it on my bedside table and went to sleep. That morning it was gone. We didn't know anything that night. The next time, we did know that there was someone in this shaft of light, entering the dark bedroom; this hesitant person standing there. George sat up and said, "Who goes there?! What do you want?" The guy said, "I'm looking for Mr. Peterson"— hence our name for him. George got up out of bed, ran after the guy in his underwear, ran down Seventy-second Street for two blocks, actually climbed up inside a building to the roof, and Mr. Peterson had already jumped to the next roof. The thing about Mr. Peterson was that he always came anyway. Those were the days when I was trying to get George to be someone; you know, to buy a pair of Gucci shoes. Mr. Peterson must have been the same shoe size, because every time I'd buy him a pair, he would steal them. Two times he stole them, and George said, "I'm not supposed to have a pair of Guccis." Frank Sinatra wanted to protect us from Mr. Peterson. I had met him just after he broke up with Mia Farrow. Chris Cerf's parents asked me to come and be Frank's date at their house. Afterwards, we all went out to a nightclub, and Frank took me home, and it turned out that he lived at the end of Seventy-second Street, across from us. He got out of the limousine and walked me to the door, and I found I didn't have my keys. He said, "Not a problem. Is your window open?" I said, "Probably." So he went up the fire escape to the third floor, goes in my window, and opens the door. Later I told him the story about Mr. Peterson, and Sinatra started coming over to visit us at strange times of the night. He gave us a gun to protect ourselves with. I didn't like having this gun around. It was in a certain drawer for years and years. One day, I got paranoid and threw it into the East River. I'll always wonder whose fingerprints were on that gun. I just wonder who had handled it. It would have been interesting to know.

PETER DUCHIN I was really fond of George, and I was in awe of some of his qualities—his energy and cheerfulness and his support of the *Review* all those years—but I never thought of him as being really serious about women. I thought that he was far more curious than serious about women. And the women I admired in the world couldn't take him seriously, either. They would joke about the idea of even sleeping with him, not to mention marrying him. They found him to be a sort of remote, slightly shy, but charming curiosity. And there was something awfully comical about George. I don't know what it was. Maybe it was a power thing, personal power, or his lack of it. A friend of mine knew George very well, and Bee and Freddy, too. He told me that he thought it never would have worked, the love affair between George and Bee, because George lacked *command*, and Bee needed that. Whereas with Freddy, their love did work in a way, because Freddy was *all* command, a sort of coiled spring of sexual command, and George found that irresistible. He needed it; *they* needed it as a couple, and she was the one who happened to have it.

DREAM JOBS AT THE *REVIEW*

JED HORNE   It was not long after all the magazine operations moved to New York in 1973. I must have been almost twenty-four. I had bailed out of a graduate program at Harvard in philosophy and was driving a cab in Boston to supplement my scrivener's wages working for an alternative weekly called the *Phoenix*. I came down to New York and dropped in on the *Paris Review* office because a friend of mine was working there. And there was George, very cordial and chatty and inquiring as to who I was and what on earth I was doing there. He pointed towards a stack of manuscripts and said maybe I ought to read a few of them while I was there. And so I read some manuscripts; and later it developed that if I was going to stick around and read some more manuscripts, maybe I would need a place to live, and George said, why didn't I take So-and-so's apartment since the whole building was going co-op, and there were some vacant spaces that hadn't been grabbed, and if I wanted to, I could rent this apartment for about a year or two, for fifty-eight dollars a month. So I said, "Fine, I'll take it." Of course, I had no furniture. George said I should take John's bed, John being John Chancellor, the newscaster for NBC at that time who had walked away from the co-op opportunity, leaving me with manuscripts to read in George Plimpton's study and my own little apartment. It had a small fire escape perch from which I could see the East River and smoke my cigarettes and think poetic thoughts and be a New York writer on East Seventy-second Street.

JONATHAN DEE   *The Paris Review* figured, in the imagination of a bookish college student like I was, as a kind of mecca. I had no idea how small an operation it actually was—it might have been in the Chrysler Building for all I knew. George was part of the allure, as a writer and also, I suppose, as a celebrity. But maybe the biggest draw, for those who wanted to be part of what Terry Southern used to call the "quality lit game," was just the opportunity to live in New York, not because there was any great advantage to it but because you knew you could at least surround yourself with kindred spirits there.

BEN RYDER HOWE   The first thing you noticed, coming to work at the *Review* office, was George's block, the last before you hit the East River. That block was incredible, with red brick sidewalks and, down at the end of it, his building, the smallest, black as coal. You'd think it was a tenement, not a warren of small luxury apartments. The street scene was bizarre, too. You had all those cancer treatment centers, with people coming there from all over the world. I remember seeing a Saudi sheikh on the promenade who was between chemo treatments, and he was out there smoking a cigarette. Or you would see someone who had just come out of Sotheby's, at the corner of York, with a two-thousand-dollar egg cup or something. Toward the river, opposite George's building, were huge, ugly apartment buildings, outside of which you might see powerful people screaming into their cell phones as they paced up and down the street. You'd see people who were obviously having secret rendezvous down on the promenade. George's building had four entries, 527 to 541, the last of which, with his apartment, gave right onto the river. It was right there under the promenade, practically at your feet, narrow as a sluice at that point, with big ships squeezing past each other between Roosevelt Island and the FDR Drive. Sometimes, at about four o'clock in the afternoon,

when you were just completely delirious from reading all the unsolicited manuscripts, you felt like one of those ships spinning on
the tide.

SUSAN MORGAN   Whenever I was there, the atmosphere of
George's apartment was a bit scuffed, unself-conscious, something
good against something decrepit. The little crummy bridge table
was always set up, and there was always a tear in the carpet, where
you thought you were going to take a header into the couch when
you walked across the room. It was a WASPy kind of thing: You
don't have something that's shiny new, you just have it because
that's what you've always had and this is perfectly good so why
should you get something new? George had very little visual sense.

BEN RYDER HOWE The *Review* office was on the ground floor,
with windows giving onto the tiny overlook of the river. There was
an intercom to George's office on the second floor, and underneath the intercom, if you looked, there was all this random scribbling on the wall, years and years of scribbling by generations of
staffers doodling while they answered George's buzz from above.
The perfectly centered fan hung over the center table, which was

Photograph by Louis Mackall.

covered with stacks of magazines and all the manuscripts that we were either reading or not reading. The building smelled old, and we had to leave when the oil truck came, you noticed the dead vermin and the cockroach traps in the cellar underneath us. The managing editor was always bumping his or her chair up against an intern's chair or two interns' chairs. There might be six or seven staffers in that room, or there might be just you. George's bicycle hung from the ceiling over some staffer's head. What George was saying, in a way, was: This is your training ground, and later you'll go on to be a big celebrity as an editor, or as a writer, or something else. That was how you were supposed to look at your experience there.

STEPHEN GAGHAN   In Kentucky, where I came from, nobody read. I mean, I was known as the kid who read books. It's kind of threatening, you know. Adults who don't read don't like young people who read. But it's through books that you feel this connection to the wider world. I didn't know how to pronounce many words because I'd only seen them printed; I'd never heard anyone use them. So you're that person, and then this guy Plimpton opens his arms to you and says, "All right, you seem like a bright young man: Here's an opportunity, what are you gonna do with it? I'm not gonna tell you what to do with it; there's no manual." There was time to write, and a social network so that when you're done writing you have somewhere to go and you didn't feel so alone. People were talking about the same things and cared about the same things.

LARISSA MACFARQUHAR   I don't know where I got this notion— probably from my parents—but I thought that once you graduated from college, life got very, very staid, and you had to wear a certain kind of clothing, and you had to attend work for certain hours of the day, and everything got very serious. A job at the *Review* could not have been more calculated to drive these notions out of your head. I think one of the first things you learn when you get there as an intern is that grown-up life is so much more fun than you had anticipated. I was hired on a beautiful, early fall day. It was very warm, and I'd worn a silk wraparound skirt to my interview,

Paris Review office: George's bicycle and
staffer Fiona Maazel.
Copyright by Sally Wiener Grotta.

and I had been hired on the spot. I was elated. Later I was walking
home along Second Avenue and felt this swishing feeling at my an-
kles, and I thought, "The trash in New York. . . ." Meanwhile my
skirt had completely untied itself and I was walking down the
street without clothes. That just seemed like part of the day. It
seemed portentous of the future.

HALLIE GAY WALDEN I was a Kentucky girl who'd just graduated from Dartmouth with a degree in English and a thesis on Virginia Woolf. I can't remember how I heard about the job, but I

was a devoted reader of the *Review.* I applied and got an interview. It was in George's living room. I was in a comfortable chair by the window, and he walked in, and I thought I had seen the most graceful, elegant man ever.

DAVID EVANIER   George called me from a plane and accepted one of my stories—I think it was "Cancer of the Testicles"—so of course that was very, very thrilling for me. He published three stories of mine very quickly, that one and "The One-Star Jew," which was in *Best American Short Stories* later and became the title of my book. So, you know, I was thrilled. It was a dream come true. I began to sort of hang out a little bit at the magazine, and I told him I was good at the slush pile. He said, "Why don't you read some manuscripts for us," so I started doing that. Gradually that turned into a kind of a job. He sent me a check for two hundred and fifty dollars a month, which, you know, I was a struggling writer and it helped. And then, gradually, he made me a fiction editor. I never really worked there. I basically worked at home.

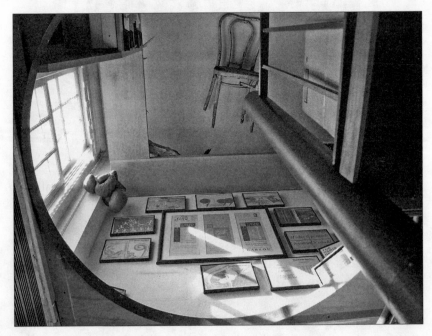

The *Review* office, up from the basement.
Copyright by Sally Wiener Grotta.

JANET NOBLE I first worked for George doing layout on a huge anniversary issue. I had been going through a terrible, terrible separation and divorce. So whenever I got to the *Review* office, which was only when there was an issue to put out, I was in a state of high anxiety. George would come down—always, like, in his socks, padding down. He was very tall and he took up whatever space there was left in that tiny office, and I remember at one point thinking that it was like being in the pocket of his gray flannel pants or something. I was never anxious for long.

BUDDY BURNISKE Max Steele, George's old friend from Paris, introduced us when George came to Chapel Hill to speak, and I told him how much I admired the *Review*. He said, "Why don't you come up and help us out?" I was at that point in my life, very much smitten with literature, when to be able to go down to the basement beneath the *Review* office and find all those old issues, I felt like I was in some secret vault at the Smithsonian. All this stuff was just kind of lying around. It was very exciting to be that close to what had been sort of the epicenter of so much good literature over a quarter of a century. Also, when I was there, I think T. Coraghessan Boyle's first story was published. And I definitely remember [Dallas Wiebe's] "Night Flight to Stockholm," because I just thought that was one of the funniest things I'd ever read. And the other thing that went on that summer was that goofy little interview with J. D. Salinger, where the woman from, I think, Louisiana went up to New Hampshire and interviewed him. Now stop a minute and think about what I just described. I was only there for, like, three months. T. Coraghessan Boyle's first story, Dallas Wiebe's "Night Flight to Stockholm," which I've seen anthologized, and Betty Epps interviewing J. D. Salinger. That's a pretty good run, and that was one summer.

ELIZABETH GAFFNEY When it came time to select the summer interns—or editors, for that matter—George certainly did not want the ugly ones. One time, when we had a really brilliant, dykey, purple-haired summer intern who was terrific—she was so smart, so well-read—numerous times over that summer, I heard him say, "Why don't we just fire her and get some charming young girl from Harvard. She's no good. She's no use to us." He couldn't have been more wrong. He just couldn't see her, because she was overtly lesbian and had purple hair.

MARJORIE KALMAN   It was a pretty WASPy crowd downstairs, but I never felt, ever, ever, ever, in this office, in twenty-five years, that anybody was made to feel uncomfortable because of their ethnicity. George and Remar came in one day after having lunch with Lee Radziwill and asked what the Yiddish word is for penis. "Schlong," I think, was the word they were looking for. They were very drunk and had obviously gone down and had a good time. God knows what the conversation was.

ELIZA GRISWOLD   Was he classist? You're not going to get a WASP to talk about class, but I'll give it a try. First of all, anybody who's going to work at the *Review* probably had some alternative source of income, because you got paid nothing. The idea was, you were getting paid in experience. So the staff came to him selfselected, in terms of their parents' ability to pay their rent, but also in terms of class. I would have hated to come into that office as an outsider—at the age we were working there it was pretty cliquish, who knew who, who'd had what experiences, a cultural shorthand I wouldn't have recognized then as class, but that's what it is.

BEN RYDER HOWE   The *Review* might have been defined as essential reading by *The Preppy Handbook;* it was the magazine for Biff with his pink Izod shirt—not the best packaging for any decade after the 1950s. I found that the staff had kind of a pathology about class. You'd see that famous photo in George's apartment, the one with Jackie O and everybody else in it, and there's only one black guy in the room, James Baldwin, and he's studying everybody. It's a black-and-white picture, and you would suppose it was an age that had passed, but it hadn't passed. There was one black guy working at the magazine for a little while. He was an intern, and he left in disgust because, at a party, someone asked him to refill their drink. That was a problem, and it had to at least be acknowledged: that in the magazine's DNA were a lot of high-

class genes, that it was a product of a particular class, with a particular desire to get at a certain goal that they thought was noble.
That had to be acknowledged. We couldn't be *McSweeney's.*

MONA SIMPSON   I think I was the first middle-class person to
work there. I worked there during graduate school, and afterwards
when I started working there more, I asked for health insurance.
This was a preposterous idea to George. He said, "Well, if you get
sick, just give me the bill and I'll pay it." And I'm sure that's true—
he would have. But I kept at it, and ultimately he did actually give
us health insurance.

OLIVER BROUDY   George didn't really understand people in
terms of class or any sort of sociological or, especially, psychological generalizations. With me it was, "Oh, here comes that computer genius! He'll know exactly what to do!" It was just a matter
of some little quirk on his computer and fiddling a wire, but I fixed
it and that made it very easy for him to apprehend me. With Steve
Clark he sensed someone he didn't have to explain certain matters
to, like boarding schools, trust funds, the virtues of *grass* tennis
courts, but I felt like I had to hold George's hand a little bit in
helping him to figure out who I was. Of course, most people re-
quire premapped avenues of apprehension to arrive at judgments,
but George's were peculiar: They were differentiated by skills, by
what you were good at, preferably *really* good at. Because only in
this way could you answer to what I always thought was a deep
need of his, which was to admire. Admiration was the key, the admiration of a skill, almost always a skill of action. George's world
was all act. So Steve played tennis really well; I knew all about
computers. Not that he *fixed* you in those skills. For example, this
photographer came once to photograph George, some random
girl from Columbia. She took her pictures of George, and then she
came downstairs and I started talking with her. She was really cute.
George had probably felt the stirring of some kind of a prurient
interest in her, too. But I ended up having a little fling with this
chick; and thereafter, that was something George could easily understand, something that he constantly referred to, adding it to the
computer bit.

ELIZABETH GAFFNEY I had just been hired on as a staff editor when George sent me to Germany to interview Günter Grass. I was very raw at that point, and it took a lot of faith to send me off to interview a Nobel laureate in a foreign language. Later, I did Lorrie Moore and Andrea Barrett. Ben Howe and I did David McCullough. I did John Guare. Those are all great interviews, and I was very proud of them, but it meant a lot to me that George thought they were good.

SUSANNAH HUNNEWELL I remember—this is so terrible—when I first started there, I was put to work copyediting a story by a future international best-selling author with a foreign-sounding name. I'd heard of him, but I'd never read him, didn't know anything about him, and so I thought that the story was a translation. This is so *embarrassing*. I was going through it, and there were all these grammar problems; I'd been to a very good girls' school in Boston, and I'd had an excellent grammar education, so I made all these suggestions and sent it back. Binky Urban, the famous agent, called and was furious. I said to her, "Well, I'm sorry, it must be a problem with the translation." She said, "Translation! It's not translated!" That was really humiliating. Those were the sorts of circumstances when George would have to step in. He never got mad, though.

ROWAN GAITHER People used to call the *Review* fairly regularly wanting George to meet foreign writers. As his assistant I answered the phone, and nine times out of ten they were people I'd never heard of. So I came up with this gatekeeping idea that George would only meet people from countries with beachfront. Because I figured you wanted to be in a situation where, wherever you go in the world, when you get there you can call from the airport and say, "We met at *The Paris Review,* can I come to your beach house?" So one day someone called and said that Haruki Murakami wanted to meet George. And I thought, "Wow, the entire country is beachfront properties! Send him over!" I had no idea who he was. So this very nice Japanese gentleman appeared at the door wearing bright red Keds sneakers. I took him upstairs. I don't think George was there. So I was struggling to find anything to say. I said, "Ah, well, I was reading *The New Yorker* the other day and there was this great story written by this Japanese author. . . ." And I told him this whole story, and he listened to the whole thing and he said, "Why, yes, I wrote it." And I said, "Oh, you did? Well, I read another one, too, in the *Atlantic.*" And I described that whole story, and he listened very quietly and he said, "Yes, I wrote that, too." So I said, "Thank you for coming."

BEN RYDER HOWE The slush pile would arrive every day; you could hear it, the big thud as the duffel bag hit the floor just outside the office. After a while it was depressing to go through it, because you realized that the average person submitting slush can't even write a covering letter, let alone a short story, but it shapes your values as a reader, because what you realize is, this is the great game, to find the undiscovered champ. Constantly, our interns would be saying, "I found something! I found something!"

JEANNE MCCULLOCH There was a sense that we were all on the cusp of something. And there was George, lending his house and his magazine and his excitement to this project. It was palpable. He was having everyone's first book party. I remember one party, when *Bright Lights, Big City* had just come out, and our whole generation of writers and editors was there. Bill Styron went up to Jay McInerney, shook his hand, and said, "That was an extraordinary book." I saw Jay's head spin, and I thought, "He'll never come off this spin."

BUDDY BURNISKE Everyone thinks of the *Review* as these golden years in Paris, but I think George did an amazing job of keeping a lot of that alive for a long time back in New York. I was twenty years old when I was there, and it seemed like every week something was happening that could be life-changing. We went to the premiere of the film *Hopscotch,* and then we went from that to Elaine's. The room was just full of Jerzy Kosinskis, or Walter Matthaus, or whoever. Or Candice Bergen falling back on a picnic blanket where Fayette and I were seated with John Seabrook, out in the Hamptons. And it's kind of like, "How do I explain this to people back home, that Candice Bergen is rolling around and falling back on our laps here at a Fourth of July picnic?" That wasn't the world I'd come from.

LARISSA MACFARQUHAR I guess a lot of people left to be fiction writers or to work in publishing, but I decided I wanted to go into magazine journalism, and George was incredibly helpful. He called people up and said, "Talk to this girl! Terribly nice girl!" I ended up going to *Spy* through Nelson Aldrich. He called up Nelson, who I knew of slightly anyway, because he knew my mother slightly, and his daughter Liberty and I went to school together. George called up Nelson and said, "Interview Larissa!" Anyway, I interviewed with them, and Terry McDonell, who impressed me greatly by smoking during our interview, and smoking menthols of all things. Nelson didn't have a job for me, but he called up Jim Collins, who he knew because Jim had dated his stepdaughter, Immy Humes, and Jim was at *Spy,* so I went to talk to Jim. George was incredibly nice. He was recommending me for the post of dogsbody, but paid dogsbody. I wouldn't have gotten the job without him. Apart from everything else, I had never even heard of *Spy.*

ANNE FULENWIDER When I got there, I wanted to be a magazine editor. I remember Elizabeth and Elissa asking me, "Where do you see yourself in ten years?" I said I wanted to be a magazine editor, and it was as if I'd said, "I want to be a businessman." It was so not what everyone else there was doing; but now, Dana Goodyear, Eliza Griswold, Andy Bellin, all ended up being nonfiction writers, which I think is a testament to George, because he made the world, the actual world, look like so much fun.

ELISSA SCHAPPELL George was very upset when I left to start up *Tin House* [a literary quarterly]. I asked his opinion about whether or not we should do it, and I made the mistake of talking to him about it at parties, after I'd had a few drinks. Then when the magazine came out, he was so mad. He said to me, "You're putting *The Paris Review* in the gutter. How can you do this? I can't believe you would betray me like this." He wrote me a letter that upset me so much. I had just lost my father, and I felt like

George was my literary father. I said, "*Tin House* exists, in part, because of you, because you're so inspiring, because of what you created, and because we love what you've done. This is something you can take pride in. You have a piece of this." He wrote me an apologetic note that said, "I love you, and I don't mean to upset you." So then we had this really tearful talk about the magazine, what he was doing and what I was doing. He said, "I go down into the office and see those kids, and I don't know who any of them are. Would you ever come back?" It was touching. In retrospect, if we hadn't both been drinking and emotional, he might not have said that, but at the time, it meant an awful lot. He still refused to call the magazine by its proper name. He'd say, "So what's up at *Tin Shack*?" and I'd say, "Well, we're coming for you, George."

TRIANGULAR DESIRE

FREDDY ESPY PLIMPTON I went out with George from 1963 to 1968, pretty much from our dinner date with the president until we were married. At first he found me an apartment in the same block of apartments as his, at 527 East Seventy-second Street. Then, after about a year or so, I moved in with him at 541 for about three years before we got married. We actually spent more time alone together than most people would think. He would write, or we would play backgammon or just rest up. We had quiet nights at home. We were living together, but we were not married. We were free spirits. And he was traveling a lot. I took it for granted that he would go out with women at every port, and he took it for granted that I would see people when he was gone.

CHRIS CERF Freddy is a very complicated woman, with a lot of demons; always has had. Adorable, and smart as hell, and gorgeous. She's a little bit revisionist these days, thinking sometimes that it should have worked with George in a way that maybe it couldn't have. She couldn't change George, but she was pretty hard on him, trying to change him. On the other hand, I'm not sure that it would have made her any happier if she'd succeeded. It seems to me that Freddy may have been more needy for control than needy for devotion, and the need for control tormented her. Sure, she re-sented George's being away so much, but it was more like a power thing, perhaps, than an emotional need to be with him. Freddy had millions of friends, too.

FREDDY ESPY PLIMPTON No, it wasn't only when he was trav-eling that we'd see other people. But what happened when he was around was really weird. I'd have dates. And most of these forays began at the apartment at 541, where, sometimes, he'd be. So this guy would come to pick me up, and while I was getting ready he'd wait in the living room, and then George would come out of his office and greet the fellow as only George could: "Oh, how do you do?" or, "Well, hello, John, would you like a drink?" And then he'd sit down and they'd start chatting each other up and having a good time. Sometimes George would even change his plans and come along. I mean, it really pissed me off. It was a very, very odd sort of relationship. There was no jealousy on either side as long as we weren't doing things for the sake of upsetting the other one, but just doing things as they came up. It was almost as though George were my dear uncle. He certainly didn't act like a jealous boyfriend. In this way, I gradually became a sort of link be-tween George and these other interesting and attractive men—and we all became great friends.

CHARLES MICHENER I think that for George the threesomes were a way of spreading—that is, diluting—intimacy. I don't think George was a person comfortable with one-on-one intimacy. He also *liked* an audience. For a great performer, two are better than one. I can see George being more comfortable in the company of men than of women. I'm not aware of any close women friends— or close men friends, for that matter. I think the idea of the three-some, in the *Jules et Jim* sense, is a very compelling fantasy for a lot of people. Freddy was beautiful, and perhaps he basked in the light of having another man finding her beautiful as well or lusting after her. I know a lot of women who'd love to be with two men. It's a very common fantasy. I've seen it more with women than with men. It's kind of a wonderful fantasy on some level.

NANCY STODDART There was a period, after he and Freddy were living together, when I would see a lot of both of them. One particularly funny night when I was staying with them, Freddy and I went out and picked up some really cute young guys, like college kids, and we brought them back and pretended that George was our father. And then, all of a sudden, all the air was taken out of our big practical joke because they all knew who George was, and they gathered around him like, you know, to listen to his stories of *The Paris Review* or stories of him doing this, that, and the other. It wasn't much of a stretch for me to pretend that George was our father. I always thought of him very much as a father figure. He gave me my wedding, actually. I mean, my own parents had very little involvement in it. And before that he was always trying to get me involved with his friend Teddy Van Zuylen, with whom, in fact, I did get involved before my marriage. Maybe George appeared to be kind of a lech to a few girls, but he was extraordinarily discreet about his sex life. I certainly didn't know about it. I don't even want to think about it. The idea of George having sex, just makes me kind of . . . eeewww, it's almost like the idea of my father having sex.

MARJORIE KALMAN George was there and cared about Freddy, but you couldn't expect him to always be home for dinner. He had a big life of his own. To make someone change was hard, if not impossible. I think George thought, "What do you want from me? You have a great life. You can do whatever you want." He had this big life, and he wasn't going to give it up for anyone. But he didn't want you to be hurt for it, either. It was neglect, but it wasn't a deliberate neglect. I always thought that he needed someone like a professional businesswoman. They'd have their life, and he had his life, and then you met up for vacation or when it's open school week or something.

PETER DUCHIN George would have loved to be looked at—the voyeur being watched. For instance, long before he was married, when I was seeing Minnie Cushing and he would take out a girl he called "the Bip," we would double-date. It would get into a "necking on the beach" kind of thing. It was no orgy—we were quite far apart—but I think he enjoyed our being there, nearby. I think he needed something to stimulate him. Whereas I could see Mr. and Mrs. Plimpton just shutting off the light and doing that which WASPs did in the twenties, a sort of quick and hasty coupling. But with George, you know he's not going to turn off the light and do that. You know, it's got to be a show.

GAY TALESE   In the seventies, America was the most sexually permissive place in the history of the world. It was quite amazing. It was the era of *Oh! Calcutta!*—full-frontal nudity on the Broadway stage, in movies, in magazines. There was *Screw,* and the advertising in *Screw,* but even in *The New York Review of Books,* with those little personal ads. It was really a remarkable time. I did the best I could to see it, enjoy it, and write about it. *Thy Neighbor's Wife* is my story, my reportage, my war-front coverage of the wayward life that was the indulgence of many, many people, in private and in public. George never wrote about it. Mostly fiction writers wrote about it. Philip Roth, John Updike. Updike is the most literary, pornographic, lyrical writer we've had—it's amazing what he got away with. He can thank pornographers for that. I've always felt that mainstream publishers and their writers owed a debt to the so-called smut peddlers who challenged the obscenity laws in court and ultimately triumphed in having these laws overturned.

PAMELA DRAPER   I met George a long, long time before I ever went out with him. It was around 1970, when I was about twenty. I met him at a party at Jim Moran's. Jim Moran was an eccentric guy, extraordinarily creative, very much like George, passionate about books and passionate about women. I'd come to his party and was wandering around this vast apartment on West End Avenue, jam-packed with people. I wandered into the study, and there was this lone man sitting behind a desk, reading a book. He said, "Hello, I'm George Plimpton," and I said, "I'm Pamela Draper," and that was the beginning of a long relationship—thirty years or more. He was having trouble with Freddy almost from the beginning. I don't know how I knew that; he certainly didn't talk about it. He opened up about his enthusiasms—literature, or music, or women in general. He could be very forthcoming about those subjects. But his sadder thoughts and feelings he didn't often express. And when you did so yourself, it was uncomfortable for him. He had a very New England upbringing. My father was the same way.

WILLIAM BECKER I don't think George had affairs of the heart, as they say. What he did do, as I did, was to go to orgies. They were called "scenes" and were presided over by a big, bearded fellow by the name of Jim Moran, one of the great characters of our time. George was much taken by Moran, and not just because of the orgies. The man was pure mischief, a lord of misrule who managed to make money at it. He was a publicist, specializing in doing crazy stunts that would get lots of news coverage for his clients. For example, when David Merrick produced *Look Back in Anger*, Moran planted a woman in the first row and had her climb up onstage and attack Jimmy Porter. It made all the papers, and the show ran forever. His orgies were informed by the same careful planning and imagination as his stunts. They happened about once a month, usually on weekends, starting at eight o'clock sharp, after which no one would be allowed up the elevator. He invited the men, whom he knew personally or were vouched for by someone he knew personally. Each of them had to bring a woman, and he planned for a week or so to be sure that she wasn't a loony or a hooker, that she was a real person. Which in fact they all were— the sort of women you might meet at Elaine's or at one of George's parties. His apartment was huge—ten rooms or more, more than enough for the ten to twenty people he invited. One of them was entirely filled with costumes—what would an orgy be without costumes? Group sex, I suppose. My costume was a monk's robe with a big cross in front, George's was that of a French country priest, with a little hat. Moran insisted on dressing all the girls himself. Drinks were available, but I don't recall anyone doing any serious drinking. No food. The rules of engagement, so to speak, were clear. You were allowed to approach anybody you wanted, but if she wanted to go off with someone else, you were not allowed to pursue her. I went to some other parties where there were people who were just dreadfully aggressive; they would push you off some girl and jump on. One fellow who did that later became a well-known American diplomat. At Moran's, things were more civilized. I remember one time when he himself was in a bedroom, down on his knees giving oral sex to a girl, when some noisy people came down the hall, and he called out to them in a booming voice, "If you want to laugh and joke or whatever, the place to do that is the library, but this room is my church, and I am at worship." And back he went to his prayers. Actually, though, there was very little at these parties to satisfy the hard-core voyeur or exhibitionist. George was of course a bit of both—New Journalist that he was—but privacy was to be had at Jim's. The orgiastic stuff was a matter of glimpses and glances, opportunity and variety, all in one place. It wasn't Plato's Retreat, a pay-as-you-come public orgy in the Ansonia Hotel, where you had three hundred people fornicating in a huge room all covered with mattresses. In any event, I always thought that George considered the "scenes" another of the many sports that he pursued.

FAYETTE HICKOX When I think about George going to orgies, I think of him not as leering with his tongue dangling out, but just as George as George. Like, okay, wow, let's see where this is going to take us.

BEN LA FARGE I had been living with a woman for over a year when she left me to marry another man, a well-known poet she had previously been involved with. George had been seeing Freddy Espy for several years, I think, and one day I heard he had left her. I called her up and asked her out. At dinner I said, "Look, I can't pretend I'm in love with you, and I know you're too unhappy about George to give a flying buttress about me, but how about having an affair?" She saw the humor of it and without hesitation agreed. Later, at her apartment, I said, "I'll bet you, once he hears about this, George will want you back." And that is what happened.

JOANIE MCDONELL Can I tell you what I think about George and women? They were like great athletes to George, like playing on a team with great athletes, and you have to understand I'm saying that with a lot of affection. George was always an admirer, first and last, and when women looked good and played well, so to speak, he was an extravagant admirer and wanted to play with them—even if they were better in his head than anywhere else. They were like—oh, Archie Moore or those guys from the Lions, like Alex Karras and Night Train Lane. Like Pancho Gonzales. It was fun for him to play with them, but I don't mean play in the unattractive sense of the word. George looked for what he thought were the best ones, or at least the ones he liked best. No, I take that back. He wasn't *looking* for anyone; he was never interested in "scoring"; girls were just always there, coming across his path. Nor did he ever try to "knock 'em off their feet," as they say. That would ruin everything. The last thing he wanted was for some girl to fall madly in love with him and ask him to leave Freddy for her—that is, to change his life in any way. He was never into heartbreaking love affairs. Or heartbreaking marriages, either: Those happened, though not to him. Of course, every little affair can't always have been fun and made him feel good about making the team. But that was okay. We all know that he never spent a day without Scotch, so he obviously needed several things to feel good. But you know what? I'm sorry to say that there came a time when, if he had to choose between women and Scotch, I think he would have chosen Scotch.

FREDDY ESPY PLIMPTON After almost five years of this, it's 1968 and I'm in a weird place where I'm not quite sure who I am or what I'm doing, or why. But by now I've gotten stubborn on the marriage thing just because it's been such an old saw, year after year after year. Now it's like "Hey, come on, let's get married and start a family, or release me to go off with somebody else!" I wasn't entirely bluffing, either. One man even asked George for my hand, sort of. He had been one of the oldest of President Kennedy's friends, a tall man with a long, pockmarked face, absolutely charming, absolutely delightful. He was divorced, and I'd been out with him quite often after we met at the party for the president. One day when I was in bed with the flu, he called and said he wanted to see me. He asked if George was there, and I said he was. He said, "Great, I'll be there in a few minutes." So he came upstairs to where I was in bed and gave me some flowers. Chat, chat, chat. Then he turns to George and says, point-blank, "If you don't marry her, I will." I was stunned. I mean, I had sort of led him on, as I am wont to do, but I hadn't led him on to the marriage point: My God, the man was older than George. I don't remember exactly what transpired after that, but we all remained friends.

DEBORAH PEASE He did everything so easily, without friction. Something occurred to him to do, and if there was no obstacle he could see, not even a categorical one—like "This is my wife, this is my mistress"—then he would do it. There were no demarcations. That way, he would be able to be married and love his wife and see other people. But even saying that makes it seem like some sort of agenda or plan or arrangement, when there weren't any. I think he just did as he pleased. Perhaps he was a little like Jack Kennedy in that way; he did what came naturally to him. If there were any hurt feelings incurred, it would not have been intended. He had a certain shallowness of feeling. He wasn't a Lothario, a lech, a womanizer. He would have genuine enthusiasm, wonderment, even gratitude—like a good boy presented with a marvelous treat—for whoever he was involved with. He often used to speak of acting in *joie,* in French, and I'm sure he knew what *jouissance* meant, too. He wasn't being pretentious, it was just that he wanted you to get past the banality of the English word. He wanted *joie* to come through in the magazine, in everything he did, not least in making love. He wanted to create joy, and he wanted to share it with his friends, who were potentially all the world. I don't think he had soul-wrenching relationships—not wrenching for him, certainly, but not for the woman, either, if he could possibly help it. He cared about that.

GEORGE'S FANTASTIC ACCESS

TERRY MCDONELL The edge George had with his journalism was how he could get access. Everyone he approached was as interested in him as he was in them, whether it was Warren Beatty or George H. W. Bush.

ROBERT BECKER George's charm was the real thing, a gift of the gods, and really him. Everyone sensed this—the athletes he interviewed, the children he entranced, the women and men who adored him. And what was the number one quality of his charm? It was curiosity, natural curiosity, and that's absolutely what George had in spades.

BOB JOHNSON I was with the Philharmonic when George played the triangle in Mahler's Second Symphony under Leonard Bernstein. There was an aura about George that was unmistakable; it was a kind of a self-assurance that allowed him, or I should say required him, to go wherever action could be found that would respond to his need to articulate. He had a great need, I think, to communicate what people do, how people feel, what they're thinking, what their backgrounds are. George identified very strongly with the members of the orchestra. He hobnobbed with us, he hung out with us. This was in 1973. He of course had his moments of awkwardness, but he was treated like an orchestra musician—including being hauled in for criticism by Bernstein. He was terrified. In fact, he said that playing in the orchestra was the hardest thing he ever did, because of the tyranny of time: In sports, you can call time-out or you can mop your brow or whatever, but in music, once your piece starts, it's not over until the measure's been played, and your part will be noted. There's nothing else like that in the world of competition. It was very unnerving.

ALEX KARRAS I don't know if George knew anything about the Lions when he made his choice to do this thing with us, but he fit right in, no problem. And usually, you know, there is some suspicion when someone comes in and really isn't a football player and is doing this or that. Guys can be rough with someone like that,

but with George they just let him come right in. He doesn't push
it, you know. He's just George. Guys would be in the room playing cards, smoking cigarettes, complaining about something, and
he'd just walk in the room, sit down, and say, "Hi, guys," and
just watch. . . . He would sing his St. Bernard's fight song. They
all made him do that, they loved it. They loved him, every one
of them. I guess management introduced him to the guys as a
ballplayer from someplace, and it worked until they saw him perform and realized he was not a quarterback. But he pretended really well. He said something about being from the Newfoundland
Newfs. They figured it out. I remember Joe Schmidt came down
and said to me, "We have really got something going on. . . ." I
said, "What is it?" He said, "George Plimpton," and I said, "Well,
he's a writer." He said, "Well, I think we're finding out he's certainly not a football player." He could tell stories. He was very
good at that. And he was able to back up the stories by going on a
football field. I remember when he played four downs against Bal-
timore, or Minnesota, or somebody, and he didn't do too bad. He
tried to pass one time and it didn't happen, but it looked like he
could possibly be a quarterback. I thought it was terrific for the
Lions to let him play with us. I remember when he put his gear on
for the first time. I guess he never played the game of football because he didn't really know anything about what he was putting
on, the hip pads and all, and the guys would tell me, they would
come in the evening and giggle a little bit and say, "George, you
look silly today." But as I say, we had gentlemen on our team,
which really allowed him to do what he did.

JAMES SALTER George wanted to do things with champions but
never boasted of it. I remember once he told me of interviewing
Muhammad Ali when he was training for some fight, and he went
to Ali's trailer and Ali had to excuse himself because someone else
was there. He said, "You're going to have to wait outside for a
while," and Wilma Rudolph, the famous black Olympic champion sprinter, came into the trailer, and they closed the door.
George said he was sitting around outside for quite a while, in fact
more than an hour. Finally, Wilma Rudolph came out and went
off. Anyway, some years later, George went to see him again and

said, "Champ, the last time I saw you was when you were down in Florida, training for the fight." And Ali said, "I remember: Wilma Rudolph." That's the story George would tell about himself. Most interviewers would say, "I'm tight with Ali. I went down and I interviewed him," and this and that, but George wasn't that way.

BUD SHRAKE   I can remember seeing George in the locker room talking to Ali. Ali always had a good eye; he always recognized someone who was way beyond average, and this was not your routine sportswriter he was talking to. When George walked up, Ali's eyes would sort of light up with this mischievous little glint, and you could tell he was getting ready to put George on, or have fun with George, or enjoy George's company.

LEON GAST   Ali always called George "Kennedy." He just thought George looked like a Kennedy. He did it even in Africa at the Ali/Foreman fight. We shot a scene at the Intercontinental Hotel where George shows up and Ali sees him and says, "Kennedy!" At that same lunch, Stokely Carmichael walked by and Ali sees him and says, "Stokely, Stokely." Stokely turns around and comes over, and Ali says, "Bundini, search him and see if he has any matches

George interviewing Muhammad Ali in Zaire a few days after he regained the championship from George Foreman. © *1974 Lynn Goldsmith.*

on him. We don't want him setting anything on fire." That was in
'74. Who else in the world could get away with that?

JOHN HEMINWAY   He and I could do the same thing in the
course of a day, but his memory and what he took away from it
was almost virtually the opposite of what I took away from it,
which was the big picture. He would often home in on one detail,
like someone's nose hairs. And he would say, "Have you ever seen
such nose hairs!" And of course I had missed it trying to get a bigger picture. What George would come away with was the funniest, greatest story of all time, and I would come back with a story
that had no value at all.

RAY CAVE   His description in *Bogey Man* [1967] of the guy in the
Port-o-Let at the U.S. Open is classic sportswriting. George is out
on the course standing next to a Port-o-Let with some guy in it.
The guy opens the door, and the door squeaks loudly, and when
he looks out, there's Arnold Palmer about ten yards away in the
rough, about to hit his shot. So the guy closes the Port-o-Let. And
he waits, and he waits, and he figures that Mr. Palmer must have
hit his shot by now. But Arnold can't stand it; he's been waiting for
the guy to finish his business and come out. He says, "George,
knock on that door!" One wonders if it ever happened. Enough
of it happened. There was probably a squeaky door.

BILL CURRY   The first day of [football] practice was no surprise,
really, but really hard for him. He looked like a big, graceful guy
on the tennis court, but he was forty-two years old and didn't run
well; he wobbled in football gear. He also had an ankle that bothered him, and he appeared to be flat-footed. It was such a struggle for him, and yet he did everything we did. So he comes out
the first day, and he's just standing there. Nobody's paying any
attention, and he announces to the coach, "I want to get in on
the drill." Well, the drill happened to be "the nutcracker," which
is man on man, one blocker, one tackler, one ball carrier. Our
coach, Don McCafferty, said, "Well, George, which spot do you
want?" "I want to carry the ball." "You sure?" "Yeah." So he
runs up in there. We had three All World linebackers, the least fa-

mous of which was Ray May. Ray would not have injured anyone purposely, but he tackled George and drove him into the ground, and when he did, George was just stunned. When he got up, he was just standing there, his arm flapping painfully. He said, "My God, look at this." So, everybody kind of looked at each other and said, "Well, that's it for him. We won't see him anymore." That afternoon he shows up, heavily taped, and comes out. He did well at the center/quarterback exchange, traditionally one of the first things you do in football practice. The center, hiking the ball to the quarterback, creates a really explosive *boom!* The ball smashes into the palm of the quarterback, including the thumb. If the quarterback is right-handed, and that right hand is the one that goes under the butt of the center, there's no way an amateur can take a snap and actually grasp the ball, but George did. When that happened, people started to take him seriously. He got respect from the guys who were already inclined to welcome an outsider, and a couple of weeks later he had everybody eating out of his hand. He never missed a practice.

MYRA GELBAND   If there was one word to describe the way George thought when he came to talk to us about ideas for articles, it would be "fanciful." Not over the top. I wouldn't say that. I mean "fanciful" in the sense that it would give him delight to think of them. He did a long piece for me once—I was his editor for probably about ten years—a lovely, very fanciful piece on an imaginary bird. He made up a bird. He wrote about going birding with these friends in Mexico, all great birders, and they made up a contest about what would be the most fabulous bird you could imagine, and he wrote about four thousand words on this, if you can imagine, and we ran it. With wonderful illustrations. But it was all based on real birds—a part from this bird, and a wing from that bird, and the beak of this bird, and the tail feather of another—it was fanciful but based on an enormous store of knowledge on ornithology. It was about all the things people who are lifetime birders want to discover.

DAVID MICHAELIS   He always said he didn't mind the constant flying off on speaking tours because he got so much writing done.

It was a real lesson. On an airplane flight he would have a legal pad open on his knee, in which he would write these beautifully simple, parsed sentences. He would drop the pad on a desk at the *Review*. I saw it several times when he walked in the door at 541 from having been somewhere. It would be completely used up, it seemed, with that lovely, straight up and down, increasingly illegible handwriting. He had a fluidity that was really an education to watch. I got the sense that he was writing out of his own idiom—he didn't have to make himself up, as he'd already done that as a kid, or so I imagine.

PIEDY LUMET   He called me up at one o'clock in the morning one night from the top of the Time-Life Building and said, "You've got to listen to this." I heard sort of a wailing noise, a high-pitched keening. I said, "What's that?" He said, "That's the wind blowing around the tower. They won't let me out because my article is past due. I have to finish my piece, so they've locked me in. Listen to the wailing." And then he went on for another thirty minutes about a very small Japanese admiral in a tiny submarine—George being tall at the top of a high, high, high, high building, feeling much like a tiny Japanese admiral, two hundred feet below the surface of the water with his periscope, trying to look out.

FREDDY ESPY PLIMPTON   People used to ask me what George was like when he woke up in the morning. What was his mood like? How did he answer the phone? How did he open the door? How did he start to work? Look, this is George Plimpton. He's done some incredible speech the night before and had a thousand people applauding him—a great night. He wakes up the next morning. He looks like hell. He's in these crumply shorts he slept in; he bumps into things; he can't smile; he's grouchy as hell. Has anybody else seen him that way? No. The wife sees it. He goes and gets his coffee and toast. By now, he would have pulled on a pair of pants, zipped up the zipper, but the belt's still open, and he's bare-chested, so he's halfway sort of gotten into clothes. He's walking around the pool table, which is littered with piles of paper, sees something, leans over, picks up a page, leans back, reads it, and puts it back on another pile across the table. He's editing his latest book as he's waking up, and he's got all this in his mind, and I watched this man nobody knew, this writer who wrote *all the time.*

BILL CURRY Let me tell you about the origin of the title of the book *One More July:* It was the early 1970s, I was home in Atlanta, and I thought I was going to retire. Then Bart Starr got his job with the Green Bay Packers, and he called 'cause he desperately needed a center. My knee was destroyed, but I thought I could play football one or two more years, so I started thinking about whether I was going to give it another shot and go up for training camp in July, like I'd been doing for most of my adult life. Meanwhile, I was interviewing for insurance jobs in Atlanta. I went into one interview with a good friend of mine, and he said, "Look, Bill, let me put this into perspective for you: If you're telling me that your passion in life is the insurance business, you'll be a marvelous representative; but if all you're doing is looking forward to July, to training camp—if this is just going to be your next July for a while, then you're wasting your time." I drove from that interview to another, again with a good friend of mine who was in the business. He sat across from me, looked me in the eye, and said, "What do you *really* want to do?" and I said, "Oh, my gosh. Bingo." I grabbed a napkin and wrote, "One more July." I said, "Excuse me, I've got the title of the book that George Plimpton and I are going to write." That's how it happened. My whole life had revolved around getting ready for the next July. Sure enough, I did it again that year, and that's when George and I got in the car and drove up there, talking and recording the talk all the way. Actually, we had been talking off and on for years, often at his parents' place on Long Island.

JONATHAN DEE The low point of my career as George's assistant came in February 1985 when he called me in on a weekend to type up the last changes on the Sidd Finch manuscript. He had me hand-deliver them to *Sports Illustrated.* I went over to the Time-Life Building and said, "I'd like to go up to *Sports Illustrated,* please." The guard said I couldn't go up—this was a Saturday afternoon, after all—so I asked if he would please deliver it to them. I handed

BASKETBALL: George at left. *Photograph © The Estate of Dick Raphael*/Sports Illustrated.

FOOTBALL: George (0) carries the ball. *Photograph © Walter Iooss, Jr.*/Sports Illustrated.

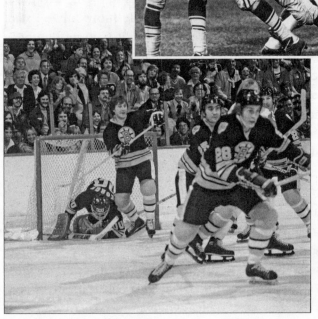

HOCKEY: George in the net. *Photograph © John Iacono*/Sports Illustrated.

TRAPEZE:
George the flying
telephone pole.
*David L. Wolper
Productions.*

SWIMMING: George with
Don Schollander. *Photograph ©
Henry Grossman.*

FILM: *Rio Bravo.*
David L. Wolper Productions.

ORCHESTRA:
The tympanist.
*David L. Wolper
Productions.*

this envelope to the security guard and I went home, thinking my job was done. It turned out that the envelope then went missing, and I don't think George had a copy of it anywhere. Come to think of it, making a copy of it was probably my job, wasn't it? Anyway, it went missing for about a day; I was out of the office and missed most of the excitement, but Jay McCulloch told me later that he genuinely thought that I had stolen it.

MYRA GELBAND   Within minutes after I got the manuscript, George called and said, "What do you think?" Now, I don't remember him being that insecure, but he hadn't written anything for us for a while, and this was so different and so secret—I mean, we didn't tell anybody about it. I said, "I'll read it on the train." I read it and I called him in the morning and said it was wonderful. He said, "Has Mark [Mulvoy] read it?" and I said, "I'm giving it to him now." He said, "Well, call me as soon as he reads it." And of course, it's not the only story you're working on when you're working for a weekly newsmagazine. So I gave it to Mark Mulvoy and said, "George wants to know what we think of it." I don't think I was even back at my desk yet when Mark—who's very compulsive about things like that—called me, laughing, and said, "I'm on page four." And it was a long piece. So I said, "Well, keep going, it gets better." I don't think he even got to the end before he called George himself. This was probably the beginning of February. It ran April first.

JONATHAN DEE   George had been a wreck while writing that piece. I was amazed to see it, because to me he was a celebrity writer, and I didn't think, at age twenty-two, that famous writers ever got nervous about whether what they were doing was any good or not. He said he had had an initial burst of enthusiasm, but then he realized what a daunting thing it is to tell a joke on a national scale. If it falls flat, you really look bad. He was worried that he had exaggerated it too much. Sidd—which was short for "Siddhartha"—was a Harvard dropout Buddhist monk in training who had accidentally mastered the union of mind and body in such a way that he could throw a baseball a hundred fifty miles per hour, which is about half again as fast as any human has ever thrown a

Sidd Finch and his creator confer.
maryannerussell.com © *'85.*

baseball, and in order to do this he had to have one foot bare and
the other wearing a work boot. As publication day approached,
George was consumed by the fear that he had gone too far and no
one could possibly fall for it. The day the issue hit newsstands—
April Fools' Day 1985—happened to be a day when he had to do
one of these goddamned speeches, in South Carolina this time. He
begged me before he left, "If anybody calls, try to keep the joke
going for as long as you can." Which made me extremely nervous.
I didn't think I could handle that at all. As it turned out, that was
a big moment in my relationship with him, because I was able to
do it, and I think he was happy to discover that I was on his wave-
length enough to be trusted to go through with something like
that. Anyway, the big morning arrived, and the phone did not
stop ringing all day long. Other journalists called. They thought
it was on the level. To give you an idea—the sportscaster at Chan-
nel Eleven, Jerry Girard, called the office and said, "I've gotten
Sidd to agree to an interview on the news tonight. Will George
come, too?" I said, "I give you my word that if Sidd is there,

George will be there." *The New York Times* called because they had sent a photographer down to the Mets' spring training facility; this guy was claiming that he had looked all over and couldn't find Sidd anywhere. I reminded them that George's story had mentioned Sidd's notorious shyness and so, on a day like this, it wasn't at all surprising that he would have gone into hiding. Senator Moynihan's office even called about it, but that one, thank God, went to *Sports Illustrated,* because I don't think I could have actually gone through with lying right to Senator Moynihan. The Common Book in the office was filled up with messages like those—pages and pages of them. I wrote it all out for him. He called once or twice from phone booths at airports to find out how it was going, but he really had no sense at all, that first day, of what a sensation it became. He was scheduled to come back home that night, and I left the book open on his desk chair so he could see what had been going on while he was away.

BILL CURRY   We were in the proofing stages of *One More July* when there was a major blowup between George and me—the only one that ever happened. One of the things that I told him about was me being a southern kid, coming from Georgia, growing up in a racist society and arriving in Green Bay for the first time, to play with the Packers. And there's Willie Davis, and Herb Adderley, David Robinson, Willie Wood, and Elijah Pitts—those guys adopted me, treated me just—I will never understand it. They were just wonderful. They took me in and helped me make the team, and we became good friends, and some of them actually ended up coming to Atlanta to visit with us, which was unheard of in those days. It was great. It changed my life. In the process, I learned something about African American culture, including their language, the nuance of profanity, such as the various derivations of the MF word and its inflections; I shared it all with George. At the time, we were drinking beer, sitting at his parents' house on Long Island; but when I saw it on paper, that language, knowing that my mother and grandmother were going to read this book . . . I remember, I was standing in the Atlanta airport, and I called George and said, "I just finished reading this, and we gotta take out the chapter on language." He said, "Take out *what*!? It's the best GD material in the book!" I said, "I don't care what it is, pal. It's coming out, because my grandmother is not going to pick this up and read it. She might die. She might croak on the spot." George's response was "You're going to turn this book into pabulum." That was his word. "It's going to be pap, pabulum." He was furious. I was furious at myself for even letting him know that I could talk like that! Bubba Smith had taken great pains to teach me the derivation and etymology of all that stuff. I just couldn't do it. George loved it, but I made him take it all out, which he thought really hurt the book. He was okay after a year or two.

PETER MATTHIESSEN   There was something about him—in those antics—that bordered on the foolish, or buffoonish almost. But that was the source of his humor, and it was wonderful. His craft was based on self-deprecation; it was the source of his charm and his wit. His wide-eyed and buffoonish look at things like the guy going in the flying lawn chair. He loved that sort of quirky thing. He's laughing at the absurdity. I think it's one of his most appealing qualities: the self-deprecation, but also the laughter at human folly.

CHRIS CERF   There's a theory that George's "amateur" was, deliberately, a buffoon. But one of the things that made these events so sweet and sad, in a good way, was that George really cared that he would do well in those games. He tried to do well, and it was heartbreaking when he didn't. For example, one of the most painful events in George's amateur-in-the-world-of-professional TV shows was being a stand-up comic in Las Vegas. His lack of success as a comic troubled him much more than his lack of success as a trapeze artist, which he did in the same series, because he figured that an erudite man of letters should know how to be funny. But of course he couldn't be funny in their way. The cultural differences between a Las Vegas comic and George were just too great. He couldn't make the break to their style. In fact, once you see him trying, you can't imagine him doing it. That's what made the show, and all the others, successful and funny, but I think George was troubled by that one. Because he fell flat on his face in something that involved intellect and presentation, rather than not being good enough at some sport or not being able to play the clarinet.

FRANCINE DU PLESSIX GRAY I thought that amateur-among-the-professionals thing was a kind of WASPy, self-demeaning sense of humor. There's a certain kind of self-deprecation to WASP humor, which George's was very much a part of. I would have thought that in the long run, it might be depressing to find yourself so repeatedly on the edge of humiliation. One might even consider the possibility that there was a masochistic ingredient in it.

JAMAICA KINCAID In his "participatory" journalism, George did something very American that Americans don't do. It is a very English tradition to take the amateur's part against the professional; but Americans are just too serious: "What? You're mining for gold? You're a gold miner." As opposed to, "Let's go mine for gold today, and tomorrow we'll be tennis pros." Yet this optimistic, protean idea of who you are is really very American. So what George did was kind of pure, really.

CALVIN TRILLIN Now, it was an important element of George's presence, in life or in books, that he made fun of himself. Of course, it took a lot of confidence to do that. To start with, there's that voice of his: It took confidence to think of it as an accent instead of a speech impediment. It took self-confidence and talent to play a piano piece at the Apollo, or to play tennis with whoever it was, Bobby Riggs or Pancho Gonzales, or to play quarterback in one of those scrimmages. But part of that self-confidence came from background. With many writers, no matter how talented they are, what George did just wouldn't work; it would be a joke. Or not a joke, it would be pathetic. George could do it because he had the background he did.

TOM BELLER Self-deprecation is fine, but in the literary aristocracy that Plimpton embodied—it's a dangerous position. Precisely because it's sort of debonair and easy, he somehow exempted himself from really trying—from what the athletes had had to do to get where they were or, for that matter, from the dangerous, emotionally daring thing that the writers he ended up publishing in the *Review* did.

JONATHAN AMES There is an aspect to his writing which seems Jewish, because Jews have mastered that kind of self-deprecation. There was a Jewish quality to the way he would put himself down in *Out of My League* and *Shadow Box* and *Paper Lion*.

SARAH DUDLEY PLIMPTON I think his books are very democratic in that what he is saying in all of them is "Look, it's me, George Plimpton, and I'm in the company of all these phenomenal athletes." He's going to fail, you know, but he succeeds in many other ways. He succeeds because he got inside that magic circle. It took great physical courage for him to go there, but he lived to write about it, and wrote about it so beautifully.

TIMOTHY DICKINSON George wrote in the great age of emphasis on the media, of the people who are making things happen for the public. George was very significantly part of that. Fifty years from now, most of the people in any of the sports he deals with will be remembered not from faded newspaper, but because a certain number of people will be reading *The Bogey Man,* or *Shadow Box,* or *Paper Lion,* or *Out of My League.* George wanted to be the man who is outclassed by the people he is dealing with but handles that with perfect grace. He brushed off the superiority of the pros on our behalf because he was a gentleman and a connoisseur. The charm of the matter was that any humiliation he suffered was a product of his own self-mocking: a preemptive strike against the superiority of others. So, in a way, they could never win against him; or if they won, it would be irrelevant. That was his charm for other people, people who knew they weren't so good: being not so good, handled with incomparable flourish.

MICHAEL POLLAN *Paper Lion* had a big impact on me. When did it come out, '66? I was fourteen, I guess. I remember I had a hardback copy that my parents gave me for Chanukah. I loved that book. But I subsequently realized, when I started teaching writing and giving interviews on my own writing, that I had been influenced by him more than I knew. I've often tried to put myself in stories, not only as a way to get a fresh perspective, but also for the humorous opportunities it opens up: It allows you to create a character who is not the omniscient journalist, but is someone who has lots of foibles and is failing as much as succeeding, and is also someone with whom the reader can identify. Plimpton understood that if you got your hands dirty in a certain way, it would be a lot of fun to write about, and you would be able to create a persona that was more accessible to the reader. I've used that trick many times. I wrote a piece about the cattle industry where I bought a steer, made myself a baby rancher. I realized in retrospect that the whole approach came from *Paper Lion*.

MYRA GELBAND By the 1980s, of course, the magazine evolved, and the kind of journalism George did for *SI*, which was his signature journalism and I would guess his most commercial, took a backseat to the type of hard-sports journalism that became prevalent in the 1980s with the advent of things like ESPN and cable television. I think it became harder for George to figure out stories that would work for the magazine, because his interests had changed, too—he wasn't gonna go suit up and play football for us, and we weren't gonna run those kind of stories. So it became a little more challenging for him to get into the magazine.

JONATHAN DEE By the late 1970s, George was spending a great deal of time on the road, giving his "amateur among the professionals" speech and making very good money at it. In the 1970s, too, of course, he was doing those David Wolper specials on TV— George as a nature photographer in Africa, George doing stand-up comedy with the greats at that game in Las Vegas. The irony is that his whole "participatory" method was devised as a way to get a better picture of the *subject*—it wasn't supposed to be about George. But over time, and more or less against his will, his celebrity became such that it overshadowed whatever else he might have wanted you to get out of the story. His persona was his livelihood, and it was also a kind of trap for him. But then that happens to a lot of successful public figures. If you want to say he was complicit in it, I suppose it was only by reason of the extraordinarily hard time he had saying no.

THE SWORD IN THE CAKE

FREDDY ESPY PLIMPTON It must have been within a year or two of JFK's death that I met Bobby Kennedy. Here was a man whose hands were trembling, who was looking at the floor, who found it hard to talk, and who couldn't meet your eyes. He was kind of short. I felt like wrapping my arms around him and saying, "It's all right, sweetie." I'll never forget that first meeting with him, because he changed over the next few years so incredibly. I've never seen anyone come out of whatever he was in, in such an amazing way. He turned into this forceful, convincing, gentle, charming person. George, of course, had known Bobby for a while. And as Bobby became more sociable, we began to see a lot of him and Ethel in Virginia. I was overwhelmed by that particular Kennedy family: twelve children, and action always going on. We went along on the Colorado River trip, with all the kids, and Freckles, the dog, and Bobby, and Jim and Blanche Whitaker. It was all about goofing around and teasing each other, taking risks. If Bobby had to go somewhere, there were times when he'd call us up and say, "You have to come with me, I'm having a hard time making decisions, maybe we can talk it through." He made the decision to run for president on one of these trips, after months of indecision. George and I were there with him on the Learjet when he finally made up his mind to go for it. He said, "It doesn't matter. This could really backfire and I could be once more known as the ruthless bastard, and everybody would just hate me. But," he said, "my belief is so strong about the war, and about the injustice done to people in this country, that I am going to run." That was in 1968, five years after George and I started dating. A whole lifetime of things happened to us in 1968. For one thing, we got married.

ANNA LOU ALDRICH Everyone had a theory or a story trying to explain the inexplicable—that is, George's getting married. Not just married to Freddy, to anyone. Most of the stories I heard were about Freddy wearing him down.

FREDDY ESPY PLIMPTON The reason I'm going on about Bobby is because during these years, George and I talked about what we should do. We tried separating from each other, and that didn't work. We always got back together again. George just didn't want to get married. One day, after he had decided to run for the presidency, Bobby called George and said, "Why don't you and Freddy come over to the UN Plaza. I need to talk to you about something." So we went over to his apartment, and he greets us and sits cross-legged in this huge wing chair. There was a couch opposite that, where George and I sat. Bobby looked so small and vulnerable, I just wanted to go over to him and eat him up. He said, "Why don't you two get married?" George said, "*What?*" Bobby said, "Ethel doesn't like it. She thinks it's bad for the kids. You're always going places together, staying in the same room, and you're not married." He said, "So I think you should get married." That's what finally pushed George into it, I think. So, shortly after that, we went down to get the marriage license, at City Hall. It was a pathetic scene, because you filled out papers at these little children's desks. Imagine George in one of those—so cramped, so unhappy. He was kicking viciously at the desk in front of him, in a rage, in an absolute rage that he was down there—he, *George Plimpton,* in a marriage license bureau—he couldn't get over it. He didn't talk to me for a few days after we got our license. He couldn't forgive me for having put him through that, and months went by before I heard anything about an actual marriage ceremony to follow the marriage license.

PIEDY LUMET I was on a ski lift at Stowe, and the guy taking the tickets said, "George Plimpton wants you to come back right now"—and it was freezing, with a big wind and eight feet of snow—"because he's getting married." I called up, and Freddy answered the phone. She sounded as if she were under a lot of stress.

Needless to say, I did not go, not in that weather. It must have been some wedding.

ANNA LOU ALDRICH Out of the blue, George called up and said, "I'm about to do this terrible thing, this insane, stupid thing, and I want you to come. Freddy and I are getting married this afternoon." Of course, Nelson and I went. It was at Joe Fox's apartment. It was a very nice wedding, but it was clear to most of us that Freddy would be unhappy very soon.

FREDDY ESPY PLIMPTON I was still working as a photostylist at the time, and on the day of my wedding I was on an early morning shoot in Central Park, wearing my scruffy jeans or whatever. We got back to the studio around noon, and Jill Krementz was there, waiting to take my picture for *New York* magazine, as the "young girl about town." So she's shooting me when the phone rings. It's Charlotte Curtis: "Darling, what are you still doing there?" I said, "What on earth are you talking about?" She said, "Just a moment, I'll call you back." So Jill and I continue, and we get a call from Joe Fox saying, "Freddy, we've decided that we're all going to meet here at four. . . ." George had forgotten to call me and ask me to marry him. He just made the decision. He didn't say anything to *me* at all. He was so terrified, he just neglected to tell me anything about it. I said to Jill, "Apparently I'm getting married at four." She said, "That's three hours away! Let's go get you something to wear." She took me to her apartment, and she was quite a bit larger than I was, but she had this Mexican wedding dress that was divine, a sixties love child wedding dress. She took up the hem, and I bought a pair of shoes, and she gave me a couple of tranquilizers, and I thought, "Boy, these make me feel okay." I was getting married. So what?

ROBERT SILVERS I have only a blurred memory of different moments of that day. It came as a surprise: I had no clear idea in advance what would happen. I seem to remember taking a taxi from *Harper's* to meet George at Tiffany's and him silently hesitating for a while and then poking his finger at a ring—no words, no jokes. Then I remember us walking down Fifth Avenue next to the park, scuffing leaves in the dusk. George seemed knotted up. He just said, "The poor girl, the poor girl." And then we reached Joe Fox's lit-up flat on Central Park South, and suddenly we were making our way into a cluster of old friends, and there was a festive glow with champagne and a minister hovering—it would all be for the best!

MAGGIE PALEY Joe Fox's apartment was in the Gainsborough, a building on Central Park South with two-story windows overlooking the park. There weren't very many of us, maybe twenty or thirty people, plus a minister. I remember George nervously trying to make conversation with me before the service, saying, "What is Presbyterianism all about? I haven't the vaguest idea."

FREDDY ESPY PLIMPTON Jackie was a very faithful friend to him: She got to the wedding on the same short notice as everyone else and brought Caroline. George, of course, was completely loyal to her, too. After the president died, when her kids were little, Jackie turned to people like George. He was so wonderful with children.

TOM GUINZBURG George decided that he would go through with it. I gather he made the decision at ten a.m.; the wedding would be at four that afternoon, at Joe Fox's apartment. It was like a squash court; the bedroom was the balcony, sort of, and beneath it was standing this group in a line, Terry Southern next to Mrs. Plimpton and so on. But they were not starting the wedding because Jackie hadn't arrived. She was coming from Hyannisport with baby Caroline. George was up there pacing around, but nobody had any confidence that we're going to have a groom, so we're taking turns going upstairs and trying to calm George, urging him to come on downstairs, the minister's here. He says, "No, we have to wait." Clearly, it's not just that Jackie hasn't arrived. He doesn't want to get married. Then it's my turn to calm him, so I'm up there thrashing around in my head for something to say—and I hadn't been married all that long myself to Rusty—so I said, "Oh, George, look at it this way: You're not ever going to be lonely again!" And George, like a wounded elephant, staggered towards

Freddy and George's wedding, 1968. From left: Robert Silvers, the minister, the couple, Willard Espy. Photograph by Jill Krementz.

me, threw his arms around me, and said, "Tombo, I've never been lonely in my life."

CHRIS CERF I was at Freddy's *first* wedding, a fellow called van Dereck Haunstrup or something, and I remember the ceremony and I remember laughing with her about it, the same day, because it was an Ethical Culture wedding, and the guy who married them didn't believe in traditional marriage vows, so he went, "Now, you guys, you're gonna be nice to each other, right?" It was really hippie. It amused me, imagining Freddy in that marriage and then, a few years later, imagining her with George Plimpton. But maybe, come to think of it, the same amount of seriousness went into both of them.

FREDDY ESPY PLIMPTON I didn't even have time to invite my mother or call my sisters. After the wedding, I told everyone, "I didn't know about this until one in the afternoon." They just looked at George like he was some kind of . . . like, How did you get away with this? He was so scared of this kind of commitment, so scared of love, of family. And forget a *real* wedding party. We went to Elaine's! That was it.

WILLA KIM   There was a big dinner at Elaine's. I remember that Billy [Pène du Bois] got up on his chair and made a whole speech in gestures without saying a word, and then everyone applauded. All these writers and their words. He was quite drunk, I'm sure.

MAGGIE PALEY   Afterwards I went with Terry Southern and Peter Matthiessen back to Peter's *pied à terre* and smoked some dope and had a good time. It was a momentous occasion. I didn't think George would be a good bet for a husband, but I didn't particularly want him to be married to anyone else. So I was sort of annoyed. I wasn't the only one.

BEN LA FARGE   One night several months later, I went to Elaine's for a nightcap—I had been one of her earliest customers, along with Frank Conroy and many others. That night I had to wait awhile, as all the tables were taken, even in the back room, where, Elaine told me, the just-married Plimptons were having their wedding party. Elaine must have tipped Freddy off, because Freddy had a plate of the wedding cake sent out to me. Some months later, Freddy and George invited me to spend the July Fourth weekend with them at a house they were renting in the Hamptons. After that, I ran into George now and then, but I never saw Freddy again.

FREDDY ESPY PLIMPTON   The next day, George had to fly to Gary, Indiana, to make a speech for Bobby Kennedy. I went to work as usual, at eight-thirty. I don't know how I did it. The telephone rings, and it's George: "You're going to have to come. I can't go alone. You're going to have to come with me." I said, "Why? What's wrong?" He said, "I feel awful, just awful. I need your help. I can't go alone." So I went. The plane was leaving at eleven, and I didn't have time to go home. George said, "Just come and be with me." So, I'm on this airplane, sitting next to George, who has grabbed on to both of my hands and is shaking from head to toe. Then I realize that he's asked me to come along so I could commiserate with him over the fact that he'd married me.

TOM GUINZBURG By the time Bobby Kennedy asked him to marry Freddy, she was pretty close to giving up on George. He didn't want to be married, and if he hadn't been taken with his Kennedy connections, I doubt he ever would have been.

FREDDY ESPY PLIMPTON We landed in Gary, Indiana, and we're met by all these women in mink stoles and mink hats and flowered dresses. They take one look at me and say, "Goodness! We need to get you something to wear!" They took us to a Quality Motel because we had to stay the night. The sign in front of the place had a big, bright yellow sun, and in the center, instead of saying, "Special Tonight: $1.99 Steak Dinner," it said, "Welcome, Newlyweds: Mr. and Mrs. George Plimpton!" *Just* what George needed. We had two rooms, so I said, "George, I think I need to be alone." And I went in the other room and shut the door. About ten minutes later I opened the door and said, "You know, we could always get divorced." And that night he made a fabulous speech for Bobby, it was incredible, everybody was cheering, and they presented us with this huge wedding cake onstage. George was given a long knife to cut the cake: He held it like this, over the cake, point down, and just dropped it into the cake. That's just exactly what happened. It sort of went *boioioing*, wobbled, and dropped onto the dais. There was an audible "Wahh!" from the audience, like he had decimated their values or something. He might have been able to tell himself that it would be funny, cutting the cake that way. Funny was to take away from sadness, or difficulty, or irritation, or negativity. So what better way to cut the fear than to cut the wedding cake in that silly way? And then, to get even further away from the fact of marriage, he took me down to the Vanderbilts' in Palm Beach for a honeymoon—can you imagine! Gertrude didn't like me at all, and neither did Hal. Hal didn't want George married; George was his beautiful young man, and he was Gertrude's beautiful young man, too. And there was I, not looking any too good! So I went out and bought myself a whole lot of Palm Beach–type outfits. I would come down after a bath, midmorning, and every single morning Gertrude would say, "Ooh, George, who is *that?* She's much better looking than yesterday's woman. She's quite charming." And I had to live with these two for five days. Why did I do it? George was himself again—perfectly charming. But he had taken me to the one haven where he knew he had someone backing him that he shouldn't have gotten married. I'm sure that he didn't think it through, but it was still not nice.

FIRECRACKERS AND SHOTS

FREDDY ESPY PLIMPTON Three days before the California primary, George and I drove through Chinatown with Bobby in his car, the three of us sitting up on the backseat, top down. Bobby was waving, waving, and these shots suddenly rang out. They turned out to be firecrackers, but George and I just fell on top of Bobby, like *that.* I've never seen anyone so exhausted and so pale and shaky as Bobby was. You just suddenly realized, My God, he's been waiting for that moment, every moment.

LARRY BENSKY The night before the California primary I went to this cocktail party at Blair Fuller's house in San Francisco. George, I think, was with Freddy, and both were traveling in Kennedy's entourage, and I remember being in Blair's kitchen, getting Blair and George, who were on different sides—Blair was for McCarthy—into a raging fight about this. I was goading them on, saying how can you say this about Kennedy when McCarthy blah, blah, blah. Everybody was standing around just enjoying this bullfight between these two partisans of these extremely, as far as I was concerned, flawed people. And then comes the next night, primary night, and Kennedy is assassinated. It was a horrible, horrible time.

KRISTI WITKER My very first job was at *American Heritage* magazine. I had been hired as an editorial assistant, but on the spur of the moment my editor decided to send me off to California to cover Bobby Kennedy's campaign for the Democratic presidential nomination. I was very naive and really didn't have a clue what I was doing, but I had been a big fan of *The Paris Review,* and through it I'd gotten to know and admire George Plimpton. When I discovered that he and Freddy were also on the campaign, I was delighted, and I spent most of the time hanging out with them. I became sort of the campaign mascot. I was young and had long blond hair and wore little miniskirts. I certainly didn't look or act much like a serious journalist. I was also anything but objective. In fact, I absolutely idolized Bobby Kennedy. The night of the California primary, I was really happy to be included in a small group of journalists that Bobby had invited to his suite in the Ambassador Hotel to watch the returns with Ethel and several of their children. And I was even more excited when Bobby asked me to his victory celebration, which would be later that night. George had a rental car, so I asked if he could give me a ride. He said, "Sure, but here's what you have to do so I don't lose you in the crowd: just hold on to my jacket when we leave the stage, because it's going to be a total mob scene and I'm going to work my way straight to the car." It was even more of mob scene than he'd imagined. I remember that when Bobby finished his victory speech that night we all started moving forward on the stage, and then someone said, "No, we're going out the back," and we reversed our direction. I was holding on to George's jacket for dear life and I wasn't aware that we'd gone into the kitchen. I wasn't aware of anything except a crush of people pushing and shoving. And then, suddenly, I heard what sounded like firecrackers. They weren't really loud, but they seemed to be in a pattern. First, there were three, then a pause, and then—during what seemed like an eternity—there were five more. I heard voices shouting, "Get the gun . . . get the gun!" and at that moment I realized with horror that we were being shot at, probably by a large number of people. Most people in the crowd began screaming and stampeding out of the kitchen back toward the hotel ballroom. But I didn't move. Everything seemed totally unreal. I remember thinking, "This can't be happening because I already have tomorrow's schedule!" And then, "Why run? If they've killed Bobby, what's the point?" The man on my left suddenly fell to the floor. He was bleeding from his head onto my shoe, and I remember just moving my foot.

And then others were shouting, "This woman's been shot!" She was right behind me, clutching her stomach, and I glanced at her and thought, "Who cares? Don't you realize that Bobby's been shot and probably killed?" At that moment, I had no interest in anyone else. Bobby was the only one who mattered. As the gunman—and now I saw that there was only one—kept firing, George and Rafer Johnson were desperately struggling to get the gun out of his hand, and finally they succeeded. We were only about four feet away and Bobby was slumped on his back on the floor. I closed my eyes and clung to George. I felt that as long as I didn't let go of him, life as it had been only moments before would suddenly snap back into place. Of course, it never did.

FREDDY ESPY PLIMPTON I was on the stairs to the left side of the stage, facing front. George was on the floor below me, taking notes. Bobby and Ethel were supposed to turn right, to go out a different way. Somebody changed the plan and had them go through the kitchen, so they turned left and passed me, where I was standing. Bobby went ahead. Rafer Johnson and Jim Whittaker, two of his three bodyguards, were around him. George and I were right there. Ethel was further behind with Rosey Grier. We entered the kitchen with a lot of people traipsing after us. It was pretty clean and open, and there were a lot of busboys standing to the left. We went past them, and one of them leaned and stretched his arm out, and Bobby reached over and shook his hand. Then Bobby turned, and this other white jacket suddenly appeared at the end of a long, shiny table and put *his* hand out and shot Bobby in the head, just like that. All I wanted to do was get a doctor. George went for Sirhan, and so did a couple of other guys, and they pinned him down. I went through the swinging doors at the end of the room and shouted for doctors, police, medics, whatever—there was no one down there. I heard a lot of gunshots in that kitchen. By the time I got back, Bobby was on the floor and somebody had given him a rosary. We were just in shock. Rosey Grier, this huge tackle, just fell apart. He started crying. He went into a nervous breakdown. George and I got him up to his room in the hotel and stayed with him. Then someone located

George and me and asked us to come to the hospital. Bobby wasn't dead yet. Frank Mankiewicz, who was his press secretary at the time, made the announcement that he wasn't doing too well. The family was filing into his room, and George and I went in, too—it was awful. There was nothing there, no sign of life in him.

BILL DOW George told us that when he was later called as a defense witness at the trial, he said that Sirhan had this look on his face when they were wrestling—I think George had his hand on his throat or something—this very peaceful look on his face and this kind of dreamlike look in his eyes. I think the reason that he was called as a defense witness is that he had told the police how calm Sirhan looked, and I think the defense was figuring that that showed either insanity or else that he didn't do it because he

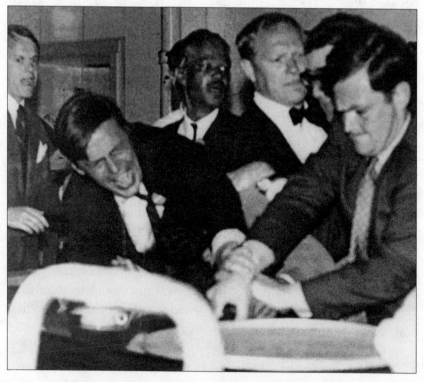

George wrestling gun from Sirhan Sirhan, June 5, 1968.
© *1968* Los Angeles Times. *Reprinted with permission.*

would have been all scared and nervous with all the commotion. I remember George telling us that when he walked into the courtroom, Sirhan had, like, this little grin on his face, and George said he was thinking, "Like, I'm going to help you, after what you've done?"

———

FIONA MAAZEL   I remember a night at a club called Life when George had so many Dewar's that he ended up weeping. I had never seen him cry, but he was telling me about the assassination of Bobby Kennedy, and he was falling to pieces. He was sobbing. I was just sitting there thinking, "I can't believe he's telling me this story," because I know he didn't like to talk about it that much. He described in such amazing detail the way they piled on top of the guy, but instead of attending to Bobby, too many people were focused on apprehending the guy. The whole experience seemed to change his life dramatically. He never wrote about it.

JONATHAN DEE   It's something, isn't it, that a man who made a career writing beautifully about his own amazing autobiographical exploits would never have touched the most amazing exploit of all, would never have written about it in a million years. I remember once I was in the *Paris Review* basement looking for something in a file cabinet and I came across a clipping of an old AP photograph taken seconds after the RFK shooting, showing two men pinning Sirhan to the ground. The caption identifies them as "Rosey Grier and an unidentified man," and the unidentified man is George. I brought it upstairs to show it to the others, and as I'm doing so, George walks in. He takes a look at what everyone is passing around, and I swear, the color just drained right out of him. It was very clear from his demeanor that he was not going to discuss it. I'm told that in later years he loosened up about that somewhat, and would actually answer questions about it if asked.

ELIZABETH WURTZEL   Obviously George didn't want "access" to Robert Kennedy's assassination, and maybe simple horror or real modesty got in the way of his ever writing about it. It was also hardly an occasion for his self-deprecating humor, or any humor, perhaps. But I was awfully close to 9/11—a wheel fell through the roof from one of the planes—and I don't think I'll ever write about it because whatever you say sounds wrong. If you make yourself sound too involved, you're not nearly as involved as the people who died. On the other hand, if you're not involved enough, you sound like a person with no feelings. So maybe that was the problem for him. It takes a really amazing writer—not to say that George wasn't that writer, I don't know that he was or was not. He might have just thrown up his hands and said, "I can't do it."

ED BARBER The first proposal that came in to me when I became editor in chief at Harcourt Brace around 1970 was something from Phyllis Jackson, who was a grande dame of agents. She was at ICM, I believe, and she represented Jean Stein vanden Heuvel. Jean had been on the Bobby Kennedy funeral train and had run up and down interviewing people. You know, get the tape recorder out and here's Milton Berle and his wife, here's Art Buchwald and his wife—this big collection of high-end people. So she had all these interviews, about three hundred of them—would I be interested in making a book out of them? Well, I could see that this was a very difficult book to put together, but I liked the interviews and signed it up. Then I looked around for somebody to work on it. First, I tried Pete Hamill, and Pete was fine with it. But he was a journalist with a unique style. He would write sizzling prose with a lot of TKs, you know, and I could see that he wasn't going to work very well, because it was going to be half horse and half cow, part interviews and part Hamill. I wanted it to be all interviews. So next I called George. George came around, we had lunch, he looked at the stuff, and he really just fell in love with it. The book was about five years too late, because the Bobby Kennedy surge had receded. But George and I set forth and divided all of these things up with Jean, who's a powerhouse. So she and George were working on it, and I was working on it a little bit, and it would go back and forth until things gradually shaped up. Those two didn't quite get on as well as they might have, but that often happens with collaborations.

$200,000 A YEAR

CHRIS CERF He needed money more than usual after his marriage, obviously, and more than that after his children were born. He sometimes had to do things that he probably thought were funny, and were, but in ways that he probably didn't appreciate, like those swimming pool commercials. My dad and George had many things in common, of which this is one. My dad did television shows when all the other publishers said, "How could you stoop to being on *What's My Line?*" My dad had all kinds of brilliant excuses about why it was good business for Random House, and so it was. But he also loved doing it. He was a ham; he loved the public eye, and I think George loved it, too. George's being on TV and in the movies delighted me, and I don't think it did him any harm at all, except among people who were hopelessly stuffy to begin with. It also helped keep *The Paris Review* going.

MONA ESPY SCHREIBER There was a time when Freddy would buy presents in New York and then go around writing little notes on them, saying, "Love, the Easter Bunny."

FAYETTE HICKOX George was already heavily into doing commercials by the mid-1970s. Jed Horne, our mutual friend, used to say, "Who is George Plimpton? Jean Cocteau or Crazy Eddie?" George really was becoming a ubiquitous figure on television. It was Dry Dock Savings Bank one week, then it was Carlsberg beer, then it was Saab. So George would drive a Saab and he'd have cases of Carlsberg, which we all drank in the office. His drink, of course, was always Dewar's. What else did he flack for? Pop Secret popcorn, though that was later, I think.

CHRIS CALHOUN He was quite skillful doing these commercials on TV. But there was something about Plimpton: He had this sort of tremendous remove, very dignified, yet I don't think he was making it ironic—and he got caught up in promoting some very silly stuff. He did a local pool ad, I remember, out in the Hamptons in the nineties, where he's coming out of the water. Nobody can look very good getting out of the water and going into a sales pitch, even in your thirties or forties, and he was in his late sixties. Anyone else would have looked like an absolute ass. It wasn't the same as looking like an ass playing pro football or something, because then there was always a fantastic book or essay to follow. But there was no story to be written about shilling for some of these insane products, there was no follow-up, there was no literary excuse. There was money. Yet he pulled it off. I think that if you saw James Salter, or even Dick Cavett, lending their names to these things, you'd think, "What a stink bomb. How much money do you need? I mean, is there anything you won't do, you old bore?" But it would never occur to you to say something like that about George. I think he had this sort of wink, this weird part of his sensibility when he's pitching these products that you're not taking too seriously, and yet he's keeping his dignity—and doing it without putting ironic quotes around anything.

SOL GREENBAUM George was concerned about his image. Thirty or forty years ago, he was offered to do Saab commercials. He told me, "I'm going to come across like a pitchman, and I'm not a pitchman. I might fail. I just don't know." I asked how much they were paying him for these commercials, and he said it was fifty thousand dollars. I said, "How long will it take to do them?" He said it was three or four days of work. I said, "George, after taxes, you'll be earning a thousand dollars an hour." He decided he would take it, and the commercials were a huge success.

FREDDY ESPY PLIMPTON He didn't want to know anything about his money. Eventually he reached a stage where he was always worried about money, I can't pinpoint when that happened, but perhaps when the second or third book had not sold as well as he had expected and we were in the middle of doing the house or something. I can't pinpoint it, but all of a sudden, he became distracted by how much money was being spent and how he was going to make enough, and all of this.

MARY JO PARKER The second summer that my sister and I were Taylor and Medora's nannies, Mr. Plimpton was concerned by how much the grocery bill was costing. They got all the food from a little Hamptons deli and had it delivered, too. It was exorbitant what they were charging for the exact same things you'd find in any old supermarket. I said to them, "Why don't we just go to the supermarket, and Jane and I can pick out the food and bring it home ourselves?" I saw it as such an easy, everyday sort of thing to do, going to the supermarket. Mrs. Plimpton was just amazed that we could go and do that. And Mr. Plimpton was very appreciative because we cut the food bill in half—*at least*. They thanked us over and over again.

SOL GREENBAUM He was so happy when he picked up a big fee, because he knew that would carry him for a while. For example, when he got a hundred-thousand-dollar advance on a book, he knew he could pay all the bills. Or when he got a new publisher. Usually in the summer, *The Paris Review* would run dry. Marjorie would say, "I don't know how to make payroll next week, George," and he would say, "Do I have any money in my account?" He would start scrounging. Once I remember he turned to Celeste Cheatham. Actually, I did it myself. She was married to one of his friends. Steve was a stockbroker, very successful. I called Celeste and said, "Steve's old friend George Plimpton's *Paris Review* needs money, and I would like you to write a check for ten thousand dollars." She sent a check. George was always able to bring in money.

DEBORAH PEASE This is how I got to be publisher of *The Paris Review*: One day, I called George to ask him if he knew of a good way I could help small literary magazines. I'd been reading them and sending out my poems to them for years, and I knew how crucial yet fragile they were. This was in 1982. I'd known George for about twenty years, but we hadn't been in touch for a while. As always, he was wonderfully welcoming. I mean, you could count on a joyous welcome if you were a friend. So I posed my question, and he made George-esque noises for an interval of about ten seconds: "Well, let's see, kiddo, gollee . . ." Then he burst out: "How about becoming the publisher of *The Paris Review*? We just lost our publisher, he's gone into rehab and his check bounced, and we don't have any money!" I shrieked and he hollered, and the gist of it was "Yes! Wow! When do I start?" That was that. "Just keep us afloat, sweet one"—he called lots of ladies "sweet one." We didn't sign a contract or have lawyers do anything official. It was all done on friendship, enthusiasm, and good faith. He sent me a dozen red roses, and the next night he took me to dinner. Norman Mailer passed by on his way out and George exclaimed: "This is our new publisher!" Mailer's response was to smile indulgently and punch a wall. A few days later, I went to George's apartment to be introduced to the team, and we all had lunch. All the editors and interns were there, sitting in the living room in a circle, everybody beaming. Things were off to a great start, and I stayed on as publisher for ten years [1982–1992].

NILE SOUTHERN We have a letter from George where he's joking with Terry about all the money he, Terry, is earning in Hollywood and how Terry ought to fly George out for a story session or something. It's true that when Terry went to Hollywood, he was making more money in a week than he'd made in a whole lifetime of writing, which was pretty surreal. George was quite aware of that. Terry downplayed it. I don't think he responded to that letter.

STARLING LAWRENCE I don't think anybody has enough money, but George really didn't. Or if he did, it was always a scramble to figure out where the next piece of change was going to come from. I remember when Norton was paying him a retainer to edit this sports anthology, and I kept calling Tim Seldes, the politest man in town, wonderful man. I kept saying, "Tim, what gives?" and Tim had no fucking idea, so we took George to lunch to read him the riot act, and he completely disarmed us by telling us the story of the man in the flying lawn chair, which was later part of a book that was published posthumously. We were at the New York Yacht Club, where you're not supposed to hoot and roll in the aisles, but I guess we walked away from the lunch thinking that we'd gotten our money's worth or something.

RED AUERBACH He was one of these people that never carry any money. He came out to my basketball camp for a week, and he's got maybe two or three dollars in his pocket. One day, he and two of my counselors go out to play golf. And he loses some and he's got to come up with eight dollars. He doesn't have eight dollars. He's got to write a check for eight dollars. I laughed like hell. How can you leave home and take two, three dollars with you?

MATTHEW BRUCCOLI I remember once, about two years before he died, we were having breakfast, and he said that he couldn't pay the printing bill for the next issue of *The Paris Review,* and he needed an infusion of money. It just so happened that an out-of-town, wealthy friend of mine was staying at the Princeton Club, and I said, "Come on, I'll take you over to the Princeton Club and introduce you to somebody I know." And within half an hour, forty minutes, George had the money for the printer.

TERRY QUINN My first visit to 541, I asked him, "How did you get all this space right on the East River? It must have cost you a million dollars." And I think he said that when he and others in the building outbid some developers for the whole block of apartments, his piece cost sixty thousand dollars. He said it was the only good financial decision he'd ever made.

LILLIAN VON NICKERN George once requested that the *Review* pay him rent at 541. We had money, someone gave us some money, and of course, immediately, it was "Well, now we can do this, that, and the other." And we did pay him rent; we paid for a while. As with everything else, it went by the boards, because the magazine didn't sustain itself. And, sadly enough, George was the one who ended up carrying all the expense, really, of that office. I can remember having about ten dollars in the checking account at a time when any bill over twenty dollars seemed a vast amount, because we didn't have it.

LARRY BENSKY As early as the mid-sixties, George kept coming up with these moneymaking schemes that seemed plausible enough—the *Review* booth at the World's Fair of '64–'65, book publishing, the Revels, the poster project. The booth I remember painfully: He paid my way to come back from Paris to help out. When I arrived George said, "Tonight we have to go out to Flushing. The fair is opening in a day or two, and our booth isn't built yet. You have to sign union contracts to get electricity and to get construction, and we don't have that kind of money, so we're just going to do it ourselves." So, we get out there, and the pile of wood to build the booth is lying there, and there's a chalk line about ten yards, fifteen yards long, from our booth to where the electricity central drop is, and it's blacktop. "We're supposed to tunnel," George says, pointing to a pickax. We did it. It took us all night, but we did it; my hands were sore and blistered and bleeding, and so were his. Some other volunteers showed and knocked the plywood and the wood stanchions up and painted it. I don't know how it got finished, but it was very festive—designed by Billy du Bois, I think. I went home and soaked my hands for a few days.

HARRY MATHEWS   George created the first *Paris Review* Editions—another moneymaker, he hoped. And the first book they

The *Paris Review* booth at the New York World's Fair, 1964.
Photograph © Richard Marshall.

published was James Salter's wonderful *A Sport and a Pastime,* which was cover-to-cover sex and did well. The second was my second novel, *Tlooth,* which was a totally weird book, but I worked on every sentence. The story that George always used to love to tell is that on pub day, they would hire a plane to inscribe the letters *TLOOTH* in the sky above New York to create wonder and bewilderment in the populace; but the winds weren't right, and it was too expensive anyway. Of course, the book—well, it didn't go nowhere, but it didn't do very well.

JOHN GRUEN   I was so pleased when George asked Jane Wilson, my wife and a great American artist, to take on his poster project. Never in a million years had Jane ever been asked to do what George Plimpton asked her to do, which was to round up every great American young artist there was to do a poster for the *Review.* Actually, she quite enjoyed it. The hard part was to get them to finish it after they said they'd do it. She was talking to Warhol, Motherwell, all the great artists you can think of. Then out came these really gorgeous posters, which I think benefited *The Paris Review* quite a lot.

DRUE HEINZ   Underwriting the printing of the poster series was the first thing I ever did for him. That was the very beginning, in the early sixties. And he said, "I have this idea to ask artists to do *Paris Review* posters. They can do anything they want, but the words *Paris Review* must appear somewhere in some form. We'll do so many of them, and then really promote them." I said yes. Before he died, he was trying to get me to find them all again, because he thought I had all the originals somewhere, and he wanted me to give them back to him to put them up at auction. I couldn't root them out quickly enough for the fiftieth anniversary benefit. In any case, the posters put us on the map. People were really keen on getting them. Now the ones I had have been given to the Morgan Library for the *Paris Review* archive.

MARJORIE KALMAN   When I first started looking after George's cash flow, I suddenly found myself having to answer questions, because he thought I might be stealing his money. He would holler at you all of a sudden, "Where's all my money going?" He knew his income, or part of it. He went to Woolworth's every year and he got a very small date book, and in that date book he wrote down where he was going and how much they paid him. He lectured a lot. As far as expenditures, I think he suffered from the same problem a lot of men do at one time in their lives, when a woman pays the bills, whether it's your wife or someone like me, where he really didn't know how much Con Edison was charging him or the telephone company—things like that; but he'd get angry, maybe once a year, and actually, when I came along, Sol said, "Oh, I'm so glad you're here, so he can holler at you now." It was the way he got information. George trusted everybody. George had a great sense of trust and allegiance; but then he'd suddenly mistrust his trustingness and get angry: "Where's all my money?"—that was a common refrain. I did initially get this feeling that I needed to go down and make details and write everything down; and then he'd forget about it. By the time I got organized, he didn't really want to hear the answer. I don't think he really wanted to be bothered with the details of taking care of his finances; he just wanted to make sure that if he trusted you, he was right to trust you. There were times when I think he would have liked me to steal, so he could be angry and go around saying, "My accountant stole millions of dollars from me!" It would have been a story for him.

SOL GREENBAUM In the late seventies, Francis became upset that George was spending a lot of money. He felt that George wasn't meeting his obligation to his family, which by that time he had— two children and Freddy—so he wanted to have a meeting with George and I. We met at George's apartment, and what came out was, he asked, "How much money does George need to live?" I said, "About two hundred thousand a year." Francis wanted to know, "What if something happened to you?" I said, "Francis, let's assume the worst: that there isn't enough money in George's estate, because he spends everything that he makes, and someone has to take care of the children. I would look to you." So I put Francis on the spot, which was not something he was used to, but he was very charming about it. He said, "I have this many millions of dollars. My first responsibility is to Pauline. I guess I have enough to take care of the children, also." I remember when I said two hundred thousand dollars, George gasped and said, "Oh no, Dad! I don't need that much." After the meeting was over, I said, "George, it was more than two hundred thousand. I brought the figure down for your father."

VI.

PUSS AND MISTER PUSS:
1973–1983

—

For some reason, that cat, Mr. Puss, was essential to George. It was as if he inhabited Mr. Puss in a way. Or maybe the cat was his familiar. Either way, he and Mr. Puss were one.

—*ANN WINCHESTER*

"ORDINARY PLEASURES"

FREDDY ESPY PLIMPTON You know, I'd hate it if you pictured this marriage as filled with nothing but parties, booze, fireworks, and wandering around. We had our ordinary pleasures, too, he and I. One thing we loved doing together was looking for stuff for the apartment, or the house in Sagaponack when we got it, stuff that looked like it had been around for generations, old WASP stuff. I went to the Salvation Army with him—we bought our big, fat, simple sofas there and just had them restuffed and re-covered. It's the way I like to do rooms, not with French antiques. Our most fun was when each thing arrived—we would try it in this place or that place, find a home for it. We also had children, for God's sake! Medora in 1971 and Taylor in 1976, and made a home for *them*. George wasn't a good father by ordinary standards, but when he was there for them, he was the best: He was terrific with children, including his own. I was less terrific for a while there, but good enough, as they say, at the beginning of their childhood and to-ward the end of it.

DAVID AMRAM The night of the Muhammad Ali vs. Joe Frazier match in Madison Square Garden, George asked me to be with Freddy, because she was pregnant with Medora, and George had to run all over the place, covering the fight. We had good seats, but LeRoy Neiman beckoned me to come hang out with him, right down next to the ring. So Freddy said, "David, go ahead." At which point José Torres, who was the light heavyweight cham-pion, also a great friend of theirs, came over and said, "Don't worry, David. She's safe with me." Freddy tells the story of how, during the fight, she was sitting on José Torres's lap, because José wanted to be certain that George's wife and baby would be safe. It was just one of those great New York nights that George was at.

FREDDY ESPY PLIMPTON   George loved a skinny little teeny-bopper-type person, so when I got pregnant with Medora, he didn't like it—the whole idea of my suddenly turning into a woman with large breasts, lactating, and my belly as big as—well, he didn't like that at all. He happened to be there the morning I started going into labor, and so, the way I recall it, we walked several blocks to New York Hospital, because somewhere George had heard that when you're giving birth, it's very good to be up and about, as he put it. I was in quite a lot of pain, so it was quite difficult to do this, but I did it. Once we got into the hospital—this was 1971, so George was at the peak of his celebrity—everyone crowded around him, and all they wanted to do was talk to him about his experiences, and they were going, "Ho-ho-ho, you better deliver this baby and write about it"—you know, things like that. So the whole birth was about George. People who were supposed to be doing things for me were being entertained by George out in the hallway. George wanted nothing to do with the actual birth. It was the same when I had Taylor. Taylor was born in August of 1976, right as some hurricane was blowing into town. Women in Southampton who were close to the end of their ninth month were asked to come into the hospital because the pressure drop of the impending storm could cause them to go into labor. So the hallways were filled with gurneys full of moaning women, myself among them. After the birth, George came in to see Taylor, and he said, "Hello, hello, hello! Good job, Puss, good job! Thank God it wasn't a *girl,* or I would have had to name her Beulah." He thought that was the name of the storm. [It was Belle.] I wanted to kick him in the teeth. Was he pleased to have a son? I don't know. He called his mother right away, and she came right out so she could be the first to hold the baby.

MARY JO PARKER   When my sister and I first started taking care of Taylor and Medora, as summer au pairs, I was surprised by how young Mrs. Plimpton was. I guess I didn't realize the age difference between the two of them. I thought she was very enthusiastic about the projects that she was doing and that she wanted the best for her children that she could possibly give them. She was a little high-strung, and very concerned that they were well taken care of. There were some days where she would just close herself off from the rest of us and just decompress or whatever. I think that's what we were there for. It was our job to take all those burdens from her—well, not "burdens," but the care of the children and other household responsibilities. The house on Long Island was a big house, and they needed people to take care of it.

FREDDY ESPY PLIMPTON I had never known what being in love was until I had Medora. Never. I had never known that heart-flipping, heart-stopping, ear-ringing, eye-bulging, heart-thump-ing . . . back in the city, I'd see the nanny pushing her up the street. I'd walk over to meet them halfway, and when I'd see that carriage coming, I would just get so excited to see her and hold her and smell her and touch her. I guess no one had ever allowed me to love anyone that much, that's what it is. But that's how much love I had. And that was news to me.

ANN WINCHESTER I spent a lot of time with them out on Long Island. I know people actually wondered why I was there; they probably gossiped. And the funny thing is, it was probably the most innocent thing in my life. Now that I look back on it, I think that George was to me like my brother had been—a passionate friend. I had an affair of the heart with my brother through our exuberant sharing of childhood. In much the same way, George and I behaved like total children inside the grown-up world of New York. We shared a huge sense of the ridiculous, which was most often channeled through the medium of Mr. Puss. And that cat took himself very seriously indeed. Freddy, on the other hand, was like my mother. She was a lot of fun, yet felt compelled to keep things tidy, and in control. She thought of herself as the adult of the group and pointed out that the rest of us were like children. And she was absolutely right, you know. Freddy was a very good mom, the den mother, the responsible adult—and yet very much up for a great laugh as well. Like my mother. With George it was total childishness. Anything less than utter childishness made his

George and Mr. Puss. © *Nancy Crampton,*
from Writers: Photographs by Nancy Crampton.

eyes glaze over. For some reason, the cat, Mr. Puss, was essential to
him. He was George's straight man. And George certainly inhabited Mr. Puss. Or . . . maybe the cat was George's familiar. Freddy
didn't understand Mr. Puss; she was good to him, looked after
him, but she just didn't get his point. The cat, I mean. He was gigantic! You could hardly pick him up, could you? I have wonderful photographs of Medora with him—and of Taylor, attacking
Mr. Puss in a tae kwan do stance. George loved him; George and
he were one. So a lot of things ended when Mr. Puss died. Certainly our friendship tailed off then.

MARY JO PARKER Mr. Plimpton seemed almost childlike when
he was with the children. He'd be very attentive, very much into
building a sandcastle or whatever it was that they were interested
in doing. When Medora was into putting on her own plays, he
would get anxious and excited to see her perform. He was de-

lighted with whatever she did. He was just enthused that he could do things with them.

FREDDY ESPY PLIMPTON We belonged to this little club, the most elite club on earth, I think, called the Devon Yacht Club. They were the most uptight group of people I've ever met in my life. No Jews, no blacks, no—and this is the seventies. It was appalling. If people brought anyone to the club who looked at all different, you could see them all whispering and glancing at you, sort of making remarks against you. Anyway, one time George had asked his circus friends from the Wolper TV series—the trapeze artist and his wife—to come out for the weekend. That's all. And then he took them next door to the Devon to play tennis, which they had never really played before. But he introduced them to a lot of people. "Hello, this is my friend. He's a trapeze artist." Anyway, he was trying to get into the Maidstone Club at this time, a place even more appalling than the Devon, because it was a great place to play tennis on grass. And the word got out that George had brought circus people—midgets—onto the tennis court at Devon. Thus he was not allowed to join the Maidstone.

MICHAEL THOMAS I've been to the Devon Yacht Club. It's in Amagansett on Gardiners Bay. Devon has sailing, which the Maidstone hasn't, and perfectly decent tennis courts. If you're blackballed at the Maidstone, as George was, and if you're George, you would join the Devon. They have these incredibly stuffy dinners on Friday night where you have to wear a necktie. Being a yacht club, they still observe the sunset protocol, cannon fire, the flag going down, members standing respectfully. I have a friend named John Alexander, a painter, who lives in inland Amagansett; he used to trap raccoons that were bothering me, then he would drive them all over to the Devon Yacht Club and release them in the garbage there.

FREDDY ESPY PLIMPTON Some of the most romantic times I had with George were our trips to Africa. We went on several safaris together. At first it was all about Hemingway. George loved

Papa Hemingway, and he wanted the experience of being a big-game hunter in Africa. He wanted the big five: the buffalo, the elephant, the lion, the leopard, and the rhino. All of Papa's trophies, he wanted. He didn't put it like that, but he said, "Papa would have loved that!" as he shot a buffalo or something. Later, I think he just wanted to see Africa. Neither of us thought we would fall in love with it the way we did. We didn't want to go home. I didn't like the idea that George was shooting animals, but I understood it and forgave it. Sometimes we'd start giggling and we'd walk off into the bush without telling anybody, like children.

WALON GREEN   George's African adventure was for a Wolper show in which George was to be a *Life* wildlife photographer and to try to get a cover picture of the largest elephant in the world, named Ahmed, who lived in the north of Kenya. Wildlife photography was just coming into its own in those days. At night we built this big fire that we would sit around, and people would come from neighboring camps. George had this kind of Jungian vortex thing, where interesting people just started showing up. Within a couple of days, this guy John G. Williams arrived, who had written *Birds of East Africa* and was taking these two ladies on safari. Then a friend of mine, who I didn't know was in Africa, showed up with this woman named Eva Motley, who had come there to make films. One night, we were telling stories around the fire, and I heard Eva Motley talking about how she'd first come to Africa. She was in the film business in England as a young woman, and she wanted to work on this film in the Congo called *The Nun's Story,* starring Audrey Hepburn. Meanwhile, George and I could hear this woman on the other side of the fire who was talking about having first come to Africa as a nun in the Congo. Suddenly it dawned on both of us that the woman who's talking about having come to the Congo to make the movie about the nun who came to the Congo is now sitting across the campfire from that very nun. It was an extraordinary moment. George was a catalyst for things like that. You went someplace and talked to people, and you would suddenly find out that there was something rather extraordinary about them. It had happened earlier, during our trip up there. We stopped at a warden's house at some park and a guy came up in a Land Rover and joined us on the porch, and we had tea and talked for a while. This guy knew all about the water-courses and the area we were going to. When he'd been intro-duced, I noticed that George perked up. I didn't even catch the name. George tried to invite him to dinner, but he got in his car and drove away. It turned out that he was this explorer named Wil-fred Thesiger, who'd written *Arabian Sands,* on the marsh Arabs, and George was thrilled. He said it was a unique opportunity to meet this guy, because he never comes where anybody can see him. Then, when we went to the coast, it happened again when he found this old guy named Barr Allen, living in the Arab section of the Lamu. He had been some big northern frontier guy in his day, back in the thirties, when it was a wild and woolly district. I can't even remember how George found him, but suddenly he said, "Oh, you must come immediately, I've found Barr Allen." I said, "Who's Barr Allen?" He knew all about him, of course.

FREDDY ESPY PLIMPTON In Nairobi, George always took me to the Nairobi Zoo's snake pit to pay homage to the Gaboon viper, which is a horrible sluggish snake that's too big to slither quickly out of your way, like most snakes do; so if you stumbled on one, it bit you, and if it bit you, you'd be dead in a matter of seconds. George felt that his chances of survival were better if he acknowl-edged it before heading into the bush. There it was: a big fat thing that didn't move at all. And there George would be, bowing to it!

WALON GREEN We wanted to get some footage of George very close to elephants, so someone suggested that we put him up in a tree, and then when the elephants gathered, he'd be six or seven feet above their heads. We got George up the tree—literally out on a limb—and the elephants came. They were right under the tree, and I was getting kind of worried about him, because they could start whacking the tree and knock him out of there. I mean, he was right over their backs, looking down at them. I can tell you he was kind of like, "I'm awfully close to these elephants right now. . . ." These are wild elephants. We had no control over any-thing, and soon they *were* rubbing themselves against the tree, moving it and shaking it, and we thought, "What if they shake it so hard, he comes falling out?" Suddenly George drops out of the tree into the middle of a herd of elephants. But that went well. We also walked him up on a pond with a huge python in it and didn't tell him it was there. Someone said, "A python! Let's catch it, George!" So he had to wrestle a python out of the pond. George would do anything. He was a good sport. He didn't like snakes particularly, but he was game for it.

ANN WINCHESTER George was there to take a picture of Ahmed that was good enough for the front cover of *Life*—not an easy feat. My main memory of him is sitting around the campfire watching him pick ticks off his legs. We were all doing it, but as George always had the most (having been tracking Ahmed in the bush on foot), we were very afraid that he would get tick fever, which you can die from.

WALON GREEN We had no problem finding Ahmed every day— he was easy to find—and for a while, though we always hoped something really exciting might happen, all George was able to do was watch Ahmed consume immense amounts of food. At Lake Manyara, however, there was an elephant named Boadicea who was guaranteed to charge. We were told she'd rush up to the Land Rover and tear up the bushes and throw them up in the air. She never actually hit a Land Rover. She always stopped short. Or so they said. But who could tell for sure whether that charging behemoth was really Boadicea? We didn't tell George the whole story. He knew it was a setup, but he didn't know exactly what the setup was. We said, "Oh, let's drive out and look at these elephants, and we'll film over your shoulder." We edged up, and edged up, and we knew Boadicea was there, and we knew that when we got to a certain point, she'd come booming out of the bush. Which she did, and we got a really great sequence.

FREDDY ESPY PLIMPTON I'll tell you one story from the Hemingway period of our trips. George and his guide went out after a rhino we had spotted some distance away. We pulled the Jeep over to the side of the road, and I got up through the top to see, and George and the white hunter and Choshi, my favorite tracker, went out, crouching down, to try to get within shooting distance—all of a sudden it puts its head up, it snorts and starts to paw the earth. I can see all of this. That rhino came at them so fast, and they looked like those cartoons of people running, with their arms pumping and their knees right up to their chests. It was the funniest thing I've ever seen. They were so embarrassed.

WALON GREEN   George wrote his own script for the Ahmed show. I kind of outlined what we would do and where we would go, and George did the rest. Nobody could write like George—same with the interviews. I never told him what to go for; he was better at reading people than I was. He'd get a good interview out of a rock. He was able to get the kind of universal nugget that connected all humanity, whether he was interviewing a good guy or a bad guy. One guy I remember bragged about shooting down elephants and watching them fall, saying how there's nothing greater than the sensation of seeing that bullet smack and to know you'd done a well-placed brain shot. But what was remarkable about it was that George managed to touch the core of the guy's passion. The same day, George could've interviewed one of the great conservationist leaders of Africa, and he would've gotten the guy weeping about the death of a salamander or something.

FREDDY ESPY PLIMPTON   Africa was an intensely romantic place for both of us. In those days, there wasn't anything out there but a silhouette on the horizon, and man, you wanted to know what it was. We loved the tents, and learning Swahili, and the problems with the funky latrines—just the ways of Africa. When we were back in New York, George would zip his raincoat and say, "*Hodi! Nataka chai?*" ("Greetings! Do you want tea?")—just like the "boy" who woke us up in the morning, unzipping the tent to bring us our tea.

TWO PRANKS

WARREN YOUNG   We started planning the Dynamite Museum in George's apartment. The formative group was George, of course,

John Train, Christopher Cerf, Michael Frith, George Trow, and Michael O'Donoghue. One of the offerings to subscribers of the museum was that you could adopt a turkey. You could adopt either an unhatched egg, which you could name, or a real live turkey that was scooting around some farmer's yard. And you would be sent a monthly status report on this turkey. Let's say its name was Claude: You would get a note saying that Claude is gaining weight fast, he's eating well, he's socializing with the other birds, mother and father are quite proud, and we have great hopes that he will be a fine, fine turkey. Each iteration would be a postcard, and you would not only have a picture of this turkey, but you would have all the vital signs and growth patterns as well. The punch line, a month or so later, would be that we regret to say that the farmer's truck rolled over Claude and we would like to know where to send the remains, or that Claude got mixed up with another lot which unfortunately are in Stop & Shop, and we would replicate the label in case they wanted to look for him there. And who was going to write these offerings? It could be Truman Capote, Norman Mailer, Bill Buckley, or a famous basketball player. George would round up the people. After many planning meetings, the whole effort was to be announced at a gathering at none other than Elaine's, where we invited a hundred and ten handpicked, creative people. I remember it went from Capote to Mao Tse-tung. The letter came from the committee, signed by George, of course, inviting them to this grand dinner, RSVP to this address, and indeed we locked up Elaine's for the night and took it over. Of course, Elaine herself was on our list—not only as our hostess, but because she was a character in her own right—but she couldn't come. We had picked the one night where she had another engagement, quote unquote, and I leave it to you to come up with the reason why Elaine would not attend a soiree like that.

FREDDY ESPY PLIMPTON   I have such good memories of the Dynamite Museum. Here in our apartment were a bunch of people I loved, having so much fun throwing out concepts and running with them. And the laughter! In those days, there was so much lightheartedness. Nobody's life had gotten too serious yet. It was more fun than anything else could've been.

CHRIS CERF   I remember Jed Harris having a wonderful idea for the Dynamite Museum, called the Bottom Party: He was going to send an invitation out to anyone whose name ended in "bottom," and he'd never tell anybody why they were invited and just let them go into the party and discover that that's what they all had in common. The basic idea was to pull off colossal hoaxes, but that's what we didn't explain properly. George strongly felt that we didn't really have to *do* very many things, we could just take *credit* for them, you know, the idea being that if something weird happened to be going on, we would say the Dynamite Museum did it.

MICHAEL FRITH   That night at Elaine's, I was mostly in the back room. I think the group spilled out into the front room, but it certainly filled the back room—jam-packed, shoulder to shoulder. We had a good dinner. I don't know how we paid for it. I remember that wine flowed freely and the room was so thick with smoke, you could barely breathe. Of course, there was this enormous sense of anticipation—"What is this all about? What is going to happen? George is gonna speak! Oh, my God, isn't it amazing we're all here? It's the cream of creative, artistic, intellectual, humorous society in America today and perhaps even the world!" There was this wonderful, electric sense of self-importance in the room. So the evening got later and later, with more and more wine, more and more smoke. Finally, as dinner was winding down and last drinks were being served, *ding, ding, ding* on the glass, and George gets up and makes this speech. All I remember was sitting there with this enormous sense of anticipation: There's no one who would be able to sell this like George. He stands up on the chair in the front of the room, over by the window, and a hush falls over the room. Everybody is just so focused. He's like, "So here we all are, to learn about the Dynamite Museum," and so on and so forth, "and it's going to be this amazing group, all of us here today, and we'll work together to . . . create . . . certain . . . items. There will be items like Mrs. So-and-so in Dubuque, and we'll let her know that she is going to get a turkey. And then every few weeks we'll send her a bulletin about the progress of this turkey!" And the room was like, "Where is this going?" Totally downhill, is where. He never really finished off with his lady in Dubuque, what she would get with this turkey, and why she would care about the life of this turkey that was being fattened up for Thanksgiving. Then he started saying that this was only one of the items, and there would be many other items, and of these items, some of them would be mysterious, some of them would be funny, some of them would be baffling. All these items. And as he went along with all these items, people started going, "Okay," looking at each other, and then they started picking up their drinks again. The level of conversation began to rise, gradually filled the room, and George, as I recall, kind of looked around and said, "Thank you very much." Everyone went, "Hurray!" And that was the end of the Dynamite Museum. But somehow it was all strangely wonderful. And the thing of it is, it could never have happened without George.

CHRIS CERF   It was profoundly embarrassing; except that as George remembered it, it became one of the funniest evenings of his life. It was so shameful, you just bled for him as he made his pitch, but he told it with such glee.

TIM SELDES   George was Tom Sawyer–ish from Exeter to the day he died. He woke me up one night many years ago and he said, "Old Tim," which is what he called me when he wanted something, "I've agreed to take my first parachute jump this morning, and I'm leaving at four o'clock, and I'd like you to come, too, because I think you should do it." And I could hardly say anything but "Oh, okay, George." Probably at around two in the morning, I finally stopped shaking, terrified, and when I woke up it was well past four, and later on that day I called George up and I said, "Well?" He said, "I decided to give you a reprieve, and you should be grateful to me that I did, it was absolutely awful." And I still don't know whether he really intended to take me with him or whether he was just poking me up to see what I would do.

TONY HENDRA   *Not the New York Times,* the parody edition of the paper we put out during the newspaper strike in October of '78—

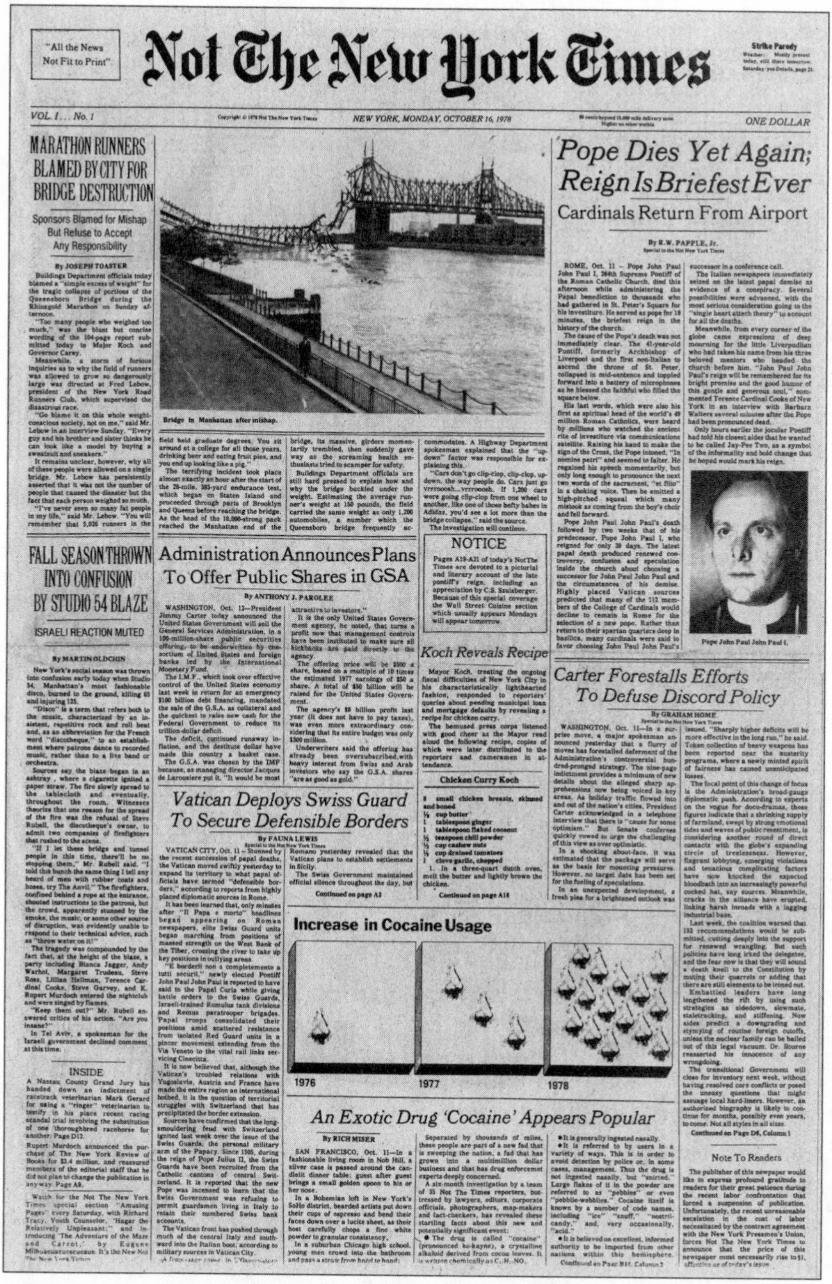

"All the News Not Fit to Print"

Not The New York Times

Strike Parody

Weather: Mostly present today, still there tomorrow. Saturday: yes Details, page 21.

VOL. I . . . No. 1 — Copyright © 1978 Not The New York Times — NEW YORK, MONDAY, OCTOBER 16, 1978 — 95 cents beyond 15,000 mile delivery zone. Higher on other worlds — ONE DOLLAR

MARATHON RUNNERS BLAMED BY CITY FOR BRIDGE DESTRUCTION

Sponsors Blamed for Mishap But Refuse to Accept Any Responsibility

By JOSEPH TOASTER

Buildings Department officials today blamed a "simple excess of weight" for the tragic collapse of portions of the Queensboro Bridge during the Rhinegold Marathon on Sunday afternoon.

"Too many people who weighed too much," was the blunt but concise wording of the 104-page report submitted today to Major Koch and Governor Carey.

Meanwhile, a storm of furious inquiries as to why the field of runners was allowed to grow so dangerously large was directed at Fred Lebow, president of the New York Road Runners Club, which supervised the disastrous race.

"Go blame it on this whole weight-conscious society, not on me," said Mr. Lebow in an interview Sunday. "Every guy and his brother and sister thinks he can look like a model by buying a sweatsuit and sneakers."

It remains unclear, however, why all of these people were allowed on a single bridge. Mr. Lebow has persistently asserted that it was not the number of people that caused the disaster but the fact that each person weighed so much.

"I've never seen so many fat people in my life," said Mr. Lebow. "You will remember that 5,026 runners in the field held graduate degrees. You sit around at a college for all those years, drinking beer and eating fruit pies, and you end up looking like a pig."

The terrifying incident took place almost exactly an hour after the start of the 26-mile, 385-yard endurance test, which began on Staten Island and proceeded through parts of Brooklyn and Queens before reaching the bridge. As the head of the 10,000-strong pack reached the Manhattan end of the bridge, its massive, girders momentarily trembled, then suddenly gave way as the screaming health enthusiasts tried to scamper for safety.

Buildings Department officials are still hard pressed to explain how and why the bridge buckled under the weight. Estimating the average runner's weight at 150 pounds, the field carried the same weight as only 1,200 automobiles, a number which the Queensboro bridge frequently accommodates. A Highway Department spokesman explained that the "up-down" factor was responsible for explaining this.

"Cars don't go clip-clop, clip-clop, up-down, the way people do. Cars just go vrrrooosh...vrrrooosh. If 1,200 cars were going clip-clop from one wheel to another, like one of those hefty babes in Adidas, you'd see a lot more than the bridge collapse," said the source.

The investigation will continue.

Bridge in Manhattan after mishap.

Pope Dies Yet Again; Reign Is Briefest Ever

Cardinals Return From Airport

By R.W. PAPPLE, Jr.
Special to the Not New York Times

ROME, Oct. 11 – Pope John Paul John Paul I, 264th Supreme Pontiff of the Roman Catholic Church, died this afternoon while administering the Papal benediction to thousands who had gathered in St. Peter's Square for his investiture. He served as pope for 19 minutes, the briefest reign in the history of the church.

The cause of the Pope's death was not immediately clear. The 41-year-old Pontiff, formerly Archbishop of Liverpool and the first non-Italian to ascend the throne of St. Peter, collapsed in mid-sentence and toppled forward into a battery of microphones as he blessed the faithful who filled the square below.

His last words, which were also his first as spiritual head of the world's 49 million Roman Catholics, were heard by millions who watched the ancient rite of investiture via communications satellite. Raising his hand to make the sign of the Cross, the Pope intoned, "In nomine patri" and seemed to falter. He regained his speech momentarily, but only long enough to pronounce the next two words of the sacrament, "et filio" in a choking voice. Then he emitted a high-pitched squeal which many mistook as coming from the boy's choir and fell forward.

Pope John Paul John Paul's death followed by two weeks that of his predecessor, Pope John Paul I, who reigned for only 38 days. The latest papal death produced renewed controversy, confusion and speculation inside the church about choosing a successor for John Paul John Paul and the circumstances of his demise. Highly placed Vatican sources predicted that many of the 112 members of the College of Cardinals would decline to remain in Rome for the selection of a new pope. Rather than return to their spartan quarters deep in basilica, many cardinals were said to favor choosing John Paul John Paul's successor in a conference call.

The Italian newspapers immediately seized on the latest papal demise as evidence of a conspiracy. Several possibilities were advanced, with the most serious consideration going to the "single heart attach theory" to account for all the deaths.

Meanwhile, from every corner of the globe came expressions of deep mourning for the little Liverpudlian who had taken his name from his three beloved mentors who headed the church before him. "John Paul John Paul's reign will be remembered for its bright promise and the good humor of this gentle and generous soul," commented Terence Cardinal Cooke of New York in an interview with Barbara Walters several minutes after the Pope had been pronounced dead.

Only hours earlier the jocular Pontiff had told his closest aides that he wanted to be called Jay-Pee Two, as a symbol of the informality and bold change that he hoped would mark his reign.

Pope John Paul John Paul I.

FALL SEASON THROWN INTO CONFUSION BY STUDIO 54 BLAZE

ISRAELI REACTION MUTED

By MARTIN OLDCHIN

New York's social season was thrown into confusion early today when Studio 54, Manhattan's most fashionable disco, burned to the ground, killing 65 and injuring 125.

"Disco" is a term that refers both to the music, characterized by an insistent, repetitive rock and roll beat and, as an abbreviation for the French word "discotheque," to an establishment where patrons dance to recorded music, rather than to a live band or orchestra.

Sources say the blaze began in an ashtray , where a cigarette ignited a paper straw. The fire slowly spread to the tablecloth and eventually, throughout the room. Witnesses theorize that one reason for the spread of the fire was the refusal of Steve Rubell, the discotheque's owner, to admit two companies of firefighters that rushed to the scene.

"If I let these bridge and tunnel people in this time, there'll be no stopping them," Mr. Rubell said. "I told this bunch the same thing I tell any heard of men with rubber coats and hoses, try The Anvil." The firefighters, confined behind a rope at the entrance, shouted instructions to the patrons, but the crowd, apparently stunned by the smoke, the music, or some other source of disruption, was evidently unable to respond to their technical advice, such as "throw water on it!"

The tragedy was compounded by the fact that, at the height of the blaze, a party including Bianca Jagger, Andy Warhol, Margaret Trudeau, Steve Ross, Lillian Hellman, Terence Cardinal Cooke, Steve Garvey, and K. Rupert Murdoch entered the nightclub and were singed by flames.

"Keep them out?" Mr. Rubell answered critics of his action. "Are you insane?"

In Tel Aviv, a spokesman for the Israeli government declined comment at this time.

Administration Announces Plans To Offer Public Shares in GSA

By ANTHONY J. PAROLEE

WASHINGTON, Oct. 12—President Jimmy Carter today announced the United States Government will sell the General Services Administration, in a 100-million-share public securities offering, to be underwritten by consortium of United States and foreign banks led by the International Monetary Fund.

The I.M.F., which took over effective control of the United States economy last week in return for an emergency $100 billion debt financing, mandated the sale of the G.S.A. as collateral and the quickest to raise new cash for the Federal Government to reduce its trillion-dollar deficit.

The deficit, continued runaway inflation, and the destitute dollar have made this country a basket case.

The G.S.A. was chosen by the IMF because, as managing director Jacques de Larousiere put it, "It would be most attractive to investors."

It is the only United States Government agency, he noted, that turns a profit now that management controls have been instituted to make sure all kickbacks are paid directly to the agency.

The offering price will be $500 a share, based on a multiple of 10 times the estimated 1977 earnings of $50 a share. A total of $50 billion will be raised for the United States Government.

The agency's $5 billion profit last year (it does not have to pay taxes), was even more extraordinary considering that its entire budget was only $300 million.

Underwriters said the offering has already been oversubscribed, with heavy interest from Swiss and Arab investors who say the G.S.A. shares "are as good as gold."

NOTICE

Pages A19-A21 of today's Not The Times are devoted to a pictorial and literary account of the late pontiff's reign, including an appreciation by C.S. Szulsberger. Because of this special coverage the Wall Street Cuisine section which usually appears Mondays will appear tomorrow.

Koch Reveals Recipe

Mayor Koch, treating the ongoing fiscal difficulties of New York City in his characteristically lighthearted fashion, responded to reporters' queries about pending municipal loan and mortgage defaults by revealing a recipe for chicken curry.

The bemused press corps listened with good cheer as the Mayor read aloud the following recipe, copies of which were later distributed to the reporters and cameramen in attendance.

Chicken Curry Koch

8 small chicken breasts, skinned and boned
⅓ cup butter
1 tablespoon ginger
1 tablespoon flaked coconut
½ teaspoon chili powder
⅓ cup cashew nuts
⅓ cup drained tomatoes
1 clove garlic, chopped

1. In a three-quart dutch oven, melt the butter and lightly brown the chicken.

Continued on page A18

Vatican Deploys Swiss Guard To Secure Defensible Borders

By FAUNA LEWIS
Special to the Not New York Times

VATICAN CITY, Oct. 11 – Stunned by the recent succession of papal deaths, the Vatican moved swiftly yesterday to expand its territory to what papal officials have termed "defensible borders," according to reports from highly placed diplomatic sources in Rome.

It has been learned that, only minutes after "Il Papa e morto" headlines began appearing on Roman newspapers, elite Swiss Guard units began marching from positions of massed strength on the West Bank of the Tiber, crossing the river to take up key positions in outlying areas.

"E borderii non a completemente a tutti securii," newly elected Pontiff John Paul John Paul is reported to have said to the Papal Curia while giving battle orders to the Swiss Guards, Israeli-trained Romulus tank divisions and Remus paratrooper brigades. Papal troops consolidated their positions amid scattered resistance from isolated Red Guard units in a pincer movement extending from the Via Veneto to the vital rail links servicing Cinecitta.

It is now believed that, although the Vatican's troubled relations with Yugoslavia, Austria and France have made the entire region an international hotbed, it is the question of territorial struggles with Switzerland that has precipitated the border extension.

Sources have confirmed that the long-smouldering feud with Switzerland ignited last week over the issue of the Swiss Guards, the personal military arm of the Papacy. Since 1505, during the reign of Pope Julius II, the Swiss Guards have been recruited from the Catholic cantons of central Switzerland. It is reported that the new Pope was incensed to learn that the Swiss Government was refusing to permit guardsmen living in Italy to retain their numbered Swiss bank accounts.

The Vatican front has pushed through much of the central Italy and southward into the Italian boot, according to military sources in Vatican City.

A front-page cover in L'Osservatore Romano yesterday revealed that the Vatican plans to establish settlements in Sicily.

The Swiss Government maintained official silence throughout the day, but

Continued on page A2

Carter Forestalls Efforts To Defuse Discord Policy

By GRAHAM HOME
Special to the Not New York Times

WASHINGTON, Oct. 11—In a surprise move, a major spokesman announced yesterday that a flurry of moves has forestalled deferment of the Administration's controversial hundred-pronged strategy. The nine-page indictment provides a minimum of new details about the alleged sharp apprehensions now being voiced in key areas. As holiday traffic flowed into and out of the nation's cities, President Carter acknowledged in a telephone interview that there is "cause for some optimism." But Senate conferees quickly vowed to urge the challenging of this view as over optimistic.

In a shocking about-face, it was estimated that the package will serve as the basis for mounting pressures. However, no target date has been set for the fueling of speculations.

In an unexpected development, a fresh plea for a brightened outlook was issued. "Sharply higher deficits will be more effective in the long run," he said. Token collection of heavy weapons has been reported near the austerity programs, where a newly minted spirit of fairness has caused unanticipated losses.

The focal point of this change of focus is the Administration's broad-gauge diplomatic push. According to experts on the vogue for docu-dramas, these figures indicate that a shrinking supply of farmland, swept by strong emotional tides and waves of public resentment, is considering another round of direct contacts with the globe's expanding circle of treelessness. However, flagrant lobbying, emerging violations and tenacious complicating factors have now knocked the expected bloodbath into an increasingly powerful cocked hat, say sources. Meanwhile, cracks in the alliance have erupted, linking harsh inroads with a lagging industrial base.

Last week, the coalition warned that 152 recommendations would be submitted, cutting deeply into the support for renewed wrangling. But such policies have long irked the delegates, and the fear now is that they will sound a death knell to the Constitution by muting their quarrels or adding that there are still elements to be ironed out.

Embattled leaders have long lengthened the rift by using such strategies as sidedown, slowmate, staletracking, and stiffening. Now aides predict a downgrading and stymying of routine foreign cutoffs, unless the nuclear family can be bailed out of this legal vacuum. Dr. Bourne reasserted his innocence of any wrongdoing.

The transitional Government will close for inventory next week, without having resolved core conflicts or posed the uneasy questions that might assuage local hard-liners. However, an authorized biography is likely to continue for months, possibly even years, to come. Not all styles in all sizes.

Continued on Page D8, Column 1

Increase in Cocaine Usage

1976 — 1977 — 1978

An Exotic Drug 'Cocaine' Appears Popular

By RICH MISER

SAN FRANCISCO, Oct. 11—In a fashionable living room in Nob Hill, a silver case is passed around the candlelit dinner table; guest after guest brings a small golden spoon to his or her nose.

In a Bohemian loft in New York's SoHo district, bearded artists put down their cups of espresso and bend their faces down over a lucite sheet, as their host carefully chops a fine white powder to granular consistency.

In a suburban Chicago high school, young men crowd into the bathroom and pass a straw from hand to hand:

Separated by thousands of miles, these people are part of a new fad that is sweeping the nation, a fad that has grown into a multimillion dollar business and that has drug enforcemet experts deeply concerned.

A six-month investigation by a team of 35 Not The Times reporters, buttressed by lawyers, editors, corporate officials, photographers, map-makers and fact-checkers, has revealed these startling facts about this new and potentially significant event:

- The drug is called "cocaine" (pronounced ko-kayne), a crystalline alkaloid derived from cocoa leaves. It is written chemically as C..H..NO.
- It is generally ingested nasally.
- It is referred to by users in a variety of ways. This is in order to avoid detection by police or, in some cases, management. Thus the drug is not ingested nasally, but "snirted." Large flakes of it in the powder are referred to as "pebbles" or even "pebblie-webblies." Cocaine itself is known by a number of code names, including "ice" "snuff," "nostril-candy," and, very occasionally, "acid."
- It is believed on excellent, informed authority to be imported from other nations within this hemisphere.

Continued on Page B16, Column 2

INSIDE

A Nassau County Grand Jury has handed down an indictment of racetrack veterinarian Mark Gerard for using a "ringer" veterinarian to testify in his place recent racing scandal trial involving the substitution of one thoroughbred racehorse for another. Page D12.

Rupert Murdoch announced the purchase of The New York Review of Books for $3.4 million, and reassured members of the editorial staff that he did not plan to change the publication in any way. Page A9.

Watch for the Not The New York Times special section "Amusing Pages" every Saturday, with Richard Tracy, Youth Counselor, "Hagar the Relatively Unpleasant;" and introducing "The Adventure of the Maze and Carrot," by Eugene Milhuacuacuescueaue. It's the New Not The New York Times

Note To Readers

The publisher of this newspaper would like to express profound gratitude to readers for their great patience during the recent labor confrontation that forced a suspension of publication. Unfortunately, the recent unreasonable escalation in the cost of labor necessitated by the contract agreement with the New York Pressmen's Union, forces Not The New York Times to announce that the price of this newspaper must necessarily rise to $1, effective as of today's issue.

Collection of Jonathan Becker.

that was the ultimate Dynamite Museum prank. Or might have been had the Dynamite Museum not flopped.

CHRIS CERF   The central group behind *Not the New York Times* was Tony Hendra and Rusty Unger Guinzburg; a guy named Josh Feigenbaum, a radio producer, who was not a close friend of George's but of Hendra's; and Larry Durocher, a Bostonian who really knew the inside of the newspaper business. And Freddy, of course. There were very active contributors, including Carl Bernstein, who wrote the lead story; Nora Ephron, who was his girlfriend at the time; Jack Egan, who did the whole financial section. We recruited an awful lot of the *Times* people, including one of their chief designers, which was one of the reasons it looked good, a guy named Richard Yeend. It had a literary group involved, too. Michael Arlen and Alice Albright and Frankie FitzGerald wrote for it. It's amazing who wrote for it, Victor Navasky and all those people. It's still my favorite thing of all the projects I've ever been involved in. It was done by seventy or eighty people working twenty-four hours a day for three weeks, mostly at George and Freddy's, all in mortal fear that the newspaper strike would end before we finished.

TONY HENDRA   I was in effect the editor in chief of the newspaper, so I knew pretty much everything that everybody wrote. The piece that sticks out in my mind, because it involves George prominently, was the lead, which was written by Carl Bernstein. As it happens, we were doing this parody at the same time as John Paul the First was dying; the cardinals were reconvening, having convened only thirty-something days earlier to elect him. So we conceived this story about the next pope, whom the cardinals would then be electing. We were going to call him John Paul George Ringo, but that seemed distracting. We called him John Paul John Paul, JP2 for short. Interesting that, because a few weeks later, John Paul the Second was actually elected pope. But anyway, the point about John Paul John Paul was that he came from Liverpool, and his reign lasted for nineteen and a half minutes. He was elected, the white smoke came out, and he died. And that was the whole story. It was a very funny story, which Carl wrote off in a corner of George's apartment. There were people everywhere working on their stories, then laying things out on that big pool table. And this was fairly late in the process, when the paper was being put to bed. We did the whole thing in a week. So Carl wrote this very funny story, and we set it in type. And then we needed a head. It was two or three o'clock in the morning, with one day to go before the paper was closed. So George and I sat down and tried to come up with this very important headline. You know, the right idea for the lead story would set the tone for the entire front page. And I said, "What do you think, George? What kind of headline should this be?" And he said, "Well, I think this is an occasion for the blindingly obvious, that kind of absurdly literal *New York Times* headline, you know." So we threw a couple of things around, and then I said, "Well, how about 'Pope Dies Yet Again.' " And he thought that was pretty funny. And then he said, "But no, no, we can't finish it with that, we've got to have at least two other subheads. Say we have 'Pope Dies Yet Again; Reign Is Briefest Ever.' " We liked that very much. And then he said, " 'Cardinals Return from Airport.' " It was just brilliant. It was just perfect. So that was the headline for our lead, and it was a classic story. Jonathan Becker shot the photo right there in George's apartment on the stairwell. I was the pope. I had a reverse collar and looked very holy.

CHRIS CERF   We got the *Times*'s distributors to sell it on the newsstand; it was on every newsstand, and it looked just like the *Times*. I've been told that Abe Rosenthal was furious, and they talked about suing us but didn't. I don't know if it's true.

TONY HENDRA   The whole event was, to my way of thinking, typically George. It was like this massive prank. We put in all kinds of wonderful jokes, like a very important little filler item which the *Times* had at the time. It was known at the paper as a "bus plunger." Somebody at the *Times* would collect these news bits about horrendous bus accidents—in South America especially— where buses would plunge off a cliff with thirty-five aboard. We had a few of those. There was another running joke: We'd note some disaster, but whatever happened, whether it was in New

York or Vietnam or Washington, the reaction in Israel would be "muted." Somehow George's spirit just permeated the whole thing. Many contributors had been conditioned by the *Lampoon,* which in the years after George's time there had a wildly extremist kind of humor. So it needed a fundamentally sympathetic but calming influence to make it work. And that was George; he actually acted as a brake on certain of our excesses. Not all the time, but some of the time.

GEORGE'S EDITORIAL TASTE AND TOUCH

MONA SIMPSON George wanted to have a staff. He didn't want people just to work for him. He wanted to have people push things to him. He wanted it to be an eclectic magazine. He ultimately wanted it to be his magazine, but he wanted things that were new, that were interesting. The magazine was unique, I think, because of his personality. I mean, usually these literary magazines reflect one intense personality like Ben Sonnenberg with *Grand Street* or Ted Solotaroff with *New American Review.* The person who does it, it's really their vision completely, and then they burn out. That's the normal way of things. George's sensibility was a bit more porous; he was a little bit more open to the variable spirit of the time and place, and for that reason, I think, he was able to stay passionate about the magazine for fifty years or more.

MOLLY MCGRANN Stories would go through a series of readers. It would start with a general reading, which was done by interns, and then if something was good, it would get passed around the office. If something was really good, the senior editors would spend time really looking at it and would either deem it worthy of George's attention or not. George would gradually accumulate this pile, and at some point he would essentially be given a deadline; he'd be sat down and told he had to go through them. Putting the magazine together went down to the wire every single time. It was exhilarating. Galleys would come in, and everyone had to sit and work on them furiously because time was so short, and decisions were being made up till the last possible moment.

JEANNE MCCULLOCH   Almost without exception, when I was there, George ushered in everything the staff got really excited about and wanted to put in the magazine. When he'd learned to trust us, I almost never came up against him saying no to something. We published some really interesting people: Michael Cunningham for the first time, Rick Moody, Jay McInerney, Susan Minot, Jeff Eugenides, Donald Antrim. It was a unique opportunity, because most of these people were also our friends, and they would come by and hang out at the parties.

DANIEL KUNITZ   The paradigmatic editorial moment with George: You come in hung over, and you feel really strongly about some story that you're certain George has not read but that you're sure he doesn't want to publish, and you go upstairs to his office, where he's sitting there in his underwear, and you're going to fight it out with him. You say, "George, I disagree with you about this." The first thing that happens is, he knows the story better than you do. He's read it three times, and he can point to specific words, phrases, this and that. He was so incredibly bright. I didn't always agree with him, but the things he said were just so on. He was a joy to work with in every way.

ELIZA GRISWOLD   As for the poetry, what would happen is, it would come into the office, and then we readers would prescreen it, and basically any letter that said the writer knew Richard Howard [the poetry editor at the time] or said something else that made it clear the person was to be considered carefully, that submission would just be bundled up and sent to Richard, who is an incredibly generous reader and reviewer of young poets. He and George didn't interact very much, because Richard did most of the poetry outside of *The Paris Review* and George didn't read the poetry. Nobody read the poetry, because there was just too much. *I* hardly read the poetry. When I left, we had a five-year backlog.

The Old Guard in 1976. Front row, from left: Maxine Groffsky, George, Donald Hall, Patsy Southgate, Rose Styron. Back row, from left: William Styron, Drue Heinz, Tom Guinzburg, Peter Matthiessen, John Marquand, Blair Fuller, Robert Silvers. Photograph by Jill Krementz.

RICHARD HOWARD   We had some difficulty with John Updike about a poem called "Three Cunts in Paris." George said to me, "Do you think we can do that?" I said, "Well, I don't think anything will happen. . . ." It was a description of a statue and two paintings in the Louvre, and it was an amusing poem. There was some French quoted in it, though, all quite incorrectly, and I wrote John back and said, "Do you mind if we do this a little differently? It won't affect the poem, but it will be correct." He wrote back saying that he didn't mind at all, that they always did that to him at *The New Yorker*. He wondered if I got extra pay for being so careful. Updike has published several big volumes of poetry by now, but he's not really a poet; he's a verse writer, and a very good one. Like Billy Collins, you know—as good as that, and a little more intellectual than that. Still, I remember George being a little hesitant about "Three Cunts in Paris," but he thought we should go ahead with it.

JONATHAN DEE   As a fiction editor, his strength and his weakness were one and the same. If you asked George in 1990, "Who are the essential American writers?" (a) that list would have been the same as it was for him in 1965, and (b) it would have been composed entirely of people with whom he socialized. I remember when we wanted to try to get Toni Morrison for the interview series in 1986, we had to explain to him who she was. He didn't read any contemporary fiction other than what he read for the magazine. He had to rely on us for that, and he took our word for it, which is pretty amazing. Who were we, you know? Just a bunch of assistants. But he knew what kind of value to put on our enthusiasm.

ELISSA SCHAPPELL   It's hard to say that there was any one sort of story he didn't like, because when you look at the range of stories he published, they were all very different. He was publishing Lenny Michaels and Lorrie Moore: one writer who dances around issues of intimacy and emotional connection and is very funny; and then Lenny, who basically is like, "I'm going to cut myself in front of you and show you the bone." I think he didn't like sloppiness or sentimentality, things that didn't make good art. He had a great eye—just look at what he bought. And he inspired loyalty in writers, too, so that they sent him their best work. When I was there the *Review* was in that little first circle: You sent your best to *The New Yorker* and *The Paris Review.*

JAMES SCOTT LINVILLE   Staff readers would come in every other week to help read through "the unsoliciteds." George would invite this crowd to spread out in his living room and give them soda or a beer. He'd explain why this task was so important, and then he'd always pronounce some instructions: "First, no stories about daughters and their mothers. It just won't work for us." Of course, a year later he published the beginning of Mona Simpson's *Anywhere but Here.* "Secondly, no stories of people dying of cancer.

That's not a *Paris Review* story." Soon enough, we showed him that story by Charles D'Ambrosio about the man driving a girl with cancer to Mexico to die. He flipped, just loved it. I said, "George, what about the . . . you know . . . ?" Of course, we gave it the Aga Khan Prize. But that was George. So he'd sternly deliver these Old Testament injunctions of what we were forbidden to publish, and then he'd turn around and be so excited about a story that was exactly that.

FAYETTE HICKOX Big ideas—War, Conservatism, Free Will, Love, any sort of theory, anything with a capital letter—just weren't his thing.

JONATHAN DEE One episode I'll never forget: We were the first magazine to see any of the stories from Denis Johnson's *Jesus' Son*. Now, I think you could make the case that *Jesus' Son* is the most influential work of American fiction in the last twenty years. The first story we got was "Car Crash While Hitchhiking," which I thought was one of the most amazing things I'd ever read. We all thought so. So we went through the usual dance where we tried to get George to read it in something resembling a timely fashion. Jay McCulloch would sometimes stick manuscripts like that into his flight bag, in the hope that he would find it by accident on the plane and figure he might as well read it. We bugged him and bugged him to read "Car Crash," and we were all very nervous about what he would say, because we didn't want to lose it to some other magazine. Finally, he came downstairs to the office one afternoon holding it rolled up in his hand. He sat down in this chair under the clock and he said, "I don't know what you guys are talking about. I just don't see anything in this. But if you feel that strongly about it, then we should do it." That was the aspect of him that people failed to appreciate; that's what kept the magazine vital for so many years. There was no reason on earth why he should have let us make those judgment calls, but he did.

BRIGID HUGHES Probably the biggest thing that we looked at in my time was the excerpt from Jonathan Safran Foer's novel. We had published a story of his an issue or two before we got the

Everything Is Illuminated excerpt. Half of the office loved it and said it was the best thing they'd seen since they'd been at *The Paris Review*. Half the office didn't like it. George in particular didn't like it. There were certain times that George didn't like something when he wasn't quite sure of his opinion, because he kept throwing it back to the staff for two or three rounds. We kept it for a while and finally said we weren't going to take it, so I sent Jonathan an e-mail, only to find out that day that *The New Yorker* had just accepted it, so it turned out fine for him.

ELISSA SCHAPPELL   He once took Alice Munro to task on the phone about some changes he wanted made in one of her stories. It was unbelievable. I thought, "My God, that's Alice Munro." It was some story that had something to do with an alien spaceship, and he said, "You're wrong. You just can't do that. It's just not right. You're wrong." I heard that he brought her to tears. But he was right.

LARISSA MACFARQUHAR   It's true that George was not involved in every last detail. On the other hand, his taste was very much the guiding force of the *Review*, and I didn't always agree with it. I felt that it was a little too conservative. I'm not some wild and woolly advocate of hypertext experimentalism or anything, but I did feel that there was a little too much of a commitment to the classic fifties American short story—the well-crafted short story. It was not just George. I felt that most of the staff of the *Review* were also fans of the classic, well-crafted story and were turned off by anything remotely pretentious, or flowery, or baroquely constructed—things that drew attention to themselves as writing, to which I could have extended more leeway. I remember disagreeing with George one time, with everyone on my side, and I think he still succeeded in getting it in the magazine, this horrendous piece of dreck by Terry Southern. I think it's called "Lamp Man." Someone recently told me that it had been sent to *Harper's* and they had the same fight. We had a huge fight with George over this absurd, pornographic story that involved a lightbulb, a peeping Tom, and an anatomically correct blowup doll. It was the most ridiculous thing, no merit whatsoever. It was so retro-porn. You couldn't take

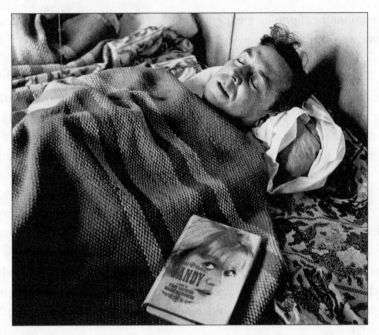

Terry Southern sleeping it off in George's guest room.
Photograph © Steve Schapiro.

it seriously as porn, it was so ludicrous. But George, loyal to the end, said, "It's Terry. We have to publish it." It was the only time he did that while I was there. If you start a magazine, it's your magazine, and you should be able to do stuff like that. And Terry Southern is a kind of awe-inspiring figure, even if he does produce pieces of absurd shit, just like everybody else.

DALLAS WIEBE I wasn't in the New York loop, as they say these days. I was stuck out here in this provincial town called Cincinnati. It's really a backward swamp down here, certainly in a literary sense. It was kind of a *de profundis* thing, you know, calling out from the depths. It was wonderful to be in *The Paris Review,* because that was away from this place. When *Skyblue the Badass* came out from *Paris Review* Editions, the dean of the College of Arts and Sciences wanted to fire me. I didn't know anything about it until it was over. There was a group in the city called the Citizens for Decent Literature; that group proliferated. It was in other cities, too. They became Citizens for Decency, and then they became Citizens for Community Values. They're still here. They're the kind of people that if they don't like what you do, they'll try to punish you. It's not just a matter of criticizing you or of dealing with you—they go after people. It's happened a lot here in Cincinnati. It's not just me. And, by the way, at the time they tried to fire me, the head of the Citizens for Decent Literature was a man named Charlie Keating—have you ever heard of him? He was the guy who ran that big savings and loan swindle out in Arizona. He got all these old people to put their savings and their retirement money into it, and then he went broke. He was the head of that. Mr. Charlie Keating.

BRIGID HUGHES George came down one morning and read an article in the paper about this book that FSG was publishing, based on a one-woman show where she played fifty different characters. So he sent away for the galleys, and he got an excerpt and said, "Isn't this great?" I did not think it was great at all, and neither did Fiona, but George was adamant about it. He thought it was different and that we really could stretch the boundaries here. I think what he thought was so new and exciting about it was that it took place at something called a "rave," which he thought we should provide a definition for at the bottom of the story. I didn't really know what to say.

OLIVER BROUDY I forget how the Richard Ford story came in. I think we must have asked for it, because only that could explain how angry Ford got. It was like ninety pages, and it was pretty shitty, really second-rate. We were all passive about it in our comments, because this was Richard Ford. Then, one day, George came downstairs and he had the manuscript with him and he started underlining sentences, pointing out that it was just bad writing, and upbraided us all for it, which I enjoyed, actually. I liked being held accountable. Anyway, George wrote a letter to Ford and basically told him that he thought the story was bad and explained why. A few days later, he came downstairs looking stricken. He confessed that he had gotten a letter back from Richard

Ford, and Ford was furious. George was deeply upset that he had pissed Ford off and was worrying aloud about how to patch things up with him, which says something about his approach to editing. He didn't want to upset people.

BRIGID HUGHES   George wrote Ford a letter at the end of the year that said something like "I'm sitting here on New Year's Eve and looking back on the past year, and I regret the way that I handled your story." Ford sent a very lovely note saying that he would never send a story again.

LORRIE MOORE   George took a story of mine, one which had already been rejected by a couple other places, and so I was completely grateful, especially since the story, "Terrific Mother," was long and had all its happiness at the end and so was unusual for me, which caused a perverse, special fondness for it in no one but myself. But George seemed to like it because he thought it was funny, which I greatly appreciated. He also very astutely noted an unnecessary scene (in getting the characters from the U.S. to Italy I actually included a scene on a plane), and so in deleting that we made the story swifter and more efficient. He did have one query, I recall, regarding the phrase "garbage night" or "trash night," one or the other. He didn't know what it meant. I told him that was the night people took out their trash for pickup the next day, and he said, rather skeptically, "Really?" But he gave me the benefit of the doubt. Though I had met him briefly once or twice—he was very tall and charming—all this took place on the phone. He was energetic and jolly and sometimes midsentence would consult with members of his staff on the significance of a word or reference, valuing consensus.

ELIZABETH GAFFNEY   My last really amazing editorial interaction with George was where we both edited the same story separately and then came together. It was this Michael Chabon novella, *The Final Solution.* I had become friends with Michael Chabon, and I was very pleased to have gotten the piece. We had never published anything by him before. It turned out to be a genre piece. It's a Sherlock Holmes story, which might not have been a hundred percent what George was expecting from his preconceived idea of Michael Chabon. It was long, one hundred pages. I read it and loved it. We took it, and this was shortly before George died, so I was editor at large at that point, but this was a project I was doing. George kept saying to me, "It needs a lot of work," and I kept saying to him, "George, it needs a very little bit of work. It's masterful." He would say, "We've got to sit down together and look at this thing." It took us forever to sit down and look at it together, but we really wanted to schedule it for this particular issue. We needed to know whether it was going to fly, because George was making rather pessimistic noises about it. He was saying the glass was half-empty, and I was saying it was more than half-full. So we finally sat down, and page after page, we had almost the exact same edits throughout this hundred-page manuscript. It was a blissful moment! I wasn't a young editor seeking his approval anymore, but there was still something so gratifying. I felt like I internalized what he had to teach me.

JEANNE MCCULLOCH George was a very good mentor, in terms of being an editor, but he was strangely unsupportive of the staff's writing. I have never heard a story of him being overtly supportive of a staffer's fiction writing. I remember about Mona Simpson's book *Anywhere but Here* he kept saying, "She's got to fix it. She can't send it out like that." She didn't "fix" it, and after it came out to great acclaim, he said, "I was in California last week, and you can imagine, they're all talking about Mona's book!" He said to me many, many times, "Kiddo, you're an editor. You're not a writer, you're an editor," which at the time was a very hard thing for me to hear, because I believed him for a long time.

JONATHAN DEE George was more paternal to some of his assistants than to others. There was a lot of talk in the office about "kiddo" status, i.e., you knew he was fond of you once he started addressing you as "kiddo." I got kiddo'd less than some in the personal assistant's job—for instance Antonio [Weiss], whom he plainly adored. I had an odd relationship with him. George wasn't threatened in the Norman Mailer sense of being threatened, where there is always someone nearby who wanted to take his crown. He was threatened because he did not like the idea of some snotty twenty-four-year-old viewing *The Paris Review,* which was his life's work, as a kind of stepping-stone or way station on the road to somewhere else. I was actually tremendously invested in the *Review* and took a lot of pride in working there. But it's true that there was something else, some other kind of literary endeavor that I cared more about, and he recognized that. Other people who worked there would go home at night and write their novels, just like me, and if they ever showed him their work in progress, looking for his approval, he could be very mean. But that never happened to me. I never showed him anything I was working on, because others there had warned me not to.

ELIZA GRISWOLD   Oh God, yes, he read my writing. I had a poem in *The Paris Review* once, and George decided he loved it. He read it on NPR, he read it at insane places. It was so sweet of him. It was a dramatic monologue about Midas, and he just loved it. Either he loved it, or he loved encouraging me. Either way, it was a pretty unique experience.

ELIZABETH GAFFNEY   I think it was hard for George to set young novelists free and to endorse them. It was a very father/child dynamic. Watch the child excel in something the parent aspired to do, and if you encourage the child to learn this skill or art form, it's complicated if the child ends up choosing something that you didn't have the balls to do or the ability to succeed at. To me, being able to edit something is an act of totally optimistic empathy. You have to be able to understand what the writer means—or rather, the best thing that the writer might mean—and then let that optimism show you how the writer might bring out the best in his or her story; and we both could read certain things that we both liked. When he could do it, he was great at it.

DAVID MICHAELIS   People projected on to him a lot of their own issues. Most likely they just fell off him; they didn't really stick. But what I always felt with George was that the kindness outweighed the coldness. I don't mean that in a Pollyanna way. I think he was crazy about the people around him. I think he really enjoyed them and had a great capacity for taking pleasure in other people, in their successes and their lives.

FIONA MAAZEL Whatever his strengths and lapses as a fiction editor, with the interviews he was unbelievable. I'll never forget—it was the third day I worked there—I transcribed a John le Carré interview, and as far as I could tell, it was junk. Then someone else put it together a little bit, and I read it again and thought, "This is so dumb." It went upstairs to George, and when it came back down from George, with all the changes, I was shocked. I had never seen anything like it. I didn't even know such things were possible. He could turn utter schlock into something magnificent because he had just the right touch and such a good ear.

VICTOR NAVASKY He didn't invent the interview, obviously, but he was a conversationalist and a performer, an oral performer, so it was appropriate that the interview should be part of the mix of *The Paris Review* and maybe the most enduring contribution that it made to literature.

JAMES SCOTT LINVILLE The interviews, of course, were his pride and joy. When I put together the magazine's archives, I took a close look at each one. Going back to the beginning in Paris, George's pencil was on every single one of them. And of course his editing was so sharp. The first thing to go, naturally, was whatever the interviewer said, because a *Paris Review* interview was about the writer, the subject. As for his approach, he preferred the most simple, practical questions rather than something high-minded. This wasn't simply George being anti-intellectual, which he could be, but that he'd recognized that the more tangible a question you asked, the more likely it was to open a door to something unexpected about the creative process.

BRIGID HUGHES There was a big file cabinet with old interviews that would just sit there for years, and sometimes George would pull one out and declare that it was going to appear. In one case, somebody called up Woody Allen and asked him a couple of up-dating questions, which he inserted; then George did one of his cutting-and-pasting jobs. All of this was done without consulting the original interviewer, which had been Kakutani. I'm not sure she even knew it appeared; but when we tried to get permission to anthologize the interview, Ben Howe, who had worked on that project, sent a letter to her, and she said no, she wouldn't grant it. So Ben called her, but she still said no. George, being George, al-ways thought that a letter from him would change everyone's minds. So he went upstairs and wrote this letter and wrote out an envelope, and thank God someone picked it up, because it said, "Nikito Kukutani." He got the name totally wrong. So then he got on the phone with her, and she lit into him for publishing the interview and not consulting with her about edits, and she didn't want it published in the first place, and she sure as hell didn't want it published ever again. Good day. George was stunned that he couldn't charm a woman into granting him permission.

MONA SIMPSON   He was very unhappy at one point with the amount of money that the *Review* had been paid for the various anthologies of interviews. Viking was paying us very little, and they were delaying publications. So Jay and I volunteered to go to this guy we knew at Simon and Schuster to see about moving our books there, and George was all for it. After an extended series of meetings, we got an offer for twenty-five thousand dollars—the current publisher was offering, I think, three thousand—and they were really going to push it and promote it. So we come to George saying, "Okay, let's sign on the dotted line, it's going to be great." Then, at the last minute, George calls our editor at the other house—basically an old friend of George's whom he'd been working with for years, who occasionally sent him tickets to a ball game. The editor sends George some tickets to the ball game and the whole deal is off. We realized at that point that we couldn't just go out in the world and do that sort of thing anymore, not even with his permission, because we found that we basically didn't have power to go against his personal loyalties. It was very embar-rassing, because Simon and Schuster was outraged that we were staying with an offer that was about twelve percent of theirs.

JONATHAN DEE The interviews were so important to me, personally, as a would-be novelist. I would work all day, and then I would take home an armload of the back issues sitting around the office, and I read all the interviews straight through. In terms of my education as a writer, there's just nothing that could have taken their place. But then in the years after I left, there was a big effort to repackage the old ones along various demographic lines—*Women Writers at Work, Latino Writers at Work*—or to jazz up the new efforts by transcribing interviews that George did onstage at the Ninety-second Street Y—*Writers at Work Live,* it was called. I just didn't buy the premise that the format had become dull. I hated live interviews, because it was the opposite of the private and thoughtful character of those interviews, to do it in front of an audience. I got mad when they started interviewing screenwriters, too.

JOHN GUARE I must say a real highlight was the day I ran into George and he said, "Oh, John, I've been looking for you—would you be interviewed for *Writers at Work*?" And I couldn't believe it. I felt there was some, I don't know, some canonization; it was Olympus, some goal that you got to that you never dream of getting to. I did it with Elizabeth Gaffney. Very intense editing, we kept going back and forth—that's what I was so impressed with, how George and Liz would go over the interview and keep specifying; you skirted over this, we want to know more about this, or we know too much about that. I mean, the editing was very line-by-line.

FAYETTE HICKOX It wasn't just the *Writers at Work* series. When you think about it, George did an awful lot of editorial work on other people's spoken words—which was fitting, wasn't it, George being such an artist of the spoken word himself. I was there when he did *Edie* with Jean Stein, his most successful "oral biography." I don't remember much about it except that one day boxes and boxes of transcripts turned up in the pool room, and there was George digging through them one after the other and being just agog at what Jean Stein had been able to pull out of people. She was an incredibly seductive interviewer.

George loved the subject, of course. He knew Edie and her parents and siblings; her grandparents were friends of his parents in Cold Spring Harbor. He knew their Society world, and he knew the Warhol world in which poor Edie rose and crashed. Also he was drawn to spectacles of failure, wasn't he, especially perhaps when they were glamorously self-destructive and involved someone of his own class. He threw himself into the *Edie* project with great gusto, but perhaps the most amazing thing he did with Jean's material was to cut up the interviews into paragraph-size bites, as he did with *Review* interviews, and then splice them together in such a way as to tell Edie's story without relying on any interpolations by Jean or himself to fill in the gaps.

> *Dear Alice—*[*]
>
> *. . . Jean started her book* Edie *with Paul Spike as her collaborator. The book was to be in the usual biographical form—she supplying the information, Paul to mold it into book form. Jean didn't approve of what had been done. She sent me a few chapters and I agreed with her. When she asked for help, I said I would only work on it on the condition that we shift the form to oral biography (the form we had used previously with* American Journey: The Times of Robert F. Kennedy*) and that she would do the interviewing and I would do the editing: the two of us were to be listed as co-authors. She agreed to this and that is how the original contract reads.*
>
> *So that's the way we worked. Of course we discussed editorial matters. I valued her opinions. . . . But the vast work of line editing, the arrangement of the chapters, the melding of one interview into the next so that it seemed seamless was mine from start to finish.*
>
> *. . . When the manuscript of* Edie *was completed, Jean and I sent it to Bob Gottlieb at Knopf. . . . I did not know Gottlieb's modus operandi at the time and when Jean and I arrived I was horrified to find him sitting on the floor of his office and flipping through the pages of our book as if sifting rather petulantly through a pile of old newspapers. I remember mentioning this to Jean after-*

---

[*] Excerpted from a letter from George to Alice Sedgwick Wohl, Edie's sister and Jean Stein's schoolmate.

wards. In fact, Gottlieb was delighted with Edie, *said as much, and I don't recall that he made any editorial suggestions except to reassure Jean, who was worried that the working title* Edie *might confuse readers into thinking they were buying a book about Eydie Gorme, that the title was fine.*

. . . What then happened was simply a power play. . . . Jean suddenly announced that she would not allow the manuscript to be published unless I relinquished my position as co-author. She would be listed as the book's sole author—this despite our agreement. . . .

After an anguished week or so I finally decided to let Jean have her way. My rationale was that she had done the bulk of the work in terms of time spent, it was her project originally, and it was finally more important to have the book appear than quibble over marquee standings.

. . . After Edie *was published I went out on tour and did my best to promote the book. Jean refused to do this—quite understandably because she isn't comfortable doing that sort of thing. Being more in the public eye, and thus able to get booked on TV and radio shows, I was left to do it. I think this increased the strain between us: it could well have seemed, being on as many shows as I was, and concentrating on the worth of the book rather than who its authors were, that I was taking too much credit. Indeed, I'm sure there were interviews during which I didn't mention Jean's name at all. The interviewer who pushed the book onto the best-sellers list was Joan Rivers on the Johnny Carson show. She talked admiringly about the book for five minutes. I don't remember saying anything.*

Frankly, I am dismayed at what has happened over the years. I've known Jean since she arrived in Paris. I liked her then, very much. She did a fine Faulkner interview. She showed a bit of muscle back then, I might add, insisting that we could only publish the interview if I made her an editor of the magazine. . . . I admire what she has done with Grand Street, *and have written her so. We have a good time when we find ourselves seated next to each other at dinner.*
[no date]

ROBERT GOTTLIEB I do know what happened between George and Jean, but I don't know that this needs to be aired twenty-five years later or whatever it is. You can say that the *Edie* experience, which started out very amicably and positively, ended in an ugly dispute between Stein and Plimpton, mainly about credit. I eventually came up with a compromise that both of them accepted.

FREDDY GIVES UP

FREDDY ESPY PLIMPTON We had this humongous apartment, as you know, but the *Paris Review* staff had it, too. We slept on the third floor, where George's original apartment had been. That's where our bedroom was, and Medora's and Taylor's, too. But the whole second floor—living room, pool room, kitchen, and dining room, everything but George's office when he was actually working in it—was open to the staff downstairs, and they loved every nook and cranny of it. Some of them were less intrusive than others. They understood that it was a private home and didn't just go roaring up there. But others would walk in without knocking—have a beer, shoot pool, whatever. I had absolutely no privacy. It was like having a burrow at the bottom of the stairs, a very busy burrow full of rabbits or something. I complained about this over and over to my therapist. I said, "I've got this situation. It's driving me crazy. I feel like killing everyone." He suggested we put in a spiral staircase to give me my own territory. And we did.

JONATHAN DEE The early eighties, when I was there, was the tail end of that marriage, and the two of them were rarely in town at the same time. On the first day of every month, in fact, I would type up for Freddy George's schedule for the month to come, his speeches, his travel plans, etc. That was her only way of knowing where he was, because I don't think they were speaking much at that point. There was a long period where by many people's standards they would not have been considered married at all. Freddy was on Long Island, trying to stay sober, while George was in New York, or else it was George on the Island and Freddy in New York. They were almost never in the same place at the same time. I don't know how long it had been like that, but by the time I got there, in 1984, that was the status quo; they effectively weren't sharing a life. It was civil, but functionally, it was a separation. That evolved slowly; and then, as I understand it, the end came quickly, because Freddy hit it off with somebody else.

FAYETTE HICKOX I can't say exactly when I first noticed that the marriage was in trouble, but I remember one dinner in the Hamptons, the thousandth time they'd taken me out to a good restaurant, when George launched into one of his tried-and-true stories and Freddy said, "Oh, George, that's so boring; do we need to hear that one again?" Her tone was utterly contemptuous. Not a good sign, contempt.

DEBORAH PEASE They were still together, or at least living in the same apartment, in '82. At the inaugural party that George gave me, the new publisher, Freddy was there looking beautiful. I remember she had a hairdo that made her look like Julie Christie in her curly phase. So Freddy was very much there, at least for that event. But what I recall most vividly, about a year later, was when I called George out in the Hamptons. Freddy answered and said, "My husband is sleeping, I don't want to wake him." She was very proprietary. People don't normally say to someone they know, "My husband is such-and-such," they say, "George is . . ." I got the sense that she was asserting herself as the primary person in his life. Maybe she was, but as things developed I'm not sure that he was the primary person in her life.

REMAR SUTTON In the early eighties, I was almost more worried than I could handle about where things were going with George and Freddy. Once, George and Freddy and the kids came down to Boca Raton, to a house we'd gotten together on the canal, a lovely Spanish-style house. Freddy was in one of those moods, fueled by too many drinks. We would be sitting there at dinner, and if one of the kids brought up the wrong bottle of ketchup, Freddy would get an edge in her voice. We would all begin to get that feeling of tension, and then Freddy would go crazy. The kids would run out of the room, and George and I would get into the car and go off someplace and leave Freddy there alone. George can't bear any type of conflict, so he just stepped away from Freddy, the kids, everybody. They lived in the same space, but that was a very tough time, particularly because George loved Freddy. But he did not know how to handle the relationship when it started going south. George is the one who got Freddy partying and brought her along way too quickly into many things in life. Then he started backing away from everything.

MOLLY MCKAUGHAN   Even in the early 1970s when I was at the *Review*, Freddy was making a life of her own on the edges of George's life. She wasn't an alcoholic yet, but I remember her telling me that she never really spent any private time with George except for in the summers. She'd say, "George will be gone for five days, and he'll come back, we'll get dressed up in black tie and go to a dinner party, then at six the next morning he'll leave again."

NANCY STODDART   The way people treated Freddy was really awful. They made it sound like he could have married anybody, but he married her. And I think some article along those lines got into either *Time* or *Newsweek:* "George Plimpton, who could have married Jackie Kennedy, Candice Bergen, some other social star . . . instead just married this photographer's assistant." It was very hurtful, as I think a lot of their marriage was. He was always center stage. It's kind of, like, you're married to the Great Man and you're the Curator of the Great Man, or the Barely Tolerated Wife of the Great Man. Whatever it is you are, you have to be in somebody else's shadow. But she chose the bed that she lay down in by choosing this guy. You know you're going to be second fiddle to him. Everybody worships him, and everybody kind of tolerates you because you've married him. Most men won't tolerate being the satellite of a great woman because, you know, their egos won't take it. On the other hand, George did not protect her, and he could have and should have. He never took her hand and said, "This is my wife."

KRISTI WITKER   I really liked Freddy. In those days I never had many plans, so I was always hanging around their wonderful town house. I loved being there. It was so much more interesting than being alone in my little apartment because there was always something going on. Strange people would come in—some circus people would walk in one door and a nun from 110th Street would walk in the other. It was always totally unpredictable and always fun. I remember thinking, "Oh, I wish I were Freddy, just to have this life—it's so interesting, so fascinating. You could never feel lonely, you could never be bored!" Of course, as time wore on, I realized that this was not necessarily the case, and perhaps it never had been.

FREDDY ESPY PLIMPTON George and I both adored Marianne Moore, but we had quite different relationships with her. She thought I was this waif, and she thought that she was necessary in my life, and I thought she was this waif and that I was necessary in her life, and it was just very touching. She saw George as an interesting and courtly man who invited her to do entertaining, if puzzling, things with him. She never seemed to realize that we were a couple. Miss Moore would invite me to visit her at her apartment on Tenth Street, where there was just room for a bed and a few shelves and stacks and stacks of books and a tiny kitchen, and she had all these odd little animals around that she collected and wrote poetry about. I would sit at the foot of the bed, and she would be propped up against the pillows. I don't know what we talked about. We always gave each other little presents. She knew I liked to paint, so she gave me watercolors. When I left, she would insist on giving me cab fare to get me home safely. I have never had a relationship like that with anyone—one of loving interest and quiet hand-holding. George wanted Miss Moore to do certain things to enhance whatever it was he was writing about. I often worried that she was too frail for such outings. When George was with Ali, for example, Miss Moore would sit there under her tricorn hat trying to think up a line for a poem that she would help Ali write so that George could write about it. Ali loved that. I remember he leaned down in this gentlemanly fashion—and he was a big man— he leaned down when everybody was sitting at a table and talked to her under her hat.

WALTER SOHIER I didn't know too much about the marriage. Freddy was a bit of a complainer and used to complain about

With Marianne Moore. Photograph by Jill Krementz.

George, but I didn't want to sit there and listen. I liked Freddy very much, and I liked them together very much. I don't think they had a very happy time. I don't know that George would be a very easy husband, probably in the same way that I wasn't, because he was probably uncommunicative, a bit indifferent. He hadn't had a warm, close family upbringing, and it's very hard for somebody without that to be a good family person; but that's just speculation. There's a lot I didn't know about George, and for all of his gregariousness, he was a very private person.

CHRIS CERF She couldn't change George, but who would want to change George? George was George. As Mel Brooks said, "You like the nose, you buy the face." Imagine that you actually could change George, and somehow he was just a great family man who gave up his lecture tours (much of his livelihood, by the way) so he could be with you, and wasn't mischievous, and didn't disappear for a week to set off the world's biggest fireworks—what's the point? That's what made him so wonderful.

CYNTHIA BAGLEY I came back to New York in 1981, and I saw George then. That's when I met Freddy. My son was then four, the same age as Taylor, so they would play together. I would keep that lad overnight, and he was so difficult, but by then I had been working with Ronnie Laing in London as a child psychologist, so I was able to deal with him, and I started trying to change his diet, to try to get him to calm down, because he had these strange eating problems. And George was just so unhappy. If you went to his house, the situation was such that even when George wasn't there, Freddy's strings were pulled so taut that you just didn't know quite where to put yourself. Without George there, it was like you were dealing with someone who was so high-strung, so on the edge of madness all the time. She *was* scary.

NANCY STODDART There was a very unattractive period where George started hanging around with this really horrible man. I was just completely shocked by the idea that somebody I really looked up to, whom I considered an older person, had gotten into a creepy drug thing—until I got into one for a brief period myself years later.

MAVIS HUMES BAIRD I remember at one point with Freddy, he was really scared. He loved her to pieces, but he was scared by how angry the exchanges were between them. It wasn't all her fault. George was an impossible person to be married to; but she would get really pissed off and start needling or getting an attitude. She's so incredibly witty, she'd come up with these barbed digs that were a riot if you didn't care about anyone's feelings. She'd sort of invite everyone to go on the ride with her. It was a treacherous social exchange—if you didn't let her know that you saw her point and that you approved of her humor, she felt hurt and betrayed by you.

FREDDY ESPY PLIMPTON Through all the bad times George and I had with each other, he never shouted, he never got angry, he simply went his own way. Sins of omission rather than sins of commission. But those are the hardest ones to bear. When you just had a baby, for example, and your husband takes off on this trip and that trip, and doesn't really acknowledge that this has happened to you, that's hard. Giving birth to Medora, then Taylor, were the biggest things I'd ever done. I mean, the whole experience was amazing for me. But I didn't get any acknowledgment from George, which is all I really wanted. And George was unable to give that to me, whom he adored—and he did adore me. I mean, he was such an acknowledging person to his friends, to the *Paris Review* staff, to strangers. Why couldn't he give some of it to me?

ANN WINCHESTER She and I had been to Disneyland with the children, and she was behaving very oddly then. It's probably the same summer that I was staying at the apartment and pretty much looking after Taylor because she was a bit off-the-wall. I was there because I was doing the sculpture for Elaine Hart, that weird lady across the road who couldn't go out. Well, one day Freddy just freaked out. She was just shaking and shaking and shaking. It was something I'd never seen before; I don't scare easily, but I was positively alarmed. No, terrified. I wanted to call an ambulance, but she absolutely wouldn't let me. I thought, "Well, it's her house and I'm her guest. . . ." But in the end I overruled her and sent her to the hospital. And I was left with the children. From there she went into detox; I think she would have died otherwise. I didn't see her again, basically. She took against me, big-time. She wouldn't see me or talk to me or anything. Fortunately, someone at the detox place told me to expect this, as it is a very common reaction to the circumstance. Apparently they can't again face the person who saw them in that desperate state—not at first and sometimes never again. I have called her over the years, but she's not indicated a wish to resume our friendship. I'm not the kind of person who lets go of old friends, and it is sad. But I am truly happy she is well.

JOYCE BARONIO I saw him sort of falling apart. I think Freddy was in Colorado at that time, in rehab, I think, and there would be these phone calls from Colorado, and he would get very upset. She could really upset him. There was something very out of control about her, and he didn't know how to deal with that. "You're supposed to be better by now," he'd say, "why aren't you better?" And I heard all the stories, from Bill Becker mostly, about how she had, you know, slept with all his friends. But George never mentioned it. He never mentioned the specifics. It just really upset him.

A. E. HOTCHNER George was an enigma, he really didn't show you a lot. George was George. He had a set persona, and that was gonna be it, hell or high water. So I know that when he and Freddy were mired in their deepest problems, Freddy was suffering over it. But not George. George was just riding through it. Not happily, but you would never know he was going through what he went through.

CHRIS CERF If someone deeply hurt George, that's not something he would talk about. He would make it into a story. It took extraordinary distress for him to be more than an anecdotalist.

JOYCE BARONIO I was trying to get him to talk about Freddy and what was going on in his life now and to try to be okay with it. So, he did that. He was just very nervous about it, what she was going to do. He could still not quite bring himself around to getting divorced, but he knew that that was pending. And it was just like some horror that he had to continually face that he had never been prepared for.

DEBORAH PEASE He did talk about it freely, Freddy leaving him. Not when there were people listening—although you never knew, when you called George, how many people were in the room— but he did say that Freddy was drifting away. I can't remember his exact words, but it did upset him. I remember him using the words *sleep over;* I mean, "When she comes to New York, she doesn't sleep over here." She was spending most of her time—all of it, really—in Sagaponack. He also told me that Freddy led a "shadow life." That's how he referred to it. And he didn't say it in an unkind way or in a judgmental way at all. But I don't think George liked shadow lives very much; he didn't understand them. When he said that, I had the feeling he just meant a diminished life. Not a clandestine life. An insubstantial life. That's how he meant it. But long before that, in the seventies sometime, I remember seeing the two of them, George and Freddy, at a little dinner party that George Trow gave in his loft down on Grand Street, before that neighborhood became so fancy. It was always clear that George was sexually available to anyone, and that evening, I felt he and I would probably get together at the end of the evening. We hadn't seen each other for a long time, several years, I think. Even in the sixties, with Freddy officially installed at 541, he never gave the impression of being unavailable. It wasn't in his nature to be monogamous. I had the feeling that Freddy was a little bit desperate, even then. I was working as a salesgirl at Design Research in New York, and they came in together, and George was not interested in being there, while Freddy was desperately trying to interest him in the merchandise. She was picking up items and extolling their virtues, and George was really bored. I'd never seen him that way before.

FREDDY ESPY PLIMPTON There came a time when things were getting out of hand. I was drinking too much and unhappy about it. I started worrying that something *bad* was going to happen, that we were going to suffer some repercussions from our behavior. That is why I moved out to the house on Long Island and lived there most of the time and went to these little AA meetings right around there. It was the only place where I didn't pick up a drink. In that apartment, I knew I couldn't *not* pick up a drink. So George and I gradually drifted apart. He met Sarah, and I, unfortunately, met another man.

NANCY STODDART I remember going to see George in the early eighties. He was speaking about something or other at a church on Park Avenue. I spent quite a lot of time with him outside the church, and he was just frantic over whatever Freddy was doing and what was going on with her. She was really circling the drain, and he didn't know what to do at that point. Apparently, she had gone and married someone. Yet he turned out to be the utter demon.

FAYETTE HICKOX She met this guy who everybody thought was fabulous, but he turned out to be a demon. That was the person for whom she left George and left behind her family, left it all behind. It was just unbelievable. Everyone thought he was saintly, amusing, handsome, great, and he just revealed himself as this really ugly, diabolical person.

FREDDY ESPY PLIMPTON I didn't just walk into George's office one day and say, "I want a divorce." He knew I was going to see a lawyer, and I reassured him that—"Don't worry, I'm not going to ask for any sort of settlement at all." Later he said, "If I thought you would ask for money, I wouldn't have divorced you."

PETER MATTHIESSEN We were going to play tennis with Jean and Steve Smith on their court in Bridgehampton, and George arrived late, very haggard. As usual, he'd failed to bring a racket, expecting others to provide it—with his celebrity had come a firm sense of entitlement. He was great fun to play with, however, very competitive yet always a good sport, cheering on his partner, even a poor one. His court manners were exceptionally gracious. He lacked speed; otherwise he was a very adept and graceful player. But this day was the only time I'd ever seen him play truly bad tennis. He kept missing and flubbing, hardly seemed to know where the ball was. We all thought he had a murderous hangover. Suddenly, he just stopped and put his racket down and blurted out, "I can't keep my mind on this. Freddy has run off with another man." He'd just learned of it that morning. He was really suffering, absolutely devastated, poor guy. We all gave him hugs, and Steve said, "I think this calls for a big pitcher of daiquiris!" He marched into the house and made the daiquiris, which we finished off while George talked out the whole thing. He was way beyond keeping his chin up. He had dropped his guard, and his defenselessness was very moving.

SOL GREENBAUM She wanted the divorce. George said, "You want a divorce, you got a divorce." She apparently had a relationship and they wanted to get married, so she was very anxious to get divorced. The settlement was ridiculous, from her point of view. As Jim Goodale, George's lawyer, put it, "Boy, did I work out a great settlement here!" and he did.

FREDDY ESPY PLIMPTON I got married—under subtle but persistent pressure, I now realize. Well, he *was* a sociopath. He set it up. He set it up so I had nothing and so he would have total control over me. After he married me, he became physically abusive, and I managed to get away from him after three months. I had no expectations of George at all, but he came right down to New Orleans to see me, to see how I was doing, to hear what happened; to be there. George was like . . . my father or a dear uncle or something.

SOL GREENBAUM After she ran away from her second husband, who turned out to be a wife beater, everything changed with respect to the settlement, though it didn't have to change, legally speaking. He left the country, and they got divorced, and then she was high and dry, so George continued to support her. He not only bought a house for her in the Hamptons, but he also arranged for her to get a generous monthly allowance to live on.

DRUE HEINZ I went down to Long Island when George and Freddy were trying to decide what to do with the house, during the divorce. George and Freddy were so sweet to each other and it went easily. They decided to sell the house, I think, and she'd get another house, where she's living now, and she's fine. George and Freddy were marvelous together. I used to feel desperate sometimes that there wasn't a real person there in George. Then I realized that, intrinsically, he *was* loving and caring. It might have been sheer upbringing, you know what I mean? Certain ways you behave, certain ways you don't. But he was marvelous in that difficult situation, so kind and so patient.

FREDDY ESPY PLIMPTON I had hurt George badly. Yet when I really needed help, when I had walked off with some crazy guy and felt destroyed and had nothing, nothing—George was the most reassuring, the most helpful, the most generous, the sweetest person. I realized how much he meant to me. What a true gentleman he was.

FAYETTE HICKOX She now lives in this little house that George got for her in Bridgehampton with wonderful views of the water . . . it's certainly a modest house, but she has zillions of birds that come every day, and she watches them and happily creates things and has a sort of spiritual side, and I think that's what she was seeking. She's freed. Her status with George was weird in a way, to the rest of the world. She was just seen as an appendage by a lot of people, whereas now she's a person in her own right. It's so nice to see someone reach serenity after such an odyssey.

VII.

GEORGE IS GEORGE TO THE END: 1983-2003

—

Did I tell you about the time I met Yogi Bhajan? The subject of my impending marriage to George came up and he grilled me about my motives. I went through the obvious responses like love and passion, but he didn't buy it. He just kept at me until I was so exasperated I said, "I'm marrying him because I have to figure out why I want to marry him."

—SARAH DUDLEY PLIMPTON

SARAH

NORMAN MAILER I was taken with Sarah. I liked her immediately. She's got it all. And I thought, "Gee, this is a lady George might really be able to have a marriage with."

JONATHAN DEE There was a great deal of gravitas when the staff was called up into the living room and told that George and Freddy were divorcing and that George and Sarah [Dudley] were romantically involved—as if that was something we hadn't already known. Truman Capote had been their beard, so to speak, because she'd been helping George with various research and transcription

Sarah meets George, Los Angeles, 1984.
Collection of Sarah Dudley Plimpton.

duties having to do with his oral biography of Capote. But the first thing I did when I came into the office every morning was to call the message service, and there would often be a message or two for George from Sarah from eleven o'clock the previous night, asking in semicoded language if now was a good time to come over; so there was pretty obviously an extraprofessional relationship there. It was all a foregone conclusion. George and Freddy had been married in name only for a decade at that point. I don't know for sure, but I imagine he was somewhat relieved that, though the marriage was broken, he hadn't had to be the one who asked for the divorce.

NANCY STODDART Sarah seems like a very different sort of person. She seems to me like a real straight shooter, like she'd be the sort of person who can kind of handle him.

PIEDY LUMET I remember seeing Sarah in Sagaponack before they were married, on a bicycle with him, and they looked fine together. I felt that he might become a little bit settled for the first time in his life. She was wearing a sarong and a bathing suit top. He looked quite pleased with himself.

SARAH DUDLEY PLIMPTON We first met in Los Angeles, where I was working for American Express, who were corporate sponsors of the 1984 Summer Olympics. They were famous for entertaining clients lavishly at sports events, whether it was the Super Bowl or the Olympics. They spared nothing. This was the eighties, so you could imagine. I had been hired to produce a series of speeches, and he was a natural for that, but I had to wrangle him. He had a reputation for getting lost. So the first time I met him, I walked into his hotel room at the Beverly Wilshire and he was stretched out on his bed in his undershorts, papers spread all around him. I mean, how many stories about George begin like that, with George appearing in his boxers? Anyway, there he was. I walked in and instantly felt that I had known him my whole life. I just . . . it was like talking to a member of my own family. I felt so at ease with him. One evening, not long into this, we were in the Beverly Wilshire bar, chatting, and he sort of reached over and put his hand on my knee. I'm so clueless, I thought, "Isn't that nice he feels so collegial?" It never even occurred to me that he was making a pass. Besides, he was still married, Freddy had just gone to her first rehab, and I was seeing two other people at the time. But he wore me down gradually. Let's put it this way, he wasn't that subtle. He wore me down, and finally I gave in. I'll never forget it because I sort of heaved a sigh, "Oh, all right."

BILLY GRAHAM   Sarah Dudley was the daughter of my parents' next-door neighbor in Cold Spring Harbor, on East Gate Road, so I knew Sarah when she was a little kid, when she was a baby; and then I didn't see anything of her for years and years. I came back to New York in 1976 or '77 for most of the summer to do a miniseries with Frank Sinatra, and while I was there I would come out to Long Island, and, by this time, Sarah was a grown-up young lady; she was twenty-five years old, I think, and quite lovely, and I used to see her down on the beach. We got friendly, and one thing led to another, and the next thing you know, she was my girl-friend. I don't think she ever actually lived out here in L.A., but we did see a lot of each other. Well, George beat me out there; I would have married her if George hadn't. In fact, at one point I was already going with Janet, who is my present wife, and Janet and I had a fight over something or other, so I flew back to New York and I called up Sarah and I said, "Come with me to London; let's get married in Westminster Abbey." I think she thought that was a little precipitous, you know. She did come to Yugoslavia with me, though, where I was doing the miniseries on Mussolini, and she spent several weeks there. That was sometime in the eighties. Anyway, we were very close, great friends. Still are.

DEBORAH PEASE   Well, I think I met Sarah only once when I was publisher. I went to the office occasionally for one reason or another, and she stopped by one day on her way to see George. I had the impression that their relationship was entirely work related—she was doing editorial work for him on the Capote book. She seemed a nice, straightforward, down-to-earth person who could be a member of George's family. You didn't have that feeling about Freddy.

SARAH DUDLEY PLIMPTON   I figured our affair would end once we got back to New York, but he began to call and ask me out to dinner. He was lonely. He didn't have anyone to talk to once the staff went home. Freddy was pretty well gone—out in Sagaponack most of the time. Taylor was there, but he was small and tended to by various people. Medora was at boarding school. Sometimes I would come over and we'd go out to dinner together at a local place. My two boyfriends drifted away. After a while, with George it became a routine: He would stop by my apartment in the evening after he'd done his rounds. It couldn't have been more convenient for him. I was next door at 531 East Seventy-second Street and had been since 1976. Sometimes I would give him supper, but most of the time he just wanted to decompress from the day. We'd sit and talk or watch the news together. It just developed from there. I kept him at arm's length because I knew he was a married man, and I didn't want to get involved with that. More than anything, I think he just wanted somebody to come home to, and I was there. Once, he bought me a microwave and stocked my refrigerator with frozen dinners so he could have supper on his way home. After a while, I began going to speaking engagements with him. Usually Friday night we would go out and he'd drag himself out of bed on Saturday mornings and get on the jitney for Sagaponack with Taylor.

MARJORIE KALMAN   From Sarah's point of view, it must have been very odd to be seeing a married man when suddenly his wife leaves him and there he is, available. She's got to ask, "Does this mean I'm supposed to marry him?" That isn't what happens, statistically speaking. But in this rare case, it did, though I think it was two years before they got married. I said to Sarah, "Where are you going to live?" She said, "I don't know." By that time she had moved to an apartment on Lexington Avenue. George was ambivalent by his own confession. She wanted to be married, and I guess there was no reason he shouldn't be married, but he was ambivalent about it.

SARAH DUDLEY PLIMPTON Here was a man who was my father's age and so much more sophisticated than I was. He would
ask me what I thought he should do about this or that—serious
things, delicate things, practical things. I was a sounding board,
true, but I always told him the truth as I saw it. I sensed that many
people only told him what he wanted to hear. I think he was very
drawn to me for that, and it was a healthy impulse on his part. He
knew he was with someone who was honest and trustworthy,
someone who would look out for him.

A. E. HOTCHNER George had been going out with Sarah for a few
years, after the divorce, and one night, we're sitting in Elaine's at
the big table in the back (the one we call the Woody Allen table),
and there were about ten of us at this table, packed in. George was
there with Sarah, and I'd been with them there at dinner a couple
of times, and I was very fond of Sarah. I said, "George, don't you
think the time has come that maybe you should be getting serious
about this relationship—how serious is this relationship, anyway?"
George became flustered; you didn't try to penetrate George's persona like that. So he sort of fumbled around a bit. He said, "Well,
Sarah and I, we're certainly going to be serious." And I said, "Well,
when's it going to happen? It's been going on for a couple of years.
Why don't you set a date?" He said, "Oh, well, I've got to get
around to that." "No I mean right now." He said, "What do you
mean, right now?" I said, "Right now, here, you've got witnesses.
Why don't you just turn to Sarah and say, Let's do it June fifth, or
whenever?" And there was this absolute terror on George's face.
Nobody had ever challenged him like that. And Sarah looked at
him, just smiling at him, as if expectant, and everybody got in on
it. "Come on, George." "Don't mislead this young lady anymore."
"The time has come." And George stepped right up and said,
"Let's get married." And he set a date. I don't think he ever forgave
me, but he invited me to the wedding.

SARAH DUDLEY PLIMPTON As for why I married him, I was
warned. "You've never been married," people would say. "George

isn't going to change; nobody ever does, why should he?" But I really thought it would be different with me. I truly did not understand how important the magazine and his social life were to him. Besides, I'd been rebelling against warnings like that all my life. So had George—we came from similar backgrounds—only he'd found a way to inhabit both worlds, the conventional and the rebellious. I wanted to learn how to do that, and he wanted someone to share it with. Periodically I would get fed up and call it quits, but then he'd pour on the charm until he got me back. With George, there was always a sense that you were going on some exotic, romantic adventure; nobody else could possibly have so much fun. You felt that this was the best fireworks show there ever was, this is the funniest cab ride I'm ever going to have, this is the best hamburger ever. We used to eat at this dive down the street, a hamburger bar with a canoe strung from the ceiling. We would go down there in the dead of winter, he in his sock-slippers with the leather bottoms sewn on, oblivious to the ice and the snow, and we would sit and eat and talk for hours, and you felt like you'd entered an enchanted world.

MAVIS HUMES BAIRD   You'd have a hard time, I think, finding any mean motive on Sarah's side of this match. She married for love—meaning, at least, that she loved him and felt herself loved by him. But she was not blinded by it. She knew much of what she was getting into—the age difference, the drinking, his infinite distractibility (by women, among other things), and so on. What she doesn't seem to have known is that she couldn't change him—*at all*. This was forgivable. There were people, a few, who thought she had changed him or that something had: the twin girls she'd had, his growing older. But George was George, a living deacon's masterpiece, all of a piece to the end. And so, as time went on in that marriage, she must have felt hopelessly naive or strangely complacent. But perhaps she was just charmed—bewitched—as only George could charm.

SARAH DUDLEY PLIMPTON   The wedding was New Year's Eve 1991, at my parents' house in Redding, Connecticut. We only had our immediate families. After dinner George, Medora, and Taylor shot off fireworks. It was a freezing cold, black night and you could hear the fireworks reverberate through the Connecticut hills. At one point a spark landed on Taylor's jacket; George always said, "I almost burned up my son on my wedding night." A few days after the wedding, we had a reception at the Colony Club in New York, which was surreal. At eight o'clock, my mother decided that it was time for everybody to go home, and she started flicking the light switch. George and I went out. We just wanted to get out of there; we wanted to be free. I'll never forget it—we went out into the night and we held hands and we skipped up Park Avenue toward home. Imagine George skipping. We were giddy.

With Sarah at San Simeon, 2001.
Photograph © Liz Gilbert.

PIEDY LUMET   Sometime not long after the wedding, Sidney and
I had a dinner for Sarah and George, and George proposed a toast.
I thought, "Maybe it will be about Sarah, or maybe me," but no,
it was a toast to his mother. Pauline must have been thrilled with
Sarah—much more civilized and presentable, from a snooty point
of view.

LAWRENCE SHAINBERG   I felt a big difference in him when he
got with Sarah. He felt much more settled down, much quieter.
He had all the same charm, but you sensed you really mattered to
him, rather than that you were his temporary excitement.

BILL CURRY   I remember when George found out that my wife
and I were going to come up to New York and bring our daughter, Kristin, and her new husband. They'd been married for less
than a year. He said, "Why, you must have dinner at our home."
He had this wonderful assemblage of people: the editor of *Esquire,*
"Satch" Sanders of NBA fame, and the Celtics. He had about ten
or twelve people, and we sat around the table and had Chinese
takeout. Sarah was putting the girls to bed. The food arrived, and
George couldn't find the dishes, and my wife, Caroline, was in
there slinging hash and getting the dishes out. So Caroline said to
George (because Caroline's an organizer, and George was totally
disorganized), "Let's just do trays and eat out of our lap." "Absolutely not!" George said. "We're going to sit around the table together so we can have a conversation." So we ended up next to the
kitchen, sitting on footstools, but George and I sat there and went
around the table and had a wonderful evening.

ANNA LOU ALDRICH   George and Sarah set up house together
about the time when the old *Paris Review* crowd began to die. Doc
was the first, then Terry Southern, then John Marquand. Eddie
Morgan and Jackie Onassis died along in there somewhere.

IMMY HUMES   George retained a tremendous amount of affection
for Doc when other people—almost all of Doc's friends—were always, at best, very tense around him. George would take his calls

and listen to him when he was in paranoid freak-out meltdown, saying things like "Get your father to call a session of the General Assembly and tell them the world is ending." And at the very, very end of Doc's life, we took him out of the hospice to go to dinner at Sarah and George's, which was just wonderful. Sarah was there—she was wonderful, incredibly nice to Doc, and Doc was very interested in her. It was tremendously sweet. You could see George's physical affection in the footage I took that night. You can see George touching him, reaching out for Doc's hand—and Doc was also physical, so they were holding hands, and there was a real palpable kind of ancient friend thing happening there. They were just jawing on about the old days. George was telling these endless stories—about Eugene Walter, "Tum-te-tum," and various disputes from the old days at *The Paris Review.*

GEORGE AS ZEUS

DAVID MICHAELIS George himself was a big part of the appeal of a job at *The Paris Review,* George as a model of how to live. Most adults, I thought, had a fixed idea of how things ought to be. George was willing to be surprised and delighted by whatever life presented him with from one moment to the next. It might be a remark someone had made to him, the sight of a beautiful girl, a story he'd just heard, or a person he'd just met, even his own responses to things—his own irritation at something, for example. "Golly!" he would cry, or, "Good heavens!" or, "Great Scott"; people were amazed at the antique purity of his expletives, but what was really amazing was the freshness and openness of the guy who uttered them. Life came at him in little packets of wondrousness. How many times in George's day did he exclaim, "Marvelous!" and mean it? Certainly more than anyone I knew. At the same time, he had what adults call "strength of character." But it was always couched, this "character," in a somewhat ironical distrust of the established system. Conventional people loved George, as everyone else did, but I imagine most of them mistrusted him just a bit—or ought to have done. The George we knew from downstairs was a subversive character. We could feel it when we went upstairs. The apartment was a place of play, or rather, it was where work turned into play; downstairs was where play turned into work. That's a dangerous place to have a summer internship, with just one easy flight of stairs between work and play.

JEANNE MCCULLOCH George presided over us, and the hordes who came before and after us, like Zeus presided over his rabble of gods and men—lecherously and jealously sometimes, but mostly with the happier forms of paternalism.

THOMAS MOFFETT I think he just liked coming downstairs every day and checking in with people and knowing what was going on. I think it kept him stimulated. Sarah always said, "George needs you guys. You keep him young."

ANTONIO WEISS The atmosphere was unexpectedly turbulent in the office. There were affairs, deceitful affairs, periods of time when the staff broke into two factions not speaking to each other. I didn't speak with one colleague for two months. There were fights over women, fights over stories. There were fights over whether or not the editors were holding the line sufficiently against George on a particular piece. I tended to agree with him.

JAMES SCOTT LINVILLE There was a time when 541 was not such a happy place, and all manner of diverse gossip swirled. Even, so I gathered, about me. Rumors (patently false rumors I should say) that I was about to leave the magazine and become a spy in Berlin, that I was slipping it to a young intern, that I'd become afflicted with a fatal disease . . . that I was about to elope with my friend Elizabeth Wurtzel. I found all this talk fairly upsetting, but George made it a point to teach me to ignore all such gossip . . . some of which he'd no doubt had a hand in unleashing. Up in his office, he adopted a sagelike pose in that Eames chair he had and offered this bit of wisdom: "James, halitosis is better than no breath at all."

Huh? I said. "You know," he explained, "just as long as they're talking about you, it's good." And then, "Heh heh." All I could manage was to shake my head and pout. Then one night I was having a drink with a woman from Random House that turned into a sort of date. At one point she stopped eating, stared at me intently, and in this serious voice asked, "Is it true you procure black transvestites for George Plimpton?" I burst out laughing, and all of a sudden I had a free feeling. I realized there was not much you could do to control that kind of thing, and better just to learn to let it slide off your back. The next morning I went to work with a spring in my step because, among other reasons, I wanted to tell him he'd been exactly right, and it was true. Well, I went up to see George and I told him, and before I could even finish he hit the roof—"She said WHAT?! Who is this young woman?!" I had to back out of his office saying, "Halitosis, George! Remember . . . halitosis!"

MARJORIE KALMAN   George used to accuse me of being good. He said, "Why are you always so good?" I didn't know what he meant. It took me years to realize it was because if he asked me to do something, I did it. I wasn't remiss. George would have preferred that we were getting high in the bathroom. When I started, Taylor and Medora were young, so we had to be careful what we did in the office, for fear that they'd pop in the door—which they didn't, I don't think. I was too good. I was obedient. George didn't appreciate that at all.

JAMES SCOTT LINVILLE   George liked there to be not too much of a division of labor, in terms of who was in charge of what. So there would always be a little bit of chaos that George could hover over. And it allowed him, like Zeus, to create a little bit of chaos as well.

FAYETTE HICKOX   When I was managing editor, I just didn't have any organizational ability. Several other people said, "Let me show you how you can organize things." But I think the only organizational tip George ever gave me was "You know, William Pène du Bois has all these wonderful cans in which he keeps his different-colored pencils."

SUSANNAH HUNNEWELL   It would be a lie to say I wasn't aware of George's constant flirtatiousness. It wasn't even flirtatiousness so much as it was the pleasure he took in your being a girl. Rather than being offended, I always thought, "Why shouldn't he flirt?" He was an obviously attractive man, so it's flattering. I never felt any pressure from him, though I'm sure he wouldn't have turned it down were it offered; but I never felt it was a come-on, just his general pleasure in being around attractive ladies.

DAVID MICHAELIS "Bring a pretty girl." He always said it when he invited me to a party, and I heard him say it to other young men later: "Bring a pretty girl." It was like an Irwin Shaw story, that lovely midcentury feeling. There was no sexism, and you felt like a million bucks because he deemed you worthy of being the kind of guy who would bring a pretty girl. I hope that doesn't sound sexy, you know? It's not like Hugh Hefner or Norman Mailer. It's much more Scott Fitzgerald, which isn't sex. It's more about the girl as a distant princess.

HALLIE GAY WALDEN Early on, I made it clear that nothing was going to happen between us, and he accepted it. I remember one surreal incident when he tried to deploy me in a fantasy he had about me and Martina Navratilova, whom I idolized. It was about the time that *Personal Best* came out, a sort of buddy movie with Mariel Hemingway that played out in a girls' track team, with all these incredibly erotic locker room shots of flashing female legs and thighs. After the movie, he said, "I have tickets to the Open. Want to come?" He must have been crafting this fantasy in his mind that maybe he could introduce me to Martina, thinking that the instant she saw me, she would just . . . What happened was, I became enthralled with his idea of getting to meet my favorite tennis player and said, "Okay, let's try it!" And because he was who he was, he was able to get us down into the lower bowels of the stadium, with the photographers waiting for her to come through. He hoped she would see us, and then he would be able to have this wonderful evening with the both of us. Well, it didn't work. She came through all right, but she had just lost one of the hardest battles she ever had on the tennis court, so the timing was not very good. We got the brush-off. From then on, the Martina story was one of his favorites, and throughout our friendship he always treated me with something like a kind and intimate paternalism.

DANA GOODYEAR Any man George's age who wakes up at ten and comes into his office in his boxer shorts is kind of saying, "I'm my own person." He was just very comfortable in his skin—and you had to be comfortable in his skin, too. But the intimacy of working and living in the same place meant that everybody there might fancy they were a child of his or like some kind of foundling who'd been taken in. The *Review* did have that kind of extended orphanage feeling. Of course, it mattered whether he liked you or not. That's what I was always afraid of—that he didn't like me. I had no reason to think so: I was just twenty-two years old and very aware of seniority and hierarchies, and I could see, just walking in there, who had the special relationships to him. But it would have made me feel self-conscious to try to befriend him in a special way. He was always my friend Taylor's dad to me. I never was adopted by him, and I never tried to be. I had my own dad. It's a weird thing to say, perhaps, but George would have been a really fun father figure—I just didn't need one.

ELISSA SCHAPPELL I spent a very small amount of time in George's life, but the people who got to enter that private realm felt very protective of him and felt like his child. He wasn't looking for that. But he could make you feel very special, and when you were talking to him, you felt very important to him. Everybody felt like he or she had this relationship with George, when in fact George had this relationship with so many people, and everybody had a bit of a hard time with that.

FAYETTE HICKOX Ah, yes, the parties. Well, I always thought of the people at those parties as divided between the herbivores and the carnivores. The herbivores were by and large the original *Paris Review* people, the Styrons, Eddie Morgan, plus George's old *Lampoon* and Porcellian friends. The carnivores were the media people, with their little laser eyes zapping past you, trying to see who might be of service to them. I remember once in that period having drinks with Bobby Fizdale, the pianist. He said, "Your problem is . . . you're in that . . . what's it called? You know, everybody talks about it . . . whatever it is . . ." And then went on, "Oh yes, you're

Book party at Seventy-second Street. From left: Steve Clark, a Batman, Molly
McGrann, Dan Glover, George, and Andy Bellin. *Photograph by Ann Kidd.*

in the *media.*" But George loved that carnivorous media world as
much as he loved the other.

MOLLY MCKAUGHAN The first party I ever went to was right
after I started. It was Medora's christening party at the beginning
of November '72. George went over to Jackie's apartment to talk
to Caroline because she was very nervous about what she was
going to say. When they showed up, Jackie was dressed gorgeously
in a long black slinky dress, and Caroline was in a plaid kilt. What
is worse for a girl with big hips than a plaid kilt? Nothing. I was
absolutely horrified. I think Caroline was all of fifteen, or fourteen, that awkward age. The party was a very small affair. Then
there were these literary parties with all of the authors—you know,
like Norman Mailer and all those guys. The one I remember best
was after Ali beat Foreman. George had been over in Zaire and
had a film of the fight before it appeared on television. He got
back from this trip and showed the film. He had Norman Mailer
there, Gay Talese, and Howard Cosell. I brought Bill Plummer,
my future husband, and my friend Tom Maloney and his wife,
Maryanne Maloney; she was at Viking. I had to step out of the

party to do something, but by the end of it, when I came back I found Maloney and Mailer wrestling on the floor of the living room. Freddy had gone to bed, and George was trying to pretend that he was the referee, and they're rolling all over the floor. They knocked over a table, and some Ming vase broke. Finally, Mailer said, "I give up," and Tom replied, "No, I give up. You're the great writer, pin me." So Mailer managed to get Tom over on his back and pinned him. George was asking them questions like a reporter, but they were both absolutely shit-faced. We got Tom downstairs, and he threw up on the side of the building, and then we got him into a cab. George would have a party at the drop of a hat. He'd say, "Call up all your pretty friends, bring them along."

JONATHAN DEE As his assistant in the early eighties, I was in charge of the parties. I felt I was the only one in New York who knew their secret—by that time, at least—which was that any time anyone ever called him and said, "May we use your home for a party?" he said yes, because he would rather have three hundred strangers in his apartment on a weeknight than be there alone. He said yes to everything, and he wouldn't even check to see if he was going to be in town. If it was a book party, the poor author and publisher would be very excited that George Plimpton was throwing them a book party, and then they'd get there and it would turn out George wasn't even in New York. It was a little embarrassing. There were three parties a week sometimes. I'd go upstairs the day before and tell George that we needed to order booze, which was always a little frustrating, because his idea of people's drinking habits was more or less frozen in time—no wine, just Scotch. The day of the party, I'd have to go up to the apartment to move the furniture around so things wouldn't get ruined and to let in the bartenders and the caterers, if there was any food, which there usually wasn't; then I'd stay there until the last drunk poet had been escorted out, so I could move the furniture back and pay the bartenders. For five years, I was at every one of those parties, from before it started until after it ended, and I got a little sick of it.

FAYETTE HICKOX Sometime before I left, in the early eighties, a piece ran in *The Village Voice* by Peter Moscoso-Gongora, who had worked in the *Paris Review* office. It was this portrait of George, like "Who Is George Plimpton Now?" It talked about how the fizz had gone out of his parties and how *The Paris Review* and George had sold out. He talked about the women at the parties with their "fuck-me shoes." I'd never heard the expression before. I looked for them, but I never could quite figure out what they were. Freddy was very concerned about the piece and was really worried about George getting terribly upset. And I guess Philip Roth happened to call; Freddy explained what her concern was, and Roth said, "I'll tell you what to do—just overreact, make it into a total drama: How awful, how could he possibly say these things," and so on. And I guess Freddy did this, and sure enough George goes, "Oh, it's all right, it's all right." But I do remember he wrote a letter to Bartle Bull, who was then the publisher of the *Voice* and a St. Bernard's boy. George referred to this—and he finished in a Queeg-like tone, saying, "My memory is long, you know," as if to say, "I'm not going to forget this, Bartle Bull." Of course, then I knew that he was going to forget about it instantly.

JONATHAN DEE   I remember one party, where Leonard Bernstein got horribly drunk and insisted on going upstairs and saying hi to Taylor, who was asleep, so Jay and I and some other staffer went upstairs with Lenny. To pacify him, we agreed to open the bedroom door so he could see Taylor; but then he went over to the side of the bed and started caressing Taylor's head. Then he started actually getting under the covers with him, at which point we pulled him off.

FIONA MAAZEL   In my day, George being around seventy years old, there were probably fewer parties upstairs, probably fewer parties for George to go to elsewhere. So, often he'd go out somewhere on an adventure of some sort, and he took the editors everywhere with him in the evening. I remember him deciding one night that what we had to do was go to a club called Life. We went in there, and it was like that Scorsese shot in the movie *GoodFellas,* where you see them walking through the restaurant, bypassing all the lines and ropes and people waiting to get in. You would walk with him all the way back to the VIP room, where he would order his Dewar's, and you'd sit and chat until all hours of the night. He loved his magazine, and he loved his staff. Whoever the staff was at the time, he loved them. He would do anything to help someone on the staff. He always hung out with them. Of course, I thought he was crazy not to hang out with his own coterie of friends, but I was happy and grateful he didn't.

ANNE FULENWIDER   One night, George took us all to Elaine's for dinner, all six or eight of us, and Doris Kearns Goodwin and her husband came in. George was introducing us all around, and Doris Kearns Goodwin sort of looked at us and was like, "You mean, all of these people work for you in your house every day?" And George was like, "Yeah, yeah, we have a great time!" And she looks at her husband and she's like, "This is what we need! We need six kids to be running around our house all the time."

The Tortola Junket. Front row, from left: James Scott Linville, Brigid Hughes, Anne Fulenwider, staffers. Back row: Egbert Donovan, restaurant owner; Steve Clark and Daniel Kunitz, staffers; George and Remar Sutton, friend.
Photograph by Mona Donovan. Courtesy of Remar Sutton.

SARAH DUDLEY PLIMPTON From my perspective, upstairs, they looked to me like a highly dysfunctional family with all its intrigue and rivalries. George used to laugh affectionately and call them "my paraplegic outfield." For a bunch of paraplegics, these kids thought their association with the *Review,* with George, was a kind of anointment.

ELIZABETH WURTZEL On the Tortola trip it was me, Jamie Linville, the kids from the *Review,* this one other guy, and George and Remar [Sutton]. There was something that struck me as just crazy about this—why was George doing this? It was hard to know whether to think it was wonderful or to think, "You really should be home with your wife and kids, being a serious adult." Looking back on it now, now that he's gone, you tend to want to look at it as all very wonderful. But we were just baffled as to why it was that he wanted to be around all these kids.

BRIAN ANTONI One time in Miami, I lost my car and we were walking through alleys looking for it. I said to George, "Take a cab, go home, I'll find the car." And he said, "No, I'll stay with you." I was afraid for him because he was older, he was all dressed up, and I was worried that somebody would mug us. All of a sudden, these three thugs came out, and I was thinking, "Oh, my God, this is the end: George Plimpton dies in the alley with Brian Antoni and it's all his fault." And then one of the thugs says, "Sidd Finch!" which was this fantasy he wrote about a guy who could pitch a ball a hundred ninety miles per hour. We stayed and had a long conversation, and he just kept saying, "I love Sidd fucking Finch."

THOMAS MOFFETT One time we all went to a Radiohead concert together. George came late. Security said, "Oh, right this way," and put him in a freight elevator with Gwyneth Paltrow. She looked up at him and said, "Oh, Mr. Plimpton, I went to Spence with Medora," and George was just smitten. He was wearing a seersucker suit at the Radiohead show, which just looked so out of place.

DANIEL KUNITZ For a number of years in the nineties we had a regular Friday night doubles game at the River Club. What would happen was we would take the last court time at the River Club at eight o'clock, and we could play for two hours, until ten, and then go up to the bar and drink. George, even in his mid-seventies, was a fantastic tennis player. Steve Clark, who was twenty-eight at the time and the best nonprofessional tennis player I had ever seen in my life, said that George beat him. He wasn't about power. He had beautiful touch. The man had serious game.

OLIVER BROUDY One day, the Underground Literary Alliance challenged us to a debate. The ULA is a ragtag bunch of bad writers who have collected together into a group whose main mission is to grouse about how excluded they are. It's hard to be angry at them and to get your back up about it, because it's really just kind of sad. Anyway, George is a good sport, and when we showed their challenge to George, thinking that he might get a laugh out of it, he said, "So why don't we go on down, see what they can do?" We were like, blink, blink, "What?" So that's what we did.

TOM BELLER Hardly anyone showed up, but I was there with some people from my magazine, *Open City*, and George was there with Team *Paris Review.* The *Times* had a reporter there, I think. Some speeches were made. Then George made the most brilliant rhetorical move I've ever seen in a public situation. Amazingly, in a classic example of how sworn enemies have so much in common, Karl Wenclas of the ULA, or someone in his gang, started going on about Hemingway. Finally, George has had all he can take and he says just one word, in that full-on, unashamed, unironic patrician accent—and the word was "Nonsense!" Three times he said it, and the third "Nonsense" fell like a sledgehammer.

OLIVER BROUDY How anyone could maintain that interest and excitement in life for so long is . . . freakish. I remember walking down the street with him once. We'd just gotten out of a play in the East Village. They were putting on *The Man in the Flying Lawn Chair,* based on George's *New Yorker* piece. Afterwards, we're walking down the sidewalk, and there's this hubbub in the East Village, and he said, "Isn't that amazing? Look what's going on in there! And in there! Everyone's doing something!" We passed one place after another, and he was just thrilled and delighted by all of the activity, and curious always.

THE MASTER OF CEREMONIES

SARAH DUDLEY PLIMPTON   Any organization that was in some way dedicated to improving the quality of life in New York City, he made himself available to. He gave very generously of his time and his energy, not necessarily his money. He didn't have a lot of money to give. In fact, I remember Russ Hemenway telling me how cheap he was, and I said, "Maybe financially, but not with his time, nor with his self." He gave time to the Explorers Club, to all the arts organizations, and, as far as I could see, to every settlement house in New York, plus PBS, the Philharmonic, the Municipal Arts Society. Some weeks it seemed like he was out every night giving a speech for some organization or other. To individuals, too, his friends and relatives, he was almost infinitely responsive. He spoke at their christenings, their birthdays, their graduations, their weddings; when they were being honored for something, when they were running for office; and then, of course, when they died. At his memorial service, a number of people came up to me saying how disappointed they were because he was supposed to speak at *their* funeral. In his time, he was master of New York's ceremonies.

NORMAN MAILER   I think if there were a rivalry between George and me, it would be at giving toasts. I have to say, he was the best toastmaster in New York. I always felt as if I were the second best, and on occasion could win. He was wonderful at toasting to people. He was sort of like Pete Maravich on a basketball court when it came to giving toasts. He could do things no one else could do. It was his sense of the particular on the one hand, and of the ridiculous on the other. There was one occasion when we were visiting a certain country and for some reason, Norris and I had been put up at a good hotel, while George was put up at another place chosen by the charity for which we were doing the reading. Well, George had a mean existence for a couple days, while we were having a splendid one, and when he found out, he was furious. But I don't think he was even aware of how annoyed he was until he got up to toast the man who had put him up in this hotel. It was George at his best. He described the quality of the sheets and the heat of the coffee in the morning, and the wonderful company. He was up in the morning all prepared to talk to a few of the wonderful people at the place, and there they were, going off in limousines and Mercedes-Benzes, while he was left alone for hours wandering around these grounds that were well kept, but not *exceptionally* well kept. It wasn't that he really *minded* when he stumbled and almost fell, because he didn't fall, and those things happen when you're walking through a garden that is kept up, but not *totally* kept up. On and on he went. He had the entire audience absolutely roaring with laughter at the guy who ran the thing. That was the only time I ever heard him do something like that. He was like a marvelous writer, taking a premise and running with it. That's where his real writing would come in. He didn't need to know what he was going to do when he started, but he had a notion of where the ridiculous was, and he would play with it. That's the true test of a toastmaster.

GEORGE PLIMPTON, SPEECH AT ANNUAL EXETER ALUMNI DIN-NER, DECEMBER 5, 2001 I think I should start off by saying that I didn't do very well at Exeter. In fact, I was a complete failure. I was asked to leave three months shy of graduation because of a multitude of sins, both academic and secular. . . . My marks were terrible. I had the strange idea that in class, even if I were daydreaming of something else, my brain was still absorbing all the material like a kind of specialized sponge, and the next day at the exam I could scratch around in the appropriate corner, in the detritus, and there would be the appropriate answers. Of course it didn't work that way, and my marks, the C's, the D's, the occasional E—the latter always in math—showed it.

These elicited letters from my father—the only letters I ever got, with his familiar, dreaded handwriting—and they were stiff with rep-

rimand. . . . *Genetically speaking, I was supposed to soar through Exeter. Wasn't the family tree full of outrageous successes? . . . And now, at the end of the line, like a caboose with two wheels missing, dragging along the ground, shooting up sparks and igniting forest fires, this. . . .*

I used to sit in study hall and curse my brain. I used to imagine taking it out of the top of my head and beating it sharply with a pencil. Why had it let me down? True, I hadn't studied, but why hadn't my brain compensated properly out of thin air? Somewhere in Melville's Moby Dick *is the line "my whole beaten brain seems as beheaded." Which is apt, thinking back on it, because my head, when I was at Exeter, was ever off somewhere else, funning it up with the heads of the few others who were having difficulty. We beheaded few, we band of brothers.*

At nightfall, I went down to the Plimpton Playing Fields and drop-kicked field goals with Buzz Merritt, just the two of us in the gloaming, often with a thin moon shining above the pines, above the river. No one drop-kicks footballs now, or did then either. Why did I do this when I should have been studying Tacitus for the exam I knew was coming up the next day? Buzz got away with it somehow, but I didn't. Sometimes, to escape the exams, I went to the infirmary. There was a secret way, which I've now forgotten, to drive up the temperature on a thermometer. If you were careless, you could drive it up to 110 degrees. I always thought Dr. Fox somehow knew, perhaps by the panicky face he was looking at, what the true trouble was, and he would put you in the infirmary for the day.

When I wasn't on detention, or probation, or sitting in study hall, I spent, at least in my final years, a great deal of time in an institution one can hardly believe existed—the butt rooms, where one learned to smoke. There was more smoke in one of those rooms than there is in the funnel of an old-fashioned locomotive. We sat in there and we were suave. I'm surprised we didn't wear green eyeshades and hats. At night I would lie in bed and, in the moonlight streaming through the window, practice blowing smoke rings. As they oozed thickly up toward the ceiling, I'd say to myself, "Wow! If only Susie Mills"—the girl who had a driver's license and drove her father's Plymouth with the top down—"could see me now!"

But what really got me into trouble were the little things I thought were funny—like sneaking in at night and turning all the benches around in the Assembly Hall because I thought it would be funny to have my classmates sitting backwards when they came in for assembly. . . . I was caught all the time. It was as if I were attached to an invisible leash at the other end of which was an authority of some kind. I'd be called in to see Dean Kerr in his offices. Shuffling in and asked to explain myself, I would open my mouth—and nothing would emerge. Sometimes in answer to a probing question of his ("Why did you think to move that stuffed rhino head?"), I would murmur, head down, "Yessir." I never looked at Dean Kerr. I didn't dare. Out of sight, out of mind. . . .

I wanted so much to succeed, to make a noise. I wrote for the Exonian, but if you were on probation you couldn't use your real name. My pen name was "Vague," thought by many to be my state of mind most of the time. . . .

I tried out for varsity sports. Bill Clark, the baseball coach, never took the care to find out that he had a youth, "a barefoot boy with cheek," who could throw a lazy, roundhouse curveball. I was cut. Football, the same. Hockey, the same. Tennis, the same. Tall as a reed, fragile as a stick, I ended up in the band playing the bass drum. . . .

I tried other things. I took piano lessons from Mr. Landers. He assigned me a Debussy piece called "Bells," as I recall. . . . The next week I appeared at Mr. Landers' quarters and sat down to play. Mr. Landers said, "Well, that's very fine, but that's not Debussy's 'Bells.' " . . .

I tried out for a play called Seven Keys to Baldpate. *They found a minor role for me, that of a young widow. . . . I was required to let out an unearthly scream, perhaps at the sight of a corpse, I've forgotten what. . . . My scream carried far out over the quadrangle, down the hill past Langdell and into the Jeremiah Smith Building, past the mailroom with its letterboxes—where in those days I received my father's letter, once a week, with its admonitions—and up the stairs to Dean Kerr's office, where he sat comfortably smoking his pipe, when suddenly this high-pitched shriek wandered in, and his blood curdled and he said aloud, "My God, what's Plimpton done now?" . . .*

My main nemesis was Bill Clark, who taught math (E–) and was the football and baseball coach. He was the master of Soule Hall where I lived that senior year. One night I was chasing Spennie Welch down the curved stairs with a flintlock musket my grandfather had given me—a relic of the Revolutionary War. As I was going down, suddenly, around the curve of the wall, on his way up to see what all the commotion was, came Bill Clark, also referred to as "Bull." He gave this little scream. I don't really blame him. The barrel-end of the musket looked like the mouth of a tunnel. A fair-sized rocket could have emerged from it. I knew I was doomed, as Holden Caulfield would say. If he had toughened it out and said, "What are you doing with that flintlock musket when you should be in your room applying yourself," it would have been all right. But he had given this little scream, and he knew that I knew, and I knew that he knew that I knew. And that was it.

Could it have been that, having failed in all departments at Exeter, I was driven in later life to compensate, to try once again to succeed where I hadn't? I've wondered, on occasion, whether these exercises in participatory journalism for which I am known were as much to show my mentors at Exeter that I had somehow managed to intrude onto the highest plateaus of their various disciplines. . . .

I have come to the conclusion that my life, whatever there is of it that might be termed successful, was indeed very much due to Exeter's credit . . . that I had somehow to vindicate myself. And I am grateful for Exeter, terribly grateful, and I wish my grandfather had never given me that flintlock musket.

ANDREW LEGGATT George always claimed that when he was at Harvard, his father gave a dinner for some of his most distinguished colleagues, at the end of which his father rose to his feet and said, "Gentlemen, my son George, editor of the *Harvard Lampoon,* will now make a funny speech," and sat down. He had not said a word to George. George claims that he said in response, "I threw my trousers out of the seventh-floor window." And then he had to think about what to say next. The point about that is I think that he created for himself the obligation to improvise.

SARAH DUDLEY PLIMPTON He told me that his beginnings as a public speaker were not auspicious. The first speech he ever gave was to Pauline's friends at the Colony Club. He'd prepared something and nervously rattled through it in about five minutes flat. Afterwards, he told me, he leapt from the podium and headed straight for the men's room. He was so mortified by his performance that he wept.

CALVIN TRILLIN   After I knew him, it was sort of as if I had always known him, because, for one thing, we took turns doing the benefit for the East Harlem Tutorial Program year after year. When I say "took turns doing," I mean we took turns being the MC or something similar. We often ended up in some kind of benefit as either the speaker or the MC or something like that. There were about four or five of us in New York who did the MC'ing—usually for events on book publishing, or the future of journalism, or something like that: George, Roger Rosenblatt, Roy Blount, Jr., and me. It was seasonal work in a way—not work, I mean it was unpaid—but I remember doing two or three in the

George, gold medal MC.

Photograph © Henry Grossman.

same week and saying to my wife, "Where the hell is Plimpton? I can't imagine why I'm doing all these benefits. He must have fled the country, knowing that this week was coming up."

P. J. O'ROURKE   George was the most effortlessly gifted public speaker I have ever seen. There is a little lake club up here in New Hampshire, call it the Wampum Lodge, and George was somehow prevailed upon to come up and speak at this club for their centennial-year dinner dance. There were fireworks involved, and I think that may have been what got George there. I picked him up at the airport, and he'd just had some operation on his eye—a sty or something. Part of his face was swollen; he obviously wasn't feeling very well. So we go over to my house and we have a couple drinks and we're having quite a jolly time out on the patio. Then we go to the club and proceed to have a cocktail hour that lasts about four or five hours, and then there's a dinner and attendant drinks. It rolls around to being about as late as it gets up there, which is to say ten o'clock. By this time we've been at it since noon. And George is called upon to speak. And I realize, just as the president of the club is introducing him, that George has not given a single thought as to what he's going to say. He knows *nothing* about the Wampum Lodge, and if it was possible to care less than he knew, he would have. And he just stands up and starts to talk! Being unable to find any connection between the Wampum Lodge and any of his knowledge or interests, he manages to tell a couple of stories that have nothing to do with anything, and then brings us around to fireworks, and then brings fireworks into the celebration of centennials in general. I don't remember a great deal of it because I myself was . . . "Friends say he needed rest" was the comment that I think would have been made about me. But he pulled this off, and it just left everybody gobsmacked, in awe of his performance.

CALVIN TRILLIN   People who are rigidly prepared can't do it very well. You have to feed off the last speaker or what's happened, or something. I think in George's case, he also had an enthusiasm that communicated itself so seductively that it wouldn't have made much difference what he said. But, in fact, he did prepare. I mean,

I was always amazed that he really sort of worked on it. I suspect George didn't say no as often as he should have. Sarah would say, "You don't really have to do it, just 'cause that guy knew your cousin at Wimpole Academy doesn't mean that you have to do his benefit, especially when it's not even a cause you particularly care about. . . ." But you know George.

HUSBAND AND FATHER

SARAH DUDLEY PLIMPTON   Accommodating me pretty soon became a huge source of resentment for him, which is interesting because he accommodated everyone else all too easily, but he couldn't do it at home. For instance, I thought it would be a good idea to find a new home when we got married, so that it would be ours together. What *was* I thinking? The apartment was just chock-ablock full of reminders of *his* life. In the office was the collection of African masks; the basket full of little totems, little birds, little medals, trophies, and other things he couldn't bear to throw away; all his plaques, his book covers, his framed reviews, the *Paris Review* posters he especially liked. In the bathroom were his photos: George in the ring with Archie Moore, blood streaming out of his nose, George pitching in the All-Star game, George at St. Bernard's, George as the "flying telephone pole" on the trapeze, George with his fireworks, George with Ali, George in the bullring with Hemingway. There were always people coming by, wanting a tour of the apartment, and when we passed that bathroom, I would say, "This is the room that George goes into whenever he feels a lapse of self-esteem." When I finally persuaded George to renovate the apartment so we could *both* live in it, he fought me every step of the way—even though it was a huge improvement. He would admit that to friends, but he never said a word to me.

FIONA MAAZEL They fought. They fought a lot. There was a lot of screaming, and he would come downstairs furious and then instantly forget it and be hilarious George. You just didn't see them interact all that much. None of us knew why he married her, or she him. None of us knew why he had ever married at all. None of us

George and Sarah with Olivia (left) and Laura (right).
Photograph © Jonathan Becker, all rights reserved.

understood it. But none of us cared about it, either. We had to deal with Sarah only when we were having another party upstairs. She hated it, hated it, hated it—then would show up, have a great time, and then be difficult about it. I heard that Freddy did the same.

SARAH DUDLEY PLIMPTON   Upstairs was separate from downstairs. He was very clear about not wanting me involved with the magazine. It helped him stay in control of the staff. He took great offense whenever I offered my opinion about magazine affairs. It was his private domain and I was not to intrude. Of course, that's an impossible arrangement because he put no limits on the staff being part of *his* household. For example, when we were first married, *The New York Observer* had a column called the "Eight-Day

Week," where they highlighted interesting parties and events in the coming week. Every party we ever gave somehow made it into that column. We might as well have had an open house, because as far as George was concerned, the more the merrier. If he sent out seventy-five invitations, a hundred fifty people would show up, most of them complete strangers. One day, we had so many people that the floor in our apartment cracked and sent the ceiling crashing down on Walter Sohier's living room just below us. I called the paper and complained. But when George got wind of my call, he was livid. He said, "How dare you ever speak to the press! How dare you tell them what to do!" Part of it was that he was worried what they'd make of it, but mostly he was outraged that I would tamper with the magic of his parties.

DANIEL KUNITZ Everything changed after Sarah moved in. First of all, she renovated the *Review* office, then the apartment, except for his office, of course, and the famous bathroom with all his photos. George was still pretty much the same guy, but the whole atmosphere changed. We used to work up in his apartment, or at least as much as we did in the office. And then, obviously, we didn't work up there. Sarah was very gracious; I never felt unwelcome up there. It was just a different situation. It was their home. Didn't George change at all? Yeah. He didn't party every night after Sarah moved in with him.

ELIZA GRISWOLD When I met Sarah, she was pretty much already at her wits' end, because I think she had—as she would say herself—assumed that things would change once they got married. And things hadn't changed. And then she assumed things would change when she had the twins [in 1994]. And they didn't change then, either. I spent a lot of time with Laura and Olivia when they were tiny little girls, which was really fun for me. That was probably one reason why, when some people had problems with Sarah, I had none, because I saw the family as coming first, and that helped relieve a lot of tension. I think I was helpful in setting some boundaries around the use of their house and the use of George's time. She liked to know before things happened, and I was comfortable with that. The people who don't like Sarah—sure, Sarah would freak out and get angry and that kind of thing—but I don't know why they cared. I think she had George's best interests at heart. In terms of George's social life, and his social schedule, he needed to rest, and he needed some time with his family, and people who opposed that—well, it always struck me as a little bit suspicious that they wanted so much from George.

REMAR SUTTON Very few people understood how close George and I were. Medora and Taylor did, and Freddy did, and some other people did. I never cared. That's why I haven't been sure if I wanted to be in the book, because my relationship with George was what we all want in life: It was a truly private relationship.

DANIEL KUNITZ Remar's a social climber, and he's somebody who wants to be friends with the rich and powerful, but I do think he gives back, and that's how he makes it happen. The way he gives back is he's a fantastic entertainer; he's willing to call in favors; he'll cobble together things to make it really great with everybody. I don't think Remar is a bad guy. I remember when he was living in that house in the country with Freddy and the children; I think he raised those children.

REMAR SUTTON I remember when I met Sarah. At that time I was up in New York probably every two weeks. And George and I had, actually, a fabulous bachelor time because Freddy was never there. And then one day Sarah was sitting in the living room with him, in the pool room. He introduced her, and for a while there, Sarah and George and I had a lot of fun together. But then Sarah became aware that I was detracting from her chance to have a relationship with George, and she was right. She realized, rightfully, that if I was going to suck up all that air, there wasn't going to be much left for her. That was when Sarah tried to distance me from George. Of course, she had to do that.

ROWAN GAITHER Remar Sutton was a real character, and he was always getting George into some sort of trouble. Remar was a wonderful guy, but he was always working an angle. After George married, it was clear to me that Remar no longer had the run of the house the way that he did. Remar had at one point left the remnants of one of his own parties around the apartment. The mess sent Sarah over the moon. Another time, Remar called me because he was trying to get me to get George to do something that Sarah didn't want George to do, and he was hectoring me to make George available to do it. I said, "Remar, I can't do that. Sarah is now George's wife. Sarah is now my boss's wife, and that's the way it is." He basically didn't ask me to do anything else after that.

SARAH DUDLEY PLIMPTON George made you feel terribly special; it's no wonder so many people fell in love with him. But some people exploited his generosity shamelessly. When Remar came to stay, the apartment became party central every night. That's fine if you're the guest, but it's insanity when it's your home. Besides, the constant partying made it hard to get any work done. George just couldn't say no to him, or anyone else for that matter. I hated always having to be the bad cop, but someone had to draw the line, and it wasn't going to be George.

BUZZ MERRITT The Dudleys, Sarah's parents, moved to Redding not long ago and built a beautiful big place and gave George and Sarah the old groundskeeper's house, very near their place, which the parents thought was going to be great. But Sarah said, "Well, you know the trouble out here is that nobody seems to recognize George, and that's bothersome." So I went up to our little local post office, and because the postmaster is a big baseball fan, I said, "You know, we've got a guy now coming here, George Plimpton." "Oh, Mr. Plimpton, gosh, I've seen him a lot." And I said, "Well, say hello to him." "Oh, I—I—I wouldn't want to do that." So I said, "Well, the next time he comes in, you tell him blah blah blah." So finally my postmaster did say hello, and he said, "Oh, Mr. Plimpton, he was very interesting, we talked for a long time." Then I said, "Sarah, we're making inroads here. The postmaster's recognized George." "Yeah," she said, "but after the postmaster, he went over to buy a paper and get some stuff at the market, and they didn't recognize him, so he was very upset."

JAY MCINERNEY   It was tough for Sarah. She wanted custody of a public figure. George was a public figure, and you can't have somebody like George all to yourself. Nobody could. She probably expected more. She and I had our ups and downs, because she considered me part of that world that was always calling George out the door, always beckoning him out into the night. I'm sure she thought that that would change more than it did.

FAYETTE HICKOX   Gene Scott, the publisher of *Tennis Week* and another late breeder, told me that he asked George how he liked being an "older dad." George said, "Well, I didn't change diapers before, and I'm not going to change diapers now." Gene was more the kind of modern dad who thought there was nothing finer in life than changing his child's diapers. I know people say that George

George with his son, Taylor, at the Indy 500, 1982.
From the collection of George Plimpton.

became more fatherlike with the twins he had with Sarah than he had been with the two kids he had with Freddy. But I don't know why people say that. When he was around, he was a very fond father with both sets of children, better and better as they grew older, learned tennis, told him about their lives and friends. But he just wasn't around very much, certainly in comparison to the amount of time I spend with my son.

BILL CURRY   I'd call him on the spur of the moment and say, "How you feelin', George?" and he'd say, "Well, I must say, the twin thing is rather exhausting." That's when the girls were really small. Caroline and I went up and participated in the twin thing. We held the girls in their diapers and all. Sarah started getting on George, saying, "Look at Bill! He's held the girls in the last two hours more than you have in the last month!" So I went and put them down. I had practice with babies—he, on the other hand, was a little rusty.

CHRIS CERF   Whether fatherhood was the center of his life—I'm sure it wasn't; but I'm sure he was great when he got around to it. He always took delight in the kids. I remember his total delight in Medora playing tennis when she was little. He would always talk about her "brown legs flashing." It always struck me: What other dad would take that away from what he noticed about his daughter, a *Lolita* reference?

JONATHAN DEE   One of the things I remember most vividly made me sad at the time: Taylor and Medora were still pretty young. Taylor wasn't ten yet. His school called the *Review* because Taylor was in the nurse's office—he had gotten sick and he needed to come home; but there was nobody upstairs, so I went to get him. I hadn't been working there that long. Taylor would have recognized me, but he didn't really know me at all. He was just a little kid, and he was sick. I felt so bad for him. I went to the nurse's office and said, "Taylor, I'm sorry, your mom and dad aren't around, but I can take you home." He just shrugged and went along with it, and we rode home without a word. We went upstairs, and I asked him if he needed anything, and he said no, he would be fine. He went to his room and shut the door, and I went back downstairs to the office.

DRUE HEINZ   George was wonderful when he came to Florida with his son, Taylor. He'd come in the middle of a week when Taylor, who was about six (I think), had been lying around all day, swimming, doing whatever. George arrived straight off the plane and looked at the boy and said, "Where are your whites?" Taylor said, "I brought them, Daddy," and went and got his tennis whites. The little boy came out looking like a replica of George. George took him straight out to the tennis courts. The boy's a crack tennis player today. George was extraordinary with children. He was always a personal friend to them.

MEDORA PLIMPTON   I think I was the first Plimpton not to go to an Ivy League school or to Exeter; I went to Tabor Academy and to Hampshire, this sort of hippie-liberal, great college. Taylor went to St. Paul's, which is pretty much like Exeter, but then he went to Reed, which is about as far away from Harvard, geographically, as you can get. And Dad was always supportive of that. He wanted us to follow our dreams and what we wanted to do. It was nice not to feel that pressure that I know a lot of my other friends felt. I had friends whose parents were disappointed that they hadn't gotten into more prestigious schools. He was always very low-key about it. You wouldn't think he would be, looking at him and hearing his voice and knowing where he'd grown up. You'd think he'd want to push his kids, but he really didn't do that.

TAYLOR PLIMPTON   I would see the other Plimptons at Thanksgiving or Christmas, and every now and then at a party at the house, but I always felt awkward at family gatherings. And I felt I had to be very proper. I felt that way with Dad sometimes, too. It wasn't easy for me to be myself, whatever that means. I think I was always a little more formal around my dad and a little more careful about what I said, but that got better as time went on. The last couple years before he died, I felt much more comfortable hanging out with him and just chatting and chilling. But he was the fa-

George and Medora at her wedding in August 2000.
Photograph © David Garten.

ther figure, the parent; it wasn't a punch-your-dad-in-the-arm
kind of relationship.

SARAH DUDLEY PLIMPTON You'd think he would be marvelous
company for a child. And he was, up to a point. When we were
first married and Taylor lived with us, his friends would come over
before they went out in the evening, and George would try to
reach out to them. But the only way he knew how to connect was
by telling stories, and you could see Taylor shrug his shoulders and
pretend to be interested. The sense of frustration was palpable. He
was proud of his father, but you sensed that he needed a deeper
connection with him. His friends all thought George was cool and
amazing, so Taylor adopted that same worshipful stance toward his
father. But I imagine there would also be great frustration at want-

ing his father to put down the facade and be real with him. But his adoration made it impossible for George to appear real to him, even if George had wanted to.

MEDORA PLIMPTON I think most kids would be sort of worried about their parent getting up and speaking at their graduation. There is a time in life when you're sort of embarrassed by your parents no matter what they do. But I was so thrilled and proud to have him up there at my graduation from Tabor, and then his speech actually blew them away. Blew his speech away, too. It was a windy day, a beautiful day in Marion, Mass., and he was standing up there, and all of a sudden a couple pages of his speech just blew away in the wind. He had to wing it, and he did a fantastic job. I was so proud, I was just beaming, and everybody came up afterwards and said, "Wow, it must have been incredible growing up with him!"

JOEL CONARROE I loved meeting his charming wife and the twins and so on, but again, I wondered if this wasn't another one of his Walter Mitty fantasies: The man at sixty-seven years old fathers two adorable children and has a beautiful wife. Why not? There's just no end to this guy and his self-inventions.

SARAH DUDLEY PLIMPTON At parties people would often come upstairs, invited or not, to view the girls. I hated that. It was as if they were some kind of curiosity to be inspected—George Plimpton's twins—but it terrified the girls. Once someone barged in while Laura was in the bath. Can you imagine? After a lot of that sort of thing, the girls preferred to take in the parties from the top of the spiral staircase—at a safe distance. I became very protective of them and tied a piece of ribbon across the stairs to discourage intrusions. They barged up anyway.

DANIEL KUNITZ He was wonderful with the kids, when he was with them. George was a wonderful role model in a lot of ways. George was such an upstanding guy. He never swore. He had unshakably good manners. He was a true democrat, small "d," and had a lively social conscience. He had these strong moral ideas about the way one lives one's life, and he was the hardest-working man I've met anywhere. When he was with the kids, he was great. I always tell people when I'm interviewed about George that his first book was a children's book. People are always shocked by that. It wasn't just that his first book was a children's book, but that he wrote several. His imagination, at its core, was childlike. His children had to have responded to that, the more so when they were young.

OLIVIA PLIMPTON   I remember he told us a ghost story about when he was sleeping in a castle that was haunted by the Gray Lady. I'm not sure if he was making this up, but he said he saw the Gray Lady, and it freaked me out. He said she was there, and she came up to his bed. It scared me so much that night, I couldn't sleep.

SARAH DUDLEY PLIMPTON   George had fantasies about the girls' future, like any other father. One morning he was sitting on the sofa with the girls, who were around four, I guess, and didn't read yet. Livvy liked to pretend to read and that morning she reached up behind them and took a book from the bookcase and started to read it—upside down—to Laura. "Helena Charles pulled herself together . . . ," she began. At which point George perked up and said, "Well, that's about as good an opening line to a novel as I've ever heard!" As for Laura, I think he saw another side of himself in her, and fantasized about her being a celebrity. Laura had different ideas: She wanted to raise cheetahs, or else become one.

OLIVIA PLIMPTON   I just always liked to watch him, even though I didn't understand exactly what he was writing. I always wanted to write something when I was little, but I didn't really do it until a couple of years ago. I've written a lot of stories, but most of them I'm not really finished with. I write the beginning of something, and then I never finish it. I just have one I've actually finished. It's called "The Treasure of the Nile." It's kind of weird. I think it's finished, but I want to add more to it.

LAURA PLIMPTON We went down to the [Review] office sometimes and bothered people and looked around. We used to go
cockroach hunting in the basement. We put on rubber gloves and
big boots and rain jackets, and we put them in little plastic bags.
We found a really big one once and brought it upstairs to show our
mom.

SARAH DUDLEY PLIMPTON After the twins were born, I stayed
at home more and more. I couldn't keep up with the social life and
still get up at six in the morning. I think he resented my being ab-
sent from his life. So he would just go out and find someone to listen to his stories. He was seventy years old and getting more
crotchety as he felt his powers slipping away. The mildest remark
would set him off: "Dammit, you always have to spoil my plans!"
"You always have to find something wrong!" "You always have to
criticize!" I wasn't criticizing him; I was merely offering a different perspective, perhaps a more realistic one, on how to get things
done. He had welcomed that in the early days, but now he saw it
all as being criticized, and he was very defensive about it. He
wanted his way, and he acted like a petulant child when he didn't
get it. This is what no one saw but me—and Freddy, no doubt. He
couldn't negotiate; it was his way or none at all. So I would get up
and walk out of the room and he would call after me, "There you
go, walking away from me again!" He would work himself up into
tears, literally, tears of rage.

SOL GREENBAUM I know Sarah was very upset, and rightfully so,
that so much of his money was going to Freddy. He paid all her
expenses and was giving money to her every month. Occasionally,
she would call me and complain that she wasn't getting enough.
He had no legal obligation to support Freddy. It was a difficult situation. Even after George passed away, she felt he didn't do enough
for her. That's typical.

SARAH DUDLEY PLIMPTON In his hierarchy of things to support, The Paris Review always came first. Then Freddy, then us. He

felt that I could support myself without him, and therefore he felt no responsibility to help me run the household. He was making some money, but his speaking engagements had seriously dwindled—his audience, the generation that had watched him play with the Lions, were old now. He had gone from making twenty thousand dollars for a speech to, in most cases, less than five. He even did a commercial for a swimming pool builder on Long Island. He was sitting in a pool, naked from the waist up, looking like the old buzzard he was. It was just humiliating, all for a few thousand dollars.

GEORGE SECURES THE *REVIEW*'S FUTURE

DAVID MICHAELIS Back in 1979, when I interviewed George for an article I was trying to write for *Esquire* about the twenty-fifth anniversary of *The Paris Review,* he clearly stated that if the magazine ever stopped, he would feel as if he had lost an important part of himself. I thought it was very genuine, his feeling. I thought he also felt that he had been left with it, in many ways. There were some hard feelings hanging over from the time when it was almost shut down by the various editors. But he had stuck with it and been very loyal to it, sort of like George Bailey with the building-and-loan bank in *It's a Wonderful Life.* And it had paid off, in the sense that everybody finally came back to celebrate when it reached its era of gray eminence. That was nice for everybody. Styron and Matthiessen, John Marquand, Donald Hall, Maxine Groffsky, all of them there in George's apartment, and they were just in heaven. I remember Jill Krementz photographing them all there. They were thrilled to be back together. It was lovely. All of them claimed pride in this beautiful thing that they had done. And all of them took a little bit of credit, when George had really been the one left holding the bag. That was when they were in their fifties, with no idea that the magazine would have another twenty-five anniversaries to go.

BRIGID HUGHES Did he want the magazine to continue? I think he did, and he didn't. I regret that we never found some way to sit down and talk about the future of the magazine with him.

At his desk, 1997.
Photograph © Jonathan Becker, all rights reserved.

SARAH DUDLEY PLIMPTON His modesty wouldn't allow him the vanity of believing that he had created an enduring brand. Neither of us could imagine that things would turn out as well as they have for the *Review.* So I told him I thought he was *The Paris Review* and that nobody could do what he did, and anything else would be imitation, so the magazine should end with him. That was the last time he ever asked for my advice about the future of the magazine.

OLIVER BROUDY We talked a little bit about whether the magazine should go on after his death, but it was a question he always dodged carefully around. It was something that touched him deeply. I think he didn't really know. He was unsure about his own mortality; the thought of death was like meeting someone he didn't understand through one of his established channels. He couldn't really fit it in somewhere. When he did, it was with that kind of British good sportingness. You saw a bit of the same thing when you talked with him about the possible death of the magazine. There was something that baffled him a little bit, and it was painful to see him baffled in that way.

BEN RYDER HOWE I thought that George's modesty got in the way of a frank discussion about the magazine's fortunes. His modesty was endless. While we were planning the fiftieth anniversary, we were talking about various ways to promote it, and we wanted him to be the focus of the celebration; but he said, "I don't want this to be about me."

JONATHAN DEE When I was there, we got to the hundredth issue, and he said offhandedly more than once, "Maybe we should stop at a hundred." Then he'd leave the office and we'd all look at each other, wondering if we were about to lose our jobs.

BRIGID HUGHES We talked about it in the late nineties. Everyone thought that George was going to live into his nineties, and we were going to be old people, and whoever he was going to pass it on to, it sure as hell wasn't going to be any of us.

JAMES GOODALE As best as I can determine, James Linville was the one who came up with, or at any rate effected, the idea of selling the magazine's archives. That money eventually helped settle the issue of the *Review*'s future. Which, in my view, was a great thing.

JAMES SCOTT LINVILLE In 1991 or so there was this massive rainstorm, and a gutter broke in back of 541. A door had been left open and water was pouring into the basement, as I saw when I went back to check on the stock of art prints. The basement back then, before it was renovated and turned into an office, was always a mess, and now it had flooded. There was water an inch deep on one side, and on the other green rat-poison pellets that were dissolving. And that's when I noticed all these steamer trunks with the magazine's old Paris address. There was our history, literary history, just sitting there, rotting. I said to George, "We have to do something about this. Researchers are going to want to study these papers, and we could sell them to a library to keep the magazine going." He said, "Ugh," as if it were all just a nuisance and all that old paper just brought back memories. I said, "Listen, I have an interest in this. If you let me do it on my own time, on weekends or whatever, and take a commission on the sale, I'll make sure it gets done." In the end, it took a good eight or nine years. For three of those years, while I compiled a massive catalog to help sell it, I had all 110 boxes of material in my living room, next door, at 535, with no space to walk around. Frankly, it was a pain in the ass to live with, and there were times I'd come home to them, with no space to walk around, and say to myself, "Ugh."

GLENN HOROWITZ   When Jamie came to me and asked if I would assist in finding a home for the archives, I agreed and George agreed, though I always suspected that George never thought there was any real value in this material. From the beginning, his perception was that this whole sale wasn't going to amount to very much.

JAMES SCOTT LINVILLE   In the course of putting together the archive, I'd bring things up to him. There was the day the early Philip Roth letters turned up, which George was always sure had been lost or sold by one of the bad-egg editors or something. And when the Hemingway letters turned up, and the Kerouac letters, I brought those into his office and showed him and he started to understand what the project was about. One that I came across was the beginning of Burroughs's *Naked Lunch,* accompanied by a postcard from Allen Ginsberg and a letter from Nelson Aldrich saying, "You have to publish this." That was the one that got away . . . or rather that was flubbed, because he hadn't published it.

SOL GREENBAUM The archives were sold to the Morgan Library. The money was put up by Drue Heinz and eventually amounted to eight hundred and fifty thousand dollars, I believe.

ROBERT PARKS The library very specifically wanted to strengthen its holdings of twentieth-century literature, and this opportunity gave us a wide range of writers over the postwar period. The *Writers at Work* interviews were a real draw for us. The documentation is extraordinary: For many of them you have the recorded interviews, the person's voice. And since the interviews were always sent back to the interviewee for editing, there's a paper as well, so you have a record of the whole process. These interviews are about creation, and they are an act of creation.

JAMES GOODALE So now, after agents' fees, the *Review* had seven hundred thousand dollars; but the question of the magazine's future still lay there. So what I told George was "I think we ought to perpetuate *The Paris Review*. It offers unequaled market access for the unpublished writer, or even for the young established writer. That's a terrific asset, particularly in a society that is going more and more money-mad and doesn't have a huge literary tradition nationwide anyway. I think you owe it to yourself to do something." George didn't believe me. He said, "You don't know what you're doing. There's never been a literary magazine that's lasted as long as this one, and there will never be a literary magazine that will last longer. You're wasting your time." But I knew that a magazine could be run by a foundation; I don't think many lawyers would have known that, but because of my own screwball background, I knew it had been done with *Harper's*. So we got George and Tom Guinzburg and Peter Matthiessen to agree to take their interest in this newfound eight hundred and fifty thousand dollars—they were owners, after all, having invested five hundred dollars cash way back in Paris—and put it into the *Paris Review* Foundation.

SOL GREENBAUM I think Peter and Tom balked a little bit about giving the proceeds from the Morgan sale to the foundation. Frankly,

I felt that *The Paris Review* was all George. These other guys had done nothing for so many years. But he said the three of them had put up their five hundred dollars for seed money and that they were stockholders. Humes, so far as I could tell, hadn't put up any money. As a matter of fact, stock had never been issued to anyone. Goodale had quite a difficult time making everything legal. In the end, the stock was valued at nine hundred thousand dollars, so they all got a nice tax deduction out of their gift.

ANTONIO WEISS   George set the foundation in place to survive him; you would never have guessed he would think about that. But he did. He sold the archives and invested the proceeds; he converted the magazine from a for-profit to a nonprofit enterprise. He endowed the place and assembled a mix of editors and close friends who could be in a position to support the *Review* financially or to lend it editorial counsel. So what is that? It's someone preparing his legacy. Now, he never said, "I want all this in place in case I should die," but it was perfectly clear to all of us what he was planning. It was surprising.

SOL GREENBAUM   It was hard for him to let go. In his heart, he didn't want to establish the foundation, but in his mind, he understood how necessary it was. He was very uncomfortable. I attended all of those board meetings. For the first time, people were making suggestions about what he should be doing. He accepted them, but he wasn't used to it. Peter, Tom, Bob Silvers, Terry McDonell—all the board members were his friends.

GLENN HOROWITZ   What made the archive so valuable? *The Paris Review* was, by any stretch of the imagination, a powerful, unique, and enduring voice in nonmainstream American literature. Most importantly, they preserved it all. As such, it was filled with chatter, at the most primitive level, the most unedited level, the chatter that made up the cacophony of American literature of the fifties and sixties and seventies, when American literature was about the only game in town that didn't lose in any sense. Letter by letter in the alphabet, it had correspondences, typescripts, the galleys of really the great names in not just American, but English literature. It was a beautifully preserved archive. It has, it seems to me, thousands of research opportunities: From the perspective of a scholarly institution, it would seem to me to suggest endless and original ways for scholarship. It's a beautiful archive, and it sold much too cheaply.

HIS "BIG BOOK"

ANNE FULENWIDER There was a myth when we were at the *Review*. I don't know if it was true or not, but there was some kind of surmise that George wasn't doing what he really wanted to do, even though he was having such a good time. There was something else that he was going to get around to doing. Some people thought it was this great novel, and some people thought it was a great memoir. I wouldn't begin to psychoanalyze George, but I do feel like there was some great mystery there about what he *really* wanted to do, and if there was such a thing, why he wasn't doing it.

MAGGIE PALEY You know that "I could have been a contender" line? I'm told it was one of George's routines. I myself heard him say it after Doc Humes's memorial service at St. John the Divine, when we all went over to Muffin's [Alison Humes's] apartment. Peter Matthiessen talked, and some other writers, and George got up and said, "I could have been a contender," and clearly to me he was saying, "If I hadn't done *The Paris Review,* I could have been a major writer." I thought he meant a novel, or perhaps a great memoir, because he was certainly major at the journalism he did write.

TERRY MCDONELL The big argument about George and his own writing was why did he spend so much time on that *Review* instead of on his own writing. When that argument came up, he'd get mad. Deep in his heart the *Review* was the place he felt most comfortable, his spiritual hideout. As a writer, he was half an inch away from Thurber—if he had cared, I mean. It would have been hard for a minute, or a week, or a year or two, but there was a short story in everything he did and wrote. But it's a mistake to think he was a Walter Mitty. Thurber if he'd cared, but not Mitty. Walter Mitty was a wimp; George was heroic.

THOMAS MOFFETT   George was on a ship in the Galápagos when he found out that he'd been offered seven hundred and fifty thousand dollars for his memoirs. I got the call first. The agent was really excited. I said, "George is on a ship. I'll try to reach him." So we got a guy on the phone, and they got the ship on the phone— it was someone speaking Spanish—and then George came to the phone and we patched him through to the agent. I think he was on the bridge of the ship when he found out about the deal. It was for a lot more than he expected, and I think the size of the advance was daunting for him. Back in New York, he would float it around the office, saying, "Should I do this? I guess I should do it." Everyone would say, "Of course you should do it."

SARAH DUDLEY PLIMPTON   I remember when the offer came in. We were sitting on the deck with Peter Matthiessen and Jean [Kennedy] Smith when George was called up to the bridge for a ship-to-shore call from New York. He was gone for a long time. Finally my curiosity got the better of me so I went up there. He was looking pale and shaken. I thought something had happened to Freddy, or the children. When he finally got off the phone, he told us he had been offered all this money to write his memoir. At first I thought he was just being modest about it. But he said, "I don't want to do this. I've already written the stories of my life, what more is there to say? It's like putting the nails in the coffin. I don't want to write about my life." He thought about it, worried about it, made notes about other people's lives, but I think he was just interested in the money. By then he was running through his savings at a pretty good clip.

WILL HEARST   Well, I do think he could have written, if he'd wanted to, a Henry Adams–type history. As Henry Adams was to the nineteenth century, George could have been to the twentieth century: "Here's how it was, here are the people that I met, here's what they thought; some of them were fools, some of them were ambitious fools, some of them were well-intentioned fools, some of them were great men." It's a shame he never wrote that book.

GERALD CLARKE I told him long ago that he should write a novel or memoir. With his connections and everything, he could have written a wonderful book on the manners and morals of his time and place and class. George knew his world as Evelyn Waugh knew his. It wasn't any of my business, but I often wondered why he never wrote such a book. One possibility goes back to the early 1970s when I was doing a piece on him for *Time*. I asked him about what seemed the great theme in his sports books, which was failure, his failures, and he made a very curious comment: "The successful man of any profession I know of somehow rues his success." I gather that toward the end of his life George got a chance—that is, a big advance—to write his memoir. It came too late for him to take advantage of it. But the possibility is that he would have been too rueful to go through with it.

PETER MATTHIESSEN Sometimes, when he thought he was unobserved, he tended to let his face collapse, let his jaw hang open like a dead man, and at these moments he looked driven, really quite awful, the saddest man in the city. I don't know how much of that I read into his expression and how much was a quirk of physiognomy. I don't think George was fundamentally depressed, but he sure looked like he was fighting something dark.

ELIZA GRISWOLD Why didn't he write the "big book"? My guess is loneliness and sadness. I think George's humor came from a much deeper sadness, as great humor usually does; and the sadness, I think, originated in a strong sense of lost possibility. It's all over his work. I think his drinking was a way to turn off a deeper question, but what *that* was I wouldn't know, and I doubt he did, either. But whatever it was, drinking did take it off, chemically, of course, but also because it was an essential enabler of his boundless social life—another wonderful painkiller.

JAMES SCOTT LINVILLE For a few years I was in a little office upstairs between George's and the billiards room. His assistant Antonio Weiss, though not much of a *Star Trek* fan, used to call it the Bridge. When George would fly off to Omaha or wherever to give a speech, I'd slip in there and sit at his desk, spin in his chair, like a kid trying on his father's shoes. Then I'd prepare to make my Important Call. One day George had gone off and left his diary sitting open right in the center of the desk. Of course I had to look. He'd written, in the center of the page, "When one goes on a journey of self-exploration, one should go heavily armed. —Verlaine." So George.

LARISSA MACFARQUHAR Even though a lot of George's journalism is about himself, it's still somehow remarkably egoless. It's self-deprecating, and that's part of it; but he's actually using himself as a vehicle to convey the sense of where he is and who he's talking about, while maintaining his respect, his great appreciation, of them. He withdraws himself out of respect. That's very hard to do and very rarely done. Usually when people are using themselves as a participatory center, a protagonist, it ends up being about them. But with George, you always have the flavor of, yes, he was there, but it's always a story about somebody else.

OLIVER BROUDY He himself was not one of the things he paid close attention to, except as this comic figure, this persona that he created for his books. It must have been baffling, perhaps painfully so, the prospect of writing a memoir. I don't know that he knew who he was. He just sort of *was,* like an idiot savant.

ROWAN GAITHER You had to sift through the stories to get down to the underlying emotion. It was always there, but often masked in a fluid style that placed you at somewhat of a remove from what you sensed was the real emotional experience. Like the *Esquire* piece he wrote about driving around Jersey City, was it, with Archie Moore, the Mongoose, looking for the Mongoose's mother. It was told with meticulous detail and with a clarity that allowed you to ignore the fact that George was actually telling a completely heartbreaking story. Or take "The Man in the Flying Lawn Chair," the story that many people who knew him seem to think was quintessentially his. The flight was a success, but the story ends with the man killing himself, all alone out in a wilderness somewhere. I'm not sure that George ever wanted to reach out and really go after the feelings aroused by those images. They would be there in the writing, but he never seemed to want them to come to the fore.

LYNN NESBIT   He could have done a great memoir of New York Society, with his wit and distant, urbane point of view—but I think it would have bored him. He would have needed to *tell* it; he needed an audience. To write, to do great writing, you have to be alone, to have privacy, a private life. He was the most thoroughly social creature I've ever known. I think George experienced private life as a terrible deprivation; I think he would have preferred not to have one. We're all social creatures to some extent, artists to the least extent, perhaps, George to the greatest extent possible.

RIC BURNS   My idea of heaven is, you'd be in some sort of wonderful place and George would simply be retelling the story of the time he was a consultant to the fireworks display for the centennial of the Brooklyn Bridge in 1983. He told me he was climbing up very high on the bridge one night, up over the harbor with one of the Gruccis, and there, out of breath, two hundred and seventy-five feet above nighttime New York, he leaned over the iron parapet and saw that on the backside of it someone had written in chalk, "You've Come a Long Way Baby, Now Let's See How Far You Can Fly." That to me is the classic George thing, where you go out on a long limb, and when you get there you find something that you could never possibly have expected. If you get to the end of the limb and the expected comes, why bother having climbed out there and brought anybody with you? He had a tremendous sense of the theater of anecdote and language, where the audience has a whole set of ideas of why you're going out on that limb and, in that context, is waiting for something completely different. George always knew that that was really a theatrical presidium in which he was manipulating your mood—the height, the image in your mind of New York—and like any good comedian or dramatic actor, he gave you something that was startling and chilling and strange, with no resolution. There was never a moral to George's stories. They were not allegorical. Which is to say, they never revolved back inward either to George or to some point or lesson. They always opened outward into the density of human experience. It's about alertness and awareness, not about presumption having been confirmed. So it's never about vanity. It's always about wonder and the world. And that's why he stayed as young as he did. If George were a piece of music, he would be an unresolved chord.

THE ONCOMING BUS

JONATHAN DEE My guess is that it would have been terribly painful for George to write his memoirs. People forget how little of George's later life was given to writing and how much to working with the words of other people—editing anthologies, editing oral biographies, editing interview transcripts. The editing of transcripts was a talent he honed from the beginning of the *Paris Review* interviews, of course, and he made them into an imperishable brand. But even many of the books nominally written by him began to feature less and less of his own actual writing. Books like *Paper Lion* or *Shadow Box* had a tremendous voice running through them, but by the time you get to later books like *One More July* or *Open Net,* he's turned the stage over to his subjects almost entirely—huge block quotes, with only a kind of stage direction surrounding them. The oral biography form was kind of perfect for him: Some of those books were truly great, like *Edie,* while others like the Truman Capote and Diana Vreeland books were slighter and more perfunctory, but the significant thing is that George himself, as an authorial voice, is nowhere in them. And then there he was at the end of his life, in the Ernest, Scott, and Zelda show, literally speaking the words of other writers.

THOMAS MOFFETT In the late 1990s, I think, George was inspired by a dramatic reading that Terry Quinn had composed out of the Nabokov-Wilson correspondence and began assembling something out of the Hemingway-Fitzgerald correspondence. George worked with Quinn on editing it in the later stages, but in the early stages, he was doing it himself. He had all these books, and he would underline the parts he wanted from each letter, then I would type them up. Then he would do another draft and put them together. There was a lot of back-and-forth, starting with the original letter, then meticulously working our way to putting it in dialogue form.

TERRY QUINN George and I had spent seven months working on a number of drafts and came up with nothing, which was probably due to the fact that we went at this from very different perspectives. His approach to the material was much more chronological, historical—a close editorial interest, I would say. Mine was much more dramatic: How will this work for an audience?

LAWRENCE SHAINBERG They did the play with Mailer as Hemingway, George as Fitzgerald, and Norris Church [Mailer] as Zelda. By the time I started talking to George about my doing an article on it, they had already done it in a number of places. It was a complicated thing because they couldn't get royalties. The Hemingway and Fitzgerald estates controlled the whole thing. So they did it for expenses. Basically, they were all in it for the love of working together.

NORMAN MAILER I don't know who literally put the show together, it may be like the founding of *The Paris Review.* Of course, there was the built-in comedy for George and myself; he was playing Fitzgerald and I was playing Hemingway. While Fitzgerald was about my height, and Hemingway was about George's height. I have a deep, growly sort of voice, while in recordings, Hemingway, to my surprise, had a fast, high-pitched voice. Anyway, I decided, since I'm half Hemingway's size, I've got to get a very big voice into it, which I did. I played him with a big, authoritative voice, a strong voice. A man who knows what everything is made of. George played Fitzgerald extremely well, and Norris, who was a talented actress, did splendid stuff with Zelda. The combination worked. First, we did it in Vermont, and then we did it in East Hampton. We did it in New York a couple of times. Then we went on a European tour: Paris, Vienna, Berlin, Moscow, and London. We were performing pro bono, for the James Jones Literary Festival in Paris, for this or that fund-raiser, and of course, for the glory of it. But then at some point, because George was always in need of money, and I, with my many children, was always in need of money, we thought we could really put this show on the road and make a fortune. It would have been sensational. Believe me, it worked. God, it worked.

LAWRENCE SHAINBERG In Europe we would come into the city, whatever city, and they'd rehearsed once or twice, usually once, and then they'd go onstage with George wearing his little orange Princeton tie and Norman in his safari jacket. Zelda in a

Norman Mailer, George, and Norris Church Mailer as Ernest, Scott, and Zelda.
Photograph © Helayne Seidman 2002.

way was the most powerful character in the play, and Norris did her in a strong southern accent.

NORMAN MAILER It was more fun than I've had doing almost anything in the theater. And we were good; the play was good. You began to feel the loss that these guys felt even as they were living it—the knowledge that they were so talented, but they were not necessarily going to get the most out of their talent; that the parts of them that were there to destroy them might prove stronger in the end than their strengths.

NORRIS CHURCH Traveling with George was just so much fun. You never knew what he was going to do. In Amsterdam, I got this call from him: "Norris, I've gone off without my script and I don't know where we're supposed to go." He was totally lost, but he always had people running after him trying to give him his tickets and his passport and things. He just jumps into the cab, his white hair flying in the wind, as someone throws the tickets after him. So, thank God, I was there. He didn't have a clue where to go to do the show; but then he always walked in at the last minute, with hair perfectly in place, and performed. It's amazing. Somehow, it always worked out. He had some kind of guardian angel chasing around after him.

LAWRENCE SHAINBERG Norman was the dominant figure. They had big press conferences everywhere, TV appearances. I remember there was one press conference in Berlin where Norman started off by saying, "The first time I came to Berlin, I got an erection when I got off the plane." That was his introductory remark. He didn't want to talk about Iraq; he was talking about China as the big threat to the United States. And George, at this press conference in Berlin, said he thought that really the best thing we could do with China, because they were so obsessed and successful with Ping-Pong in the Olympics, was to send a lot of tennis rackets over there. Then some reporter from *Stern* came up to him and said, "Mr. Plimpton, I want you to know that your remark about the tennis rackets is the most intelligent thing I've heard all through this conference."

NORRIS CHURCH I think we might have gone on, doing Zelda, Scott, and Ernest, touring South America, doing Broadway, taking our show on the road forever. We never knew how ill he was, and there he was, at the end planning a trip to Cuba. We weren't able to go, but he said, "Oh, I'll pick up some actors on the plane. It will be fine." I'm sure it would have been.

SARAH DUDLEY PLIMPTON He would bicycle everywhere, white hair flying, no helmet. I can't tell you how many helmets we bought him and tried to place on his head. I can't tell you how many scrambled brain stories I told him. He absolutely refused to wear a helmet. His excuse was that, well, if you went to a restaurant, you would have to check it. That's pretty lame. Anyway, he loved having that long white hair flying in the wind. And he loved having people shout from the sidewalks, "George, where's your helmet?" So many people would tell me they saw George riding his bicycle downtown without his helmet. This is the child in him. He used to tell me how, when he was pedaling home from the Racquet Club or the Brook, he would go up Lenox Hill on Park Avenue to Seventieth Street, and then he would always see if he could coast from Park down to York. Imagine a seventy-year-old man seeing how far he could coast downhill on his bicycle. That's pure George.

RICHARD PRICE The last time I saw George was the most memorable experience I had with him. There was a guy, Flip, from Gotham Book Mart. The Gotham Book Mart had won box seats at Yankee Stadium, and Flip decided he was going to call a couple of writers. It was me, Flip, George, and Don DeLillo, a strange combination of characters going up there. Flip is this crazy bookstore guy, and DeLillo's like the gray ghost, slim as a blade, and the whole way up there, George was saying, "I have this idea for this great series of books! We're all going to pick a mineral. . . ." I don't know what he was talking about. He was saying, "We're going to have this adventure! And I'm going to have writers write backwards!" We got there, and I've never had seats like that in my

George on his evening rounds.
Photograph © Ron Galella.

life; you could see if Derek Jeter had popped that zit yet. But the game wasn't really that interesting. By the sixth inning, Don had left; and by the seventh, George and I left. So Flip was in this empty box seat. I shared a gypsy cab with George back into the city, and he was still coming up with all these ideas: "Let's join the Afghans! No, let's set up a soccer field in the Tora Bora Mountains!" It was probably August. It was the only time I was ever alone with him.

THOMAS MOFFETT He went to the doctor a lot. He seemed preoccupied with checkups. His main doctor, Dr. Cox, was across the street. He had to go for a colonoscopy on my birthday, the summer before he died. He was joking about dreading going and doing this thing. He said, "Listen, they tell me they need someone to come get me afterwards. Sarah's away. Can you?" I said, "Sure." When I walked over, the nurse said he was still waking up, and I just remember seeing his feet come down. He was looking for his shoes. He walked out and sat down, and he was utterly charming about it. He was saying, "That was a terrible procedure. I'm sorry. It's your birthday, kiddo. What an awful way to spend your birthday." We walked back toward 541, and he was saying, "How old are you? Twenty-five, that's a great year. I remember when I turned twenty-five." Then he started telling me about when the first review for *Paper Lion* came out, I think because he was getting ready to go to his reunion with the Lions that fall. He said he was so hung over. He was in a hotel room somewhere, with one of the worst hangovers he ever had. He said, "But I knew then that my life was going to be different."

BILL DOW   I was forty-seven, a freelance writer in the Detroit area, where I grew up. That Detroit Lions team from the early sixties was the team that I grew up with, and *Paper Lion* was, of course, one of my favorite books. As a freelance writer I'm always looking for ideas, tying in articles with anniversaries and so forth; and so in July 2002, I decided to call him up out of the blue, and to my amazement, I was put right through to him. So I said, "Mr. Plimpton, do you realize that next year will be the fortieth anniversary of your '63 Cranbrook training camp with the Lions?" He said, "Oh, my God, that's really something." And I said, "Would you ever consider coming back to Detroit for a reunion of that team? Perhaps it could be for a charity dinner or something like that." He said, "Oh, I'd be delighted to, if you could do something like that. Those were the favorite times of my life." So I decided, what the heck? We were able to get twenty-eight of his teammates to come back, including Alex Karras—and, you know, Alex was pretty much estranged from the organization; he hadn't done anything with them since he left. It took some prodding, because he's not used to doing that type of thing. The only way he came back was because of George, I know that. The next day, the players were introduced at halftime at the Lions game at Ford Field, and among the last group of players that were introduced were the Fearsome Foursome—Roger Brown, Darris McCord, Sam Williams, and last was Alex Karras, who got a big ovation. And then the next person introduced was Joe Schmidt, who's kind of like *the* legendary Detroit Lion—Hall of Fame player, former coach of the Lions. And George was the last one introduced, and I am not kidding, he got the loudest ovation. I mean, Karras got a really good ovation, and Schmidt did, too, but the look on George's face, the smile, it was just priceless. He was certainly surprised by it. He waved to the crowd, and I could tell he got the biggest kick out of it. At the dinner, of course, he said a few words, which included a couple of stories, one that was typically George, somehow, about how he was in the airport in Texas and this guy with a cowboy hat on recognized him and told him that *Paper Lion* was the only book he had ever read in his life.

PETER MATTHIESSEN   George was inducted into the American Academy of Arts and Letters only a few months before he died. The timing was great because it really meant a lot to him to be recognized as a real writer, not merely an editor. The academy has a category for people who make significant contributions to the arts, and he certainly qualified for that as well, but he deserved membership as a writer. That series of Mittyesque sports books is masterful, sui generis, and very droll in his fine, self-deprecating way. And here and there his well-turned sentences are truly lyrical and poignant—that last page of the prizefight book, the young boys on the airstrip in Zaire, is my own favorite. There had been resistance to his membership; it might have stemmed from the fairly buffoon-ish image conveyed by those unfortunate TV ads and the like. Even in the wonderful amateur-among-the-pros books, there was something about his role that bordered on the foolish. But wasn't that the true nature of his humor? His most appealing quality as a writer, perhaps also as a man, was his affectionate response to human folly.

SARAH DUDLEY PLIMPTON   About six months before George died, he was having one of his usual evenings at the Brook Club. I believe it was after dinner, he was sitting in the bar and he rose to go get another drink, and his blood pressure dropped and he passed out. As he came crashing down, he hit his head on the table and was knocked out. He was also bleeding quite profusely. The paramedics were called. Now, George had done another little amateur-among-professionals stint with the fire department, so whenever a fire truck went by as he was walking down the street or riding his bicycle, they would shout out, "Hey, George!" which he took such delight in. Anyway, the paramedics from the local firehouse came, and they recognized him instantly, and they were slapping his cheeks and calling to him, "Hey, George! Wake up!" The maître d' at the Brook Club took great exception to this, and he turned to them and said stiffly, "At the Brook Club, sir, we refer to him as 'Mr. Plimpton.' " The aftermath wasn't so funny. We had an intervention to get him to stop drinking. It worked for a month, a long time considering that hardly anyone showed up. Some were afraid of losing his friendship or love; many truly believed he didn't have a problem; but most of them, I think, had become dependent on George's high spirits and their friendship wouldn't be the same if they confronted him.

DENTON COX George stopped drinking for thirty days as a result of the intervention. And then I received a letter from Sarah saying that he had begun drinking again. I feel that he had a resentment that never went away as a result of it—and I don't know at whom it was directed. That intervention, which was so valuable and ought to have made a really big difference, didn't make a difference after a month or so, and it left him feeling resentful.

THOMAS MOFFETT In the weeks after he fell, he was more uneasy on his feet. He would ask me a lot, "Do I seem okay?" That always struck me as weird. He seemed very concerned about whether he came across differently; he acted a little bit older after that. He seemed to be a bit more cautious; but he would still play softball, which made Sarah nervous. So of course, George would go out and pitch at these softball games, which probably wasn't the smartest thing, but that was George. The idea of not being able to do something well was really painful to him.

SARAH DUDLEY PLIMPTON   In the Galápagos he'd slowed down considerably. He was very forgetful and quite spaced out. I would compensate for all that by doing things for him, whether it was buying equipment or packing his bags or filling out forms. He hated me doing that because it reminded him that he couldn't do it himself.

FIONA MAAZEL   You remember how he hung his bike up in the *Review* office? Well, I sat underneath it, and how he hung the bike up became an indicator of how sick he was becoming. We would all sit there and be very nervous, because it was taboo even to offer to help him. We would stand back and watch his arms shaking as he tried to hang this bike, and it just got worse and worse. It was awful. But even when you saw George looking weak, you didn't think it was serious. He didn't seem like he was ever going to die.

OLIVER BROUDY   That summer, we were playing *The New Yorker* at softball. I always play catcher because I'm half-blind. Michael Crawford, who's one of the *New Yorker* cartoonists, was up at bat. He swings, and in swinging, he swung the bat backward and launched it and nailed me right in the forehead. I had five stitches in a hospital. The plan was to retire after the softball game to some dive on the West Side. Despite this injury, the blood and stitches, I rejoined the team. George was there, and everyone was gathered around. I walked in, and there was a big roar of welcome because I was the wounded player. George turned around in his chair and saw me there and was so moved that he reached his arms up to me to hug me and started crying. Some little door opened and he saw something there, though I'm not sure how much of it had to do with me.

SARAH DUDLEY PLIMPTON   I think the staff believed he was Superman. In your seventies, you can't go out nightclubbing every night without suffering the consequences. His body began to betray him and it got harder to maintain that exuberant persona. He managed to keep up a pretty good front for the kids downstairs; he was new to them. For most everyone else, the same old routines, the same old stories, wore pretty thin. Toward the end of his life, he struck me as desperate. He didn't know how to drop the mask, but he kept going on the staff's adoration. He certainly wasn't getting much of it from me anymore.

PATRICIA STORACE What was Ichabod Crane–ish about him was speed and the comic aspect. But also a sense of fear, I thought —trying to outrun mortality. Or trying to outrun adulthood, if that's possible. Or limitations: That could also be what he was outrunning. And in that way, I don't see him as just jovial and self-assured; I see him as someone who is conscious of some risk.

HALLIE GAY WALDEN He came to my Dartmouth twenty-fifth reunion two months before he died. We couldn't pay his normal fee, but he did it as a favor for me: "Anything for you, Hallie Gay." So I went up and spoke about him very briefly and sat down, and George got up, and he sort of shuffled to the podium. He didn't look all that well. He looked frail, and I had never seen him look frail before. His nose kept running, there were little drops on the paper from his nose that he didn't even notice. That, and his elbow having gone through his houndstooth jacket. It was a very conservative crowd, and he stood up and launched into talking about me, and when I first worked for him, and how people used to line up on the sidewalk and jump to try to look in the *Paris Review* window. My face was red, and then he launched into his usual speech about participatory journalism, and everyone was kind of looking around, and I was watching everyone, and it didn't seem like it was going over as well as I thought it should, for the first five minutes of his talk. A lot of the people were from the business sector and didn't know much about literature, and they were kind of like, "Who is this guy?" Then he started this tale, and people started clapping, and everyone started smiling and laughing. There were eight hundred people there. It was a huge audience. People were roaring back in their chairs, and George said, "I'm rambling now," around the forty-five-minute mark. "Maybe I'm going on too long?" And people stood up and said, "No, keep going!" When he finished, he got a standing ovation. He just stood there, and he came to the edge of the stage, and he looked frail, and he gave this exceedingly humble bow, just bowing ever so slightly as they gave him this ovation, and I started to cry, because he looked so humble, like he was surprised that his speech had gone over so well.

JAMES GOODALE   Let me tell you about our planning for the fiftieth anniversary benefit for *The Paris Review.* Well, here we are, a foundation, and someone said, "We're having a fiftieth anniversary; why don't we use it to make some money?" We all knew without saying that George had thrown Revels for fifty years and never made a penny. What were we going to do about this? We organized ourselves into a sort of committee which would meet every now and then on the phone to see if we could help George and to make sure George was really going to bring in the money. But every time we got on the phone or got in the meeting, George would talk for about five minutes, then walk out of the meeting, so we had no idea of what he was doing. We threw up our hands. We really began to get concerned as we got closer to the event because it was getting larger and larger and larger, and George seemed to be doing more and more and more of the work. We did everything we could to try and stop him from doing that, and I really think that overexertion had something to do with his heart attack. In the end, we took in a hell of a lot of money, though. We took in eight hundred thousand dollars. *The Paris Review* had never seen more than seventy thousand dollars.

THOMAS MOFFETT   He was really busy on the day he died. First thing in the morning, he did a spot for Conan O'Brien, some audio thing. He had lunch with someone trying to raise money for something at Harvard. He came back to the office and then had rehearsals for the Ernest, Scott, and Zelda play. He was going to do the play in Cuba. That was the last time I saw him, when he went upstairs for the rehearsal. He went out that night, then he died in his sleep.

MICHELE CLARK   I don't think he ever thought he was successful. I don't think he thought he was successful at all. In fact, when we went to look at Cipriani's Forty-second Street for the Revel—

we had already booked it, but George hadn't seen it yet—he walked in and his face just fell. He looked so upset. I said, "What's wrong?" He looked at me and said, "We'll never fill this space. This many people aren't going to come out for *The Paris Review.* I don't know what we're going to do." He was very genuinely worried. We had four hundred and fifty people already signed up, which was a very respectable number, when he passed away. That was about two and a half weeks before the event. And we ended up with eight hundred and thirty-five, who brought in eight hundred thousand dollars, maybe a hundred times the previous record for a Revel. The night before he died, he spent two hours with us, going over the invitation list. He was incredibly worried that nobody was going to show up. We already had a very successful turnout by then. But he was still worried. So he called people that night, right there on the spot. He sat there and went through the Common Book to see who'd called and who hadn't been called, and he made phone calls. So it was incredibly shocking that he passed away that night, because I thought for sure he would hang on through this party.

PAT RYAN   There was a wonderful irony to the last night I saw George, which was at a dinner party we gave at our apartment. Everybody else went home, exhausted. George stayed and stayed. Suddenly there was this noise outside—we live facing the Statue of Liberty—and George says, "I think that's fireworks." And we went out on the balcony and watched. It must have been midnight.

DONALD HALL   George called me from New York the night he died—I think it was about five-thirty. We talked on the phone sometimes. Often he wanted me to advise him on a new poetry editor or on something that was coming up on the magazine. My name is still on that masthead, after all those years, and he did occasionally consult me. This time he wanted me to go to the fiftieth anniversary party, and of course I was the first call to get to. I should have been there. I just couldn't bear it. Physically, it cost me too much. So I said, "Oh no, I won't do that. I like it up here." He tried to persuade me, but not terribly hard. He was not a guilt maker. We talked away. It was a typical conversation in that I felt good afterwards. It was pleasant, even though I was saying no.

DENTON COX He died in his sleep from a catecholamine surge, resulting in sudden cardiac arrest. I don't know whether we could have found something that would have prevented the episode. What you must know about George's health is that he had an enormous burden of vascular disease—his arteries were heavily laden with plaque from cholesterol, which were monitored yearly. Though he quit smoking when he first came under my care—till then, he had been smoking for twenty years or so—his diet was quite poor. And his blood pressure was terribly high—a problem that went on for years. . . . Just understand that the ever vigorous George, who we saw zipping around on his bike and sparring with champions, had a great deal of physical vulnerability. In any case, there are fifty thousand deaths in the United States every year, between four and eight a.m., from sudden cardiac arrest following a catecholamine surge—in people who don't even have heart disease. It's not entirely understood why the surge happens. Perhaps it goes back to our early ancestors, who needed to wake up alert and ready. At any rate, the body puts out a great deal of adrenaline, the heartbeat becomes irregular and then stops. For George it was an ideal way to go.

———

ROY BLOUNT The only unlikely thing he did, the only thing that seemed out of character, was dying. It didn't seem like the sort of thing he would do.

SARAH DUDLEY PLIMPTON Thursday had been a pretty typical day. The fiftieth-anniversary issue was put to bed a few nights before. I had a terrible cold and had gone to bed at about five in the afternoon. I remember George coming into the bedroom saying, "Laurance Rockefeller's downstairs, why don't you come down and say hello?" I had to beg off. They went out to dinner at Petaluma, which is just up the street, and he came home a few hours later. The next morning I woke up just before seven. George slept like a stone when he took sleeping pills, so I always had to check and see if he was breathing. That morning, I leaned

Paper Lion reunion, September 2003. © *Tom Albert Photo.*

over to wake him and he didn't move. I looked at his face and knew he was gone. I had sensed for some time he was dying and I would panic when I had trouble rousing him in the mornings. So this time, I thought, "Oh, you've finally done it." I just held him. Olivia and Laura were waking up and I told them to hurry up and get ready for school. Livvy just stood there, so I said, "Dad's very sick and I want to call the doctor. You go on to school." She started to cry saying, "He's dead, isn't he? I dreamed that he died." The paramedics arrived a few minutes later. They started to try and resuscitate him. I was frantic because I knew he was gone and that would have been the last thing he wanted. The paramedics had set this activity in motion and I wanted it stopped. I begged them to stop. Finally they did. I sent them away and brushed his hair and sat with him for a while. He looked so beautiful. The girls were called back from school and I had them come in and sit with him. Laura picked up a toy Canada goose that George had given her for Christmas the year before. She sat it on his forehead and gave it a honk. George would have liked that. It was the sort of thing he would have done.

THOMAS MOFFETT The week after he died, there was a family-only gathering upstairs. We assumed we weren't going to be invited up, because it was for family, but at the last minute, Sarah came downstairs and sweetly and emotionally said, "Listen. You guys are family, and I want you to come up and join us."

EPILOGUE:
BLESSED GEORGE,
WHO COULD BLESS

—

FAYETTE HICKOX Odd people would come to George's parties, like one friend of his who is utterly malign—whatever's the opposite of benign. I remember that he came to one of George's birthday parties and slipped into George's own office, took the *Social Register,* and carefully cut out the page with George's name on it and then handed the volume to him, without that page, as a present. Pretty surreal. He's writing a book about George himself, he told me. He said, "I'm critical of George. I don't say nice things about George; but no one ever did me more favors."

WALON GREEN I know a guy who is a well-known screenwriter—a brilliant, well-educated guy who taught in the Ivies for a time. However, when his wife is impressed by someone, he has to trash that person. So Ann, my wife, called her and said, "We're having dinner with George Plimpton. Do you and [let's call him] Bruce want to come?" and Bruce's wife said, "I'd love to meet George Plimpton." As soon as I heard she'd said that, I thought, "Oh boy, this'll be Bruce on his bad behavior." Still, I'd put George in the room with anybody. I thought, "I'll just clue him in a little bit." So when we picked him up, I said, "Bruce So-and-so is a very smart guy, but I don't know how well he's going to behave tonight. It should be interesting for you." So we got there, and sure enough, Bruce started taking all these shots at George. His wife got so mad, she grabbed my wife and went and locked the two of them in the ladies' room and went into a full tirade that you could hear outside the restroom. Meanwhile, Bruce was going at it with George. But interestingly enough, not only could Bruce not get to George, but George never showed a flicker of being offended. Bruce was trying to elicit some sign of dishonesty, and it just wasn't there. Bruce basically thinks that everybody is a liar, a phony, and that he can expose them. But he couldn't find any of that in George. He just couldn't find it. George was an incredibly intuitive reader of people. He could see where they were going and head them off without them even being aware of it. Here was this difficult person out to savage him, and George let the guy in the end come around and savage himself. My wife was immensely impressed. You could say it's the patrician attitude, but it wasn't that. I've seen aristocrats deal with situations like that, and they feel, "Well, I am who I am, and so what?" But George was actually much better than that. Bruce was blowing professorial credentials all over the place. I remember him saying something about Robert Penn Warren, telling him that he, Bruce, was the new Hemingway. George didn't say anything. He just let this guy go on until finally the guy thought, "What kind of jerk am I?" Then out loud, he said to George something like "I guess what you're thinking is, maybe I shouldn't be saying that about myself." Now, I'm not sure if George meant to have this effect by being silent, but the fact is, he actually made this guy a better person that evening.

EDMUND WHITE   When Ned Rorem first proposed George for the American Academy of Arts and Letters, I seconded it, then unseconded it. That's true. Ned said, "Won't you do this for me?" and I loved Ned, so I said, "Okay." And then I thought about it: "What's he ever done that's so great? I mean, why should he be in the American Academy of Arts and Letters? He's sort of an 'after-dinner speaker,' not a major American writer." And I think the American Academy, unlike the French Academy, actually has very good people in it. I think they really are the best writers. Recently they've been getting in bad people, even the old ones, people like Garrison Keillor. But I remember that when he did get in, George gave this talk at the winter dinner where new members are invited to speak. People usually get up and say, "I'm terribly honored, and it's much too good for me." But George got up and gave a real after-dinner speech, and it was charming and people cooed. He was that kind of person who would make cultured older women coo, like, all the pouter pigeon crowd.

JACK RICHARDSON   I remember I saw him once hosting an homage to Mickey Mouse on TV. It had something to do with Mickey Mouse. I don't want to say he was a Walt Disney shill. I don't know what drove him. He had the ability to, as they say today, morph into other people, to try on these roles for about a minute. It was a clever gimmick, and it brought him fame, money, and the love of beautiful women, the same things that would drive anybody else. I don't think I could go any deeper than that.

FAYETTE HICKOX   We're always ready to suspect "social" people, aren't we? Their charm and good manners can seem false and manipulative, sometimes with good reason. And when the other guy is so extravagantly blessed with social virtues and graces as to be, like George, a blessing to everyone around him, a few people may actually need to see him as a phony. Plus, there's the inevitable wrinkle that people like George will often seem to be promising more than they can possibly deliver.

NORMAN MAILER   "Socialite" is a word that's pinned on upper-class WASPs; but he was a social light, if you will, because he was a point of focus. I think what was extraordinary about him is that he was like a socialite of the greatest possible inclusiveness. In other words, he invented performances involving himself but held them wide open for others in a way that no one else had ever dreamed of. He had the life he wanted to have, which was no small gift for the rest of us. At his memorial, speaking extempore, I came up with an idea that I hadn't thought of before—about love. There are many people we love in New York in a pure way; and many people in New York who we remember with love. We might only see them twice a year or once every five years; it didn't go anywhere; we didn't have deep relationships with them, but it didn't matter. We loved them. That is the way I loved

George, and still love George. So many people loved George. It's possible that he was loved in that manner more than anyone else in New York. It's even more possible that he loved more people in that manner than anyone else in New York.

FREDDY ESPY PLIMPTON   Once he was not legally bound, or in any way bound, to another person he was attracted to, then he could get close to them and be endearing, and he wasn't scared, and he was truly George. George's love was uninhibited. It knew no bounds. There wasn't enough space in the world for it, and there weren't enough different ways that he could feel it, for real. Except for marriage, of course.

RIC BURNS   We didn't know exactly what we had in him. He understood something, at a deeper level than walking around, about what it is to be alive, to be there at the end of your own fingertips. The miracle of personality is so tied to real time. That's the thing: He had an amazing personality, and it existed in real time. That's where his artistry was, and that's why he won't be remembered maybe for his books, but for the spirit that he had in every interaction. And it's gone. Once it's gone, there is no way to convey what that was to somebody.

OLIVER BROUDY   I've been thinking about this a lot, the mystery of George's personality and character. He really seemed like he wasn't quite on the same plane. I'm sure you've heard this a lot. When you actually had his attention, you felt like there was a shift in the weave of things. You felt like some spotlight had been turned on. It was a hyper-real moment. To the last days, I felt like that: highly self-conscious, highly aware.

HAROLD BLOOM   I don't like to think of myself as pugnacious or aggressive, but I suppose, for one reason or another, I have struck a lot of people as being pugnacious or aggressive. But George was one of those rare people I ever knew who I wished I could have a blood transfusion from. I would have been a much better human being, I always felt, and a lot easier to be with, or live with—even for myself to live with or be with—if I could have had some transfusion of that essential quality, which was absolutely authentic in George. And it's so difficult to describe. It's too banal to call it just goodness, but it was goodness: absolute goodwill.

CHARLES MICHENER   There was always a sense of astonished admiration in George. He was astonished by everything. He would often say, "Could you believe" something. "Could you believe that!" There was a note of incredulity. "How remarkable! How astonishing! I couldn't believe it!" After which his astonishment would often give way to admiration. George was the greatest, most effective communicator of infectious admiration I've ever known.

GEOFFREY GATES   What was unique about George's presence was that whenever you saw him, or came up to him, or went to his apartment, it seemed that everything was fine. Things were fine, and in his presence, you began to feel the same way. There's no one else in the world I've ever known like that. He was enchanting, literally.

PAMELA DRAPER   I had one experience with George that literally changed my relationship with him forever. It happened when George was visiting L.A., where I was temporarily living. It was a Sunday night and he suggested that I accompany him to the Playboy Mansion. George and I had some drinks and then he led me down to the swimming pool and through an archway of enormous rocks into what was called "the grotto." Inside, the light was all muted gold and purple and orange with wisps of steam meandering upwards from the surface of the water. There were ledges in the rocks where you could perch like a mermaid. Here you had a house full of people several hundred yards away and not a single, solitary soul was there but us. George said, "Let's go for a swim." We flung off our clothes, dove in, and splashed around. Then George pointed to a passage in the stonework, and in moments we had swum into the outdoor pool. It was very, very late at night. It was dark, but the pool was all lit from the depths, and it was magnificent to swim about and breathe the night air. All of a sudden, George said, "Let's go into the tunnel now." I was startled. "What tunnel?" "Well," George said, "there's a tunnel down there. If we dive down and go through this tunnel, we'll come back out in the grotto." I looked down and about three feet below the surface of the water there was a narrow opening. It was lit but, again, it was three feet underwater. It was not like a tunnel where you could surface for air, and once you got in, you couldn't exactly turn around and try to get out. You had to make a commitment to get to the other end. I said, "George, I'm not going to do that. I can't do that. I can't swim underwater. I don't even want to put my head under. I'm not good at it." He said, "Oh, sure you can." We didn't have to do this, but once George knew I had this tremendous fear of it, it intrigued him. We went back and forth, as I remember. "Nothing will happen to you. I'll be there." "No, no. I'll drown, I'll die, I can't do it!" "I'll keep my eye on you. Nothing will happen!" If you're scared of something, you really have to do it, he said. He of course would do anything; the harder the challenge, George would do it. I wasn't George. I didn't want to go underwater, I didn't want to die. But with George I had to believe I wouldn't. I mean, there was no way we'd have come to be friends if I were a wimp. Right? I took a deep breath, dove down, and followed him right through the tunnel. Every three seconds or so he turned his head back to make sure I was okay and I nodded. After what seemed to me an endless time underwater, holding my breath, I surfaced inside the grotto. He was so pleased with empowering me, and I was so pleased with my accomplishment, we clapped hands and laughed and laughed and the noise echoed from the top crevasses of the grotto, which made it even better. "Damn, I was scared," I said. George laughed some more and got me to say I'd do it again. We were alone. We celebrated. We rejoiced in that experience and in each other.

NORMAN MAILER At eighty-two, I've gotten to that point where urination has become one of my preoccupations. In other words, I am never, ever in a place for long without knowing where the bathroom is. In St. John the Divine, where George's memorial service was held, I had explored the joint, so I knew that the men's room was like a quarter of a mile from where I was sitting, all the way down in the basement. So when the service ended, I headed for a side door, and I passed Phil Roth. Phil and I have had an edgy relationship for thirty or forty years. He said, "Where are you going in such a hurry, Norman?" and I said, "Well, I have to tell you, Phil, I've got to urinate. When you get to my age, this becomes a desperate matter. In fact, let me warn you, when you get to my age, you're going to be looking around for telephone booths in which you can relieve yourself." And Phil said, "Norman, I'm there already," and I said, "Well, Phil, you always were precocious." And then we both laughed. It was the first time in our lives that we had both laughed together. I attribute this to George's spell.

PETER MATTHIESSEN   When you hear some of the adulation poured over the iconographic George, it's tempting to say, "You didn't know George"; but those of us who saw his human frailties loved him more. We knew who we loved, we knew who we had there. When he let his guard down, he was heartbreakingly touching.

SARAH DUDLEY PLIMPTON   Everybody downstairs in the *Review* office felt that in some way they were blessed and that this was a gift that he had given them to pass on. I definitely felt this after he died. He taught me how to give. He taught me how to open my heart when it seemed the blackest. Many of those twelve years of marriage were hugely painful for me, and for him—after all, his life was beginning to slip away from him, which he found unbearable. I had to pull out all the inner strength I could possibly summon. He was a teacher, he really was a very gracious teacher. I like to think that the best of him is still with me.

FREDDY ESPY PLIMPTON   The reason I use the word *Bodhisattva* to describe George is because his generosity was such a quiet, understanding giving. And he never asked for anything in return, ever.

PIEDY LUMET   This is a story about George's graciousness, or something more than that. He asked Leslie, my daughter, to be godmother to Medora. Leslie was stunned. She didn't understand why or wherefore. She was young, maybe twelve, and shy, but she loved George. So Chris Cerf read something that was incredibly funny, and Francis read a dazzling thing that George might have written, and Caroline Kennedy read something fine. Leslie said, "I can't get up in front of all those people." I told George, and he said, "It's okay, it's fine." And then George spoke for Leslie and said, "Leslie would like a Zen breath for Medora, so I'm going to sound this gong," and it went *bong,* and it was beautiful—the contrast, the quiet, then the single sound. That was typical of him. He was perfectly accepting of how you wanted to be and made it right—his uncommon grace.

NORMAN MAILER His nature was to keep everything open, keep every possibility open, because who knew when someday or other there wouldn't be a huge payoff. Not for himself, but for the sheer spirit of amusement. You see, this is what I got to understand about him last of all. It was that there was something immensely impersonal about George—he wasn't doing it for himself, he was doing it for the spirit of the universe. Or rather he was doing it for the spirit of the occasion, because if you improve the spirit of the occasion, maybe that wouldn't be altogether bad for the spirit of the universe. I think that's as close as he came to mystical philosophy.

FAYETTE HICKOX I called his home on the day I found out about his death, and someone I didn't know answered. I said, "I should just say that George was so nice to me, so kind to me," and she said, "He was kind to everybody!" Like, good-bye! And I was like, "Wait a minute, no, no, he was especially kind to me! Don't you realize?"

George, Being George is not a biography. Not according to any common use of the word. No would-be biographer, for example, need be put off his own project by the existence of this one. On the contrary, he or she should be delighted with this trove of anecdotes, judgments, and feelings, all nicely prepared for quotation, like spices for a proper meal.

Moreover, such is the nature of this kind of book, whatever it's called, that one can easily imagine another editor taking the raw material I worked with and fashioning out of it a very different account of George's life. In fact, one can easily imagine scanning the thousands of pages of transcribed interviews that we've assembled, plus any number of additional ones, plus any number of comments on the interviews, onto a Wikipedia-style site from which might be made an infinite number of books like this.

What I can't imagine is what, collectively, to call those books. I only know what it's like to put this one together. People would ask me about that while I was doing it, and the metaphors came easily to mind. I'd say it was like making a collage, a mosaic, a documentary biopic, a New England farmers' wall. But mostly, toward the end, it seemed like pasting thousands of scribbled Post-it reminders on a tailor's dummy.

I liked that one. It captures the pastiche character of what I was doing. And with it, a suggestion of a treasure hunt—the reader plucking one little clue after another off the poor dummy's body. It also captures the peculiar experience of reading a book like this. Reading *Edie*, I remember being enticed to go on and on, enchanted, as I met all these different people having their say about her. Each fragment of their talk brought its own special note to the hunt for who she was, and whatever note it brought, it held me for a moment as I tried to imagine the speaker—who *he* was, what his interest in her was, whether I'd like him if we met. A book like this is a twofer: You learn something about the subject, George or Edie; but you also, at the same time, get to play an intriguing game of hide and seek, of glances and glimpses, with the people who are telling you about them.

So what kind of book is this? In the end, I'd say it's a kind of literary party, George's last, so to speak, where everyone, including the reader, is gossiping about the host. That is to say, where everyone is more or less consciously working his or her way to some understanding of the good life—a *social* book, in short, about a supremely social man.

The project began in the imagination of Amanda "Binky" Urban, our agent, who persuaded Sarah Dudley Plimpton, George's widow and literary executor, to commission it. Binky then sold the idea to Bob Loomis, the legendary Random House editor. That much was accomplished not long after George's death in September 2006. The following June, eight of us convened for the first of six or so planning meetings at George's apartment. Sarah presided over these meetings with skill and humor. Chris Cerf, John Heminway, Fayette Hickox, Ben Howe, Jeanne McCulloch, Susan Morgan, Jonathan Dee, and I developed a general list of potential interviewees, from which each of us selected people we particularly wanted to interview. The original list numbered over 400 people, of whom 374 were actually interviewed, and their words transcribed on disk and hard copy. Of the 374 only about 200, unfortunately, will see their contributions in print.

We also came up with some basic rules for the project at those meetings. The most important of these was set by the oral biography we chose as our model: George and Jean Stein vanden Heuvel's *Edie*, about Warhol's 1960s superstar. This was oral biography at its purest, which meant that George's story, like hers, would be told exclusively in the words of the interviewees, with no editorial intrusions other than, of course, the massive intrusion of selecting and arranging those words (for reasons of space, context, intelligibility, etc.) in the first place. I'm responsible for that, as George and Jean were in *Edie*.

All of us at the planning meetings were friends of George, many of us friends of each other through George, and all of us would probably say, at the very least, that George was the most exhilarating person we'd ever met. We loved him for that, but also for his faults: To most of us, even these seemed liberating. This disposition might have led us, as interviewers and editor, to favor the sunniest memories of our protagonist, and to scant the sorrows and damage that personal liberation sometimes entails, not least on the liberator. But this hasn't happened. Interviewers were free to ask any sort of question, and interviewees were encouraged to offer any sort of answer. Sarah Dudley Plimpton was so emphatically *not* the stereotypical "guardian of the flame" in this process that I, her interviewer, was sometimes stunned by her candor. Her aim, like mine, was simply to gather the most telling account of George's life and character.

I should say something about the winnowing by which some contributors' text-bites made it into the published book and some did not.

The first step was to manage the logistics and finances of all that interviewing: nudging people to sit down and do the interviews, having them transcribed (by no fewer than twenty-three transcribers), getting the raw transcripts to me, and arranging for everyone to be paid. This hugely complicated job fell to Jonathan Dee, the novelist, journalist, and former *Paris Review* staffer, and he did it without a glitch or a whimper. Then, as the interviews came in, I would mark them up with marginal notes and signposts indicating what text-bites I wanted to keep and under what heading I wanted to keep each one. Then, with all the interviews in and cut up, at least on paper, three extremely well-organized young poets,

Diana Fox, Anne Yoder, and Cate Peebles, helped me copy the text-bites into the computer, each with its designated interviewee and topic, each on its own separate piece of paper.

Day after day, for more than a year, I conducted a triage around my dinner table, sorting and re-sorting those sheets of paper according to some mental map of where I thought they might "do." I wish I could say that my choices were guided by some principle, but, looking back on it now, the process seems thoroughly anarchic and invidious: Whose account was more vivid, more amusing, more idiosyncratic, more complete, more powerful, more affecting, more useful in advancing the story of George's life?

The map seems awfully arbitrary, too. Chronology was of some help, especially for George's early years. But after he returns from Paris and settles down in New York to construct, incredibly swiftly, virtually every feature of the life he loved, chronology becomes almost irrelevant. One can't even say that his life "went on"; it unfolded like a flower, or perhaps like one of his adored "chrysanthemum" fireworks, going off on radiant lines that hardly changed from day to day. There was the *Review* to edit and the staff to hang out with; games to play at the Racquet Club; books and articles to write for anyone who would pay for them; New York ceremonies to MC; girls to make love with; and always, from every direction, the endlessly seductive pull of friendship to respond to. The only big changes in his life that followed chronology were his marriages—which, notoriously, hardly changed anything in his life. His apartment might grow and grow: More wall space would disappear behind more posters, pictures, photographs; more furniture and souvenirs would accumulate; more rooms, whole stories, would be added. Children would be added. But George, being George, remained George.

This astonishing continuity of character and activity accounts for the loose, baggy later chapters of this book—as it does also for the absence of chronology in the post-1973 subchapters on *The Paris Review.* Members of the staff—interns, editors, publishers, and "the business side"—appear in them without regard to when they appeared in George's life. They do follow one another thematically as the staffers speak of themselves starting out on the job, of George as an editor, of George as a boss, and of George's last years. But George was George: the man they worked for in 2003 was much the same guy that an earlier generation worked for in 1973.

The book is dedicated to "the contributors," as it should be. Without their witness, the protagonist of the book would not exist. Without their eloquence, humor, and insight, the book would not exist—we would have dumped it long ago. There are two contributors, however, whose accounts of George must have been painful to give, and to them, Freddy Espy Plimpton and Sarah Dudley Plimpton, I am especially grateful.

Beyond these two, I want to acknowledge my thanks to a whole roomful of people who gave me, and not only through their interviews (or, in a few instances, any interview), insights and puzzlements about George without which this fascinating man would have appeared even more mysterious than he does in these pages. At random: Norman Mailer, Sarah Gay Plimpton, Bob Silvers, Peter Matthiessen, Peter Duchin, John Train, Jonathan Dee, James Scott Linville, Bill Wadsworth, David Michaelis, Jeanne McCulloch, Oliver Broudy, Maggie Paley, Marion Capron, Buddy Burniske, Fayette Hickox, Tom Martin, and Diana Fox. I'm also grateful to three Random House editors, Abby Plesser, Millicent Bennett, and Frankie Jones, for crucial last-minute help with collecting photographs, releases, contributor biographies, and only they know what else. Heartfelt thanks, also, to the three poets who helped me input the text-bites, without whom I would have certainly gone mad.

Finally, I want to thank two noncontributors whose efforts on behalf of the book were, in that new old word, "existential." Amanda Urban conceived of the idea that George, and readers, would be well served by an "oral biography." Rather more daringly she conceived of me as the editor of it. Bob Loomis, the editor's wonder-working editor, has been drowning in accolades since entering a second half-century of almost mythic accomplishment at Random House. I will say only that every suggestion he gave me in the making of this book was astonishingly deft, as simple to carry out as it was delightful to see on the page. And he delivered these suggestions with a combination of authority and deference that I wouldn't have thought possible in his or any other profession. Perhaps his most brilliant proposal was his last. It was also the one he put no authority behind, and which I resisted long into the production process. It's the text-bite with which I end the book. He thought it would be perfect, and it is.

Nelson W. Aldrich, Jr.
June 17, 2008

NOTES ON CONTRIBUTORS

After Paris and New York, BEE DABNEY ADAMS returned to Massachusetts, where she raised her son and continues to draw, paint, and find ways to encourage young people to explore the arts.

KATHY AINSWORTH, when she is not traveling, lives on an island in Scotland.

ANNA LOU ALDRICH first met George Plimpton in the mid-1950s when she went with Doc Humes to a party at Bee Dabney's apartment. She now divides her time between New York and Stonington, Connecticut.

NELSON W. ALDRICH, JR., is the author, most recently, of *Old Money: The Mythology of Wealth in America*. He first met George during his 1957–1958 stint as Paris editor of the *Review*.

JOAN AMES is a writer living on Martha's Vineyard, and a first cousin of George's.

JONATHAN AMES is the author of four novels and four essay collections, the latter including the forthcoming *The Double Life Is Twice as Good*.

DAVID AMRAM, as he has for more than fifty years, travels the world as a conductor, soloist, bandleader, composer, visiting scholar, and narrator in five languages. Over the years he has worked with Thelonious Monk, Willie Nelson, Charles Mingus, Leonard Bernstein, and Jack Kerouac.

KURT ANDERSEN is author of the novels *Heyday* and *Turn of the Century*. He's also host and cocreator of *Studio 360,* the Peabody Award–winning weekly public radio program, and writes a column for *New York* magazine.

BRIAN ANTONI first met George twenty years ago in the Bahamas. He is the author of *Paradise Overdose* and *South Beach*.

RED AUERBACH was the legendary coach of the Boston Celtics when George, for one glorious moment, played with the team.

MAVIS HUMES BAIRD practices addictions and trauma therapy, combining neurological, behavioral, spiritual, and body-centered approaches. A short list of her extended family relationships would locate her as a daughter of Harold (Doc) Humes and Anna Lou (Humes) Aldrich, as stepdaughter of Nelson W. Aldrich, Jr., and as little sister to Alison Humes and big sister to Immy Humes, Alexandra Aldrich, Liberty Aldrich, and Arabella Aldrich. She spent time with George off and on during several periods of their lives.

EDWIN BARBER served as editor in chief at Harcourt Brace, and as director of both the college and trade divisions at W. W. Norton & Company. He worked with George Plimpton on four books, notably *The Norton Book of Sports*.

JOYCE BARONIO, a 1976 graduate of Yale, was introduced to George at a book party for her first volume of photographs, *42nd Street Studio,* in 1980. She exhibits with the Howard Greenberg Gallery in New York.

ROBERT BECKER was eighteen years old when he started working with George in 1977. He is the author of *Nancy Lancaster: Her*

Life, Her World, Her Art and is writing a book about nineteenth-century American missionary families in Hawaii.

WILLIAM BECKER was instrumental in assembling the collection of Janus Films and its sister company, the Criterion Collection. He is chairman of both.

TOM BELLER is editor and cofounder of Open City Magazine and Books, and creator of the website Mrbellersneighborhood.com. He is the author of three books, *Seduction Theory* (stories), *The Sleep-Over Artist* (a novel), and *How to Be a Man* (essays).

LARRY BENSKY was Paris editor of *The Paris Review* from 1964 to 1966. He is well known for his work with the Pacifica Radio station KPFA-FM in Berkeley, California, and for the many nationally broadcast hearings he anchored for the Pacifica network.

HAROLD BLOOM, Sterling Professor of Humanities at Yale University, is the author of twenty-eight books. His best known include *The Western Canon, Shakespeare: The Invention of the Human,* and *The Book of J,* as well as his pioneering study *The Anxiety of Influence.* He is a MacArthur Prize Fellow.

ROY BLOUNT, JR.'s forthcoming book is *Alphabet Juice.* He is a panelist on NPR's *Wait Wait . . . Don't Tell Me!,* a columnist for *The Oxford American,* and president of the Authors Guild.

OLIVER BROUDY is an ex-managing editor of *The Paris Review,* and now a freelance writer living in New York City.

MEREDITH M. BROWN practiced law from 1966 to 2004 at Debevoise & Plimpton LLP (as the firm is now known), where he chaired the mergers and acquisitions group and the corporate department. Early in his career, he worked closely with Francis T. P. Plimpton. Brown has written many books and articles on legal topics, several articles on American history, and *Frontiersman: Daniel Boone and the Making of America.*

MATTHEW J. BRUCCOLI was the Emily Brown Jefferies Distinguished Professor Emeritus of English at the University of South Carolina and president of Bruccoli Clark Layman publishers. He was the author or editor of one hundred volumes on American authors.

After serving in the Navy, DOUGLAS BURDEN became one of America's top ski racers and competed internationally until a near fatal ski racing accident in Italy in 1954 ended his career. He continued playing tennis and golf and became "coach" to friends and family. He passed away on January 26, 2008.

BUDDY BURNISKE was a *Paris Review* intern in the summer of 1990, after which he returned to Chapel Hill to study English. When he died in 2006, he was a tenured professor at the University of Hawaii.

RIC BURNS is an Emmy Award–winning writer, director, and producer of documentary films. Among his best-known works are *New York: A Documentary Film, Coney Island, The Donner Party, Andy Warhol,* and *The Civil War,* on which he collaborated with his brother, Ken Burns, and Geoffrey Ward.

CHRIS CALHOUN met George at a *Paris Review* party in 1985 and became a contributing editor to the magazine shortly thereafter. He is a literary agent in New York City.

MARION CAPRON worked for the *Review* in the mid- to late 1950s. She has lived in Haiti and, most recently, in Florida.

RAY CAVE assigned and edited stories by George for *Sports Illustrated* beginning in the mid-sixties. Their close working relationship continued for a decade. In 1980, as editor of *Time,* Cave persuaded George to help cover the Summer Olympics in Moscow, an assignment that upset the culture of *Time* but not Plimpton's prose.

CHRIS CERF has been a contributing editor to the *National Lampoon* and an award-winning (Grammy and Emmy) contributor to

Sesame Street. He is president of Sirius Thinking, Ltd., and is currently producing *Between the Lions* for PBS.

BRONSON WINTHROP CHANLER knew George at Harvard. He was George's investment adviser until 1968, when he moved to Rhinebeck and became a country gentleman.

MICHELE CLARK knew George Plimpton for fifteen years and worked briefly at *The Paris Review.* She is a business development consultant who lives and works in New York City.

TOM CLARK edited the poetry section of *The Paris Review* from 1963 to 1973. His latest book is *Light and Shade: New and Selected Poems* (Coffee House Press, 2006).

GERALD CLARKE is the author of *Capote*, the biography of Truman Capote, and *Get Happy: The Life of Judy Garland.* He also edited a book of Truman Capote's letters: *Too Brief a Treat.* He lives in Bridgehampton, New York.

JOEL CONARROE, an author and editor, is president emeritus of the John Simon Guggenheim Memorial Foundation.

BERNARD F. CONNERS, a former publisher of *The Paris Review,* is a novelist and entrepreneur. After the Army, Conners was an FBI agent in charge of night operations of the Chicago and New York divisions.

DENTON COX was George's primary-care physician for many years. He was murdered in 2007.

BILL CURRY played pro football from 1965 to 1974 and later spent seventeen years as a head coach in the college ranks. He is now an on-air game analyst for ESPN.

JONATHAN DEE is the author of four novels, most recently *Palladio*, and a staff writer for *The New York Times Magazine.* He worked at *The Paris Review* from 1984 to 1990.

CLEM DESPARD first met George in 1949 when he joined the *Harvard Lampoon.* He was occupied in various business endeavors until 1981 when he began doing artwork (box constructions). He is represented by Gallery Henoch in New York City.

MILTON DEVANE graduated from Exeter (where he was acquainted with George but did not know him well) and from Yale. He attended King's College, Cambridge, with George, and thereafter, following three years in the Navy, he attended law school and practiced law in New Haven, Connecticut.

TIMOTHY DICKINSON, famed among journalists as a polymathic "source," was a friend of George's for more than thirty years. He lives in Washington, D.C.

BILL DOW organized the 40th Anniversary Reunion of the 1963 Detroit Lions ("Paper Lion") team. It was held just four days before George's death. He also wrote the afterword to the 2003 and 2006 editions of Plimpton's bestseller *Paper Lion,* published by the Lyons Press.

PAMELA DRAPER is a single parent and personal chef in Manhattan. Her professional background is in theater, dance, and the arts; her family background (of great interest to George) includes Paul Draper, the tap dancer, Ruth Draper, the monologist, and Dorothy Draper, the interior decorator—respectively her father and two great-aunts.

PETER DUCHIN is America's preeminent dance-band leader and the founder of Peter Duchin Entertainment. A successful recording artist and author, he is also honorary chairman of the Glimmerglass Opera and a member of many boards.

OSBORN ELLIOTT was editor of *Newsweek* in its glory days, and subsequently served his hometown of New York in many capacities, including that of deputy mayor.

DAVID EVANIER was hired by George as a *Paris Review* reader in 1976, and from 1979 to 1986 he was a fiction editor and, later, a senior editor. His books include *The Great Kisser, The One-Star Jew,* and *Making the Wiseguys Weep: The Jimmy Roselli Story.*

JULES FEIFFER is a cartoonist, playwright, and children's book author/illustrator. Among his better-known works are his play *Little Murders,* his film *Carnal Knowledge,* and his Pulitzer Prize–winning sociopolitical cartoons, which ran for forty-two years in *The Village Voice.*

BRUCE JAY FRIEDMAN is a novelist and short story writer, best known perhaps for *A Mother's Kisses* and The Lonely Guy stories. He lives in New York.

MICHAEL K. FRITH was the *Harvard Lampoon*'s president just fifteen years after George. He was an author/illustrator and a Random House editor/art director, and then, for twenty years, art/creative director, executive vice president, of Jim Henson's Muppets.

ANNE FULENWIDER became George Plimpton's assistant and an editor at the *Review* in 1995. She helped him complete his biography of Truman Capote, which was published at the end of 1997. She is senior articles editor at *Vanity Fair,* and lives in Brooklyn with her husband and daughter.

BLAIR FULLER and George Plimpton became lifelong friends as undergraduates at Harvard. A short story of his appeared in the second issue of the *Review,* and he has been an editor at the magazine for more than fifty years. His most recent nonfiction book is *Art in the Blood,* a history of the Fuller family's seven generations of American artists.

ELIZABETH GAFFNEY worked with George for over sixteen years, beginning as a *Paris Review* intern in 1988, ending as a director of The *Paris Review* Foundation when he died. Her novel *Metropolis* was published in 2005.

STEPHEN GAGHAN's screenplay for the film *Traffic* received an Academy Award in 2001. Most recently, he wrote and directed the Oscar-nominated *Syriana* (2006). He worked as an intern at *The Paris Review* in the early 1990s.

ROWAN GAITHER was an associate editor of *The Paris Review* and assistant to George Plimpton from March 1991 until August 1992. After leaving the *Review*, he attended Harvard Law School and now practices law in New York City, where he lives with his wife and two daughters.

LEON GAST is a nonfiction filmmaker best known for the Oscar-winning *When We Were Kings*, a documentary about the 1974 Muhammad Ali–George Foreman heavyweight championship fight in Kinshasa, Zaire.

GEOFFREY GATES was born in Manhattan, where, since graduating from Princeton, he has worked in the investment business. He now lives in New Jersey with his wife, Wende Devlin.

MYRA GELBAND was a senior editor at *Sports Illustrated* magazine from 1982 through 2001. She is now a freelance writer and editor. She lives in Connecticut with her husband and two children.

JAMES C. GOODALE, a New York City lawyer, has represented *The Paris Review* since 1980, and also represented George Plimpton from that time until he died in 2003. Before then, he was vice chairman and general counsel of *The New York Times*, which he represented in the *Pentagon Papers* case.

TONI GOODALE has been part of the New York City literary and journalist scene for many years. She is a past board member of the PEN American Center and is the founder and president of Goodale Associates, a capital campaign-fundraising firm in New York City.

DANA GOODYEAR is a staff writer at *The New Yorker* and the author of *Honey and Junk*, a collection of poems published by W. W. Norton in 2005. She lives in Los Angeles.

ROBERT GOTTLIEB has been editor in chief of both Simon and Schuster and Alfred A. Knopf, as well as editor of *The New Yorker* from 1987 to 1992. He is now a critic for *The New York Observer*.

PHILIP GOUREVITCH is the editor of *The Paris Review* and a long-time staff writer for *The New Yorker*. He is the author of *Standard Operating Procedure* (2008), *A Cold Case* (2001), and *We Wish to Inform You That Tomorrow We Will Be Killed with Our Families: Stories from Rwanda* (1998). He lives in Brooklyn.

BILLY GRAHAM was a classmate of George's at St. Bernard's School in New York. After graduating from Yale, he began a career in television and film directing. He lives in Malibu, California, with his wife, Janet.

FRANCINE DU PLESSIX GRAY was born at the French Embassy in Warsaw, Poland, and raised in Paris. The most recent of her twelve books are *Simone Weil* and *Them: A Memoir of Parents,* which won the National Book Critics Circle Award for Autobiography. Gray's biography of Madame de Staël is scheduled to be published in October 2008.

WALON GREEN, a writer/producer in television, worked as an executive producer and writer on *Hill Street Blues, Law & Order, ER,* and *NYPD Blue.* As a screenwriter, he is best known for the Western classic *The Wild Bunch.* Green also produced and directed the feature documentary *The Hellstrom Chronicle,* which won an Academy Award in 1972.

SOL GREENBAUM was George Plimpton's personal accountant for more than thirty years. He works at Jacques M. Levy & Co., Certified Public Accountants, in New York.

ELIZA GRISWOLD was George's assistant and associate editor at *The Paris Review* in the early 1990s. She is a New America Foundation fellow and award-winning poet and journalist living in New York City.

MAXINE GROFFSKY started her career in publishing in the editorial department at Random House. Paris editor of *The Paris Review* from 1966 to 1973, she has been director of the Maxine Groffsky Literary Agency since 1975 and lives in New York City with her husband, Winthrop Knowlton.

FELIX ("BUTCH") GRUCCI, JR., is the CFO of Fireworks by Grucci and of Pyrotechniques by Grucci, and a former U.S. congressman.

JOHN GRUEN is a critic, writer, and photographer whose latest book, *Callas Kissed Me . . . Lenny Too! A Critic's Memoir,* was published last April by powerHouse Books.

JOHN GUARE, whose plays include *House of Blue Leaves, Six Degrees of Separation,* and *Landscape of the Body,* received the 2004 Gold Medal in Drama from the American Academy of Arts and Letters.

TOM GUINZBURG, a cofounder of *The Paris Review,* joined the Viking Press in 1953 and became president in 1960. Chairman of the American Book Awards in 1982, he also served as senior consultant to Doubleday & Co. and Turner Publishing. He was a governor of Yale University Press from 1968 to 2004.

DONALD HALL was at Exeter and Harvard with George, and became the first poetry editor of the *Review.* He was the fourteenth U.S. Poet Laureate and is the author of eleven books of poems, most recently of *Without* (1998) and *White Apples and the Taste of Stone* (2006). He lives in his grandparents' old farmhouse in Wilmot, New Hampshire.

WILL HEARST is a partner is in the venture capital firm Kleiner Perkins Caufield & Byers and a member of the board of directors of the Hearst Corporation.

HUGH HEFNER was born in Chicago. He is the founder, editor in chief, and chief creative officer of Playboy Enterprises.

DRUE HEINZ, for fifteen years the publisher of *The Paris Review*, is a prominent patron of the arts in her husband's native Pittsburgh and around the world. In 1981, she established the Drue Heinz Literature Prize, which is a nationally known prize for short fiction and includes publication by the University of Pittsburgh Press.

RUSSELL HEMENWAY is the director of the National Committee for an Effective Congress, founded in 1948 by Eleanor Roosevelt. He serves on many civic boards and writes and speaks often on politics and public affairs.

JOHN HEMINWAY fell in love with the wild places of the world in a career writing books and making documentaries. Today he is doing what he can to protect them. Along the way, he has earned many awards, including a Peabody, a duPont-Columbia for journalism, and two Emmys.

TONY HENDRA is a writer by trade, an actor occasionally, and an editor when the need arises. His friendship with George was sustained by vinous lunches, shared interests (they were both charter members of the storytelling group the Moth), and mutual literary respect.

FAYETTE HICKOX is a creative director and writer, living in Weston, Connecticut, with his wife, Auste, a painter, and their son, Cal.

PATI HILL is a writer and artist, and an early contributor to *The Paris Review*. Her latest exhibition was "Vers Versailles," shown at the palace in 2004. She lives in Sens, France, and is currently working on a memoir of Diane Arbus, a friend since they were in their twenties.

JED HORNE was a slush pile reader at *The Paris Review* soon after the magazine moved from Paris in 1973. He is the author of *Breach of Faith,* about Hurricane Katrina, and *Desire Street,* about a Louisiana death row case. He lives in New Orleans with his wife and sons.

GLENN HOROWITZ is the proprietor of Glenn Horowitz Book-seller in New York. He has brokered the sale of the literary archives of Norman Mailer, Don DeLillo, Vladimir Nabokov, and many others.

A. E. HOTCHNER is a writer, best known for *Papa Hemingway* and (among George's friends) *Everyone Comes to Elaine's*. He partnered with Paul Newman for the Newman's Own line of food products.

RICHARD HOWARD is a translator, critic, and poet. He teaches literature at the School of the Arts (Writing Division) of Columbia University. He was the poetry editor of the *Review* for eleven years.

BEN RYDER HOWE, a writer, was an editor at *The Paris Review* from 1995 to 2005.

BRIGID HUGHES is the founder and editor of the Brooklyn-based literary quarterly *A Public Space*. She was managing editor of *The Paris Review* from 1995 to 2005, succeeding George Plimpton as editor after his death in 2003.

ALISON HUMES is a magazine editor at *Condé Nast Traveler*. She and Rory O'Connor have two sons, Ciaran and Aidan O'Connor.

IMMY HUMES is a daughter of "Doc" Humes, whom she calls the "Instigator" of *The Paris Review*. She is an Academy Award–nominated documentary filmmaker, and her recent film *Doc,* about her father, features George, along with Norman Mailer, William Styron, and Peter Matthiessen.

SUSANNAH HUNNEWELL is the Paris editor of *The Paris Review*. She currently lives in Paris with her three sons and her husband, Antonio Weiss, whom she first met as an intern at the *Review.* Antonio's pursuit of her was successfully orchestrated by George.

BOB JOHNSON left his post as solo horn player with Leonard Bernstein's New York Philharmonic in 1969 in order to found the New York Philomusica in 1971. George joined its board in 1973 and later became president.

MARJORIE KALMAN-KATZ took care of George's personal finances for almost twenty-five years but forgot to get tips on playing pool.

ALEX KARRAS was a six-time All Pro with the Detroit Lions and in 1970 was named to the All-Time Lions team and the All-Time Big Ten team. His movie credits include *Paper Lion, Against All Odds, Blazing Saddles, Porky's,* and *Victor/Victoria.* With his then wife-to-be, Susan Clark, Karras formed a production company, and he starred in 150 episodes of the long-running TV series *Webster.* He is the author of *Even Big Guys Cry, Alex Karras: My Life in Football, Television, and Movies,* and *Tuesday Night Football.*

WILLA KIM was married to William Pène du Bois, *The Paris Review*'s first art editor, and was in Paris for the magazine's launch. She is a theater designer with many awards, including Tonys, Drama Desks, Emmys, and the Theatre Hall of Fame.

JAMAICA KINCAID writes novels, memoirs, and books and articles on gardening. *The Autobiography of My Mother* was published in 1996, *Among Flowers* in 2005. She teaches writing at Harvard.

DANIEL KUNITZ was managing editor of *The Paris Review* from 1995 to 2000. He has written about art for *Harper's, Slate, The New York Sun,* and many other publications.

BEN LA FARGE, a professor of literature, is a former chair of the Division of Languages and Literature at Bard College.

TED LAMONT, a friend of George's since St. Bernard's, is an economist who helped administer the Marshall Plan after World War II. He is the father of the Ned Lamont who won Connecticut's Democratic nomination for Senate from Joe Lieberman.

STARLING LAWRENCE is the editor in chief of W. W. Norton & Company, which published many of George Plimpton's books. He also had the pleasure of playing tennis with George, and of witnessing, at a charity event, his astonishing mastery of bowling, a sport which he claimed never to have bothered with. He may have been telling the truth, but no one quite believed him.

PHOEBE LEGERE has released seven CDs of original music and is currently head writer and host for *Roulette TV,* a New York City show about experimental art and music. She recently appeared on Nickelodeon's comic children's show *The Naked Brothers Band.*

SIR ANDREW LEGGATT's relevant claim to fame is that he roomed with Plimpton during their second year at King's College, Cambridge. Their activities included night climbing, jousting in punts, and writing letters to *Country Life.* He is a retired judge of the Court of Appeal in England.

JAMES SCOTT LINVILLE, a *Paris Review* editor from 1984 to 2001, is now a screenwriter and journalist. He lives in New York and London.

CHRISTOPHER LOGUE won the 2005 Whitbread Poetry Award for *Cold Calls,* the latest of his much admired "accounts" of the *Iliad*—*War Music, Kings,* and *The Husbands.* He succeeded in Paris, as George did not, in publishing two novels of porn with the Olympia Press. More recently, in Britain, he wrote for *Private Eye.*

PIEDY (GIMBEL) LUMET first met George while he was at Harvard. In 1954 in Madrid, she introduced George to Ernest Hemingway. She lives in East Hampton and New York City.

FIONA MAAZEL's first novel, *Last Last Chance,* was published in March 2008 by Farrar, Straus and Giroux. She was an editor of *The Paris Review* from 2003 to 2005.

LARISSA MACFARQUHAR is a staff writer at *The New Yorker.* She was an intern at *The Paris Review* for six months from 1991 to 1992.

NORMAN MAILER was born in Brooklyn in 1923. In a career spanning almost sixty years, he wrote thirty-seven books of fiction, nonfiction, essays, poetry, and criticism. In 1969, he won the National Book Award and the Pulitzer Prize for *The Armies of the Night.* Mailer received another Pulitzer in 1980 for *The Executioner's Song.* For many years he lived in Provincetown, Massachusetts, with his wife, Norris Church Mailer. He died on November 10, 2007, in New York City.

NORRIS CHURCH MAILER played Zelda Fitzgerald to George's Scott and her husband's Hemingway on their tour of Europe and the United States in the play *Zelda, Scott, and Ernest.* Married to Norman Mailer for twenty-seven years, she is the mother of two sons, stepmother of two sons and five daughters, and has one grandson and one step-grandson. Her second novel, *Cheap Diamonds,* was published by Random House in August 2007. She is also a painter.

HARRY MATHEWS settled in Europe in 1952 and lived there, chiefly in France, until 1978. Married to the French writer Marie Chaix, he now divides his time between Paris and Key West. His most recent book is *My Life in CIA: A Chronicle of 1973* (Dalkey Archive Press, 2005).

PETER MATTHIESSEN is a novelist, naturalist, and journalist. Among his many much-acclaimed books are: *At Play in the Fields of the Lord, The Snow Leopard, In the Spirit of Crazy Horse,* and *The Shorebirds of North America.* A one-volume version of his trilogy of novels beginning with *Killing Mr. Watson* was published in 2008.

JEANNE MCCULLOCH is a former editor at *The Paris Review* and a founding editor of *Tin House* magazine and Tin House Books. Her work has appeared in *The New York Times, Vogue, O: The Oprah Magazine, The North American Review,* and *The Paris Review* among other publications. A forthcoming memoir will be published by Bloomsbury USA.

JOANIE MCDONELL is the author of several books and screenplays. She lives in Amagansett, New York, and New York City.

TERRY MCDONELL edited George Plimpton at *Rolling Stone, Smart, Esquire, Men's Journal,* and *Sports Illustrated.* They also traveled together on various "literary expeditions." In the 1990s, Plimpton asked him to help with *The Paris Review,* for which he now serves as president of the Board of Directors.

MOLLY MCGRANN was a *Review* intern in the 1990s.

JAY MCINERNEY is the author of seven novels, including *Bright Lights, Big City,* his best-selling 1984 debut. Among his other novels are *Ransom* (1985), *Brightness Falls* (1992), *Model Behavior* (1998), and *The Good Life* (2006).

MOLLY MCKAUGHAN worked for George from October 1972 to August 1976 as his assistant, and later as managing editor of the *Review.* Since then, she has been ME of two short-lived national magazines, *Quest* and *Next,* a senior editor at *New York* magazine, a freelance writer and poet, author of *The Biological Clock* (1987), and a program officer at two national foundations, the Commonwealth Fund and the Robert Wood Johnson Foundation. She lives in Montclair, New Jersey.

BUZZ MERRITT knew George for seventy years. They met as "small boys" at St. Bernard's School and carried their friendship to Exeter. They kept in touch throughout their lives.

DAVID MICHAELIS is the author of the national bestsellers *Schulz and Peanuts: A Biography* and *N. C. Wyeth: A Biography,* which won the 1999 Ambassador Book Award for Biography, given by the English-Speaking Union of the United States. He worked at *The Paris Review* as a summer intern in 1976 and 1977.

CHARLES MICHENER was George Plimpton's editor at *The New Yorker.* He was senior cultural editor at *Newsweek,* editor in chief of *The Movies,* and a frequent contributor to national magazines. He is currently working on two books—a study of Cleveland, Ohio, entitled *The Hidden City,* and an oral biography of Robert Altman.

THOMAS MOFFETT was an associate editor at *The Paris Review* and George Plimpton's assistant from 2000 until George's death in 2003. He is a screenwriter living in New York City.

LORRIE MOORE is the author of the short story collections *Self-Help, Like Life,* and *Birds of America*. She has won the O. Henry Award and the Rea Award. Her story "You're Ugly, Too" was selected by John Updike for *The Best American Short Stories of the Century*. She teaches at the University of Wisconsin–Madison.

SUSAN MORGAN is a writer who lives in Los Angeles, California, and Edinburgh, Scotland. She is a contributing editor for *Metropolitan Home,* author of *Joan Jonas: I Want to Live in the Country (And Other Romances)*, and recipient of a 2006 fellowship from the Graham Foundation for Advanced Studies in the Fine Arts.

JOAN DE MOUCHY has lived in Europe since 1955. Assistant Paris editor of *The Paris Review* for eight years, she then married Prince Charles of Luxembourg and lived in that country until his death. Returning to Paris, she married the Duc de Mouchy in 1978. For the past thirty-five years, she has been running the Dillon family vineyard, Château Haut-Brion.

VICTOR S. NAVASKY, the longtime editor and publisher (and now publisher emeritus) of *The Nation,* is chairman of the *Columbia Journalism Review* and was the founder of *Monocle* magazine. His books include *Kennedy Justice, Naming Names, A Matter of Opinion,* and (with Christopher Cerf) *The Experts Speak: The Definitive Compendium of Authoritative Misinformation* and *Mission Accomplished! Or How We Won the War in Iraq*.

LYNN NESBIT is a literary agent in New York City.

JANET NOBLE laid out issues of *The Paris Review* in the early 1980s, during the last days of "cut and paste" production. She is a playwright and screenwriter living in New York City and working part time at *The New York Review of Books*.

P. J. O'ROURKE is the former editor of the *National Lampoon*. He spent fifteen years as a foreign correspondent for *Rolling Stone* and currently writes for *The Weekly Standard* and the *Atlantic*. He is the author of twelve books, including, most recently, *On "The Wealth of Nations."*

RON PADGETT's most recent books of poems are *How to Be Perfect* and *You Never Know*. He is also the author of *Oklahoma Tough: My Father, King of the Tulsa Bootleggers*.

MAGGIE PALEY worked closely with George on *The Paris Review* and other projects during the 1960s. She's the author of *Bad Manners*, a novel, *The Book of the Penis*, nonfiction, *Elephant*, a chapbook of sestinas, and many magazine articles and book reviews.

ROBERT PARKS is director of Library and Museum Services at the Morgan Library & Museum in New York.

DEBORAH PEASE met George Plimpton at a debutante party in Newport, Rhode Island, in 1961. Her books include *Real Life*, a novel (Norton, 1971), and *Another Ghost in the Doorway: Collected Poems* (Moyer Bell, 1999). From 1982 to 1992, she was publisher of *The Paris Review*.

FREDDY ESPY PLIMPTON was George's first wife and the mother of their daughter, Medora, and son, Taylor. She lives on a pond in Bridgehampton, New York, where she is an avid bird-watcher and nature lover. She is an artist and photographer who especially enjoys the company of her children and grandchildren.

LAURA AND OLIVIA PLIMPTON are George and Sarah Plimpton's daughters, fourteen years old, attending school in Manhattan.

MEDORA PLIMPTON, the eldest child of George's first marriage, lives in Starksboro, Vermont, with her husband, Spencer Harris, and children, Addison and Tanner. She is pursuing a career in nursing and enjoys volunteering as an EMT-I for a local ambulance. Medora is an avid skier and cherishes spending time with her family in the outdoors.

OAKES PLIMPTON, born in 1933, is George's youngest brother, retired now, but still active in farming enterprises, coordinating the local farmers' market in Arlington, Massachusetts, where he lives with his wife, Pat Magee; his son, Robin Plimpton-Magee, lives in New York.

RUTH TALBOT PLIMPTON was married to Francis Plimpton's half-brother, Calvin. She is the author of *Mary Dyer: Biography of a Rebel Quaker*. She lives in Westwood, Massachusetts.

SARAH DUDLEY PLIMPTON is George's second wife and the mother of their twin daughters, Laura and Olivia. She likes to think her early jobs in wilderness survival, special events, and publishing were excellent training for life with George. She has edited a posthumous collection of his writing, *The Man in the Flying Lawn Chair*.

SARAH GAY PLIMPTON is George's only sister. After majoring in biology in college, she went on to medical school. After three years, she took a year off to reconsider, and George suggested she work for *The Paris Review* in Paris. She worked with Patrick Bowles (then the Paris editor of the *Review*) for two years, 1962–1964. Then she began to write and paint, which she continues to do in New York City.

TAYLOR PLIMPTON, George's son by Freddy Espy, is a freelance writer in New York City.

MICHAEL POLLAN interned at *The Paris Review* in 1974. He is the author of several books, the most recent of which are *In Defense of Food: An Eater's Manifesto* and *The Omnivore's Dilemma: A Natural History of Four Meals*, named one of the ten best books of 2006 by *The New York Times* and *The Washington Post*. Pollan is a contributing writer to *The New York Times Magazine* and is a Knight Professor of Journalism at UC Berkeley.

RICHARD PRICE is the author of eight novels, including *The Wanderers, Clockers,* and *Lush Life,* and the screenwriter of ten feature films including *The Color of Money* and *Sea of Love.* He was a co-writer on the HBO series *The Wire.*

TERRY QUINN is a novelist, biographer, playwright, and opera librettist. He co-authored, with George Plimpton, two dramatic dialogues that have toured the United States and Europe. George played the role of critic Edmund Wilson in three productions of his play *Dear Bunny, Dear Volodya: The Friendship and the Feud.*

JACK RICHARDSON, a critic and playwright, lives in New York City.

JAMES RIGHTER is an architect practicing in Boston.

ANNE ROIPHE is the author of the novels *Up the Sandbox* and *Lovingkindness,* the memoir, *1185 Park Avenue,* and many columns and essays, chiefly from a feminist perspective.

PAT RYAN followed Ray Cave as George's editor at *Sports Illustrated.* After leaving *SI,* where she had been a researcher, writer, and senior editor, she was the first woman to edit a Time Inc. weekly (*People*), and at the end of the '80s, was the editor of the monthly *Life.*

DEWITT SAGE is a prizewinning (two Peabody Awards) documentary filmmaker. Much of his work has been for PBS's *American Masters* series ("Winter Dreams," on F. Scott Fitzgerald) and for WGBH's *Frontline* series ("Broken Minds," on the treatment and mistreatment of schizophrenia).

JAMES SALTER is the author of *The Hunters,* which drew on his experience as a fighter pilot in the Korean War, *A Sport and a Pastime,* published by Paris Review Editions, and *Dusk and Other Stories,* which won the PEN/Faulkner Award in 1989.

ARAM SAROYAN's poems have been extensively anthologized. His most recent collection is *Complete Minimal Poems.* He has also written a memoir of his father, William Saroyan.

ELISSA SCHAPPELL was senior editor of *The Paris Review* in the early 1990s. She is an author, essayist, and cofounder of the literary magazine *Tin House*. She resides in Brooklyn with her husband and two children.

MONA ESPY SCHREIBER is Freddy Espy Plimpton's twin sister. She was married to a diplomat and lived all over the world. Now divorced, she is the mother of four children. She has a BA in English from Tulane University and has worked mostly in educational and nonprofit institutes.

GENE SCOTT was tagged with three labels: "Tennis's Renaissance Man," "the most controversial figure in the game," and "the conscience of tennis." He was a member of the U.S. Davis Cup team, and was inducted posthumously into the International Tennis Hall of Fame in 2008. He died in 2006.

JEANETTE SEAVER has written four cookbooks, including *Jeanette's Secrets of Everyday Good Cooking* and, most recently, *My New Mediterranean Cookbook*. She is the wife of Richard Seaver, and, with him, publisher of Arcade books.

RICHARD SEAVER was a founding editor of *Merlin* in Paris in the 1950s, where he first met George. For many years, before founding Arcade Publishing with his wife, Jeanette, he was the editor of Grove Press and of the *Evergreen Review*. He has also edited collections of the works of Samuel Beckett and André Breton. He and his wife live in New York City.

TIM SELDES met George at Exeter, where they were the starting pitchers on the only freshman class baseball team ever to finish higher than fourth place. Seldes went to work at the literary agency that represented George's literary work, and they remained connected until his too-early death.

MARY LEE SETTLE was the author of eleven novels, including the Beulah Quintet saga and *Blood Tie,* which won the National Book Award in 1978. In her youth, as a New York actress and model, she tested for the part of Scarlett O'Hara in *Gone with the Wind*. She died in 2005.

LAWRENCE SHAINBERG's novel *Memories of Amnesia* was edited by George Plimpton and published by Paris Review Editions in 1988. He is also the author of the novel *One on One;* a nonfiction book, *Brain Surgeon;* and a memoir, *Ambivalent Zen;* as well as a *Paris Review* essay, "Exorcising Beckett."

EDWIN ("BUD") SHRAKE is a novelist, screenwriter, former newspaper columnist, and longtime feature writer for *Sports Illustrated*. He became friends with Plimpton at the Ali-Liston fight in Miami in 1964. Shrake lives in Austin, Texas.

ROBERT SILVERS cofounded *The New York Review of Books* with the late Barbara Epstein in 1963 and continues to be its editor. He was Paris editor of *The Paris Review* and is a member of its editorial board. Last year Silvers received an honorary doctor of letters degree from Harvard University.

MONA SIMPSON was senior editor of *The Paris Review* in the early 1980s. She is the author of four novels: *Anywhere but Here, The Lost Father, A Regular Guy,* and *Off Keck Road.*

FARWELL SMITH was a classmate of George's at Exeter and Harvard, where they worked on the *Lampoon* together. He is a rancher and land preservation activist in Montana.

WALTER SOHIER was a lawyer who practiced most recently at the bar of the International Court of Criminal Justice in The Hague.

NILE SOUTHERN is a writer and filmmaker living in Boulder, Colorado. He is coeditor with Josh Alan Friedman of *Now Dig This: The Unspeakable Writings of Terry Southern, 1950–1995,* and author of *The Candy Men: The Rollicking Life and Times of the Notorious Novel Candy.*

NANCY STODDART met George when she was still in high school through Christopher Cerf, who was a friend of a classmate's older sister. She went to Sarah Lawrence College, worked in the fashion business in Rome and Paris, and returned to New York to marry Peter Huang. George gave Nancy her wedding party at his house. She then went to work at Atlantic Records. After her divorce and career in the music business, which included being a BMI-affiliated songwriter, she moved to California to write scripts and was employed by HBO to write a biopic. She is a Writers Guild of America member and has been hired to write other scripts, which were unproduced, including one for Barry Sonnenfeld. She went back to decorating starting in the 1980s. She is still a designer today.

PATRICIA STORACE is the author of *Dinner with Persephone: Travels in Greece; Heredity,* a book of poems; and *Sugar Cane,* a children's book.

ROSE STYRON, widow of the late novelist, is a poet, journalist, and human rights activist.

WILLIAM STYRON, a native of the Virginia Tidewater, was a graduate of Duke University and a veteran of the U.S. Marine Corps. His books include *Lie Down in Darkness, The Long March, Set This House on Fire, The Confessions of Nat Turner, Sophie's Choice, This Quiet Dust, Darkness Visible,* and *A Tidewater Morning.* He lived, with his wife, Rose, for most of his adult life in Roxbury, Connecticut, and in Vineyard Haven, Massachusetts. He died in 2007.

REMAR SUTTON was a columnist for *The Washington Post* and is the author of five fiction and nonfiction books. Sutton is founder of several national consumer rights task forces, and lives in the British Virgin Islands and Denmark.

JAMES SYMINGTON, a St. Bernard's classmate of George's, served four terms in the U.S. House of Representatives, representing Missouri's Second District as a Democrat, after holding several other posts in government, including U.S. Chief of Protocol in the Johnson White House. He is a lawyer in Washington, D.C.

GAY TALESE is the author of twelve books, including *A Writer's Life, Thy Neighbor's Wife,* and *The Bridge.* He knew George Plimpton beginning in 1957. He and his wife, Nan, live in New York City.

MICHAEL M. THOMAS first met George Plimpton in the late 1950s and they remained good friends thereafter. Thomas has been a museum curator, an investment banker, and, since 1980, a writer. He has published seven novels and contributed to innumerable periodicals, including *The Paris Review.* From 1987 to 2004, he wrote a weekly column, "The Midas Watch," for *The New York Observer.*

JOHN TRAIN succeeded George in 1949 as president of the *Harvard Lampoon.* After receiving an MA in comparative literature, he moved to Paris and became a founder and managing editor of *The Paris Review.* Train's more than four hundred columns and twenty books cover such subjects as investments, foreign policy, naval warfare, and Oriental rug symbols.

CALVIN TRILLIN has been a staff writer at *The New Yorker* since 1963. He lives in New York.

NANCY TUCKERMAN was the longtime spokeswoman for Jacqueline Kennedy Onassis, her former roommate at Miss Porter's School in Farmington, Connecticut. She was White House staff coordinator during the Kennedy administration. With Nancy Dunnan, she revised and updated *The Amy Vanderbilt Complete Book of Etiquette* in 1995.

RUSTY UNGER (GUINZBURG) has been a New York–based magazine and book editor and writer, as well as a film executive. She has written for television, motion pictures, and many national publications.

WANDA URBANSKA, with her husband, Frank Levering, runs a large cherry and apple orchard in North Carolina. She is also an editor, publisher, and writer of books for people who are looking for a simpler life.

TEDDY VAN ZUYLEN, after many years of living in Paris and the Netherlands, now lives in London, where he is writing a memoir of his parents.

GORE VIDAL is an acknowledged master of the satirical, historical, and political novel (often all three at once), a list of which would deprive other contributors of their due fragment of space. His critical essays on literature and political culture, most recently *Perpetual War for Perpetual Peace,* continue to delight readers and enrage the powers that be.

LILLIAN VON NICKERN was the business manager of *The Paris Review* from George's move to New York in 1954 until her recent retirement.

HALLIE GAY WALDEN is producer of a forthcoming PBS documentary on the Thoroughbred. A Dartmouth College and Columbia Law graduate, Ms. Walden was managing editor of *The Paris Review* (1980–1985).

ANTONIO WEISS is the publisher of *The Paris Review* and an investment banker with Lazard Frères in Paris. He was George's "aide-de-camp" and an editor at the *Review* in the late 1980s.

EDMUND WHITE is best known for the gay trilogy *A Boy's Own Story, The Beautiful Room Is Empty,* and *A Farewell Symphony.* He teaches writing at Princeton.

KATE ROOSEVELT WHITNEY has been a teacher of young children and is a social worker.

DALLAS WIEBE is the author of many works of fiction, including *Skyblue the Badass,* published in 1969 by Paris Review Editions. He won the *Review*'s Aga Khan Prize for Fiction in 1978.

ANN WINCHESTER studied sculpture at Oxford and worked in Paris on large civic sculptures for Paris, Buenos Aires, and San Francisco. She met George in 1971 during the filming of *Plimpton!*

Adventures in Africa. She now lives in London and is directing an animated musical drama, *This Immortal Coil.*

KRISTI WITKER was a reporter for CBS News and ABC News and an anchor and reporter for WPIX in New York. Her articles and photographs have been published in numerous newspapers and magazines.

ELIZABETH WURTZEL's journalism has appeared in *New York* and *The New Yorker,* and she has published three books: *Prozac Nation, Bitch,* and *More, Now, Again.* She lives in Greenwich Village.

WARREN YOUNG, after happily enduring the Dynamite Museum disaster, less happily saw to the development and abandonment of a Sunday supplement, *Three to Get Ready,* by its corporate sponsor, CBS. Since then, for twenty-seven years he has been running the publishing efforts of the Boy Scouts of America, located in Irving, Texas.

BOBBY ZAREM is a publicist, best known for having created and executed the "I Love New York" campaign, which, he likes to think, literally saved the city of New York. His clients have included Dustin Hoffman, Cher, Diane Keaton, Diana Ross, and Michael Douglas, among many others. He was born and raised in Savannah, Georgia, and graduated from Andover and Yale.

JAMES ZUG is the author of four books, most recently *The Guardian: The History of South Africa's Extraordinary Anti-Apartheid Newspaper.* He was a reader at *The Paris Review* from 1997 to 1999.

Books by GEORGE PLIMPTON

The Rabbit's Umbrella *(juvenile)*

Out of My League

Writers at Work: The *Paris Review* Interviews, *Volumes I–IX (ed.)*

Paper Lion

The Bogey Man

American Literary Anthology, *Volumes I–III (ed.)*

American Journey: The Times of Robert F. Kennedy *(with Jean Stein)*

Pierre's Book *(ed.)*

Mad Ducks and Bears

One for the Record

One More July *(with Bill Curry)*

Shadow Box

Sports *(with Neil Leifer)*

A Sports Bestiary *(with Arnold Roth)*

Edie: An American Biography *(with Jean Stein)*

D.V. *(with Christopher Hemphill)*

Fireworks: A History and Celebration

Open Net

The Curious Case of Sidd Finch

Poets at Work: The *Paris Review* Interviews *(ed.)*

Women Writers at Work: The *Paris Review* Interviews *(ed.)*

The Best of Plimpton

Chronicles of Courage *(with Jean Kennedy Smith)*

The Writer's Chapbook

The *Paris Review* Anthology *(ed.)*

The Norton Book of Sports *(ed.)*

The X Factor

Truman Capote

Beat Writers at Work

The Writer's Chapbook: A Compendium of Fact, Opinion, Wit,
and Advice from the Twentieth Century's Preeminent Writers

Playwrights at Work: The *Paris Review* Interviews *(ed.)*

Pet Peeves, or, Whatever Happened to Doctor Rawff?

Home Run *(ed.)*

Latin American Writers at Work: The *Paris Review* Interviews *(ed.)*

George Plimpton on Sports

As Told at the Explorers Club: More Than Fifty Gripping Tales of Adventure *(ed.)*

Ernest Shackleton

The Man in the Flying Lawn Chair and Other Excursions and Observations

INDEX

Page numbers in *italics* refer to illustrations.

ABOUT THE TYPE

This book was set in Bembo, a typeface based on an old-style Roman face that was used for Cardinal Bembo's tract *De Aetna* in 1495. Bembo was cut by Francisco Griffo in the early sixteenth century. The Lanston Monotype Company of Philadelphia brought the well-proportioned letterforms of Bembo to the United States in the 1930s.